GHOST ROCK

Front Range Rock Climbs Near Calgary

3rd edition

Andy Genereux

Rocky Mountain Books

GHOST ROCK
Front Range Rock Climbs Near Calgary

3rd edition

Andy Genereux

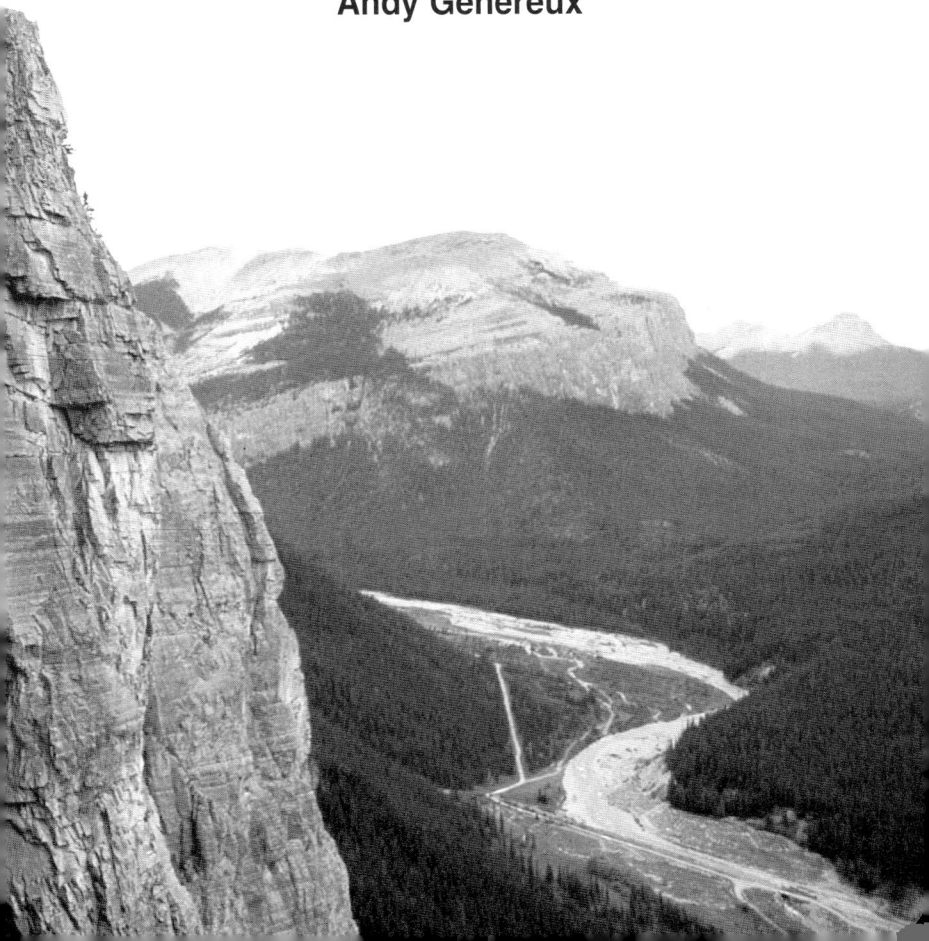

Front cover: Chas Yonge turning 40 and cranking the third ascent of "Alberta Jam"
Photo: Andy Genereux.
Back cover: James Blench on "Gunslingers in Paradise", Wild West Wall. Photo: Roger Chayer.
Title page: Some people call him the Fred Beckey of the Ghost. We refer to Fred as the Frank
Campbell of everything non-Ghost. Frank on pitch two on the second ascent of "Separated Reality."
Photo: Joe Josephson.

Photo credits not otherwise acknowledged:
Chris Perry: 24.1, 24.2, 36, 37, 39, 47, 51, 54, 65, 67, 98, 118, 184, 188, 190, 221, 223, 264,
284, 303, 309, 312, 321.
Joe Josephson: 27.1, 27.2, 46, 53, 56, 74, 243, 251, 283, 316, 325.
Andy Genereux: 25.2, 26.1, 26.2, 29.1, 84, 90, 141, 171, 178, 193, 204, 237, 257, 270, 298, 324.
Brian Spear: 30, 31. Frank Campbell: 305, 307, 310. Jon Jones: 71, 260, 262. Stewart Midwinter:
41. CMC History by Chic Scott: 25.1, 26.3. Trevor Jones: 23, 28. Brad Wrobleski: 180.

We acknowledge the financial support of the Government
of Canada through the Book Publishing Industry Development Program (BPIDP) and the support of the Alberta
Foundation for the Arts for our publishing program.

Published by Rocky Mountain Books
Surrey, British Columbia
Printed and bound in Canada by
RMB Kromar Printing Ltd., Winnipeg

National Library of Canada Cataloguing in Publication Data

Genereux, Andy, 1959-
  Ghost rock : Front Range rock climbs near Calgary / Andy Genereux.

  Includes index.
  Previous ed. by Joe Josephson, Chris Perry and Andy Genereux.
  ISBN 1-894765-42-7

  1. Rock climbing--Alberta--Ghost River Valley--Guidebooks. 2. Rock
climbing--Alberta--Waiparous River Valley--Guidebooks. 3. Ghost River
Valley (Alta.)--Guidebooks. 4. Waiparous Creek Valley
(Alta.)--Guidebooks. I. Title.
GV199.44.C22A4545 2003   796.52'23'09712332   C2003-910410-9

TABLE OF CONTENTS

Introduction

The Climbs

Maps

The Ghost is a special place. It has long been considered a quiet, adventurous and even spiritual place to explore. Part of the pleasure of the Ghost is the virtually unrestricted access for much of the area (except for Banff National Park and the Ghost River Wilderness). This may also become the Ghost's downfall. Utility workers, oil and gas companies, abuse-rehab programs, family campers, four-wheelers, motocross & quad riders, native groups, the military, hunters and climbers have all run roughshod over the Ghost landscape year round. For the most part, this has historically been a very congenial and respectful coexistence. With continued increasing demand it would be naive, however, to expect that the present state of affairs will not change. The Provincial Government is now in the process of doing a land use study of all Crown Lands north of the Trans Alta Access Road and north of the Ghost River. This will directly apply to all areas north of the access road to where it meets the Ghost River drainage at the bottom of the big hill. This will include all areas north of the Ghost river drainage north into the Waiparous drainage. This will directly effect crags like Bastion Wall, Alberta Jam and Silver Tongued Devil Crag. How this will effect access and use is still to be determined in the near future through several public forums. Anything might be possible, from the road somehow miraculously being upgraded or worse, closed. If the wrong politically connected person gets a hold of land rights and services like toilets and campgrounds get established, or if a myriad of other developmental nightmares get started, the Ghost will undoubtedly be the scene of an ugly fight. I believe it is important for us as climbers to establish a strong and respectful stakehold in the future of the Ghost. The Alpine Club of Canada and The Calgary Mountain Club are both actively involved in the process to see that we as climbers maintain access and have some control over what results from the decision making. It seems consensus that most people that use the Ghost (including non-climbers) do not want to see the present status change too much. Therefore it is extremely important that we all treat the area well, not be obnoxious or pester other visitors, respect the national park and forest service regulations, not make a mess of the campsites (or worse, burn the area down), and not harass wildlife or otherwise destroy the fragile ecosystem.

Numerous features come to a dramatic union in the Ghost River to produce a most unique and unforgettable rock-climbing arena. There are over 35 linear kilometres of steep cliff line in the region. In June and July when the wildflowers are in bloom, it is simply beautiful. Plus, the remote and relatively wild nature of the Ghost Valley adds a strong adventure component that has as much to do with the climbing as the routes themselves. There are no highways or railroads visible from the Ghost. Aside from the occasional small airplane flying through Devil's Gap or the whine of ATVs, you will be left alone to the sounds of wind, rivers and your partner(s).

By local standards, the Ghost has climbing on above-average rock. To date, however, it is still woefully underdeveloped. Although this has been changing, since the last guide in 1997 the amount of climbing has almost doubled. Trails are becoming more defined and many of the climbs have now had multiple ascents. Although the Ghost has one of the longest climbing histories in the area, it would be fair to claim that the present state of development is still well behind that of the Bow Valley. However, this is not a bad thing to be sure. There are more climber visits than ever before but for the most part one can still have the place to themselves. The traditional scope of Ghost River climbing scene has been changing with the addition of more pure sport climbs with several being multi-pitch. However, the Ghost still remains a strong bastion for traditionalist climbing. Traditional routes still continue to go up at a blistering pace. This variety of climbing style makes the Ghost a unique venue, one that looks to the past but embraces the future. The melding of ethics and styles leaves for a broad spectrum of climbing, "with a little something for everybody's taste".

The abundant crags that make up the Ghost River rock climbing are only a small part of the mountains found there. For those inclined, there are several alpine rock climbs described beginning on page 320.

Included in this book is a chapter on the rock climbs of Waiparous Creek beginning on page 303.

The Waiparous Creek area lies to the north of Black Rock Mountain, and along with its tributaries, is pretty much the most northerly extension of the Ghost's dramatic cliff lines. It is, however, considered a totally separate venue because getting there makes the rest of the Ghost seem casual. Until recently, Frank Campbell and partners were the only regular climbers to tap into the vast resource of quality limestone found there. This has changed very little with only one new major route by a party not involving Frank. With several visits by others to repeat several of Campbell classics this area is just starting to get a bit better known. The author is eternally grateful to Frank for divulging what was for years his "secret" spot. The information given here is strictly to catalogue what has been done. I hope to present an introduction to the area and foster dreams of adventure. However the information is not conclusive or guaranteed to be accurate Frank has been known to forget things from time to time. And until the access improves, the area gets more visits, or more climbs are completed I leave it for your own exploration and discovery.

ACKNOWLEDGEMENTS

A special acknowledgement has to go out to **Joe Josephson** for his major effort as the lead author on the previous 1997 "Ghost Rock". Joe was the driving force to collect and compile the information and main reason the last guide came together. With out his previous effort and determination the Ghost wouldn't be the climbing area it is today. "Jo-Jo's" previous work is strewn through out this guide. With his gracious permission I have been able to incorporate much of his past work through out this guide and built on it's foundation. I make no pretence to pass this previous work of Joe's as my own. Joe with out your footsteps to follow I would have been lost thanks again.

We the climbing community are truly indebted to Joe for his past energy and time. I for one hope he comes to visit soon from his home in Montana so we can revisit some of the many excellent climbs of the Ghost River maybe even look at several new lines the list is long and time is short. Cheers Joe.

Also **a special acknowledgement** goes out to **Chris Perry** one of the original fathers of Ghost River climbing. Chris put out the first guide to this area in 1980. It was this original guidebook that brought others and myself to the Ghost for the first time. Chris has also contributed heavily to the 1997 guide as well. He has produced many of the photos and route descriptions that have inspired a generation or two to get out there and explore and establish some of the fine routes the Ghost has to offer. These inspirations are only possible because Chris has continued to share his stories and climbing experiences from a 30 year plus love affair with the Ghost.

Like Joe Josephson much of his previous work is strewn through out this guide with out his former footsteps and dedication, the Ghost wouldn't be what it is today. Chris is presently flushing out all the lost routes and new climbs for a new Banff Rock Guide and didn't have a lot time to put into this version of Ghost Rock. Without his previous contributions this book couldn't be what it is. I am greatly indebted thanks again Chris.

The author is also indebted to the support and information from the following individuals: A huge slap on the back goes out to longtime Ghost pioneers Dave Morgan, Trevor Jones and Frank Campbell for sharing their routes, photos and stories (buy them a beer when you see them!). We appreciate Glen Boles for permission to reproduce information from his venerable, green guide *Rocky Mountains of Canada South*. Others who have assisted in providing information and photographs are: Don Vockeroth, Jon Jones, Paul Stoliker, Chas Yonge, Andy Skuce, John Rowe, Tim Pochay, Paul Valiulis, Grant Statham, Dale Bartrom, Keith Haberl, Albi Sole, Brian Wyvill, Chris Kalous, Al Pickel, Shawn Huisman, Shelly Huisman, Jamie McVicar, Brian Spear, Ken Wylie, Stewart Midwinter, Greg Fletcher, Rick Felber, and The Calgary Mountain Club World News.

All of the routes in this book are on limestone. Most of the Ghost River climbing is on Eldon Formation, which is the same as Yamnuska. (The other formation present is Cathedral-Phantom Bluffs.) As a result, the climbing is similar to that on Yam and mainly follows steep crack lines. Overall, though, the rock is better than the Bow Valley and in many cases it is exceptional. Alongside the crack lines there are vast quantities of sweeping, compact, water worn walls that have begun to produce some fine, if not prickly, face climbs. The better climbing tends to start in the moderately hard grades (5.9 and up), although there are a number of quality 5.7s and 5.8s.

Beware that the rock can be brittle and seemingly solid holds have on occasion been known to snap with little warning. Keep this fact clearly in mind when attempting new routes or soloing. As well, most ledges will be scree covered and it is therefore advisable to wear a helmet. Rough-jagged cracks, textured arêtes, bulging walls, razor-sharp ripples and square edges combine throughout the Ghost to produce what is, arguably, some of the best limestone climbing in the Canadian Rockies. Until recently all of the climbing had been developed on walls varying from slabs to slightly overhanging and ranging in length from 15 to 360 meters. Now climbers are reaching out to the modern styled radically overhanging ground to push both single and multi pitch climbs. See the individual chapters for the specifics on each cliff.

Gear Protection

Unlike most local limestone areas, the Ghost is blessed with a lion's share of great crack climbs making camming units and wired nuts desirable. One can come to the Ghost with nothing but a rack of quick draws but you will miss out on major portions of what the Ghost has to offer. Every effort has been made to determine if a route requires the use of pitons. If in doubt, particularly on the older, obscure climbs, a standard rack, a selection of 4-6 pins up to a 1/2" angle will usually suffice.

A **standard rack** would include a set of wires, a full set of camming units to 4", including a few smaller "TCUs," and a few Tri-cams™ and/or Hexes depending upon your personal preferences. You would be wise to have several long slings in a selection of 14-16 quickdraws. As well, efforts have been made to indicate if any unusually wide protection pieces are helpful or if climbs require multiples of any particular sizes.

As the camming units come in a variety of different models and changing preferences there has been no effort made to translate from one brand of camming unit to another nor to measure the width of every crack. What you read is what I have been given by the contributing climbers or previous author's or I have personally experienced myself. There has been no attempt to give explicit gear placements and a pitch by pitch blow of what gear is required on a climb. Diagrams will detail crack sizes and the opening description will detail if certain types of gear would be useful like TCU'S or if multiples are required. If very little is known about a climb it usually gets designated as having gear to 4 inches. This means that you could find placements up to that size but how many and specifically what is required I leave

Type of Climbing

up to you to discover. If a climb is detailed as requiring a **standard rack**, this usually means you will require extensive gear placements that will range wildly as to size. It also means the pitches will most likely be longer requiring many quick draws and it is advisable to have several longer slings to avoid rope drag on these routes. If a climb is recommended to use double ropes this refers to double rope technique where you split two half-ropes to eliminate rope drag and is particularly useful on some of the wandering multi pitch climbs. Topo diagrams attempt to detail all known fixed gear i.e. pitons and bolts. This information may not always be accurate, someone might have removed gear or it might have fallen out or the original information might not have been accurate to start with. If you find inaccuracies contact the author so that future information can be corrected. The Ghost has always been about having a little bit of adventure and to that end I give you the general specifications for gear but I leave it up to you to figure out the how, when, where and specific use of that gear. None of the information is perfectly accurate and local limestone is notorious for accepting adequate protection for one party and none for another. Use your own judgment.

Ropes

Over the years the Ghost has been largely a traditional area. To that end several climbs still demand the use of double rope techniques. I have attempt to detail on which routes this technique would be useful. It requires two half-ropes, which are split to remove excessive drag and provide better protection while clipping into gear by reducing potential fall distances. However these techniques require skill and knowledge and I leave it to you to acquire these attributes before attempting to actually use this technique while climbing. Even in this day of ultra-equipped sport routes many of the Ghost's activists maintain some degree of commitment and adventure in their routes (This is the Ghost after all!). As a result, there are few areas where only one rope will suffice. The 1997 guide stated "only one full-length route in the entire Ghost River that was equipped for 25 m rappels—this being "Dirty Dancing" on North Phantom Crag. This has changed somewhat but it's still not the norm. There have been several additions in recent years that can be rappelled using a single 60 m rope. They include: "Planters Valley East" which now has the normal rappel equipped for 30 m rappels and the route "Cashew Sunday", the multi pitch sport route "Smoking in the Boy's Room" to the right of "Dirty Dancing". The right side of Silver Tongued Devil Crag has many new three and four pitch sport routes, all of which can be descended using a single rope. Bastion Wall also has two climbs that can be rappelled using a single 60 m cord, "Rave" & "Men of Fashion". It also possible to descend from West Phantom Crag with one rope via the Bonanza Descent Gully but if the waterfall is flowing or you need to back off your route, you will be in trouble. Some of the big crags have walk-off descents but again, if you need to back off your route…. Most of the sport/cragging areas also require an extra rappel line. Be sure to check out all the details in the individual chapters before you commit yourself.

Note: Most multi-pitch climbs do not have fixed belay or rappel anchors. If you need to back off such a route you will probably appreciate having a few pitons or extra wires/hexes along and several long knotted slings.

Fixed Protection

People have been climbing in the Ghost for over 30 years. As a result, the area has been influenced by various and widely different climbing styles. Many of the older routes have little or no fixed protection and if they do, they are typically pitons. Fixed pitons can loosen quickly in the local climate and/or may not have been well-placed to begin with. It is recommended to test all fixed pitons with a hammer before they are trusted. **Do NOT** test bolts with a hammer.

Some routes have bolts for belays or for protection. Bolts on the older climbs (pre-1993) are pretty much all 5/16" self-drill concrete anchors with shear and pullout strength of about 2000 kg. On these, you will find a variety of hangers. They range from home-made aluminum (up to the late eighties) to home-made steel and modern stainless steel brands. Note that on some of the older cragging routes at Kemp Shield and Sentinel Bluffs the home-made aluminum hangers have exceptionally small carabiner holes (0.5" diameter). A selection of small profile carabiners is required. Otherwise you can feed a wired nut through the hole and clip the wire so the nut jams against the hanger. Beware that it is unknown whether this procedure affects the strength of the hanger or the wire.

To date, the authors have not heard of a 5/16" self-drive bolt failing. Although there are no formal tests or accounts of failures, it seems the bolts themselves are fine but it is the cap screw that presents the weakest link. In the early days they were plain steel cap screws with either Allen-key heads or standard hexagonal heads. These are susceptible to rust and should be replaced with newer case-hardened, aircraft-quality cap screws (identified by the star pattern on the head). Unfortunately, these older cap screws most often break while attempting to unscrew them. If this is the case the entire bolt should be replaced. Several of the older climbs have had fixed placements upgraded. This is time consuming thankless job and is appreciated. However, as a common courtesy every effort should be made to discuss with the first ascensionist (if possible) any changes that may require the moving or in some cases adding fixed gear to established climbs.

Note: Virtually every pre-1996 self-drive bolt are of imperial thread. The 5/16" imperial Rawl bolt is no longer made and it seems only the metric 10 mm "Petzl" bolt is available. Be aware of this and have the right threads when performing your civic duty to the community.

In recent years, the somewhat stronger 3/8 "Hilti" quick bolt (or equivalent) has been introduced on both sport climbs and multi-pitch routes. In fact, the Ghost is where the style of drilling with a power drill on lead was developed in the Rockies (see History). The modern standard is now going towards a 3" X 3/8" or 3" X 1/2" stainless steel quick bolt with stainless steel hanger and fixed belays having stainless steel ringbolts or Rap hangers. So if you enjoy clipping those beefy bolts and

Andy drilling on lead. Photo Fay Wilkinson.

convenient rappel stations but are not active in building climbs there is a way for you to contribute. The **Association of Bow Valley Rock Climbers (TABVAR)** is a non-profit organization who have supported many of the new routes being done in recent years in the Ghost. Much of what has been done would not have been possible without the support of TABVAR. To help make sure that climbs are maintained, new routes continue to go up with good protection. Every one who uses the resource should put a little back into it. **You as an individual can really help** to make this possible. The organization (TABVAR) is climber funded and supported, donations can be made to: TABVAR, 79 Rosary Drive NW, Calgary, AB, T2K 1L4 or check out there web site at TABVAR (The Association Of Bow Valley Rock Climbers) **www.strongholdclimbing.com**

OTHER SOURCES OF INFORMATION

The World Wide Web (Internet)
Various individuals and climbing related organizations maintain sites on the World Wide Web that may contain updated information on new routes and access in the Ghost. Next time you're up late with nothing better to do, check out the following resources.

Rocky Mountain Books: www.rmbooks.com

Rock n' Road: www.rocknroad.com/

The Calgary Mountain Club: www.geocities.com/Yosemite/4163/

The Alpine Club of Canada: www.culturenet.ca/acc/

TABVAR (The Association of Bow Valley Rock Climbers)
    www.strongholdclimbing.com

Rock Solid (Brian Spear) www.rocksoildgide.com

Live the Vision (Cody Wollen) www.live-the-vision.com

Alberta Forestry Fire Bans Alberta www.alberta.firebans.com/

HAZARDS

The Road

The access road is perhaps the most legendary and maligned aspect of the Ghost River. This rough, pot-holed, washed-away, mud-filled, rock-infested endurance test is what has kept the Ghost River a relatively unvisited rock climbing venue. Many a muffler and oil pan have been sacrificed over the years. In the past, the road's reputation was far worse than it deserved. The author has seen just about every type of vehicle in the Ghost including everything from Buicks, Westfalias, 4WDs and mobile homes to taxi cabs (some don't make it back in the same condition). More recently, the road was graded the first time in ten years, (2 years ago) this has improved the conditions somewhat. However, the road has been gradually falling back into a worse state of disrepair. Check out the "Getting There" section on page 19 for more details. Good luck!

Rockfall

As per any rock climbing area, particularly on limestone, rockfall can occur at any time. The biggest concern is climber-generated rockfall by the leader or other parties above. Helmets are highly recommended for all multi-pitch routes and many of the shorter cragging routes, particularly Borderline Buttress and Sentinel Bluff.

Naturally-occurring rockfall can also happen, sometimes on a catastrophic level. Check out the devastation below Epitaph Wall that occurred sometime in the winter of 1996. If faced with these circumstances, blame it on fate and pray for the best. The high winds common to the Ghost can also dislodge scree or blocks from

A classic Ghost River climbing experience–Ghost car camping. Photo: Jamie McVicar.

ledges or the top of the crag. Clumsy mountain sheep have also been known to torment climbers with rockfall. Despite all these warnings, rockfall is the exception, not the rule.

Ticks

The Ghost has a high resident ungulate population. Mountain sheep are abundant and moose, deer and bear are also common. As a result, spring time in the Ghost also means Rocky Mountain wood tick time. They are abundant from April (earlier if it is warm) until late June. The area around West Phantom Crag is particularly bad as it faces south and is relatively warm and dry. Ticks usually don't attach themselves right away and will be found crawling around your clothes and neck for up to several hours. It is recommended that you check all your gear and clothing closely as soon as you arrive at the car. If you still find one when you get home, flush it down the toilet, not the sink (believe it or not they'll get caught in the trap and crawl back out (they are tough little buggers). To date, the serious condition called Lyme disease, which is common elsewhere, is not known to exist in this area.

Rats

Bushy-tailed wood rats (*Neotoma cinerea*) or more affectionately known as pack rats, are common although you may never see one. The smelly, offending nests that are commonly seen on Yamnuska are strangely absent in the Ghost. However, if you leave any gear at the base or are looking for a rappel sling, expect to find tattered threads. Carry fresh rappel slings and don't leave chewable gear overnight at the crags.

Bears

The Ghost is bear country. Both black bears and grizzlies live in and frequent the area. When camping, store all food in the car overnight and while out climbing. Take precautions not to spill or pour excess food and drinks on the ground as the smell will attract bears. Dump grey water and leftovers in a fire pit and burn it. Not only does it keep the bears away, but it helps preserve the fragile (and often over-used) campsites. For more information on avoiding bears, consult one of the many popular books on the subject.

Weather

Wind is the main ingredient throughout the Ghost. Even the high south-facing crags can turn icy with a stiff breeze. It is advised to carry plenty of pile layers and a wind jacket on most days. The Ghost seems to enjoy the same "rain shadow" effect found on Yamnuska. It may be raining (or snowing) in Banff/Canmore, but the thunderheads seem to break up as they get blown through the narrow valleys of the Ghost only to reform over Calgary. Nevertheless, the winds will be violent, the temperatures will drop, and if a storm does hit the Ghost be prepared—they are usually severe.

Regulations

Just about the only regulations governing present climbing areas concern Banff National Park. It is illegal to camp or drive beyond the park boundary in Devil's Gap. Park wardens regularly perform border patrols and if you are caught camping or driving in the park it will result in a nasty fine and you'll give the rest of us climbers a bad name. The Park boundary is obviously marked by yellow pickets and a cut line. The following crags and climbs lie within Banff National Park: Planters Valley, Spectre Crag, The Arrowhead, Wild West Wall, Kemp Shield, Bonanza, Grey Ghost Wall, Epitaph Wall, Spirit Pillar and Borderline Buttress. The remainder of the Ghost region is crown land where there are few or no governing regulations. Note this may be changing as the area is under review. One area that does have some regulation is the Ghost River Wilderness, which begins 10 km west of the North Ghost parking and far from most climbs in this book. All that is asked is that everyone show some decency and respect for the land, each other and the fragile ecosystem that makes the Ghost such a wonderful place to be.

Registration

Technically, for climbs within Banff Park you can register with the warden service. This would entail driving two hours out of the way to Banff. Plus, rescue in the Ghost is difficult at best (see below). In other words, registering is not a realistic option.

Rescue

If you require a rescue, don't expect much, if any help. It is a one hour drive just to get to the nearest phone. Cell phones sometimes work. The coverage is very spotty so don't count on it. The Banff warden service is responsible for rescues within the park and Kananaskis Country personnel are responsible for all other areas. Remember this is a remote and difficult area and rescues cannot be undertaken as they might on Yamnuska or around Banff. Helicopters, medics and rescue personnel may take many hours or days to reach you if they can at all. If you get into a bind the only ones around to help you will be you and your partner(s)—so don't! For the sake of completeness here's the number: In an emergency, first try **911** before Kananaskis Country Emergency **(403) 591-7755** and RCMP, Cochrane **(403) 932-2211**.

Guides

If you want to climb in the Ghost but don't have the vehicle or the experience to go on your own, there are numerous qualified guides and schools in the Calgary, Canmore, Banff area that have strong knowledge and experience of the area. I do not think one better than the other so I leave it to the individual to seek out their service of choice.

Top: Camping in the North Ghost with a view of Mount Aylmer
Photo: Jamie McVicar.
Bottom: The view from the top of Phantom Tower looking south.
Trevor Jones and Orient Point. Photo: Joe Josephson.

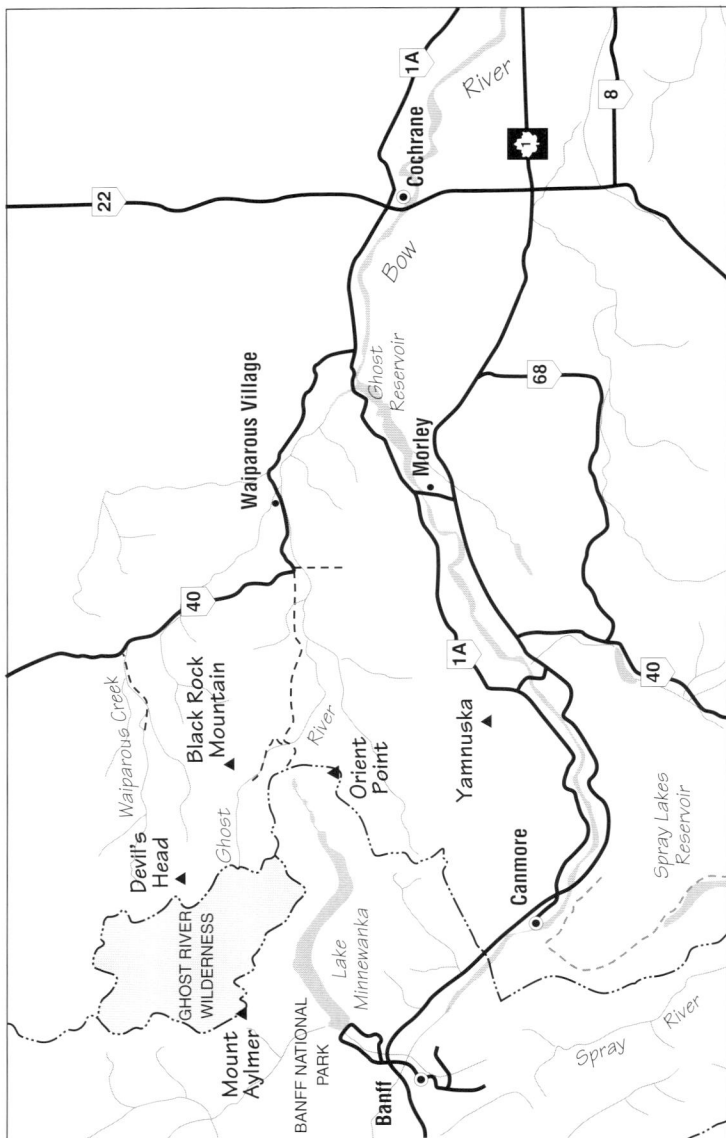

Because finding your way around the Ghost can be a taxing experience for the newcomer, access will be described in three stages. The first, "General Access", will get you from either Calgary or Banff/Canmore to the Big Hill that provides access to all the areas in the Ghost drainage. There are three main parking areas, all diverging from the Big Hill described in the introduction to each of the main areas. The third stage, "Approach Details," will take you from your car to a specific crag. The approach details for each cliff can be found in its individual chapter.

General Access

The Ghost can be reached in 60 to 90 minutes from either Calgary or Canmore.

From Calgary, head west on Highway 1A (Crowchild Trail) to the town of Cochrane (your last chance for gas) and a four-way stop junction with Highway 22. Continue west through the stop for 13.4 km to a right (north) turn on to the Secondary Route 940 (Forestry Trunk Road), also known as Highway 40.

From Banff/Canmore, the quickest route is to follow the Trans-Canada Highway east to the Chief Chiniki/Morley turn-off and follow the Morley Road north to the 1A highway then turn right. SR 940 is another 15.5 km east (4 km past the Ghost Reservoir).

Once on the SR 940, continue northwest for about 25 km to a gated gravel road on your left about 100 m **beyond** the junction with **Richard's Road** (just after the road makes a sharp turn to the north). Be sure to re-close the gate if you found it that way. Just as you turn onto the gravel road, there will be a large ranch house on the hill to the right. Bear right at a fork after 3 km, just beyond a small bridge. Follow the rough, ever-worsening road for another 13.5 km to the infamous Big Hill overlooking the Ghost River Valley (running north to south at this point) and Devil's Gap (straight ahead). From the bottom of this hill you will have to decide in which valley you want to climb. Going right takes you to the "Ghost River Valley" and the "North Ghost". Turn left to go into "Devil's Gap" and the "Minnewanka Valley." The Anti Ghost takes the trail to the right 100 m before going down the Big Hill.

Most vehicles will be able to reach the top of the hill, and if yours isn't up to the rigours of the Ghost itself, park in a clearing on the right at the top of the hill. Devil's Gap is about a 30-minute walk from here. If you wish to climb on the more northerly crags without a vehicle, a mountain bike is recommended.

It is important to note that the Ghost River floods almost every spring. The riverbed along the base of the Big Hill is usually dry but can at times be a raging torrent with two to three meters water. If this is the case, don't even attempt to cross by car or foot. More importantly, these floods change (i.e. eliminate) roads, carve steep banks and give the Ghost its sometimes deserved reputation for difficult access. At present (2003) it is recommended that you have good vehicle with good clearance or a 4WD. Other types of vehicles have been used but they usually return a lot worse for wear. Faint tracks and roads abound in the Ghost. If a section ahead looks impassable, you can usually find an alternative. Take your time and if in doubt, scout ahead or walk. All parking areas are a 15-30 minute drive from the Big Hill if you don't get stuck.

CAMPING

Camping

One of the best features of the Ghost is the abundance of good, free camping, making this an ideal destination for the weekend. You can camp anywhere in the Ghost outside of Banff National Park, which prohibits any camping or overnighting. There are, however, several established campsites where most people reside. They are located as follows: 1) at the bottom of the Big Hill on the left, 2) along the park boundary in Devil's Gap, 3) next to the river near the Black Rock Mountain hiking trail, 4) at the old CMC campsite near Wully Wall, and 5) in the clearing near the start of the Bastion Wall approach. These areas are marked on the maps on pages 34 and 176. All of these areas have numerous little niches and clearings that make for fine camping.

Water

Except for the Big Hill campsite, all sites have access to water most of the summer. During spring runoff or flood, there will be water near the Big Hill. Before spring thaw and late in the season the river in Devil's Gap will dry up. To the authors' knowledge, all water in the Ghost is fit to drink as is. If you are unsure or concerned, boil or filter it.

Fire

Most well-established campsites will have fire rings, many of them outlandishly big. If you have a fire, please use an established ring. **Do not** make new fire rings or build fires directly on the ground. The ground cover in the area is very fragile. Some areas, particularly Devil's Gap, are starting to get picked clean of dead wood. **Do not cut down any trees for firewood, either live or dead-standing.** Find dead fall or better yet bring your own. During extreme fire hazards, the forest service may restrict camp fires on all crown lands. As there are no services in the Ghost, you are responsible for knowing when fires are disallowed.

Call the Renewable Sustainable Resource Development at (403) 297-8800 or for fire bans call 1-800-FYI-FIRE. To report a fire call toll free 427-FIRE.

Human Waste

There is only one outhouse in the entire area, located at the start of the "Black Rock Mountain Hiking Lookout" trail. When nature calls, walk at least 200 m from any streams, climbing or camping sites and find an out of the way place, preferably in the trees. It is best to bury your waste in 6-8 inches of topsoil and burn the toilet paper. Better yet, desecrate a trash bag and carry it out with you. At the very least you should burn the paper. The most popular campsites in Devil's Gap are beginning to see white flowers (toilet paper and tampons) scattered through the trees. In general, however, waste has not been a big problem.

Please—it is up to us to keep it that way.

Garbage

Put only combustible material into a camp fire. This **does not** include plastic, tin foil, tin cans or batteries. If you do burn tins to rid of food odours, clean them out in the morning and pack them out with the rest of your garbage. Hey—this is car camping, there are absolutely no excuses. By keeping our impact minimal and our profile low, we can do our part to help maintain the unrestricted access we now enjoy. but more importantly we can endeavour to preserve the fragile ground cover and ecosystem of the Ghost. Besides, none of us really want to find a pigsty when we go camping. This attitude applies to the crags as well, pack out all used tape, slings, butts, etc. from your visit to the cliffs.

Season

The climbing season generally runs from early-May to mid-October, give or take a few weeks on either end. Recent years have seen this extend into mid December on southern aspects on sunny days. West Phantom Crag, Phantom Bluffs, Wully Canyon and Silver-Tongued Devil Crag and the west end of Bastion Wall will have the longest season owing to their southern aspects. Because of the generally low snowpack and high winds, the rock dries out very quickly and rarely seeps. The defining features in the spring will be when the snowdrifts in the road melt away and the river is passable—see General Access on page 19. In the fall it is common to climb into late October or even November and December depending upon location, air and wind temperatures. During the winter (sometimes in mid-October) the Ghost offers an abundance of fine waterfall ice climbing. See Joe Josephson's *Waterfall Ice Climbs in the Canadian Rockies* fourth edition.

Limitations of this Book

This book is intended for the experienced climber only. It is not a manual of instruction, but a rough, if not incomplete, guide to the routes. It assumes that the reader is already proficient in the use of climbing techniques, route finding ability, hardware and protection, the use of a rope or ropes and has climbed before on natural rock in the out-of-doors. Whereas this book contains much useful information, it does not take the place of skill and good judgment. Every word in this book is the subjective opinion of the authors and is not guaranteed to be 100% accurate. You, the readers, are responsible for, but not limited to, the following factors: your own safety and health, your ability to find the start of a climb, finding the route on any climb, your ability to judge the difficulty of the climb or any individual move on any piece of rock you may encounter, your ability to safely climb any piece of rock you say you are going to climb, your ability to descend or back off any cliff you find yourself on, your own decisions in life and climbing and, your ability to have fun.

Brian Spear and Ken Wylie up high on first ascent of Ardent Heart. Photo: Keith Haberl.

Despite the limited number of established climbs verses the "Bow Valley", the Ghost has always enjoyed being near or at the forefront of local style. In the 30 plus years of recorded climbing history, numerous styles and ethics have reared their head or been initiated on Ghost River rock. These run the gamut from traditional ground-up ascents, to pre-inspected sport climbs, evolving into multi-pitch rappel bolting, to on-lead, on-sight bolting with a power drill. Sometimes all of the above while rope soloing.

Rock climbing began in the area in the late sixties when members of the newly formed Calgary Mountain Club (CMC) held a series of club camps in the Minnewanka Valley. This early exploration was not documented and old pitons found later remained a mystery for many years. Some information was unearthed recently during an interview with Don Vockeroth, one of the most prolific Rockies climbers of the 1960s. Climbs had been done mainly on the lower cliffs (now called Phantom Bluffs) but according to Don, no records were kept because "any climb with less than five pitches was considered to be practice." It is likely that the pitons found on "Bandidos" and "The Grooves" on Phantom Bluffs and on the Spirit Pillar date from this period. Other members of this early group included Lloyd MacKay, Bernie Schiesser, Gunti Prinz, Deiter Raubach and Klaus Hahn.

Chris Perry

The first major climb, also unrecorded and a mystery for many years, was the "Texas Peapod" by Don Vockeroth together with P. Robbins in 1971. Nothing else happened until 1975 when the area was rediscovered by a new generation of CMCers who were unaware of the earlier exploration. Acting on a tip from that venerable source of new route potential, Urs Kallen. Chris Perry and Trevor Jones drove in for a look. From the top of the Big Hill, the sight of the Minnewanka Valley with its steep and, in some cases, overhanging walls, seemed like a promised land—a "limestone Yosemite." They were particularly struck by a large face directly above the old RCMP cabin in Devil's Gap (now burnt down), which had an appealing crack line curving up its centre. The face was reminiscent of the Dolomites where both of them had recently climbed. Not wasting any time, the pair returned the following weekend with Andy Dunlop and Martyn White to climb the now classic South Face of Phantom Tower. Once on top of the tower, with rain turning to sleet and approaching darkness a problem arose they hadn't counted on—how to descend the huge cliff bands that extended in both directions without an apparent break. Eventually the South Phantom Crag Descent Gully was found with just enough light to reach the base of the cliffs.

For the next few years development proceeded at a rapid rate. The overall quality of the rock was significantly better than that of the Bow Valley and there were numerous crack and corner lines that offered good natural gear and piton protection. The mostly expatriated British climbers considered bolts unethical and this limited the scope of development. Jack Firth and Canadian, Pat Morrow, joined Chris and Trevor to produce seven multi-pitch climbs by the end of 1975. A report by Chris Perry in the Canadian Alpine Journal summed up the enthusiasm at the time. The term "Limestone Yosemite" was used and the article ended with a tongue-in-cheek quote, that "In a few years time when Calgary climbers talk of going to the 'Valley' they'll mean the Ghost River Valley."

Regular CMC camps-cum-parties took place and the number of devotees increased as did the quality of the climbs. Prominent additions were Bugs McKeith, Jeff Upton, Albi Sole and perhaps most of all Nigel Hellewell. Access was even more difficult than today so the action centred close to the CMC campsite on North Phantom Crag and Wully Wall. But when "Bonanza" was climbed in early 1976 with its exciting descent by a single rappel, this helped open up the spectacular south-facing cliffs above Devil's Gap. "Grey Ghost" was climbed by Trevor Jones and Jack Firth and the well-known British climber Pat Littlejohn added "Banshee" along with local Ian Staples. The 1976 season culmi-

Jack Firth

nated in North Phantom Crag's superb "Crack-A-Jack" (5.10b) by Jack Firth and Jeff Horne. This came closest to their ideal of a "limestone Yosemite."

The pace continued during the 1977 season with a collection of outstanding new climbs. The moderate "Consolation," added by Chris Perry and Martyn White, boasts excellent rock and an outstanding position and has remained one of the most travelled routes in the region. Many of the others like "The Wraith," "Thor," and "Satan" were largely the work of Nigel Hellewell. "Thor" follows a coveted three-pitch corner on "Bastion Wall". Most of the first pitch had been climbed by Chris Perry and Mike Sawyer, but before the duo could return, they were scooped midweek by Nigel and Jeff Upton. Depending upon who you talk to, "Thor" is anywhere from solid 5.10a to 5.10c and

Nigel Hellewell

is considered the classic hard route of the seventies era. The few bolts now on the route were added on subsequent ascents.

It is important to note that "Thor" and the earlier "Crack-A-Jack" were all originally graded 5.9 because that was believed to be the max of their abilities. It was a bad habit that continues to cough up sandbags well into recent years. Nigel was the first to break free and delivered the 5.10 grade with his rarely repeated "Satan" (5.10b) on "Bastion Wall". This was perhaps the first route in the Rockies to deliberately be given such a distinction.

The following season would prove to be a watershed in Ghost River climbing. "Wully Wall" and "Sentinel Crag" were the favoured venues although a few obvious lines

Albi Sole

were mopped up on "Phantom Tower", "North Phantom Crag" and "Bastion Wall". Chris Perry and Nigel Hellewell continued to lead the fray with a number of challenging routes on "Wully Wall" in the so-called 5.8-5.9 range. Another "old style 5.9" called "Big Willy" was added by Bugs McKeith and Alan Burgess and may still be unrepeated. Meanwhile, Albi Sole and Greg Spohr polished off the obvious "Cy-

Andy Genereux

clops" (5.10b) on "Sentinel Crag", only the second declared 5.10 in the valley. Not only were the 1978 climbs among the hardest in the Ghost, they would prove to be the last major routes of the seventies.

In 1980, Chris Perry produced the first Ghost River guidebook, which included some 40 climbs. It was hoped that the book would help continue the development and encourage others to visit the area. Instead, it marked the end of an era. How could they have seen that the eighties would usher in a revolution that would change the landscape of climbing around the world?

In 1981 the area was visited by Jeff Marshall, a young, somewhat controversial Calgary climber (Jeff drilled the Rockies first rappel-placed bolt at Wasootch in 1982) he would later do many significant firsts in the Bow Valley. En route to "Phantom Tower" he stopped at "The Haystack" and climbed the original, run-out version of "Teenage Wasteland" (5.9 R), the first recorded climb on the lower bluffs. Jeff also has a penchant for spectacular falls and on an early attempt to repeat "Thor" he fell 25 meters on the second pitch managing to break Al Pickel's knee at the belay. Jeff later climbed "Thor," but he lost the second ascent (also without bolts) to another young Calgarian, Andy Genereux, along with Bill Rennie. Andy would begin to figure very prominently in and eventually dominate Ghost River climbing.

Despite these movements, only a handful of new climbs were done in the first few years following the guidebook. The focus remained on traditional style and bolts were reluctantly used, if at all, even on the short routes. However, in 1983 climbers began to launch out of the cracks and corners and on to the sweeping, less-

Chas Yonge

obvious expanses of compact grey rock. Naturally, the Grey Ghost Wall was the prime location and "Ziggurat" (5.10a) was climbed by Chris Perry and Chris Dale in September. The following month Chas Yonge, along with John Rollins, found the amazing "Mantissa" (another 5.9 sandbag) now rated 5.10c/d R also on the "Grey Ghost Wall". These routes, however, remained dictated by the availability of natural protection and the willingness of the climber to push their limits and began the next era of development, which could be described as the "runout years." Prominent players were Dave Morgan, Andy Genereux, Andy Skuce and Jon

Jon Jones

Dave Morgan

Jones, although others had their moments of being "out there." Bolts were used only sparingly and placed on lead but the focus had switched from the big cliffs to the shorter, more accessible cragging areas around Phantom Bluffs and Sentinel Bluffs. Some of the notable, if not exciting, routes from this period were: "Revelations" (5.10a), "On the Border" (5.10b), "Achilles" (5.10b) and "Imbroglio" (5.10d) at Phantom Bluffs, and "Softly, Softly" (5.10b), "Prickly Fear" (5.11b) and "Last Mango in Paradise" (5.10c) all at Sentinel Bluffs. Some of these routes have since been retrofitted with new and/or more numerous bolts.

Frank Campbell

It was Morgan who first brought the 5.11 grade to the Ghost with the ultra-classic "Alberta Jam" in 1982. This challenging offset crack remains the hardperson's plum and although it is only 5.11b/c it took several years to receive the first known on-sight ascent which was possibly by Brian Balazs a local Calgary talent. The years 1983 through 1985 saw an important change in local values that eventually led the way to the modern sport climbs of the present era. The main Ghost activists in this new pursuit were Andy Genereux and Jon Jones who were amongst the innovators of the ethic in the Bow Valley. They established many of the first routes to be cleaned and bolted on rappel. But in these early days of this new ethic top roping was rarely employed and run-outs were intentionally created to simulate on-sight placements with certain amounts of boldness built in. Prime examples of this early but short-lived ethical style are "The Chimera" (5.10c/R) and "Rhydd" (5.10b), both at Borderline Buttress. It has only been through the adamant insistence of Genereux that "The Chimera" has to this day retained its original character as most others have since been retrofitted.

Beginning around 1985, true sport climbing tactics began to take hold in the Canadian Rockies. The Ghost was no exception and the movement was toward closely placed bolts, pre-inspection and top roping. A small group of activists had the Ghost to themselves as a private playground as it were. They put up the majority of the new routes. The group consisted of Dave Morgan, Jon Jones, Andy Genereux, Chas Yonge, and Andy Skuce.

With the new bolting ethic many of the hard short face routes were tamed. Morgan was quickly joined by Genereux to firmly establish the 5.11 grade. Between them with a variety of classic sport routes like "Cryin' Mercy" (5.11b), "Edge Clinger" (5.11b) and "Boy Wonder" (5.11c). These routes culminated in the spectacular arching dihedral "Sunset Boulevard" (5.11c/d) and the region's first 5.12, "Superwoman's Wildest Dream" by Genereux in 1989.

During the mid-eighties the Ghost also became a Mecca for waterfall ice climb-

Trevor Jones

ing. The undisputed leader of this movement was Frank Campbell. During that same period Frank began to look at the untapped traditional-style rock climbs. Along with Paul Stoliker and several other friends, they developed three completely new areas: Planters Valley, Spectre Crag and Silver-Tongued Devil Crag along with numerous climbs in the Waiparous Creek drainage. Many of these routes cleaned up on classic, obvious lines and filled a much-needed void for quality, moderate climbs.

The breakthrough, multi-pitch route of the mid-eighties was found on Epitaph Wall. The prominent right-leaning grey streak was for years considered the best line in the Ghost. However, the early activists didn't use bolts and thus didn't con-sider climbing the route's immaculate yet compact rock. In 1987, "Creamed Cheese" (5.11a) finally fell to the determined efforts of Brian Gross and Choc Quinn with the minimal use of bolts (not for the faint at heart). This monumental route has bold run-outs on 5.10 terrain and is generally considered to be one of the better tra-ditional styled classic routes. It's still considered real feather in your cap to complete this tic. In the same vane is the previously underrated "Mantissa" put up by John Rollins and Chas Young preceding this route by 3 full years. It was just as serious, if not more so and only marginally less difficult. Because of its original 5.9 grading and low key promotion the climb fell into ob-scurity to only be recently rediscovered and given its rightful place as an early Ghost River classic.

Joe Josephson

The dawning of the nineties saw a continued development of sport climbs in the established areas as well as the incredible Kemp Shield. But it was Andy Genereux's multi-pitch "Dirty Dancing" (5.11d/12a) that was the most outstanding addition in 1991. With four back-to-back 5.11 pitches and the later he added two optional 5.11-5.12 approach pitches. Until last year it remained unrepeated. The climb was started traditionally on lead, but owing to a crack filled with mud, this method was abandoned in lieu of rappel bolting and cleaning. Because of overgrown cracks and short sections of loose rock, this proved to be the style of choice for several other first ascents of the steep faces in the area. Nevertheless, "Dirty Dancing" was the first multi-pitch route to be completed from the top down in the Ghost.

One of the most consistent activists over the years has been one of the original Ghost veterans Trevor Jones. In 1990, he and Blob Wyvill extended the now up-graded "Crack-A-Jack" to the top of North Phantom Crag with four excellent pitches of "Separated Reality" (5.10b/c). Later in 1992, along with Joe Josephson, Trevor added a major variation to the long-lost route "The Wraith" (5.9). As well the pair established numerous cragging routes in the Spirit Pillar and Phantom Cracks area. To date Trevor has remained active with a variety of partners putting up moderate traditional lines like "Angelua Vicia" (10a) on Phantom Tower, extending an earlier variation of the "South Face" as an independent line to the top of the tower. Another traditional effort was "The Bat and The Raven" (10b) in Wully Canyon filling a much-needed void in the moderate traditional scene.

Inspired by Trevor, Jo-Jo continued to unearth some notable-but-forgotten gems at Sentinel and Silver-Tongued Devil crags and added his own "Tough Trip Through Paradise" (5.10b) with Bruce Hendricks in 1993. This was the first ascent of the heretofore unclimbed South Phantom Crags.

Soon after the first ascent of "Dirty Dancing," a new style appeared; one that has created some of the finest multi-pitch climbs in the Rockies. The style is ground-up, bolting on-lead with a power drill. In 1993, Genereux and Tim Pochay opened the gates with their

Tim Pochay

instant classic "Southern Exposure" (5.11a) on Grey Ghost Wall. Genereux was the driving force behind "Windmills of the Mind" (drilled on-lead without hooks at 5.11b), "Zephyr" (5.11a), the Rookie (5.11a) and "Wully Sport" (5.11b/c). This latter route includes one of the harder crack pitches on local limestone. Although all of these routes require natural gear, they are predominantly protected and belayed from bolts. By using the drill, climbers have been able to stray away from the natural cracks and corners that generally hold the loosest rock, and by climbing them from the ground up, these routes preserve a large adventure component.

In pure Ghost tradition, however, older values have continued to ring true. Traditional styled routes continue to go up at the same pace as modern bolted sport climbs, with the addition of "Prosopopoeia" (5.11b/c) on Epitaph Wall in 1995 by Keith Haberl and Shep Steiner. Climbed between bitter August storms in a one-day effort, the pair used only one bolt on this committing route that finished up "Creamed Cheese" in the pouring rain and darkness. It was one of the hardest, traditional, multi-pitch routes done in the Ghost. In 1998 Keith with friends Chris Robertson and Brian Spear climbed another traditional test piece "Forbidden

Andy Dunlop, Trevor Jones and Martyn White on an early CMC trip in 1975, resulting in the first ascent of Phantom Tower. Photo Chris Perry.

Planet", 5.11d, on "Bastion Wall" using minimal bolt placements. This baby took a concerted effort over several attempts to establish the climb. Bolts were both hand drilled and put in with a power drill. All efforts were ground up, on the forth and final day all pitches were redpointed. The similar but slightly easier route "Babarella Psychadella" just to the left was cleaned and bolted partially on rappel showing that a mix of the two styles could coexist; one no better than the other. The only thing being lost is the experience by the first ascensionist of charging up into unknown ground.

Since then Keith Haberl and Brian Spear along with Ken Wylie and several friends have put up six more multi pitch routes to "storm the bastion" as it were. Some are in the traditional motif while others resemble sport routes with some gear. This group also established the only new route in the "Waiparous Drainage" since the last guide, "The Ardent Heart" 5.10d another offering in the finest traditional style.

The hardest technical climb to date in the Ghost is the traditional test piece "Dionysus" 12.d/13.a/R put up in 1999 by Ben Firth the son of Ghost pioneer Jack

Ken Wiley

Firth. Ben has a desire to seek out difficult bits of rock and work them out using the available protection. This can leave for some heady moments as you look at the potential to hit the deck doing the crux moves. This necky and bold style looks back to British roots and the hard problems done on gritstone.

There is another unusual style that was started in the Ghost by Andy Genereux, that of rope soloing to put up new climbs. He has also carried this ethic into the Bow Valley establishing major routes on Yamnuska. This requires total commitment and confidence in ones ability. Andy has continued to lead the way with this style with several roped solo efforts both ground up and rappel bolting then rope soloing the route. This all started on the "Haystack" with the climb "Solitaire", 1989, completed with a dubious self-belay system using "jumars". The introduction of a device called the "soloist" has allowed Andy to push a lot harder. This style continued with classics like "The Nutman" 5.10d established ground up using a power drill all bolts drilled from free stances and "Cashew Sunday" 5.11c rap bolted and rope soloed in a day. The ethic has culminated with "The Gods Must Be Angry" 5.11d/12a in 2002. This climb was started ground up including the hardest pitch, then was completed by rappelling to clean and bolt, then rope solo the upper four pitches in a single day.

Sport climbing has also continued to progress, not at the expense of, but in conjunction with the traditional climbing scene. To date only small selections of the potential for sport climbing have been touched. The primary venues have been Wild West Wall, Spirit Pillar, Phantom Bluffs, Silver Tongued Devil Crag the Dirty Dancing area. The former has, to date, produced some of the finest sport climbs in the Ghost, highlighted by Pochay and Genereux's mega-classics "Blade Runner" 5.12a and the spectacular "Dreams of Verdon" 5. 12a. This latter six-pitch route was completed in 1996 from the top down after several efforts over three years. With four pitches going at mid-5.11 and one 5.12, "Dreams of Verdon" is the hallmark sport climb of the Ghost. Two more recent routes of this nature were put up to the right of Dirty Dancing in a couple of solo bolting efforts by Andy Genereux the best being "Smoking In the Boy's Room" 5.11c which sports 5 mid–5.11 pitches with an optional 12a/b fourth pitch. There has been a raft of development on the right wall of STD Crag by a group headed up by Shawn Huisman and Jamie McVicar. From 1999 to date they have established 11 three– and four–pitch sport routes in the mid 5.10's to low 5.11 range. There has been a great deal of debate on the close spacing of bolts on these climbs. Again there was a bit of an outcry but the popular nature and the great climbing have quieted most of the critics. These climbs have filled a need for excellent although well (over?) protected multi pitch sport routes Giving the Ghost something for everyone's taste.

Brian Spear

As late as the early nineties you could characterize climbing activity in the Ghost as follows: 95% of all people rock climbing in the Ghost did the classic "Bonanza" and that route might have seen five ascents a year. Which didn't add up to a whole lot of climbers. Slowly that has begun to change. "Thor," "Southern Exposure," "The Wraith" and even "Creamed Cheese" have begun to see enough ascents that they can't be kept track of. The past seven years since the last guide have seen the volume of routes double with many different styles employed. The Ghost is no longer a backwater of Canadian Rockies climbing, it has moved beyond the golden age. Today it is not unusual to see people from the United States or Eastern Canada enjoying the Ghost. The Ghost is now ready to take its rightful place as a major venue in the main stream of Canadian Rockies rock climbing.

Today there are nearly 400 routes with 165 climbs being multi-pitch now established in this wonderful area. The surface has hardly been scratched and the potential barely explored. Classic climbs await those with a spirit of adventure and who still want a challenge in their climbing experience.

Some people think guidebooks will ruin the Ghost. Indeed, this version of the guide will most likely increase traffic. But if we all adhere to a standard of decency and respect, the Ghost will remain a perfect place to camp, to seek adventure and to enjoy the experience of climbing in one of the Rockies truly special places. This guide will hopefully continue to inspire others to explore, experience and treat the Ghost with the same admiration and respect I have given it. The author has almost 25 years of experience in the area. The reasoning behind this book is to share the wonders and joy's of the Ghost climbing.

USING THIS GUIDE

The climbing areas will be described in a clockwise sequence starting with the southern crags and moving north. The climbs on each cliff (except for noted exceptions) will be described in a left to right fashion. Unless indicated, all directions for approach, while climbing, and for rappelling will assume that the climbers are facing the rock. For downclimbing, directions assume that climbers are facing out.

The Parking Access and Approach Details in each chapter take you from the standard parking area to the base of the cliff only. To find your way to the Ghost, please refer to the "Getting There" section on page 19.

When available, we have included topos. It is important to note that because a route does not have a topo it doesn't mean that it's not worth doing. The reason for no topo is probably because the authors could not get adequate information. New topos and updates to existing ones are greatly appreciated.

A star system is used to indicate route quality. The range is from one to three stars. Three stars indicates a classic in the style. Two stars refer to an exceptional climb of a given type. One star indicated a very good climb. All of the star ratings refer to and are compared to climbs in the Ghost River only. No comparison or illusion toward other climbs or areas is intended. If a climb does not have a star rating it does not imply that the climb is not worth doing. It simply means that there may not have been enough information or a consensus to arrive at a star rating. If I know a route to be truly poor, I will tell you.

Consider the following story. In 1992, two Calgary climbers went to climb the then obscure route "The Wraith." After two attempts (one thwarted by a rainstorm) they finished the route (a possible second ascent) to find what is perhaps the most sustained and best 5.9 route in the area including Yamnuska (it was originally graded 5.8). The moral of the story is this: the Ghost has a reputation for coughing up forgotten gems (another one was "Duveinafees," rediscovered in 1996). A third gem would be "Mantissa" rediscovered in the late nineties. One reason many of the older routes don't have stars is because not much is known about them. If you happen to find a forgotten gem, do a new route, or have corrected information on any established route, please contact the author at the following address:

Andy Genereux, 4828 Nordegg Cres NW, Calgary, AB T2K 2M5
or via Rocky Mountain Books, #4 Spruce Centre SW, Calgary, AB T3C 3B3

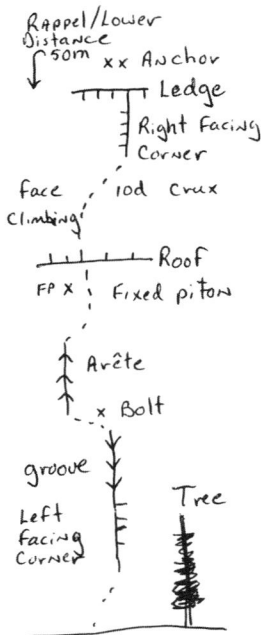

Ben Firth on-sighting "Blade Runner." Photo: Paul Valiulis.

Devil's Gap

A map of the Devil's Gap area showing climbing crags and landmarks, including: The Big Hill, The Peanut, The Drip Route, three-way intersection, Black Strap, Orient Point, South Phantom Crags, Phantom Tower, Morning Glory Tower, Kolbassa Wall, Border Bluffs, Phantom Crag East, West Phantom Crag, Bonanza Descent Gully, Spectre Crag, Planters Valley, DEVIL'S GAP, Lakes, Ghost, Costigan's Boil, BANFF NATIONAL PARK, and Lake Minnewanka. Compass showing N direction. Parking areas marked with P.

Orient Point is the most easterly of the peaks on the south side of the Minnewanka Valley. See the map on page 34. It is a massive and complex mountain, surrounded almost entirely by cliff bands. Aside from the climbs in Planters Valley, however, only three rock climbs have been established. Each climb is unique, if not bizarre. They stand testimony to the exploration of Ghost pioneer Frank Campbell. The three climbs are described below and those in Planters Valley are covered in the Devil's Gap section starting on page 39.

Frank has recently been back at work on Orient Point along with the original "Bulky Boy" Rick Felber. They are known to be working on several short routes at a cliff east of the waterfall ice climb "The Big Drip" on the eastern reaches of the "Point." So far none of the climbs have been completed but one is bolted and several projects have anchors. The approach depends on your 4X4-capability. From the three-way intersection take the river road (south fork) far as you can. Follow trails south until below the "Point". It takes between 45 minutes to an hour and a half to reach the cliff. You will have to get specific details from the boys to find out what toys to bring.

"The Peanut" is an intriguing pinnacle located in a notch between a much larger outlying pinnacle and the east ridge of Orient Point. It is only distinguishable as a separate feature when viewed from near the three-way intersection at the entrance to the Minnewanka Valley. From here, it is located approximately due south. It has a long approach and is perhaps a climb to do just "because it is there."

"The Drip" was done to serve as an approach to "The Big Drip," a waterfall ice climb that forms in one of the large bowls on the east side of Orient Point, north of "The Peanut." This huge curtain of ice rarely extends down past a halfway ledge and is usually reached via a lengthy approach from above. This three pitch rock route was established to access the ice from below on warm and sunny winter days.

The remaining climb, "Black Strap," was completed for more conventional reasons— it climbs an interesting feature on generally good rock. It is currently the only climb on a large band of cliffs that angles slightly up and left across the east side of the northern subsidiary peak of Orient Point. The cliffs face the access road directly when viewed from between the Big Hill and the three-way intersection and are situated immediately below the summit of the subsidiary peak. A huge open corner at the apex of a large scree cone breaks through the cliff band just left of centre, and immediately left of this is a buttress with a rounded nose of rock on its left side that extends almost to the top. A shallow, right-facing corner system forms the right side of the nose, and at the top of this on the right is a prominent, square-cut overhang. This overhang, and one on the opposite side, form two "eyes" above the "nose." "Black Strap" climbs the corner to the top of the nose and continues up to the top of the cliff. Despite its relatively long approach, it is reported to be a worthwhile route.

The extensive cliff bands on Orient Point have received little attention because many of them face north and east and are relatively difficult to access. The area around "Black Strap" and the waterworn walls above the ice climb "Wicked Wanda" appear to be the most promising areas for new climbs many of the potential projects look to be moderate traditional lines which await exploration.

Orient Point

A. The Peanut
B. The Drip
C. Black Strap, see opposite

Approach Details

Approach for the first two climbs is described from the three-way intersection mentioned in the Devil's Gap parking access, see page 40.

The Peanut 5.7, 15 m, gear to 2"

F. Campbell & O. Miskiw, June 1987

This climb definitely has the worst ratio of good climbing to approach length than any other in the guidebook. However, the appeal of this little pinnacle, tucked in a distant notch, is undeniable. If no one else will go, ask Frank, he is probably good for the second ascent!

From the three-way intersection, head due south on the River Road and park as close as possible to the gully on the north side of the notch. Take the line of least resistance up through the trees and then climb the gully (4th class) to the notch. Climb the wall on the left (east) side of the pinnacle to a piton belay at the top.

Descend by rappel.

The larger outlying pinnacle can also be climbed at easy 5th class.

The Drip 5.8+, 95 m, gear to 4"

F. Campbell & P. Stoliker, 1986

This route lies in the left hand of two major bowls, readily seen from the top of the Big Hill, on the east face of Orient Point. At the three-way intersection, head south on the River Road for almost 2 km to a small drainage that comes down from the two bowls. Hike directly up the drainage and at a Y-junction, follow the left fork up into a bowl below the waterfall. Scramble up to the top of the scree/snow cone on the right of the waterfall and begin slightly to the right.

1) 5.8, 40 m. Climb up for a few meters and then traverse left to a large flake. Either squeeze up the more secure, inside chimney or go up the outside of the flake to the top. Continue up a left-facing corner to a piton belay.
2) 5.5, 10 m. Move right across a ledge to a fixed rappel station by a right-facing corner.
3) 5.8+, 45 m. Climb up and right to a bolt and then go back left to some small flakes. Move up to a piton and continue past two bolts (5.8+) to a groove on the left. Go up this to a fixed station on a big ledge. This ledge leads left to the waterfall.

Descend the route in two 55 m rappels.

Black Strap

Orient Point

Black Strap* 5.8, 200 m, gear to 4"
J. Rowe & F. Campbell, May 1984

This interesting climb has had several ascents. However, the description given below was "interpreted" from two slightly contradictory sources. As such, pitch lengths are approximate so do the climb expecting a grading sandbag.

The approach is reportedly not as bad as it looks. Start at the park boundary as for other climbs in Devil's Gap (see page 40 for parking access). Walk south directly up the cut line marking the boundary to a large cairn at the top of a hill. Continue south for about 50 m to an east-west horse trail that goes along the bench a few hundred meters above the valley floor. Follow the horse trail left to a point below and slightly right of the large scree cone noted on page 37. Walk up through fairly open trees and continue up the right side of the scree cone to some house-sized blocks near the top. Move over to the left side and then scramble up and left (3rd class) following ledges past the outside of some small pinnacles (ignore an obvious gully on the right). Move up and left over a short step to the end of easy ground, below and about 6 m right of a right-facing corner. The main upper corner on the right side of the "nose" is now some distance up and to the left, out of view.

1) 5.8, 45 m. Move up and traverse left into the corner. Climb the wide crack in the corner to below a loose-looking section (#11 Hex), and then traverse left on to the edge and go up to a small belay.

2) 5.6, 40 m. Easy climbing leads up and left into the main corner system.

3) 5.8, 45 m. Climb the crack in the corner to a steep section and then move out left to belay.

4) 5.7, 30 m. The next pitch climbs the left wall of the corner to the top of the "nose." Go up left across the wall and then back right for a short distance to a see-through crack. Climb the crack and continue up past loose blocks to a good crack that leads to easy ground and the top of the "nose." Move right to a fixed belay and rappel station immediately left of the large roof.

5) 5.7, 40 m. Make a short, loose traverse left and then go up to a block at the base of a crack. Climb the crack to a tree belay at the top of the cliff.

To descend, move across right (north) to a good tree with a small cairn above and rappel past a large overhang to the fixed station at the top of pitch 4 (45 m). The second rappel leads to a ledge system (45 m) on the right wall of the corner; walk north along this to the next station (bolt and piton). Continue down past a third fixed station, at a ledge (40 m) to easy scrambling at the base of the cliff (30 m).

Devil's Gap or the Lake Minnewanka Valley is the premier rock climbing venue in the Ghost River. This owes mostly to the southern exposure of the cliffs on the north side of the Gap. These are consistently the highest cliffs around with perhaps the greatest potential for more quality routes. Of the eight major walls on the north side, each one reaches at least 200 meters in height with several striving for well over 300 meters.

The four easternmost formations are spurs off the Phantom Crag massif and are the only formations with recorded climbs. Each are separated by gullies of varying size and character. They are from east to west: 1) Phantom Tower, 2) Epitaph Wall and Grey Ghost Wall, 3) Bonanza Wall and Wild West Wall and 4) Spectre Crag. The Epitaph, Grey Ghost, Bonanza and Wild West walls are known collectively as West Phantom Crag (see photo page 65).

Spectre Crag is the most-westerly of any developed venue. The large wall that is the continuation of Spectre Crag to the left remains untapped. Perhaps the most intriguing formations beyond here are the two massive caves that form the bottom of a 330 m cliff (perhaps the highest in Devil's Gap) just above the second Ghost Lake. There are two projects that climb cracks out right of these caves both are up a couple of pitches. These are near the waterfall ice routes "Dr. Heckle" and "Mr. Jive." With a mountain bike, they can be reached in about 45 minutes from the park boundary. Southern exposure and a reasonable approach should hopefully see this area bloom in the next few years.

On the south side of Devil's Gap, I have considerably less to say. Most of the walls face due north and with the high winds common to this part of Ghost they are likely to be rather cold. However, this side of the valley does hold numerous cliffs on several levels as well as one of the most consistently overhanging sections in the entire Ghost.

Devil's Gap

This spectacular cliff looms over Lake Minnewanka and appears to overhang 50 m out of 200+!

Yet aside from Planters Valley on the west side of Orient Point there are no other climbs established on the south side of Devil's Gap proper.

Parking Access

Devil's Gap, also known as the Minnewanka Valley, gives access to the following crags: Orient Point, Planters Valley, Spectre Crag, West Phantom Crag (which includes the Arrowhead pillar, Wild West Wall, Kemp Shield, Bonanza, Grey Ghost Wall (Storm Tower), Epitaph Wall and Spirit Pillar), Phantom Tower and the various Phantom Bluffs.

At the bottom of the Big Hill, turn to the left and go a short distance to a break in the bank that puts you into the riverbed. Follow various cobblestone roads south until it is possible to cross near the south end of a large gravel embankment after passing several boulder breakwaters set at 90-degree angles. Beware of the steep bank climbing out of the river. Follow a good road south for about 100 m to where it turns west. Shortly after the road turns west there is a **three-way intersection**. At this point the Banff Park service has attempted to erect a sign indicating the approaching park boundary and some previously published descriptions for the area include this sign. However, the sign rarely lasts more than a few weeks before vandals or strong winds dispatch it to the garbage pile. The sign has not been up for a few years now.

The first branch referred to as the "River Road," turns due south (left) and leads along the east side of Orient Point for an indeterminate distance. The remaining two offshoots both lead into Devil's Gap.

The middle branch turns left, goes down a bank, across the flats, then winds through the trees and takes a deeply rutted track (requiring a narrow wheel base or high clearance) for another 2 km to a large sign indicating Banff National Park. At the boundary make a sharp right turn and go a short distance to a meadow near the river. Park here—it is illegal to drive west beyond the Park Boundary huge fines can be levied. Driving farther west doesn't get you much closer to the climbs anyway. Be careful in the spring when this road can be muddy or drifted in with snow.

If you go straight from the three-way intersection the road picks its way across gravel flats following the heaviest travelled track along to a large diversion bank, follow this to a break on the left that gives access to the above-mentioned meadow area near the "Banff" park boundary. Marked by yellow pickets and a cut line. The straight-ahead variation has recently been the better option to reach the boundary parking but it still requires you have adequate power/traction to not get bogged down in loose cobblestones and gravel. If either of the options sounds iffy—walk.

Planters Valley is the only major climbing area, to date, on the south side of the Minnewanka Valley. The quality of the rock on established climbs is well above average and only a few of the routes have been repeated—beware of grading sandbags. The area is characterized by predominately crack climbing and a small selection of pitons is recommended for most routes. The climbs are located on cliffs along both the east and west sides of the valley. They are all before (north of) a narrow canyon that leads through to the upper drainage and the "Peanut Gallery" ice climbs. The cliffs are referred too as East and West Planters walls. Descriptions will start on West planters wall and go anti clock wise (right to left) around the valley as this is the way you will encounter the climbs as you ascend the valley from Devils Gap. See map on page 34.

Approach

From the large sign at the park boundary, follow the Lake Minnewanka trail west, crisscrossing a rough gravel track for the first kilometre or so. Stay on the main trail on the south side of the valley until directly opposite the Planters Valley drainage (15-20 minutes). A faint trail cuts left (south) through an open, treed flat to gain the creek bed. Follow the creek drainage up stream to the climbing areas. There is usually some water seeping through the rocks in the lower part of the valley although it may dry up in hot weather. With the exception of Cacahuete Crag all climbs in the Planters Valley require about an hour to approach from the car.

West Planters Wall

A. South End
B. Central
C. Right
D. North End
E. Cacahuète Crag

This small cliff is found on the right (west) side of the Planters Valley. It is the first cliff you see on the right side of the stream after several minutes travelling up stream. It takes about 20 to 25 minutes to get there from the parking at the Banff Park Boundary. At present there are four traditional routes described from left to right. There are no fixed anchors at this time so bring fresh slings to use for rappelling off trees. Of note is slot canyon that leads west around the corner from this crag, it has some excellent promise for one and two pitch routes on the (right) south facing side.

Sous le Vent* 5.8, 30 m, gear to 4"
L. Nicholls & S. Midwinter, August 2002

Climbs the face left of the obvious corner capped by stepped roofs on the right end of the cliff. Below the roofs climb to the corner then traverse left for three meters then continue left and descend on committing moves then up to a tree belay. Descend by rappelling 25 m from a tree.

Dénouncment** 5.8, 20 m, gear to 4"
L. Nicholls & S. Midwinter, August 2002

Located two meters right of the big corner on the right end. From a shallow scoop climb a crack up and into a v-shaped groove. When level with the base of the tree five meters to the right, traverse right along a blocky section to the tree belay. Descent is by rappel from slings around the tree.

Rapprochement 5.8, 50 m, gear to 4"
L. Nicholls & S. Midwinter, June 2002

Climbs the shallow left facing corner to the tree belay in the middle of the face. There is a second pitch that continues in the shallow corner from the tree and climbs to the top but is a less desirable outing. Descent is one 50 m rappel from a tree or two shorter rappels that require a single 60 m rope.

Mon Chiot 5.6, 40 m, gear to 4"
L. Nicholls & S. Midwinter, August 2002

Climbs the v-shaped corner to a small tree, pass this and continue on scrappy ground to a large tree at 40 m, Rappel to descend from a sling on a tree.

CACAHUÈTE CRAG

A Sous Le vent *	5.8	gear to 4"
B Denouncment **	5.8	gear to 4"
C Rapproachment	5.8	gear to 4"
D Mon Chiot	5.6	gear to 4"

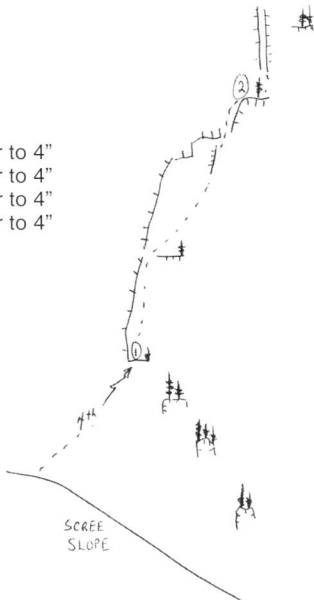

WEST PLANTERS WALL, NORTH END

Forage For Porage *   5.7
160 m, gear standard rack to 4"

Forrage for Porage* 5.7, 160 m, gear standard rack to 4"
L. Nicolls & S. Midwinter, September 2002

The climb is located on the lower angled northeast-facing corner of the West Planters Wall. Located north of a deep slot canyon that cuts deep into West Planters Wall. This moderate angled wall has excellent potential for moderate traditional lines before the wall turns into the overhanging north face. Locate three small tree islands that rise up the wall just left of centre. The route starts just left of the highest Tree Island. The rock is lower angled and has lots of cracks, which allows for several options on the climb, take the line of least resistance. See photo page 41.

Approach

Approach as for "Planters Valley" (page 41). From where the trail forks to head south into the Planters Valley stay on the main trail and continue west. From this point the wall with the three small tree islands and the descent are clearly visible to the west take a moment to survey and plan your day. Travel west on the main trail to a fork that heads to the dry lake. Stay left on the main trail for another 200 m to a small scree fan that crosses the trail. Head up this staying on the right side, then take large sized scree to head up to the main wall. Traverse left, climbing the slope along the base until it is possible to traverse right onto the wall just to the left of the highest of three small tree islands. Topo page 43.

1) 5.6, 35 m. Go up a crack in the corner above to a ledge with a small tree. Move up the corner to a second ledge and small tree and belay at a natural stance.

2) 5.7, 35 m. Continue up the v-shaped groove until below a roof. Move right onto the face then up into a gully at the bottom of a broad chimney. Angle up and right to a ledge and a tree belay.

3) 5.5, 40 m. Climb the shallow v-shaped chimney to the top of a ridge, easy ground leads up and right to the base of a shattered pillar with a steep crack that slits the face.

4) 5.7, 50 m. Climb the steep crack up the pillar 5.7 be careful passing a couple of suspect blocks. Easy ground heads up and right to a short step then into a corner to the top.

Descent: is by traversing left then down through trees keeping a large slot canyon on your right as you descend. At a cliff band a 50 m rappel from trees is required, then continue down and follow the wall left to the base of the route.

The Scar* 5.9, 150 m, gear standard rack to 4"

J. A. Owen & F. Campbell, June 1987

Towards the north end of West Planters Wall there is an area of grey slabby rock bounded on the right by a big slot canyon. Bordered to the left by a corner and a steep yellow wall. Immediately left of the yellow wall there is a striking, right-slanting corner system, capped by a large roof. "The Scar" climbs the corner system and exits to the right around the roof.

Approach

Walk south up Planters Valley to a large scree gully directly below the climb. Continue up the creek for a short distance to a large talus slope, ascend through trees right of the talus, and then follow a ridge between the talus slope and the scree gully to reach the main cliff just left of a lower cliff band. Traverse right along ledges above the lower cliffs and then go up to an alcove at the base of the main corner. The first pitch climbs a short buttress on the left side of the alcove to gain the main corner system above.

1) 5.7, 25 m. Beginning just left of the main corner line, climb the wall into a large right-facing corner and follow it to a belay ledge by a block on the left.

2) 5.5, 30 m. Traverse right and down slightly then climb up to gain the main corner system and climb up easily to a good ledge on the right side where the wall steepens (bolt).

3) 5.9, 40 m. Climb up and right onto the steep face and continue up past a bolt to an overhang. Move left to overcome the overlap (5.9), then continue up using a vertical crack. Belay on the right (bolt).

4) 5.8, 35 m. Continue up the corner passing a bolt on the right wall, stay with the corner to a stance on the right below the large roof.

5) 5.6, 20 m. Climb up and trending right below the roof, climb to the top and belay off trees.

Descend by rappelling from trees at the north end of the cliff, just beyond the section of grey slabby rock. Careful choice of tree location, slings and two 50 m ropes are required.

A. Acorn-er
B. Third Movement
C. Second Movement
D. First Movement
○ Rappel Anchors

Nutcracker Sweet: First Movement* 5.8, 115 m, gear to 4" & pitons
P. Stoliker & L. DeMarsh, Aug. 1987

Despite mostly excellent rock the climb is, in places, difficult to protect without pitons, most noticeably on the first pitch and the final corner. Start about 5 m right (north) of the apex of the scree cone.

1) 5.7, 35 m. Climb up to a scree ledge. Follow steps up and left to another scree ledge. Move up and left along the ledge to an alcove (piton—hidden at the back of small edge) roughly 7 m below and slightly left of a large corner crack (Second Movement).

2) 5.7, 40 m. Step left from the belay and move up for about 4 m to the bottom of a finger crack. This crack is 3 m left of the large crack on the "Second Movement." Make a few moves up the finger crack then take a difficult step left to easier ground in a corner. Go up to a large ledge with a **rappel chains** pass this and move left along the ledge and follow an obvious corner to a small ledge at the bottom of a crack to belay (1"-2.5" friends useful for the belay).

3) 5.8, 40 m. Climb the crack to a loose block. Climb up right on big holds then step left, over top the block to a large ledge (be careful not to disturb the block). From the left side of the ledge, climb a slanting corner to a ledge. Step up to a piton and continue right into an open book with a tiny crack. Stem the open book (crux—knifeblade pitons recommended) to the fault line and step right to a bolt/piton belay with **rappel chains**.

Nutcracker Sweet: Second Movement** 5.8, 100 m,
gear standard rack to 4"
P. Stoliker & L. DeMarsh, Sept. 1987

This climb starts just left of "First Movement" and crosses it at the first belay and again just before the fault line.

1) 5.8, 25 m. Climb the steep left-trending crack about 5 m left of the apex of the scree cone and then continue up and right over easy steps to belay as for "First Movement" (piton).

2) 5.8, 45 m. Climb the wide crack above and slightly right of the belay. Continue up easier cracks to a ledge at the bottom of an inside corner with a large crack 3 m to its left. Climb the corner and then step left to the base of another corner at the top of the wide crack. Move up this to a good belay in an alcove a few metres higher.

3) 5.8, 30 m. Climb straight up for 3 m and then left for 7 m to rejoin "First Movement." Follow the "First Movement" for a short distance to the open book about 7 m below the fault line. The original line moves left for 2 m, then up and left over a slab (often wet) to the fault line. It is recommended, however, to finish straight up the corner as per the "First Movement."

Nutcracker Sweet: Third Movement * 5.8, 95 m, gear to 4"
P. Stoliker, L. DeMarsh & M. Haden, Oct. 1987

Start about 20 m left of the top of the scree cone and scramble up and left for 30 m to the bottom of two cracks.

1) 5.7, 40 m. Climb the steep right-hand crack, past loose-looking blocks for about 4 m to a ledge. Move up and right over easy ground to the base of a large crack in a left-facing corner. Follow the corner to a ledge below a finger crack.

2) 5.8, 45 m. Climb the crack to a ledge and then follow "First Movement" up to the fault line.

Acorn-er* 5.9,120 m, gear standard rack to 4"
P. Stoliker, L. DeMarsh & M. Haden, Oct. 1987

The climbing in the upper corner is interesting and well protected. Start about 50 m below and left of the scree cone at three small trees, below and slightly to the right of the main corner.

1) 5.3, 40 m. Follow a blocky corner up and left to the first awkward section.

2) 5.6, 45 m. Continue up the corner for about 7 m to easy ground. Move up and right and then climb yellow rock on the left to a ledge about 10 m below a huge roof.

3) 5.9, 35 m. Move up and right to a ledge. Avoid the next ugly-looking section of the corner by moving right on the ledge, then climbing a groove back left. Follow the obvious jam-crack up and around a roof to the fault line.

4) 5.4, 40 m. Traverse right along the fault line to the Nutcracker Sweet descent.

This area extends south from the prow line left of the "Nutcracker" area to where the cliff diminishes to allow access to the upper drainage the canyon containing the ice climbing. The first climb "Pistachio Pillar" is located at the approximate centre of this area. It climbs the right side of a prominent pillar that ends at half height on the wall. Above the treed slope 50 m south of the pillar are two climbs "Wall Nut" and "Nuts and Bolts". The right facing stepped corner above the left edge of the treed patch is "Peanut Dogleg".

Approach
There is a stepped buttress located just to the south (left) of "Peanut Dogleg" which extends almost down to the creek drainage. Scramble up scree slopes immediately north (right) of the buttress to reach the trees below the main cliff near "Peanut Dogleg," a prominent right-facing open book leading up to stepped overhangs that trend up to the right.

Descent
The three most southern climbs descend the buttress, by two 50 m rappels from trees 40 m to the south of "Peanut Dogleg".

Pistachio Pillar* 5.8, 45 m, gear to 4″
G. MacRae, M. Sennick

Climbs an obvious right facing pillar that rises to half height on the wall. It is located roughly in the centre of the area referred to as the South End See photo page 51. You find this climb 50 m north (right) of "Wall Nut". Traverse the base of the wall right past the treed slope, then a blocky sparsely treed ground climbs up and right to the base of the pillar.

1) 5.8, 25 m. Climb the right side of the obvious pillar. Stay with the corner until it is possible to belay in the corner opposite a small tree (a natural stance).

2) 5.7, 20 m. Continue to the top of the pillar then to the top of a large flake belay on gear.

Descent: The first ascent team rappelled off the flake simultaneously from opposite sides, single strand leaving no anchor (reminiscent of the Needles). It is recommended that ringbolts be installed to accommodate an easier rappel in the future.

Wall Nut* 5.10a, 115 m, gear to 4″
P. Stoliker, F. Campbell & M. Haden, July 1987

This recommended route has sustained climbing on generally good rock. It may be better to split the last pitch to minimize rope drag. Start about 45 m north of "Peanut Dogleg" at a small tree a few metres off the ground in a short crack.

1) 5.9, 50 m. From the crack, climb easy steps up and left to a left-facing corner. Go up this to its end and then make an awkward move left to a point 10 m below the base of a large V-slot and crack system (30 m). Climb a short wall past a bolt and then step left into a hand crack. Follow this until it is possible to move onto a weakness in

A. Peanut Dogleg
B. Nuts & Bolts
C. Wall Nut
D. Pistachio Pillar
O Rappel points

51

the steep wall on the right. Continue up to a belay, located on a good ledge (piton) in an alcove at the top of the wall.

2) 5.4, 15 m. Move left along the ledge and belay at two small trees.

3) 5.10a, 50 m. From the right-hand tree, climb a steep wall (5.9) and then easier ground to below a small overhang (piton). Make a tricky move right around an outside corner to a small ledge below a roof (bolt) with a smooth wall on the right. Move right and up with difficulty to a jug and climb the corner above to the top.

Nuts and Bolts 5.10b, 130 m, gear to 4″
P. Stoliker & S. Brucke, July 1988

This route starts left of "Wall Nut", crosses it at half height, and then finishes on mediocre rock up and to the right. Start 10 m left of "Wall Nut" at a right-facing corner. Below is the original description.

1) 5.8, 35 m. Climb the corner for about 7 m to a ledge. Move up and left past a piton and then traverse right to a bolt and wired nut. Climb up past a second bolt to a 2-bolt belay just below a left-facing corner.

2) 5.10b, 30 m. Move up with difficulty past a bolt to a crack in the corner and follow this to the ledge on pitch 2 of "Wall Nut" (piton). Traverse easily right and down a ramping ledge to gain a piton belay in an alcove at the top of the first pitch of that route.

3) 5.7, 40 m. Move up and right over easy but loose rock, and then go back up and left on better rock to a tree.

4) 5.6, 25 m. Climb a corner to the top.

Note: The best option on the South End of the wall starts by climbing "Nuts and Bolts" to where it crosses "Wall Nut" and then follows that route to the top. This gives a fine, sustained, three-pitch climb (5.8, 5.10b, 5.10a **).

Peanut Dogleg* 5.8, 95 m, gear to 4″
P. Stoliker & J. A. Owen, June 1987

"Peanut Dogleg" follows the obvious corner/roof line noted above.

1) 5.8, 45 m. Climb the open book to a good belay ledge about 10 m below a roof.

2) 5.8, 50 m. Continue up the corner and then follow the roof to the right until one can finish up a narrow chimney. Easy climbing leads to trees at the top.

This is a fine cliff and for the most part faces west. The sun finds this wall from the climb "The Almond" north from about noon and stays there until late in the day. There are several water streaks that may stay wet until mid-season (between "Coconut" and "Macadamia"). The early probes onto this great wall tended to look at the obvious natural lines. In the past few years there have been two new lines completed that take advantage of the fantastic waterworn rock between the more traditional lines. However there are still large areas of quality grey-water-worn rock as well as several overhanging sections that remain untouched.

With the retrofitting of the rappel route to allow for 30 m rappels, this will allow most parties to climb on this wall using a single 60 m rope. Be aware other than the route "Cashew Sunday" if you are forced to retreat you will require a second rope or be leaving behind a lot of gear for others.

Approach

There are several options and all of them involve at least a little bit of scree bashing. With increased traffic a reasonable trail should become established. The normal approach is to follow the creekbed up to the canyon where the east and west walls converge and then follow a faint game trail back north along the base of the cliffs. Alternatively, a narrow gully cuts through the lower cliff bands and allows access directly to the north end of the wall. This gully also makes a convenient descent route. It is directly across from "The Scar" route on the West Planters Wall.

The climbs are described from right to left as access is normally from the creekbed at the south end of the cliff.

A. Pecan Pump topo p.64
B. Coconut & Macadamia
F. Born to Chimney

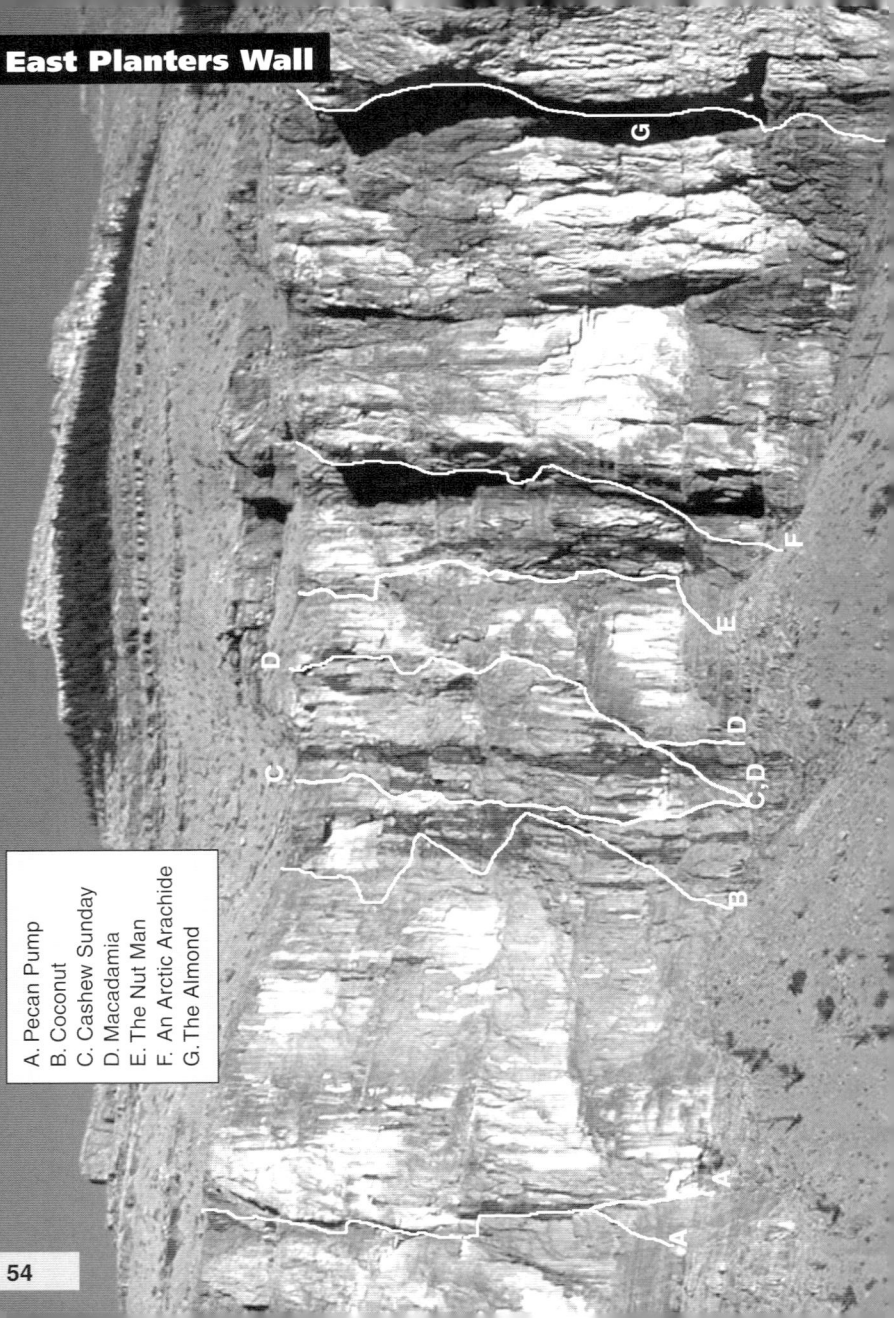

A. Pecan Pump
B. Coconut
C. Cashew Sunday
D. Macadamia
E. The Nut Man
F. An Arctic Arachide
G. The Almond

Descent

The recommended descent for all climbs except "Born To Chimney" is via a fixed rappel route situated about 20 m left (north) of "Macadamia" and about 30 m right (south) of "Coconut." See photo page 56. Four 30 m rappel stations implementing stainless bolts and ringbolt hangers (thanks to TABVAR see page 13) now replace the old corroded self-drive 50 m rappels. **Note:** the rappels are very steep and some are very close to a full 30 m make sure to tie knots in both ends of the rope before rappelling. The top station can be tricky to reach if the rock is wet. There is a second set of ringbolts a few meters north of the rappel route for the route "Cashew Sunday". This route can also be rappelled using four 30 m rappels. However it is very steep and parties will have to back clip pitches 4 and 2 to reach the anchors. The third option is to use the two 55 m rappels of the "Nut Man" located 15 m south of "Macadamia". If in doubt, walk off right (south) as for "Born to Chimney" via easy scree slopes into the canyon where the east and west walls converge.

Born to Chimney 5.7, 175 m, gear to 4" or bigger
P. Stoliker & M. Brolsma, May 1987

The name speaks for itself! "Born To Chimney" was the first route climbed in Planters Valley and has been recommended to those "with a liking for caving."

The climb follows a large, right-facing chimney that begins one pitch above the ground. It climbs the right side of the large pillar/buttress formation near the south end of the cliff. Three crack lines offer access to the ledge at the base of the chimney. Begin below the centre of these, a short distance right of the chimney. See photo page 53.

1) 5.6, 50 m. Climb the centre crack line up to the ledge.
2) 5.5, 35 m. Move left and climb a short step into the chimney. Belay 15 m higher, at the back of the chimney just past a large chockstone.
3) 5.5, 40 m. Chimney up past two large chockstones and step onto a ledge. Climb up a short step and then move back into the chimney. Follow this to a large chockstone (poor protection).
4) 5.7, 50 m. A few meters above, the chimney is blocked by another large chockstone. Pass this on the outside (5.7) and then climb over loose blocks to just below the final chimney. Move right for 5 m to an easy crack (piton), and then go up and left to the top.

The Almond** 5.9, 165 m, gear standard rack to 4"
P. Stoliker & M. Haden, Sept. 1989

"The Almond" climbs a large left-facing corner system about 180 m north of "Born To Chimney" and about 150 m south of "Macadamia." On the right wall of the corner there is a very striking crack line that, on closer inspection, turns out to be off-width. The main corner does not extend to the ground but begins at a ledge about 25 m up the cliff with a small tree on its left side. Start at the base of the lower wall, below and slightly right of the tree, beneath a small patch of yellow rock.

Macademia

A. rappel route
B. Macadamia
C. The Nut Man
D. An Arctic Arachide
O Rappel Anchors

1) 5.9, 25 m. Climb a steep wall on jugs, past a small patch of loose yellow rock to a bolt. Follow a flake up and right (piton) to a ledge below a short corner/crack. Climb this and continue up left to the tree. This pitch may be avoided by scrambling up from the left.

2) 5.9, 50 m. Walk right to a finger/hand crack in an open book about 5 m left of the main off-width crack. Climb the open book to a ledge and then move left and climb a corner past a piton to a roof. Pull over the roof (bolt) into a niche and then move right into a widening crack on the left side of a pinnacle. Climb up for about 2 m and gain a small ledge on the steep wall to the right of the pinnacle. A couple of difficult moves on superb rock leads up to a juggy face then to a crack set at a more forgiving angle. Follow the crack to reach a two bolt belay at the top of a large pinnacle (sustained 5.9).

3) 5.8, 35 m. Move 2 m right to footholds on the wall to the right of the off-width corner-crack. Make a tricky move straight up past a bolt then follow easier ground just right of the corner/gully. Belay on the right (bolt and pitons) just before the climb steepens.

4) 5.9, 55 m. Follow the chimney/corner to the top.

An Arctic Arachide* 5.10a, 125 m, gear to 4"
P. Stoliker & F. Campbell, July 1989

"AAA" follows a large left-facing corner system about 110 m north of "The Almond" and about 40 m south of "Macadamia." A steep move on the second pitch is the only difficulty on this generally easy route. The rock is solid and waterworn. Scramble up from the left to the start of good rock at the base of the corner.

1) 5.8, 40 m. Move right and climb the centre of a steep ramp, the left side of which leads to a wide crack. At about 30 m, climb a short corner/crack and then make a tricky step left to a ledge. Belay up under a roof (piton).

2) 5.10a, 50 m. Move left across a slab and climb a short step up and right. The corner ends at a steep wall broken by two crack lines and then continues above. Climb the left-hand crack (piton, 5.10a) to a belay at the top of the steep wall (piton).

3) 5.5, 35 m. Follow the corner to the top.

The Nut Man** 5.10c, 110 m, gear to 4"
A. Genereux, July 2001

This climb was established ground up via rope solo over a five hour push. The new "Macadamia" rappel route was put in the same day. This is another wonderful addition to mid grade climbing in the Planters Valley. Located 20 m to the right of Macadamia it follows excellent rock for most of the climb. It can be rappelled with two 55 m ropes from ringbolt stations. To start the climb follow a fourth class right slanting ramp for 5 m to gain a large ledge and a single bolt for the belay.

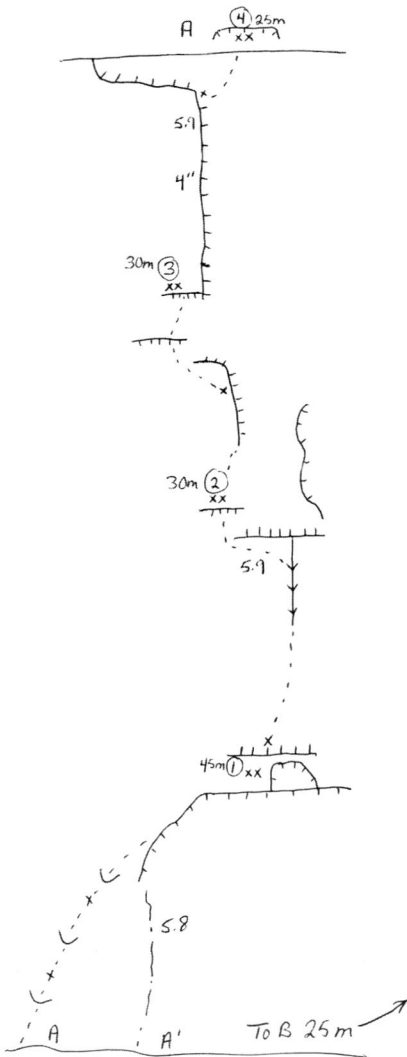

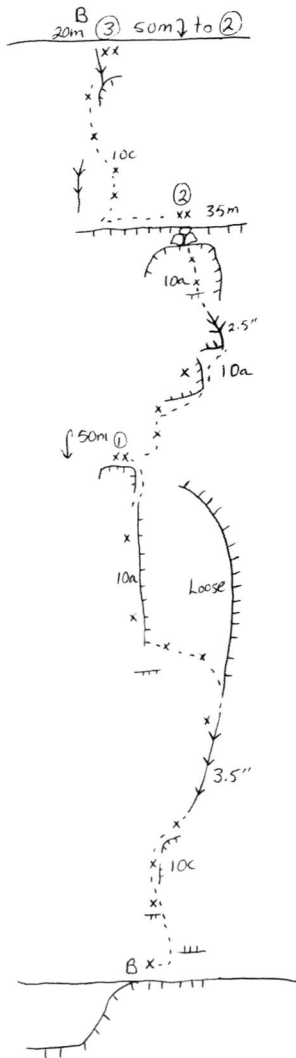

A Macadamia ***   5.9, 130 m   gear standard rack to 4" or bigger
A' Macadamia Direct Start ** 5.8   wires, small cams
B The Nutman **   5.10c, 110 m   gear to 4"

1) 5.10c/d, 50 m. Start right of the belay, make hard moves up a shallow groove, then left to a small foot ledge and a bolt. Sustained climbing leads up the groove past a bolt and gear placement to gain a 5.8 right leaning corner. Climb the corner above for 10 m to a bolt below a shattered section. Move left on big holds to a bolt then into a second small hidden corner. Climb this corner past two bolt's (5.10a) to a crack, which leads to the bolt belay on a small ledge.

2) 5.10b, 35 m. Climb the face up and right of the belay to a bolt. Hard moves climb directly up to a second bolt, then Move right to a short right facing corner. Clip the bolt on the left and make an awkward move right around the roof to gain a flaring slot. Climb the slot to a bolt on the face juggy holds lead straight up past a bolt to the top of a large pedestal. Easy ground over big blocks straight back for 5 m to a large ledge and a two-bolt belay.

3) 5.10b/c, 20 m. Traverse left along the ledge for 5 m (not hard but use care) to a bolt. Climb straight up to a bolt on sustained ground. At the second bolt move left into a shallow groove climb up the groove then right to a fourth bolt then follow the crack to the top the belay is ring bolts to the right.

Descent: Rappel the route using two 55 m rappels from ring bolts on pitches 3 & 1, or go left (north) 30 m to the Macadamia rappel four 30 m rappels.

Macadamia*** 5.9, 130 m, standard rack to 4" or bigger
P. Stoliker & F. Campbell, June 1988

"Macadamia" is one of the better moderate climbs in Planters Valley. The rock is good and the climbing is sustained at the 5.7/5.8 level. The route is located at the approximate centre of the wall. The climb ends at the obvious overhanging arch at the top of the wall. A left-facing corner leads up to the right side of the arch on the last crux pitch.

1) 5.8, 50 m. The climb begins directly below the arch at a ledge. You are presented with two options on how to start the first pitch: the first is from a clean ledge at the base of the wall climb the right leaning groove past two bolts up to a blocky ledge. Option two the **"Macadamia Direct Start"** is a few meters to the right and climbs up a set of thin hidden seams that give good protection on natural gear. Climb directly to where the groove meets the blocky ledge. Traverse up and right on the blocky ledge to a bolt belay.

2) 5.9, 35 m. Climb the overhang above the flake (piton) and follow a corner up right. Make a tricky move left to gain a large ledge system and belay (bolt and pitons) directly below the prominent corner of pitch 4.

3) 5.8, 30 m. Climb the yellow corner on the right and traverse left past a piton to a good ledge. Continue up for 5 m and belay at the right-hand end of a second ledge at the base of the final corner leading up to the overhanging arch.

Frank Campbell on the spectacular, final pitch of "Macadamia" during the first ascent. Photo: Paul Stoliker.

4) 5.9, 25 m. Climb the corner sustained (large gear) to a piton at the top and then swing out right from below the roof and up to the top of the cliff. Located on a small band of rock a few meters above the main wall is a fixed piton belay.

Cashew Sunday*** 5.11c or 5.10d, 120 m, gear to 4" and long slings
A. Genereux July 2000

The first new route established in the Planters Valley for almost a decade, a real shame considering the potential particularly on the East Planters Wall. This line was originally rap bolted and rope soloed. Unhappy with the difficult third pitch that was out of context with the other pitches Andy returned a week later with a partner and established the third pitch variation on-sight, which overall makes for an excellent 10+ adventure. The 11c direct version of the third pitch is excellent but a full number grade harder than the rest of the climbing on the route.

The climb starts of the clean ledge a few meters left of "Macadamia" and climbs the face past three bolts to a crack. The route follows several weaknesses up excellent rock.
1) 5.10b, 30 m. Climb up past three bolts to an overhanging crack. Awkwardly enter the slot and make a difficult move follow the wide crack to a semi hanging ringbolt belay.
2) 5.10a, 30 m. Leave the belay on the right by taking a series of finger cracks up to a groove, follow the groove to a step with a ringbolt belay.
3) 5.10c or 11c, 30 m. Climb the corner above the belay for 3 m then move left onto the face, sustained past two bolts, left to gain easier ground. Take a short ramp/corner to an overhanging wall, make strenuous move to gain a sloping ledge. From here climb the bulging face above past five bolts (11c) or alternatively move right a few meters (long slings required for rope drag) and climb the shallow left facing corner (10+) then back right along ledge to the belay.
4) 510d, 30 m. Move right to a short overhanging corner, make well protected but exposed, arm taxing, moves out right on juggy holds to gain a shallow right leaning ramp. Move along the ramp for 5 m then wind your way to the top steady mid 5.10 climbing on a mixture of gear.

Coconut* 5.8+, 135 m, gear to 4" double ropes recommended
P. Stoliker & F. Campbell, Sept. 1990

"Coconut" winds its way up steep ramps and ledges about 40 m left of "Macadamia" and tops out at a notch to the left of a large yellow roof. Start below a steep, right-trending ramp.
1) 5.6, 55 m. Follow the ramp on good holds for a full rope length. Move up to a ledge and go left along the ledge to a bolt belay.
2) 5.8, 40 m. Climb an easy wall up and left for about 8 m and then go back right up a steep corner (2 pitons) to easy ground. Move left along a ledge that soon ends and then step up to another ledge and belay.

Cashew Sunday

Cashew Sunday ***   5.10d or 5.11c
120 m, gear to 4" long slings

Note: When rappelling the climb using a single 60 m rope back clip pitches 4 and 2 to reach the belays.

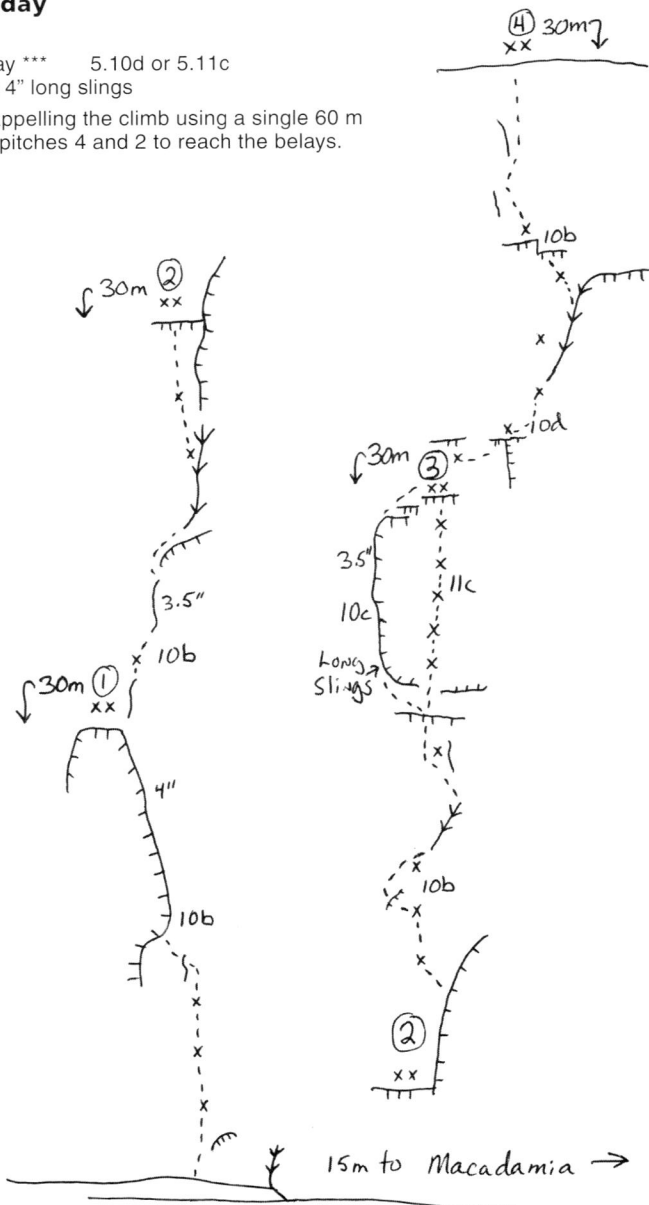

④ 30m
xx

10b

x-10d

30m ③
xx

3.5"

10c

11c

30m ②
xx

3.5"

10b

Long
Slings

30m ①
xx

4"

10b

②
xx

10b

15m to Macadamia →

3) 5.8+, 40 m. Continue up and left for about 7 m and then move back right over loose blocks to a bolt directly above the belay. Traverse right to a corner, go up this and continue straight up on excellent rock to a fixed belay at the top (2 pitons).

Pecan Pump*** 5.10b, 145 m, gear standard rack to 4"
P. Stoliker & M. Haden, Sept. 1990

This excellent route follows a prominent left-facing corner about 120 m north of "Macadamia." It features sustained 5.9/10a climbing in the lower corner-crack and steep, "pumpy" face climbing higher up. The rock is excellent throughout, making the climb one of the best in Planters Valley.

Originally you would start the climb from the left and scramble over ledges up and then right to the foot of the main corner. In 2001 A. Genereux and J. Marshall climbed the direct start to the corner that makes the climb more consistent and protects nicely on natural gear.

1) 5.10a, 50 m. Follow the corner-crack on excellent rock to a good belay (2 pitons) in a niche at the base of yellow rock. This pitch can also be reached via an easier-looking ramp from the left with spacious pro which joins the corner after a third of a pitch.

2) 5.10b, 45 m. From the niche, move left and up for about 4 m to a bolt. From here you have an option to climb straight up to a seam. This thin crack takes small gear and goes at the same grade as the Pump 3 m left but now you have reasonable protection. Or climb the "Pecan Pump" original by reaching up left to a jug above a roof and make a strenuous sequence of moves up for 3 m, this option is a bit sporty. Move back right into a groove, up this to below a roof and make thin moves right into a corner. Climb a short wall on the right and then follow the corner/crack up and left to a large ledge at the top of the steep climbing. Note: most parties choose to rappel from here.

3) 5.6, 50 m. Continue straight up to a sit-belay behind a large boulder on the scree slope.

Pecan Pump

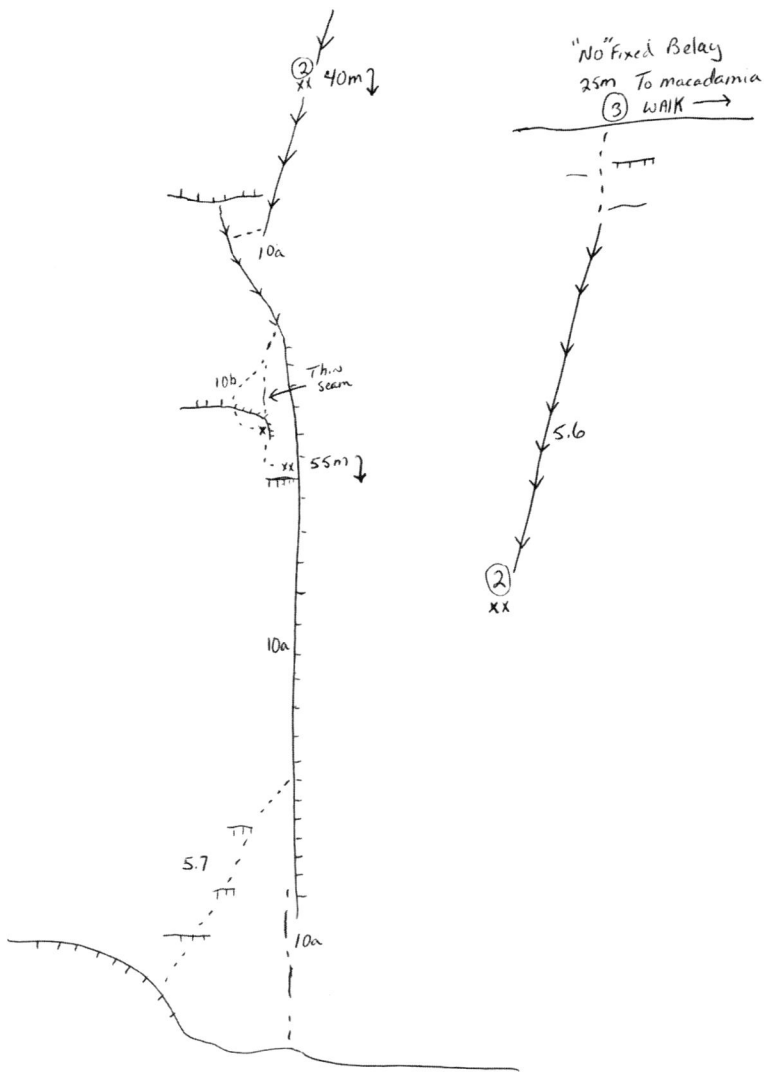

"No" Fixed Belay
25m To macadamia
(3) WALK →

(2)
xx 40m ↓

10a

Thin seam

10b

x

xx 55m ↓

5.6

10a

(2)
xx

5.7

10a

10a

Pecan Pump ***   5.10b, 145 m   Standard rack to 4", RP's & TCU's

A. Spectre Crag
B. Wild West Wall
C. Kemp Shield
D. Bonanza
E. Bonanza Descent Gully

F. Grey Ghost Wall
G. Epitaph Wall
H. Phantom Tower
I. Border Bluffs

J. Kolbassa Wall
K. Morning Glory Tower
L. East Phantom Crag Summit
M. Mount Costigan

This is the most westerly of the established climbing areas in Devil's Gap. Directly opposite Planters Valley there is a deep gully that breaks through the main cliff band. This is the location of the ice climbs "Aquarius" and "The Recital Hall." Located left of "Aquarius" is Spectre Crag and to the right is the Wild West Wall area of West Phantom Crag. The Spectre Crag routes are on the grey section of cliff and are visible from the parking area at the park boundary. The crag has been climbed upon sporadically since the time of the first ascents and more traffic will likely establish several of the climbs as classics, particularly "Hoss" and "Spectre's Knife." No one has yet looked at the more blank sections of the cliff, some of which are very steep. Pitons are advisable for all the routes on Spectre Crag. See photo page 65.

Approach
From the park boundary, follow the Lake Minnewanka trail west, as described in Planters Valley (page 41). After about one kilometre, instead of forking left toward the south side of the main valley, continue straight following the Gravel Trough Road to gain the riverbed near the first Ghost Lake. The lake may be dry later in the year and may also be reached by following the riverbed directly. Cross over to the north side of the river near the lake inlet and move west to the base of the "Aquarius" drainage. Hike up through fairly open trees and then move over left on easy slopes to skirt around the lower cliff band. Continue up and then left through sparsely treed, broken ground. During spring runoff, this approach may require a considerable amount of snorkeling. If so, approach by continuing west from the Wild West Wall. See pages 71 & 73 for details and contour north around the "Aquarius" drainage between Spectre Crag and the Wild West Wall. Allow about an hour and twenty minutes for this option.

Descent
For "Ponderosa Right", "Spectre's Knife" and "Hoss" it is possible to rappel the routes from fixed anchors (bring slings). Otherwise walk right (north) along the top of the cliff to the highest point and then continue down to the east for about 100 m into a bay. Three airy rappels from conveniently placed trees lead to the base of the cliff. The first rappel is a full 55 m. See photo page 67.

Ponderosa Right* 180 m, 5.9+, 180 m, gear to 4" and pitons
F. Campbell & J. A. Owen, May 1987

"Ponderosa Right" and "Left" start at the left end of a treed ledge about one pitch up the cliff. The ledge is reached by scrambling up easy ground on the right and then moving over left. From part way up the fourth pitch the Right or Left finish may be taken. Each is described separately.
1) 5.7, 30 m. Either climb the right-hand crack that overhangs slightly at first or follow an easier corner on the left to a fixed belay station.
2) 5.8, 45 m. Continue up a corner on the left passing a small overhang lower down to a horizontal break in the wall.

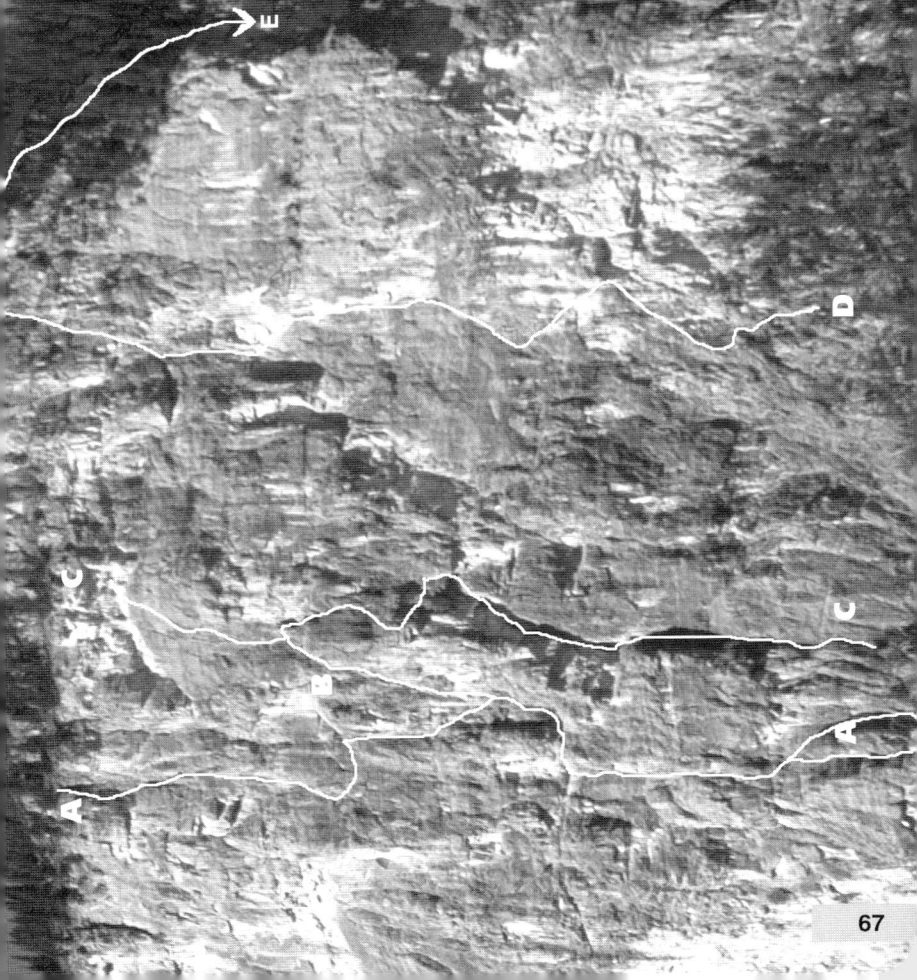

A. Ponderosa Left
B. Ponderosa Right
C. Hoss
D. Spectre's Knife
E. tree rappel

3) 5.7, 15 m. Traverse right around a buttress to an alcove with a tree and fixed belay.

4) 5.8, 55 m. Climb a break on the right side of the tree for about 10 m and then continue up a chimney to a fixed belay almost at the top of a pinnacle.

5) 5.9+, 35 m. Climb a break in the face, above and slightly left of the pinnacle, then follow a crack in the slab above to a fixed belay under an overhang just below the top.

Ponderosa Left 5.9, 220 m, gear standard rack to 4″ and pitons
F. Campbell & J. Rowe, May 1987

"Ponderosa Left" moves left and continues up to the top of the cliff from part way up pitch 4 of "Ponderosa Right."

1-3) As for "Ponderosa Right."

4) 5.8, 45 m. Climb a break on the right side of the tree for about 10 m (as for "Ponderosa Right") and then continue up and left following a crack system on good rock to a sloping ledge below overhangs.

5) 5.6, 35 m. Move down and left to gain another crack system and follow this to a belay.

6) 5.8, 55 m. Continue up the loose crack system to the top.

Hoss* 5.9+, 190 m, gear standard rack to 4″, and pitons
P. Stoliker & L. DeMarsh, Oct. 1987

"Hoss" follows a large right-facing corner topped by a huge block, just right of "Ponderosa Right." It joins that route at the top of a pinnacle, about three-quarters of the way up the cliff. The climbing is interesting and on generally good rock although two large blocks on pitch four require special care.

Start 10 m right of "Ponderosa," directly under the main corner, about 8 m below a tree growing horizontally out from a ledge.

1) 5.7, 50 m. Climb up to the tree and continue up the corner above to a ledge. Move up past a piton to a higher ledge and then go up right past a loose rock into a crack. Follow the crack until it steepens and then move up and left across a slab to a belay (bolt and piton) in the main corner.

2) 5.8, 20 m. Continue up the corner to a belay (piton and wired hex) on a ramp at the base of a wide crack in a huge corner.

3) 5.8, 25 m. With gardening tools at the ready, climb the crack for 5 m and then move right onto the face. Climb up to a bolt and then back left into the corner at the top of the steep section. Follow the corner for 5 m and move right onto the face again. Climb up to a ledge and move right and up to belay (bolt) at another ledge about 4 m below a roof and a large loose block.

4) 5.9, 35 m. Move around the roof with care and follow face holds to a bolt directly below the huge block at the top of the main corner. Pull over the block on its right, traverse left below overhangs, and climb up and left to belay on a ledge at the top of the overhangs.

5) 5.6, 25 m. Climb the crack above and follow an easy gully to the top of a pinnacle (junction with "Ponderosa") and fixed belay on the left side.

6) 5.9+, 35 m. Climb a break in the face, above and slightly left of the pinnacle, and then follow a crack in the slab above to a fixed belay under an overhang just below the top.

Spectre's Knife** 5.8, 180 m, gear to 4", and pitons
J. A. Owen & M. McKellar, Aug. 1987

This climb starts about 50 m right of, and 25 m higher than "Ponderosa." The first pitch begins at a tree just below a small ledge with two trees growing close together. The trees are about 7 m in height and one is a "school-marm" with two trunks. The climb goes generally straight up, following a faint crack system through the blocky-looking, grey bottom section, then through yellow rock and an easily visible, short fist-crack, and finally between yellow and grey rock in a left-facing corner system to the top. Recent activity has uncovered an optional start pitch to the left, which might prove to be a better option. **See the topo** and make your own decision.

1) 5.7, 45 m. Gain the ledge above the belay and climb a crack on the right for about 3 m Move left for about 5 m and climb up trending right in cracks and grooves until just below the yellow rock. Continue up and right to a small ledge just out of sight on the right, at the start of the yellow rock.

2) 5.8, 45 m. Move up a short distance on yellow rock and traverse left for about 5 m on small holds to a ledge at the base of the fist-crack. Climb the crack and continue up and left on face holds. Go back right over easy ground to belay.

3) 5.7, 50 m. Move straight left for about 4 m to gain a corner, go up this, and continue up following the obvious line up the left facing corner between yellow and grey rock. Move left to belay at the base of a shattered pillar (piton belay). Note double rope techniques are useful on this pitch.

4) 5.8, 40 m. Step left and climb the shattered pillar to the "Knife," a sharp 12 m outside corner. Climb the knife (first on the right and then on the left), and go straight up steep cracks, followed by an easy gully up and right to a tree belay at the top.

Spectre Crag

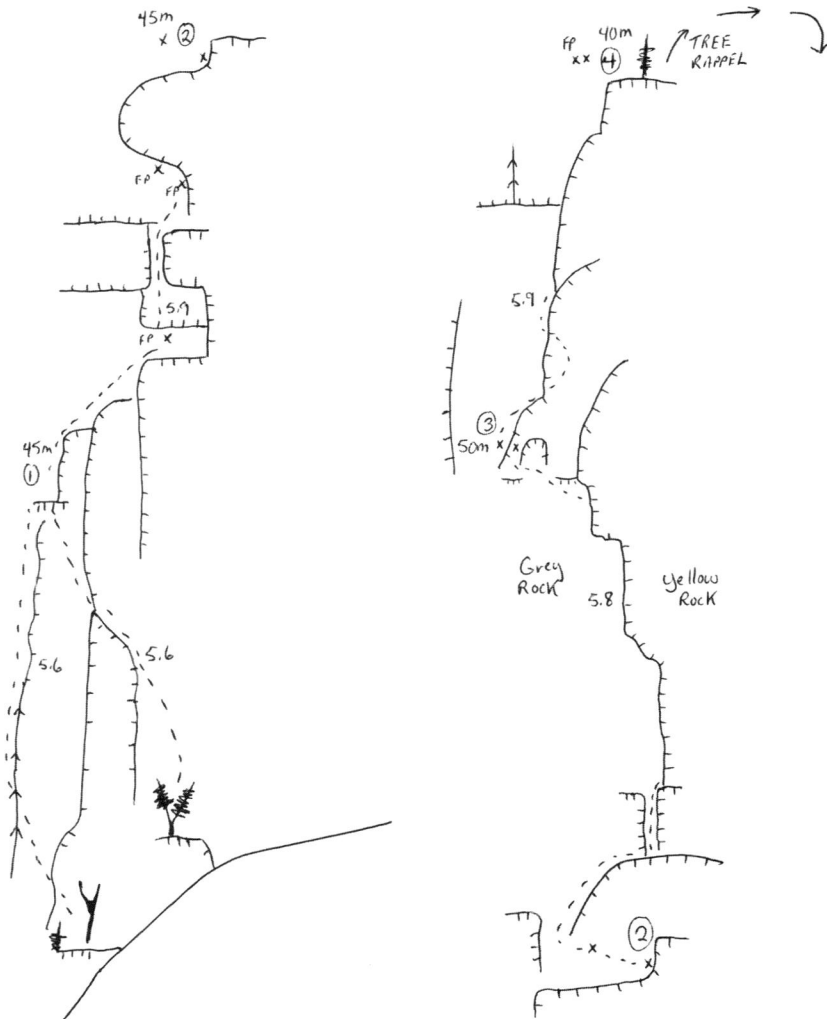

Spectre Knife ** 5.9, 180 m, gear standard rack to 4"

Slings required to rappel route.
Belay anchors could use new bolts
to replace existing fixed gear.

West Phantom Crag is the premier multi-pitch limestone crag in the Ghost if not all of Alberta. Indeed, the selection of ultra-classics is numerous, and so is the potential for new, modern routes. A straightforward approach, the southern exposure and a consistent 250-300 m height will ensure it maintains its status for some time to come.

The cliff is one-and-a-half kilometres long and is separated into six distinct areas. They will be described from west to east: Wild West Wall (including the Arrowhead), Kemp Shield, Bonanza Area, Grey Ghost Wall (including the 7 pillars of Wisdom) and Epitaph Wall (including Spirit Pillar) and Phantom Tower.

Approach

The entire West Phantom Crag is serviced by one approach. Leave your car at the Banff Park boundary in Devil's Gap. See page 39 for details to this point. Walk and/or wade downstream (west) along the riverbed. About 100 m beyond the park boundary (identified by yellow pickets) there is a treed gulch that breaks through the hillside on the right. Look for a faded, red sling on an aspen tree. Follow a trail up the gulch to where the angle lessens and it starts to curve around to the east. Hike up switchbacks on the steep hillside to the left. Continue into more open terrain to gain the crest above and follow the trail to a fork with a cairn, stay left. The right fork of the trail goes to the Phantom Bluffs "On the Border" cliff. Continue along left fork to where the trail steepens onto a scree slope, make several switchbacks and pop over a small rock band about 30 m below the main crag. You will be directly below the right side of the Grey Ghost Wall. The routes "Southern Exposure" and "Windmills of the Mind" are looming directly above.

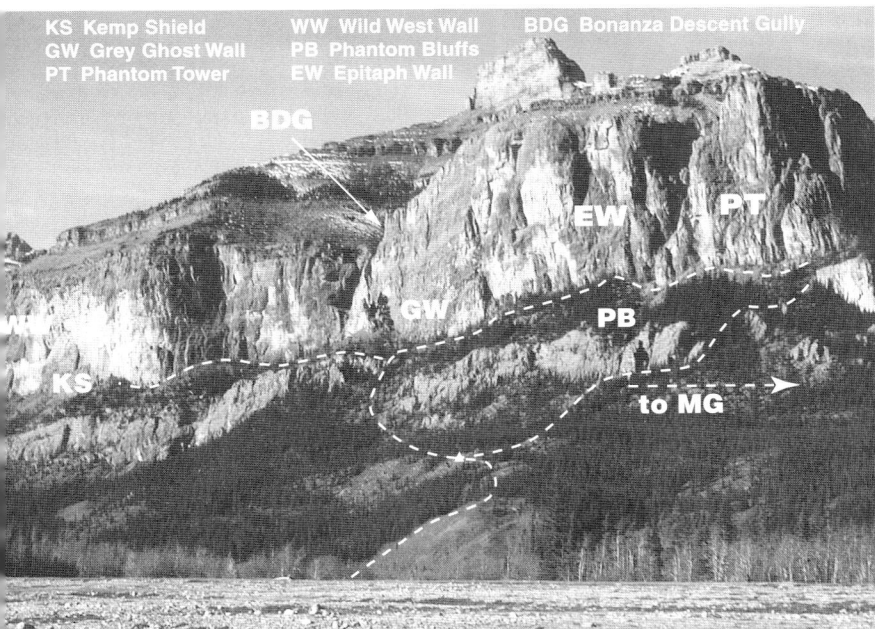

KS Kemp Shield   WW Wild West Wall   BDG Bonanza Descent Gully
GW Grey Ghost Wall   PB Phantom Bluffs
PT Phantom Tower   EW Epitaph Wall

Bonanza Descent Gully

From here a short trail switchbacks up to the base of the wall to arrive at the start of "Southern Exposure." The Grey Ghost Wall, Epitaph Wall and Phantom Tower are all reached by hiking directly uphill to the main cliff and following a trail right or left along the base to your intended route(s). The Seven Pillars of Wisdom, Bonanza Descent Gully, Bonanza Area, Kemp Shield, the Arrowhead and Wild West Wall are all found to the left by staying on the trail and traversing left after popping through the small band of rock. Follow the trail as it flattens out and contours across the hillside. After 200 m or so, the trail curves into an amphitheatre known as the Bonanza Descent Gully, home of the route "Ghost Town Blues." Above the trail, as it turns into this amphitheatre are some shattered pillars situated in front of and to the left end of the "Grey Ghost Wall". These are referred to as "The Seven Pillars of Wisdom" the tallest being Storm Tower which has three routes.

Bonanza Descent Gully

Of the multi-pitch routes that reach the top of the crag, only one, "Zephyr," is equipped for a rappel descent from above ("Dreams of Verdon" stops short of a loose, low-angled section leading to the top). The common descent for all other routes is down the Bonanza Descent Gully. This is located at the head of the amphitheatre between Grey Ghost Wall and "Bonanza."

To help avoid confusion, the following description will assist in finding the proper rappel point when descending from above. From the top of your route hike to the large bowl directly below the East Phantom Crag Summit. Once in the bowl, descend into a narrow scree gully. Follow this down to a level area with some large boulders. At this point the gully splits into the two grooves. The right-hand one (skiers right, looking down) is typically a flowing waterfall. Don't go down this one! The left-hand one is the proper descent. Scramble down this groove to a scree ledge with a small live tree and three dead ones. If in doubt use a belay to downclimb this section. Although you can't see it, you are on the edge of a 60 m cliff. From the live tree (bring a sling, because the rats will eat any that are left) rappel 20 m to a small stance with a cabled bolt anchor. From here a 50 m, mainly free-hanging rappel will reach the ground. **Note:** it is hoped that new ringbolt rappels will be installed in early 2003 look for these just after this guide is published.

A single rope rappel is possible. Some 5 m below and to climber's left of the cabled anchor there is a chained anchor—rappel here from the tree mentioned above. A 25 m rappel will reach a second chained anchor from which there is another 25 m rappel to the ground. See the topo for "Ghost Town Blues" on page 96. If the waterfall is flowing, this option will be unequivocally unpleasant.

Wild West Wall marks the far west end of West Phantom Crag. It presents consistently steep and compact rock and will likely be the scene of some really hard multi-pitch routes. Several projects are underway, but owing to the extreme time, hard-work and money commitments involved, only one has been completed. Nevertheless, the number of one, two and three pitch routes along the base and on the Arrowhead make for a fine, yet mostly harder, sport climbing venue. Avoid the area on super-hot days. This can be a great early and late season venue due to the southern exposure, however wind can be a problem on many days.

Another impressive wall lurks around the corner to the left overlooking the "Recital Hall/Aquarius" drainage. There is a very impressive overhanging bolted project that climbs the obvious line to a big cave at half height located near the back of the drainage on the west facing wall. It climbs up to a large cave then out its right side back along the lip and takes the obvious line to the top of the wall. This seven-pitch project has been under way for three years and is showing signs of being near completion.

Approach
Follow the West Phantom Crag approach as for the Bonanza Descent Gully. See page 71 for details. Continue west (left) along the base of the cliff on a good trail. After about 100 m the trail climbs to the side of a scree cone that marks the route "Bonanza." Continue across the scree cone, then down around the corner and through a patch of gnarled, bleached trees. In the open area beyond these trees is the distinct Kemp Shield. The wall left of the Kemp Shield is generally known as the Wild West Wall. The Wild West Right covers everything east of the Arrowhead to the left end of Kemp Shield and Wild West Wall Left covers everything left of the Arrowhead to the western reaches of the wall. The Arrowhead is the obvious detached pinnacle located roughly in the middle of the wall. Wild West Wall can be reached in about 15 minutes from the Bonanza Descent Gully (45-50 minutes from the park boundary). The routes will be described in a right to left fashion as this is the order in which you will encounter them.

Descent
All but two of the established routes are sport climbs and have fixed stations. Only "Dreams of Verdon" and "Cowboy's Don't Cry" will require double ropes to descend.

Wild West Wall

A. Dreams of Verdon
B. The Arrowhead
C. Smoking Gun
D. Cowboys Don't Cry
E. Cowboy Up
F. Snerty & Me

In the last guide there was only one route on this section of cliff. There have been several excellent additions in the past few years to make this wall a day trip destination on its own. It starts about 100 m west of the "Kemp Shield" and it's right side defined by a large leaning pillar with an obvious right facing off-width crack called "Snerty and Me" and runs 150 m west to the "Arrowhead" pillar which defines the left boundary.

Orange Peel*** 5.11a/b, 25 m, fixed gear
A, Genereux, Aug. 2002

Climbs the orange face just to the right of the off-width crack "Snerty and Me". Take the blocky access ledge left towards the leaning pillar to a single bolt belay. Climb the excellent prickled orange rock above on sustained face climbing.

Snerty and Me** 5.10c, 50 m, fixed gear
A. Genereux, Oct. 1998

This was the last climb Andy completed with his faithful dog Fergie (a.k.a. Snert) in attendance. It was put up on-sight via rope solo with a power drill. It climbs the obvious off-width on the right side of the pillar all bolts are located on the main face. Easy climbing leads up left on a blocky ledge to a single bolt belay. Climb the off width crack by staying to the outside and stemming and face climbing rather than mangling your body inside the wide crack, making this is really a fun climb, really! Two 25 m rappels descend down the outside on the main face left of the corner.

Cowboy Up** 5.11c, 10c, 55 m, fixed gear
A. Genereux, Oct. 2002

Located 15 m left of "Snerty and Me" and starts in a corner on the left side of a blocky pedestal. Climb the left facing corner to gain the bulging face. Sustained climbing (solid 5.11) past several bolts to a bolted belay. The second pitch is excellent but a full number grade easier and finishes at the top of the pillar with "Snerty and Me." For the five ten climber the upper pitch could be climbed in conjunction with an ascent of "Snerty and Me" by rappelling to the anchor above pitch one and then climbing back up.

Project-Sidekick
Has a bolted anchor and is halfway between "Back in the Saddle" and "Cowboy Up".

Back in the Saddle*** 5.11a, 32 m, fixed gear
A. Genereux & T. Pochay, Jun. 1995

This interesting face climb was established on lead and began the development of what appears to be a very promising piece of rock. The name was spawned from the fact that this was the first route Tim Pochay climbed after a miraculous recovery from a serious avalanche incident on Mount Athabasca. **Note:** this climb is a rope stretcher pay close attention to the ends of your rope when lowering or rappelling!

Wild West Wall, Right

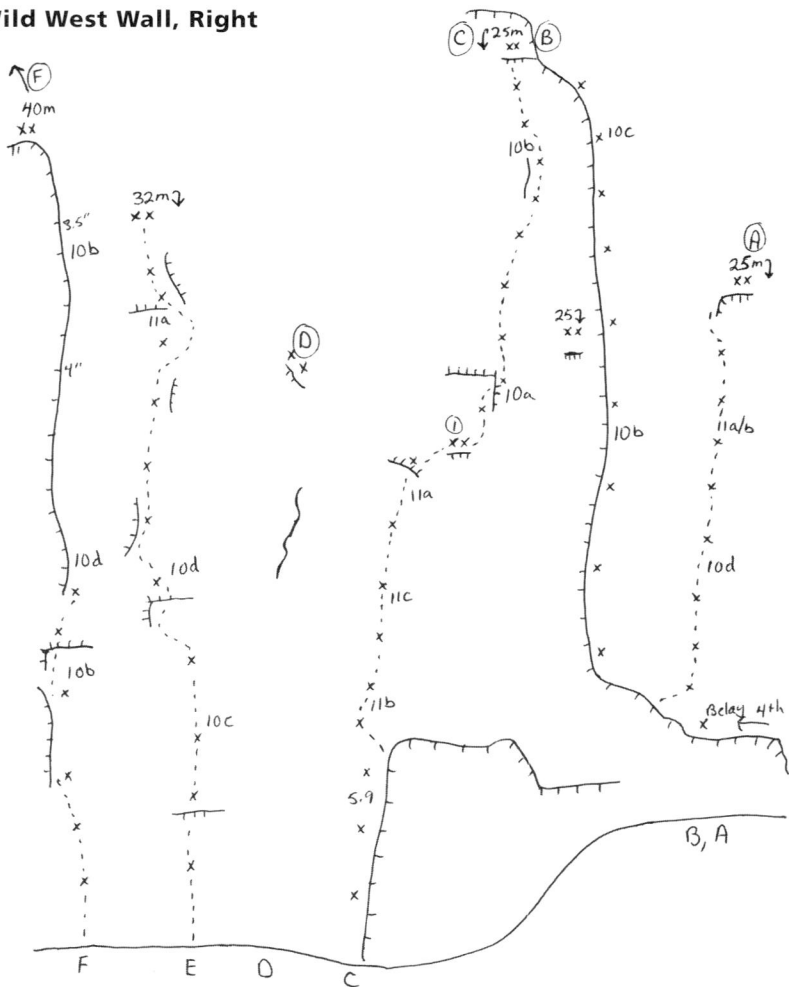

WILD WEST WALL, RIGHT

A Orange Peel ***   5.11a/b, 25 m
B Snerty And Me **   5.10c, 50 m
C Cowboy Up **   5.11c, 5.10c, 55 m
D Project Sidekick
E Back in the Saddle ***   5.11a, 32 m
F Cowboys Don't Cry **   5.10d, 5.8   90 m, gear rack to 4"

Cowboys Don't Cry** 5.10d, 5.8, 90 m, gear standard rack to 4"
A. Genereux, Jul. 2000

Climbs the corner to the left of "Back in the Saddle". Thinking the climb would be in the 5.9 range Andy started to establish the route ground up rope solo using hand drive bolts. After 20 m he encountered a very large suspect block. To avoid this nasty, he traversed onto the route to the right, climbed this for a couple of bolts then back into the corner to place a bolt (which is all possible when using a "Soloist" device one doesn't have to worry about rope drag). Anyway when he rappelled down to check out the block it cut loose and totally destroyed his rope one of the lower bolts and a quick draw sending him home with his tail between his legs.

He returned a few months later, again rope soloing this time armed with a power drill he completed the first two pitches of a project he hopes one day will reach the top of the wall. The first pitch is very good addition to the cragging circuit and involves excellent, steady 5.10 on mostly natural protection and is 40 m long. The second pitch is bit scrappy at a much easier grade. From the top of the second pitch 3 rappels down "Smoking Gun" is possible using a single 60 m rope.

Smoking Gun* 5.12a, 5.10b, 5.10a, 90 m, gear to 2.5"
A. Genereux, Jul. 2001

Locate a black painted hanger on the main wall 15 m east of "The Arrowhead" pillar. Climb the sustained first pitch past six bolt's then traverse right on easier stepped ground to the shallow corner. This corner is much easier but offers excellent climbing over two pitches to a large ledge sharing the belay with "Cowboy's Don't Cry". The first pitch still requires a separate anchor at the top of the hard section to avoid the easy traverse right. There is an arching project starting from the left that it is hoped will provide a more consistent start for the upper two pitches.

Project: Hang Em High
On the main wall slightly east of the "Arrow Head Tower" find six bolts heading up and right in an arching line to try and join "Smoking Gun" at the traverse above the hard first pitch. The name comes from the fact Andy almost hanged himself via a gear sling attached to the drill and around his neck, when a key hold broke while drilling on lead.

The Arrowhead

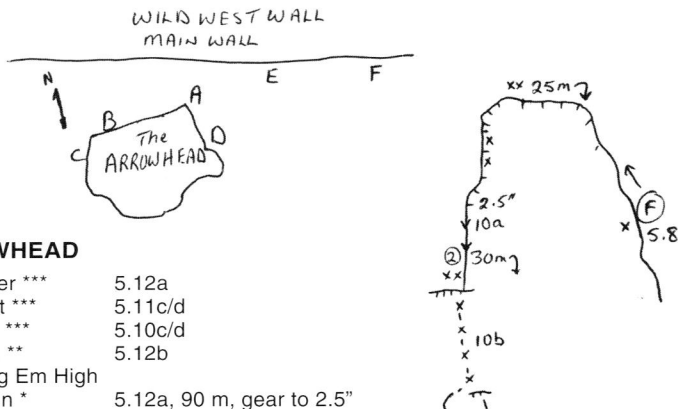

THE ARROWHEAD

A Blade Runner ***	5.12a
B Vision Quest ***	5.11c/d
C Hi Ho Silver ***	5.10c/d
D Solar Winds **	5.12b
E Project Hang Em High	
F Smoking Gun *	5.12a, 90 m, gear to 2.5"

WILD WEST WALL, RIGHT

F Cowboys Don't Cry 5.10d, 90 m
G Smoking Gun * 5.12a, 5.10b, 5.10a, 90 m
    gear to 2.5"
H Project Hang Em High

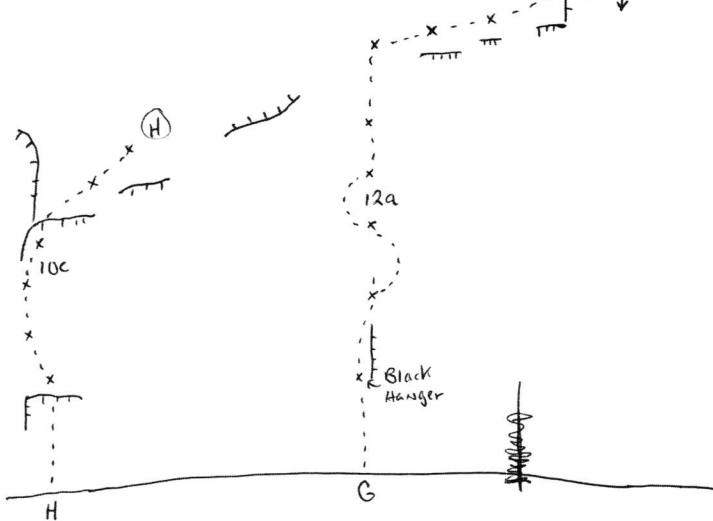

The Arrowhead

The Rockies are full of detached pillars similar to the Arrowhead. None, however, is known to rival the quality of this outstanding feature. Dave Morgan started on the Arrowhead in the late eighties and placed the first two bolts on what is now "Hi Ho Silver." After seeing no activity for several years on this line, Andy Genereux, with prodding from Tim Pochay, started up the route placing a bolt on lead. When it came time to place the next bolt the power drill would not operate forcing a bolder runout than anticipated to the top of the tower. The route was later retrofitted and is a classic. The main reason to finish the route, however, was to get on top and bolt an amazing overhanging arête on the northwest corner of the tower. "Blade Runner". Both Andy and Tim constructed the route. It was Tim who powered up the arête first to receive the coveted first redpoint in September of 1993. Despite the breaking of several (non-crucial) holds, it remains one of the best 5.12's in the Canadian Rockies.

Solar Winds*** 5.12b, 20 m, fixed gear
T. Pochay & A. Genereux, 1994

This is technically the hardest route on the pillar. It climbs the east face with a devious crux sequence between the second and third bolts followed by sustained 11d/12a climbing above.

Blade Runner*** 5.12a, 20 m, fixed gear
T. Pochay & A. Genereux, Sept. 1993

"The Blade" climbs the right side of the superb, clean-cut arête on the NE corner of "The Arrowhead". The crux is low down at the first bolt with strenuous and sustained 11+ climbing to the anchor.

Vision Quest*** 5.11c, 20 m, fixed gear
A. Genereux & T. Pochay, 1996

This companion route to "Blade Runner" climbs the NW arête and north face to the left. The lower third is very technical and requires a variety of techniques. The remainder offers "endurance climbing" to the top.

Hi Ho Silver*** 5.10d, 20 m, fixed gear
A. Genereux & T. Pochay , Sept. 1993

This interesting climb follows the left edge of the west face and is harder than it looks. Be prepared it stays in your face all the way to the top.

How the West was Won 5.8, 30 m, gear to 4"
A. Genereux, 1994

This gear route, which climbs the right-facing corner at the right of the lower wall, was used to establish anchors for the other climbs to the left. The rock is of dubious quality and the climb is probably better forgotten.

Gun Slingers in Paradise** 5.11a, 25 m, fixed gear
A. Genereux & T. Pochay, 1994

Found on the main wall 25 m west of the "Arrowhead." This route gives excellent steep, sustained fingery face climbing through three crux sections.

abandoned project
Three bolts behind the tree between "Rock Doctor" and "Gun Slingers in Paradise."

Rock Doctor** 5.11d, 25 m, fixed gear
T. Pochay & A. Genereux, 1996

This fine, but somewhat squeezed route lies immediately right of the arête, which defines "Dreams of Verdon." Although it has a separate anchor, it can be used as a variation first pitch to that route.

Dreams of Verdon*** 5.11d/12a, 220 m, fixed gear, double ropes required
A. Genereux & T. Pochay, Aug. 1996

This impressive route begins on the arête below the right edge of a massive roof and continues for a total of six pitches. The rock is good throughout and the climb ranks as one of the most outstanding multi pitch sport routes in the Canadian Rockies. Above the second pitch, two 50-metre ropes are required to descend.

Pitch two was established in a four-hour, unplanned aid fiasco. It was originally thought it might go at 5.11 but there are a few less holds than anticipated. Later the pair returned, this time from the top of the crag, and added three pitches from the top of pitch one, the second of which found easier climbing to the right of the original project. Time constraints stalled the project for a couple of years. A final push in 1996 established the last two pitches. The climb has now been climbed several times and most parties feel the sustained last pitch warrants the stiffer 5.12a grade. Several parties have found the first pitch to be quite stiff for the stated grade. If you climb straight up after the third bolt it's more like a 12b sequence. Attacking the arête from the left side and making a difficult high step was how the pitch was graded.

Project 220 m
A bolted project that follows excellent grey rock located 20 m right of an obvious right facing corner at the west end of the wall and about 30 m left of the big roof ("Dreams Of Verdon" is located on the right end of this roof). Bolts head up the steep and stiff looking face to a chained anchor. This climb is being established top down by Keith Haberl and

WILD WEST WALL, LEFT

Dreams Of Verdon *** 5.11d/12a, 220 m

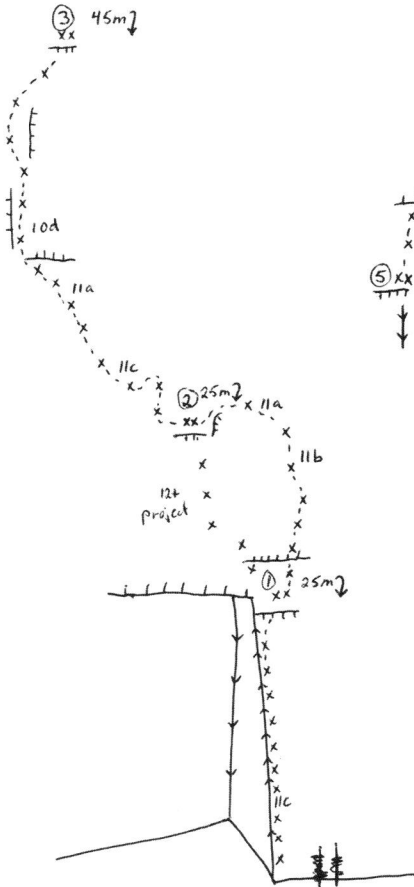

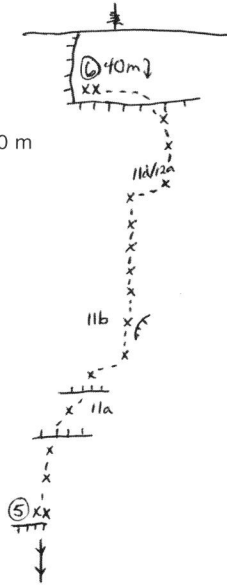

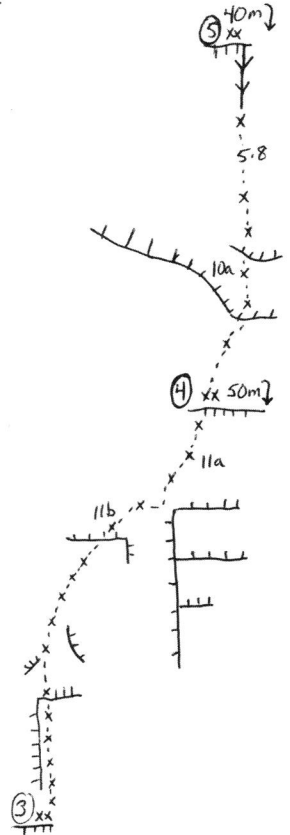

⑥ 40m↓
xx

11d/12a

11b

x 11a

⑤ xx

④ 40m↓
xx

5.8

10a

④ xx 50m↓

11a

11b

③ xx

③ 45m↓
x

10d

11a

11c

② 25m↓
xx x 11a

11b

12+
Project

① xx 25m↓

11c

Wild West Wall, Left

Richard Jagar and it is unknown if any of the pitches are completed at this time. This has been an ongoing project for a few years.

Project 220 m
Continue around the corner from the Wild West Wall into the "Aquarius" drainage near the north end of the west facing wall from the tip of a small scree cone a bolted line climbs up to an obvious cave then to the top of the wall. This ongoing project is the work of Daren Tremaine and Ryan Johnstone. It is reported near completion and may come in around the mid 5.12 range.

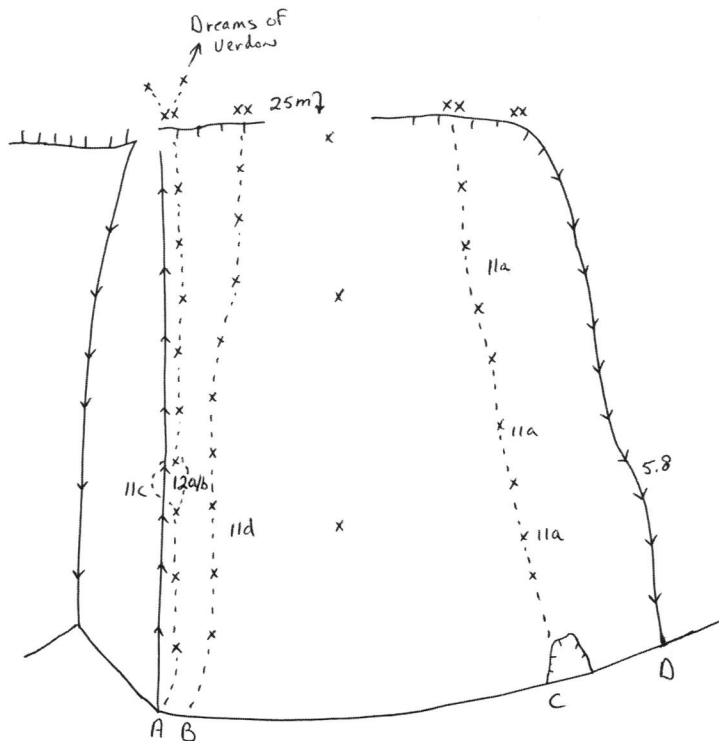

WILD WEST WALL, LEFT

A Dreams Of Verdon ***   5.11c or 5.12a/b, 5.11b, 5.11c, 5.11b, 5.10b, 5.12a, 220 m
B Rock Doctor *   5.11d, 25 m
C Gun Slingers In Paradise*** 5.11a, 25 m
D How the West Was Won   5.8, 35 m, gear to 4"

Situated at the base of a tremendous 300 m wall, this is a most unique feature. Centuries of water pouring off the summit overhangs have etched an immaculate slab of compact stone surrounded by overhanging yellow rock. The slab is named in memory of the late Dennis Kemp who on a visit from England during the summer of 1986 helped Dave Morgan pioneer several routes in the Ghost.

Kemp Shield suffers from unusually finicky conditions. In the spring watch out for dropping ice from the huge overhangs. During rainy periods and times of snow melt, it is hopelessly wet from water running off the top of the crag. During hot spells, you will roast or die from heat exhaustion. There are no trees to provide shade and the overhanging walls contribute an albedo effect that adds to the already inciting black rock. Early summer and fall are good times to check out these routes.

The compact rock and lack of features make what few routes have been done unusually technical. On some of the routes dust can be a remnant from the constant water battering. Despite some impressive efforts, large expanses of unclimbed rock remain and the area holds plenty of interest for future exploration. Of the ten routes produced to date, Ghost pioneer Dave Morgan established all but two. Most of the climbs are above average and the crag is a recommended destination for a day. Many of the hangers here are home-made and require small profile carabiners. See the "fixed protection" section of the introduction on page 11.

Climbs have been established in two separate sections of the cliff, as you approach from the east the right end has several routes, then just left of centre marked by a yellow streak are three more routes. The last two routes are located on the extreme left edge of the "Shield". See photos pages 65, 84 & 90, and accompanying topos pages 86 & 88. All climbs will be described from right to left as this coincides with the direction of approach.

Approach
The Kemp Shield is an obvious apron of dark rock located between "Bonanza" and Wild West Wall. It is reached in 10 minutes by walking west from the Bonanza Descent Gully or 40-45 minutes from the park boundary. See the West Phantom Crag introduction on page 71 for more approach details.

Descent
All routes are descended by rappel, many requiring two 50 m ropes.

Climbs on the right-hand section of the cliff are described as you encounter them from right to left. The west end of this section of the Shield is marked by an obvious right-facing corner at the boundary of grey and yellow rock.

A. Kemp Wall, Left, p 88
B. Kemp Wall, Right p. 86

Boldly Go** 5.10c, 45 m, gear wires & TCU's
D. Morgan, B. Huseby, T. Jones, E. Trouillot & A. Pickel, 1990

This enjoyable and well-protected route climbs a thin finger crack in the centre of a flat, poorly defined pinnacle located above ledges about 20 m up the face. The start of the route is about 18 m left of the extreme right end of the Shield, below a shallow groove that begins about 6 m up the face and leads over left to the base of the upper crack. The crack requires a good selection of small gear.

User Friendly** 5.9, 45 m, gear to 4"
D. Morgan, B. Huseby & A. Skuce, 1990

"User Friendly" climbs the left-facing corner on the left side of the upper pinnacle of "Boldly Go." It is entirely bolt-protected except for one large gear placement at the top of the off width crack in the corner (#3.5" to 4" Friend). The addition of a bolt at this point is recommended to make the climb match its name. The climb begins about 5 m left of "Boldly Go" and goes up to the ledge system below the upper corner via a V-shaped alcove in the lower wall. Unknown to Dave at the time of the first ascent the lower half of the route had been climbed without bolts by Andy Genereux and made for a bit of fun around the campfire playing with Dave's ethical beliefs.

Tradesman's Entrance* 5.8, 50 m, gear to 2.5"
D. Morgan & B. Huseby, Aug 1986

This route was originally used to access the upper part of the Shield and to place the bolts on "Scaremonger" and "Cryin' Mercy." It begins about 10 m left of "User Friendly" and just right of a prominent, right-facing corner that begins a few meters above the ground. Move up and left past a bolt (5.8 to the corner, and go up this moving right at the top over small ledges (bolt high up on left) to the base of a crack in a second right-facing corner (bolt). Climb the steep corner (gear to 2") until it closes at a ledge on the right. Move up on to the ledge and step right (crux) to easier ground. Continue up past a bolt and climb an easy corner to a bolt belay and chains on a flat-topped block.

Scaremonger** 5.10c/R, 50 m, gear wires & TCU's
D. Morgan, B. Huseby & D. Kemp, Aug, 1986

This aptly named route climbs a shallow crack in the steep face above and slightly left of the lower corner of "Tradesman's Entrance." The crack is difficult to protect and a good selection of small/medium gear is recommended. Climb "Tradesman's Entrance" as far as the bolt at the top of the lower corner. From here, move up and left with difficulty around a bulge to a bolt and continue left to the base of the shallow crack. Follow the crack moving right and up at the top to a short, right-facing corner. This leads up to the rappel anchors at the flat-topped block of "Tradesman's Entrance." At the top of the crack it is tempting to move right on to "Tradesman's Entrance" and the addition of a bolt at this point is recommended to encourage use of the original finish.

Cryin' Mercy*** 5.11a/b, 50 m, fixed gear
D. Morgan & B. Huseby, Sept. 1987

"Cryin' Mercy" is one of the best routes on the Kemp Shield. It typifies what the crag has to offer—steep, continuously technical face climbing on excellent rock. The route has several difficult sections and the location of the crux seems to be a matter of opinion. Begin a few meters left of the lower corner of "Tradesman's Entrance" and angle up left following the line of bolts. The route continues up the steep face and exits up a right-facing groove. The upper part is runout but relatively easy.

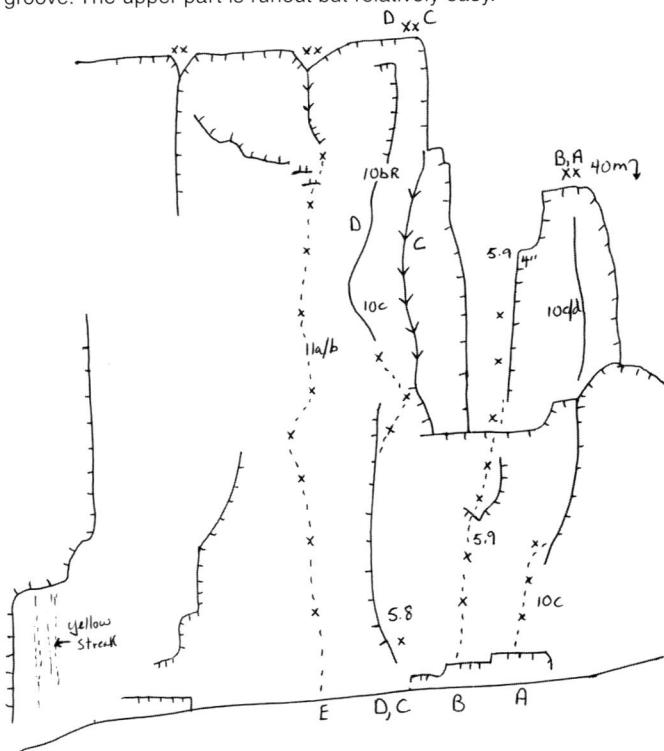

KEMP SHIELD, RIGHT

A Boldly Go **	5.10c, 25 m	small wires, TCU's
B User Friendly **	5.9, 25 m	4" cam
C Tradesman Entrance*	5.8, 40 m	gear to 2.5"
D Scaremonger **	5.10c/R, 45 m	wires, TCU's
E Cryin Mercy ***	5.11a/b, 45 m	

The left side consists essentially of two parts. The first comes just after the mid point of the Shield and has one major route, "Big Rock Traditional," and its two variations, "Shred" and "Fool's Gold." These climbs are best located by a prominent ledge about 12 m above the ground and about 20 m left of the lowest point at the base of the cliff. The second part is located at the left edge of the Shield and consists of two sport routes established by some visiting American climbers from Colorado. Both routes share the same start then diverge at the fourth bolt. The route moving out to the right is an ongoing multi pitch project "Premonition" that continues on the wall above the Kemp Shield.

Fool's Gold** 5.11c/d, 40 m, fixed gear
D. Morgan & T. Freeman, 1990

This very technical route follows a faint, ochre-tinted streak that leads directly to the belay at the top of pitch one on "Big Rock Traditional." The technical crux is low down but the bolts seem widely spaced higher up as you near the anchor. It makes an excellent route when combined with the second pitch of "Big Rock Traditional."

Shred* 5.12a, 15 m, fixed gear
D. Morgan, B. Wyvill & G. Powter, 1993

A short, technical route that climbs the wall a few meters right of "Big Rock Traditional." It gains the right end of a small ledge system extending out from the top of the groove.

Big Rock Traditional* 5.10c, 70 m
D. Morgan, B. Huseby & K. Hines, 1991

This interesting climb was established in traditional style, with all the bolts being drilled by hand on-lead. The route required a number of attempts spread over two years and much patience from Dave Morgan's wife Bev who belayed him on many of them.

Begin directly below a short groove that leads to the prominent ledge noted above. The first bolt is a long way up and steady climbing is required to reach it. Continued technical but protected climbing then leads up past a second bolt and the groove to the ledge. From here, traverse right and up to a ramp that angles rightwards to a small ledge and chained anchors. The second pitch climbs the steep wall on the left to a short groove and belay ledge above. The upper part of the shield is lower angled and the route does not continue beyond this point.

Kemp Shield, Left

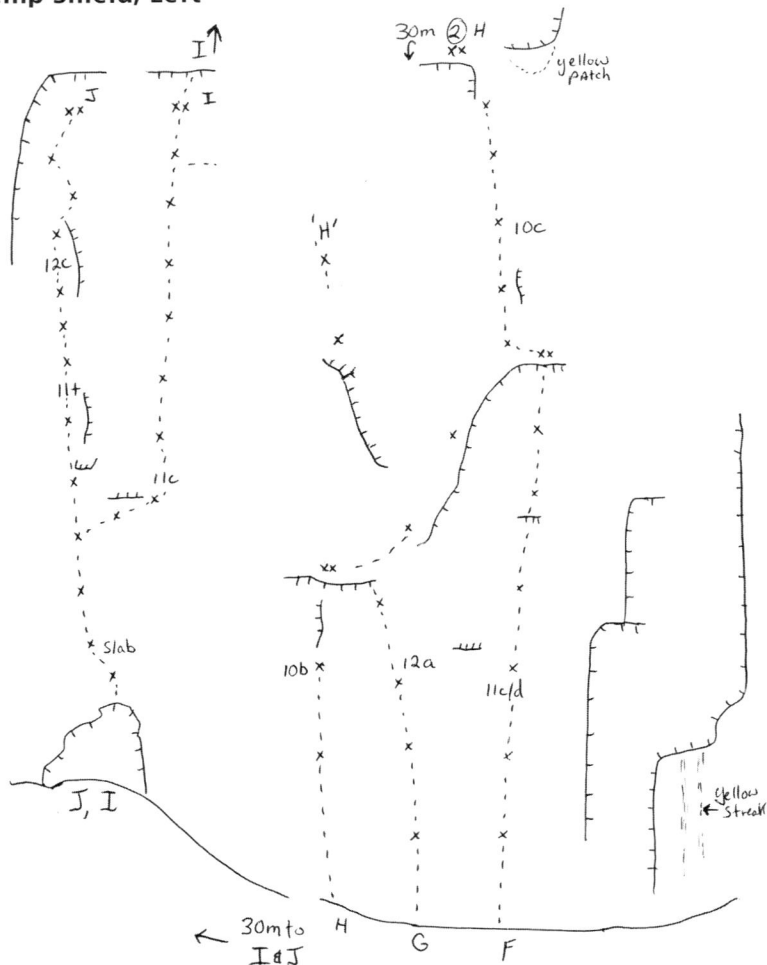

KEMP SHIELD, LEFT

F Fools Gold **	5.11c/d, 40 m
G Shred * 5.12a, 20 m	
H Big Rock Traditional *	5.10c, 70 m
H' Project	
I Premonition **	5.12a, 105 m
J Side Project ***	5.12b/c, 30 m

Premonition** 5.12a, 105 m, fixed gear, double ropes recommended
C. Kalous & A. Porter, Aug. 2002

This is an ongoing project with the first four pitches complete. It has been established by a couple of Colorado climbers over three-week period. Located on the left edge of the "Shield" find a line of bolts on the face just to the right of a broken corner that defines the west end of Kemp Shield. Start off a blocky pedestal to a tilted slab and follow bolts upward. At the fourth bolt "Premonition" heads out right for two bolts then up the slabby face. Gear required: allow 14 draws, with several long slings, double ropes needed to rappel from pitches 3&4. The climb will be 6 pitches when completed to the top of the wall. The upper two pitches have anchors and are partially bolted but are not complete at this time. The pair hopes to return in 2003 to complete this project. The first two pitches make for some excellent 5.11 climbing and could be completed using a single 60 m rope.

1) 5.11c, 30 m. Climb up from the top of the pedestal after four bolts traverse right (long slings) and climb the impeccable rock to a bolted anchor at the top of the "Shield".

2) 5.11b, 20 m. Climb up the slabby orange rock above the "Shield" to a bolted anchor.

3) 5.12a, 20 m. Go up two bolts then move left across a suspect section of lower quality rock. Then head into an overhanging corner to a bolted anchor (note these are not rap bolts continue up the next pitch to rappel).

4) 5.11b, 15 m. Follow bolts up and right into an overhanging corner to finish on a small stance. This pitch and pitch three can be combined using double ropes (like the pitch detailed above the anchor has regular hangers, you will need slings to rappel and you must back-clip several bolts to reach the stations below when rappelling pitches 3&4).

5) & 6) Are incomplete at this time. The grade is expected to come in around the mid 5.12 range.

Side Project** 5.12c, 30 m, fixed gear
C. Kalous & A. Porter, Aug. 2002

The route climbs the left edge of Kemp Shield. Climb off the pedestal on sustained technical climbing through a couple of bulges. Long slings might be useful to alleviate drag, altogether I counted 13 clips but I might have missed one. Chris and Allan likened the climbing and quality to the hard routes of the Arrowhead.

A. Dreams of Verdon
B. The Arrowhead
C. Cowboys Don't Cry
D. Snerty & Me
E. Kemp Shield
F. Ju-Jube
G. Bonanza Area

This area lies between the Descent Gully and the Kemp Shield. Only one climb goes to the top of the main crag and it checks in near the top of the list for quality in the moderate traditional styled category. This, of course, is the ultra-classic "Bonanza."

The first ascent of the climb was rather uneventful except they couldn't believe just how good the crack was and they kept yelling down to each other about their fortune. The infamous traverse was discovered simply by going around the corner "for a look." Soon they spied the foot ledge leading back right and the big holds just kept coming.

To get off the climb, they then headed down what is now called the Bonanza Descent Gully. Knowing that the rappel would be tight with only 45 m ropes, they downclimbed to the lip (site of the present cable anchor) and as they threw the ropes it was getting dark, raining hard and the ropes just disappeared into space. Chris Perry launched over the edge with nothing more than "two small bootlace-sized pieces of nylon" to use as prussiks as a last resort. He could only see about halfway down the cliff and the ropes didn't reach the ground but he was encouraged by the fact that at least they were laying on easier-angled rock. At the bottom of the ropes, a pendulum right and a jump onto the rising scree slope turned a potential epic into just another day in the Ghost.

Approach

All routes in this area are listed relative to "Bonanza." Approach as for the rest of West Phantom Crag and the Descent Gully. See page 71. Continue west (left) past the Bonanza Descent Gully for about 200 m to an obvious scree cone. Near the top of the scree cone there is a prominent chimney that forms the left side of a large 45 m pinnacle. This is the start to "Bonanza." There is a bolted route on the face to the right of this chimney.

Descent

Hike right across scree and around the corner to a less exposed treed slope on the east-facing bowl above the Descent Gully. Traverse the slope to the right toward the back of the bowl. Cross the first small gully/stream (this ends in a steep waterfall) and continue right into the next major scree system. Follow this down and into the Descent Gully. See page 72 and topo page 96 for the remaining details.

Project Unknown 40 m, fixed gear

A bolted line that appeared on the face to the right of the "Bonanza" chimney around 1999, its origin, quality and grade are unknown at this time. It appears to be reasonably sustained, climb past 11 bolts to a ring bolt anchor.

Opposite: West Phantom Crag, West.

Bonanza Area

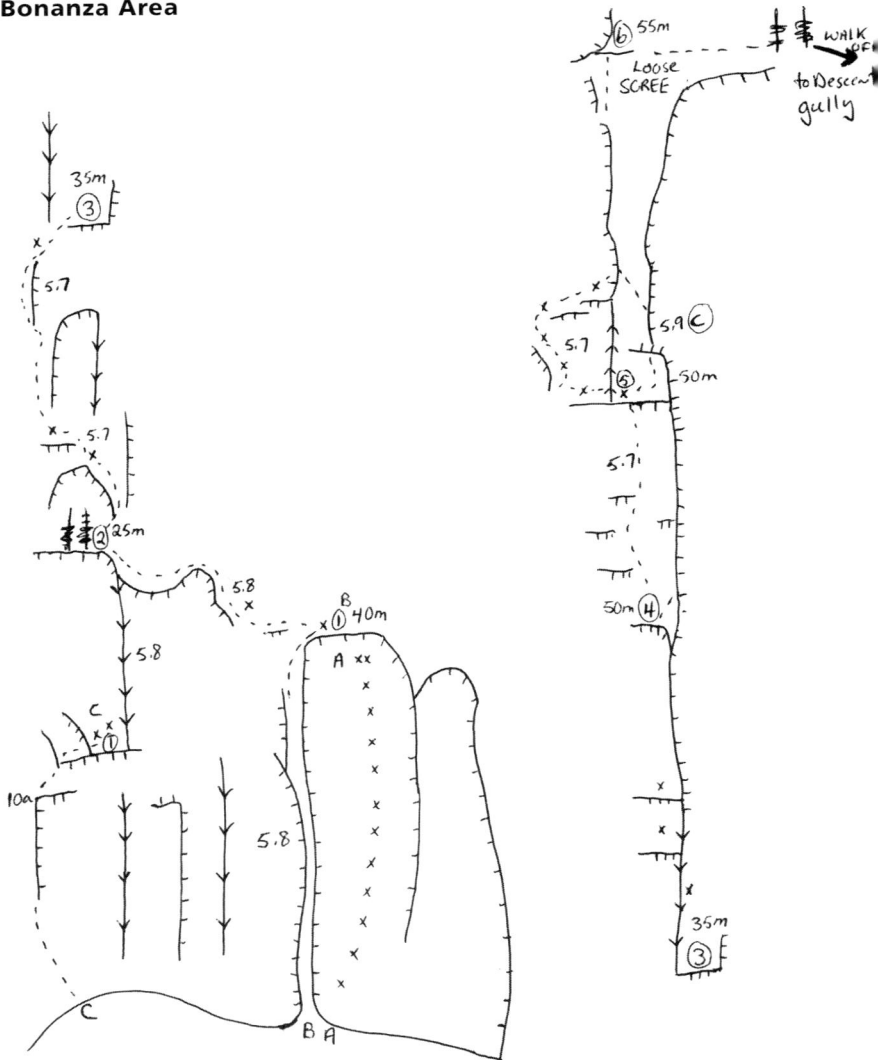

BONANZA AREA

A	Project	unknown, fixed gear
B	Bonanza ***	5.8, 260 m, gear standard rack to 4"
C	Bonanza Direct	5.10a, 60 m, gear to 4" & pitons

Bonanza*** 5.8, 260 m, gear standard rack to 4"

C. Perry & M. White, June 1976

"Bonanza" lies in the only major corner line left of the Descent Gully. West Phantom Crag makes an uncharacteristic bend at this corner and as a result, "Bonanza" faces almost due east. Accordingly, it loses the sun much earlier in the day than the rest of the cliff. In the right light, the splitter crack in the middle of the climb is easily seen in the back of the corner. Such sustained and relatively uniform cracks are a rarity in local limestone. And the devious traverse near the top adds spice and will challenge your rope work. Enough said, have fun….

There are many different ways to piece together the pitches and everyone I have talked with seems to have their best way. There are numerous stances with good natural cracks. The belays indicated on the topo are only one option and are for reference only. Use your own judgment based on the length of your cord and the rope drag you encounter. Pitons are not necessary.

1) 5.8, 45 m. Climb the left-facing chimney, which is easy at first and then turns steep and narrow. There are two possible ways to attack the wide crack that is probably the crux of the climb; either stem across it committing or squeeze into it feel safer and struggle. Take your pick.

2) 5.7, 30 m. From the top of the pinnacle (piton), traverse left on a small foot ledge to a corner. Go up this and across left to a tree belay on the large ledge below the upper corner.

3) 5.7, 35 m. A subsidiary groove on the right (directly behind tree belay) is followed for about 10 m before a traverse diagonally left can be made into the main corner. Interesting climbing on good rock leads to a small stance.

4 & 5) 5.7, 100 m. Follow the steep and sustained corner on excellent crack climbing for two 50 m pitches to a ledge below the obvious overhang in the upper section of the corner (piton on the right). There is a small dead tree on this ledge.

6) 5.7, 50 m. Traverse left around an outside corner and onto the face. Follow small but good holds across (pitons) to a small corner and go up this to a ledge with two pins. Follow a good foot ledge back to the right (piton) to the main corner. Either belay here or continue up to a higher ledge and belay there. Long slings and two ropes are useful on this pitch. Alternatively, you can split the traverse by belaying at the ledge with two pins before moving back right to the main corner. A 35 m pitch from here will reach the top.

6) alt, 5.9, 50 m. Climb the main corner direct past the overhang, going at 5.9 it is reported to be excellent. Stay with the corner and climb to a belay at 50 m in indistinct cracks before traversing right on the scree. This is an excellent option although a harder alternative. It takes out some of the rope handling concerns of going out left.

Bonanza Area

7) 5.6. An easier pitch leads to a scree slope at the top. The length depends upon where you belay at the end of pitch 6. This can be combined with the lower pitch using good double rope techniques. The top belay requires some ingenuity, but can usually be found at the base of the rotten cliff band above the scree slope. If not, traversing right across the scree into trees usually knocks lots of loose rock down the climb and really pisses off your partner and other parties that might be below.

Bonanza Direct 5.10a, 60 m, gear to 4" pitons recommended
F. Campbell, D. Stefani & N. Stefani, July 1994

A better name for this route might be "Bonanza Indirect." The first pitch involves a major traverse and is hard to protect without pitons. It was also originally graded 5.8+! There is a direct groove that would go with some bolts, which would make for a better start but the grade would still be stiff in relation to the pitches above. The fixed piton belay at the top of pitch one provides the final rappel point for parties backing off "Bonanza."

The route starts just to the left of the top of the scree cone and below an obvious left facing corner about 10 m off the ground. From the top of the corner traverse across right to a larger corner system that leads to the traverse on pitch 2 of the normal route.

1) 5.10a, 30 m. Climb a faint break in the slab that leads to the corner and climb the corner (15 m). From the top of the corner (watch for some loose rock) traverse right across a small bay of compact rock to thin crack on the right wall. Climb up the crack for 3-4 m to where a small ledge leads right to a larger belay ledge (pitons).

2) 5.8, 30 m. Climb the corner directly above to join the normal route on the easy traverse leading left. Follow this and belay on the treed ledge.

Rock n' Robin 5.9, 35 m, gear to 4"
T. Jones & R. Stark, Aug. 1991

About 30 m left of the start of "Bonanza" where the scree slope starts to descend. Locate a short, left-facing corner that starts about 7 m up the cliff and leads to a ledge with a small tree on the right.

Beginning below and left of the corner climb the slabby right wall of a short groove. Trend up and right to the base of the corner. Go up this past an old piton (crux) and continue up the crack with excellent protection to a stance at the tree on the right. Rappel from the tree.

Opposite: Martyn White crossing the infamous pitch six traverse during the first ascent of "Bonanza." Photo: Chris Perry.

Bonanza Descent Gully

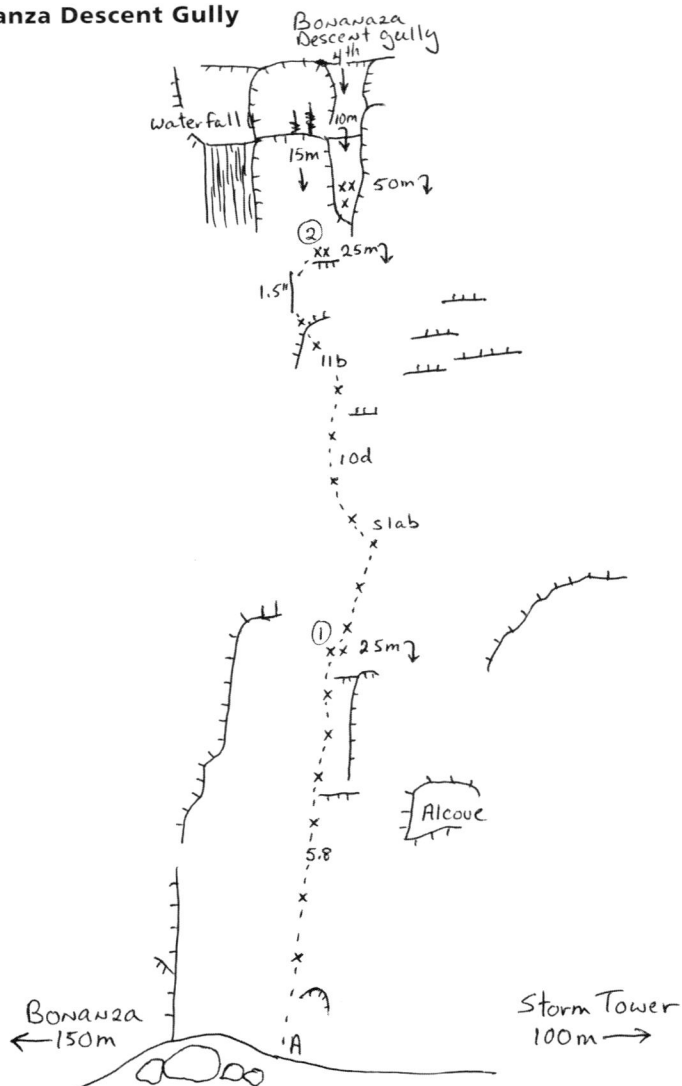

Bonanaza Descent gully
4th

waterfall

10m

15m

50m

② xx 25m

1.5"

11b

10d

slab

① 25m

Alcove

5.8

Bonanza
←150m

Storm Tower
100m→

A

BONANZA DESCENT GULLY

A Ghost Town Blues ** 5.8, 5.11b, 50 m

Ghost Town Blues** 5.8, 5.11b, 60 m, fixed gear
K. Haberl, R. Jaeger & D. Orr, 1994

"Ghost Town Blues" was first done strictly as an access to the top of the crag. The climb is wet until mid-season. When dry, the bottom pitch is 25 m to a chained anchor. This is a good moderate pitch, which could be combined, with other moderate pitches on "Bonanza" and "Storm Tower" for a good day of cragging. The upper pitch is substantially harder and could use a bit of optional gear in a crack after the last bolt. The first 5.8 pitch (25 m) can be done on its own or continue up the thrilling second 5.11b pitch, which has sustained steep climbing through the upper half.

An early attempt at "Ghost Town Blues" in poor conditions. Photo: Trevor Jones.

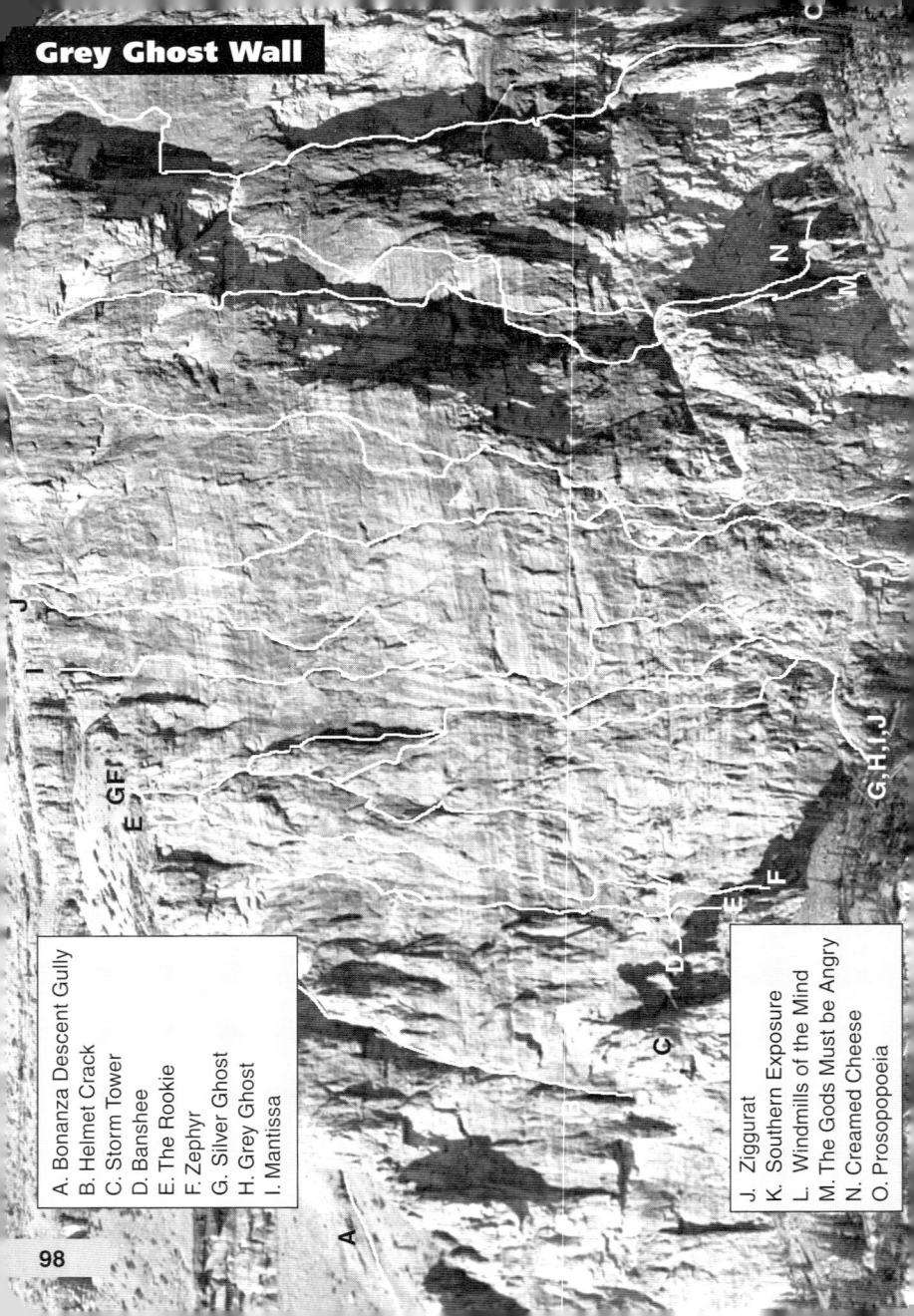

A. Bonanza Descent Gully
B. Helmet Crack
C. Storm Tower
D. Banshee
E. The Rookie
F. Zephyr
G. Silver Ghost
H. Grey Ghost
I. Mantissa

J. Ziggurat
K. Southern Exposure
L. Windmills of the Mind
M. The Gods Must be Angry
N. Creamed Cheese
O. Prosopopoeia

GREY GHOST WALL

This section of cliff is named for obvious reasons. It presents a uniform-looking wall that is some 200 m to 300 m high and almost solid grey throughout. Naturally, it has a high concentration of quality, multi-pitch climbs. It is bounded on the left by the Bonanza Descent Gully and on the right by huge, stepped overhangs of yellow rock that extend almost the entire height of the crag. The Grey Ghost Wall itself can be separated into two parts by the left-slanting diagonal break of the route "Grey Ghost." To its "Left Side" the cliff is somewhat shorter and more broken "The Seven Pillars of Wisdom" sit in front and to the left end of this part of the wall. The Grey Ghost Wall, Right Side consists of a steep slab of sweeping, compact rock. If you were to climb on only one multi-pitch venue in the Ghost, this would be it. Every route except for "Helmet Crack" and "Grey Ghost" is highly recommended.

Approach
See the West Phantom Crag introduction on page 71 for details. The trail nears the base of the cliff directly below the route "Southern Exposure." When the trail contours left toward the Bonanza Descent Gully, continue straight up for 50 m to the base of the crag. It takes about 35-45 minutes to hike from the parking area at the park boundary.

Descent
The standard descent is to hike left (west) and rappel the Bonanza Descent Gully. See page 72 for details and topo page 96.

"Zephyr" is the only route on the crag that is equipped for a rappel descent that can be approached from the top. It requires double 55 m ropes and care has to be taken not to hang your ropes up on the big ledge two-thirds the way down the second rappel. Since "Banshee" and "Grey Ghost" both end at this same top anchor, the "Zephyr" rappel could be used. As well "The Rookie" and "Silver Ghost" top out just to the left and both routes can easily utilize this rappel route. This rappel could also be used as a descent from other Grey Ghost Wall or Epitaph Wall routes. As you hike west along the top of the crag toward the Descent Gully, you will encounter an easy slab approximately in the middle of the Grey Ghost Wall. Near the bottom of the slab is the only pine tree in the vicinity. The top anchor of "Zephyr" is found at the edge of the cliff in a shallow gully formation just below (west) of the tree and slab. It is advised that you climb "Zephyr" to figure out where this rappel line is located and if in doubt use the Bonanza Descent Gully.

A collection of shattered pillars, named by Trevor Jones who with nothing better to do while belaying, meticulously counted them to arrive at the name for these features. They lie in front of the Grey Ghost Wall towards the left end between the climbs "Helmet Crack" and "Zephyr" and are separated from the main face by a scree gully that slopes down to "Southern Exposure". The largest pillar located on the southwest corner of the "Seven Pillars" formation that is known as "Storm Tower." It houses the only routes to date found on the "Seven Pillars". The remaining pillars show little scope for new routes but one never knows.

Storm Tower, South Face

The classic "Matterhorn" shaped tower has an impressive south face with easier possibilities on the east side. The steep south face had three routes established in the fall of 2002. There are several good possibilities for more routes. To date there are a couple of active projects.

Approach

To access the tower take the trail that heads to the "Bonanza Descent Gully" as the trail rounds the corner towards the "Descent Gully". "Storm Tower" is directly above, head up the shoulder through a small boulder field to the south face of "Storm Tower" about 70 m above the trail.

Wind and Flurry* 5.8, 25 m, fixed gear

A. Genereux, Nov. 2002

Located on the left edge of the south face it starts steeply then rolling ground to a sidewalk belay ledge. Start up an overhanging slot with 2 bolts on the right side. Move past the second bolt with an awkward move to gain the right wall. Climb the rolling grey rock past six bolts to a second crux then onto a good ledge with rap bolts.

Snowflakes of August** 5.11b, 25 m, fixed gear

A. Genereux, Nov. 2002

Climbs the sustained and devious bulging face between "Wind and Flurry" and "Thunder and Lightning how Frightening" and shares the same boardwalk ledge as "Wind and Flurry" but has it's own rap bolt anchor.

Thunder and Lightning How Frightening** 5.9, 28 m, gear to 4"

A. Genereux, Nov. 2002

Climbs the obvious large left leaning crack, which splits the centre of the south face of Storm Tower to a rap bolt belay in a bay where the climbing eases. The crux is short and the climb consists of mostly 5.7 to 5.8 climbing.

Lightning Bolt Crack 30 m (project)

This is the obvious steep right leaning finger & hand crack 2 m to the right of "Thunder and Lightning How Frightening". This excellent line still requires some cleaning but should be completed by spring 2003. This climb has an anchor on a ledge 3 m above and 5 m right of the above-mentioned route.

Riders in the Storm 30 m (project)

The left leaning hand crack located on the right side of the south face. It starts behind a small spruce tree. This project has an anchor but still requires extensive cleaning.

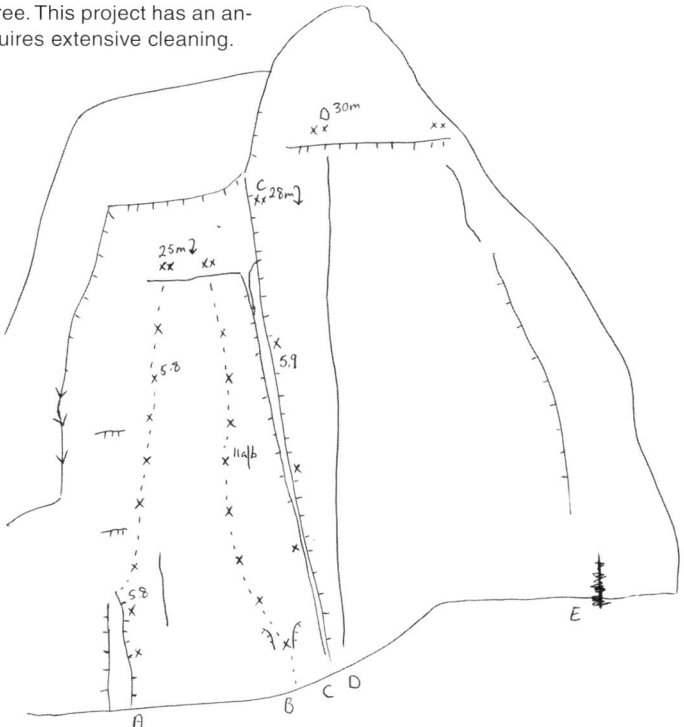

STORM TOWER, SOUTH FACE

A Wind and Flurry *	5.8	
B Snowflakes of August **	5.11b	
C Thunder and Lightning How Frightening **	5.9 gear to 4"	
D Project Lightning Bolt Crack		
E Project Riders In A Storm		

Helmet Crack 5.8, 180 m, gear to 4"

J. Firth & J. Upton, June 1979

About 150 m right of the Bonanza Descent Gully near the top of a scree slope and immediately left of "Storm Tower" the largest tower on the west end of the "Seven Pillars of Wisdom" at the base. Locate a deep corner leading up to a gully in the upper part of the cliff. The climb follows the corner all the way and is mainly 5.6 with a 5.8 roof near the top.

Approach for "Zephyr" and "The Rookie"

"Zephyr" is a modern route that climbs the face on the right side of a wide, dished corner system of "The Rookie" and is left of "Grey Ghost" break. It is possible to follow the base of the cliff left from "Southern Exposure," however, this entails a healthy scree bash. It is better to follow the trail west as for the Bonanza Descent Gully for 200 m or so to a point directly below "Storm Tower" the largest pillar, part of several large, detached pinnacles and blocks known as "The Seven Pillars Of Wisdom." Scramble up the talus and around the right end of the tower into a scree gully. "The Rookie" starts just below and "Zephyr" begins in an irregular crack 25 m right, about halfway down the scree gully.

The Rookie*** 5.11a, 200 m, gear standard rack to 4"
double ropes recommended
A. Genereux and J. Kaufman, Oct. 1998

Done in a single one day push ground up, using a power drill, a single battery and no hooks. This climb is similar to "Zephyr" in grade and style and makes for a good companion route. Completing both in a day could be a worthwhile objective for a strong party. Due to some miss-information on the first assent, as to the amount of rope available to complete the second pitch. The team returned for a second visit and moved the two middle belay's higher to better locations and added a couple of more bolts.

Start near the top of the scree gully behind the "Pillars of Wisdom", 25 m left of "Zephyr". Locate a bolt on the face 5 m above.

1) 5.7, 45 m. Climb past a bolt in grey rock up to a shattered pillar. Move past the pillar on the right (loose) to gain a groove climb this to a bolt then take intermittent seams to a good ledge. Locate a single bolt belay where the ledge meets the right facing corner. Note the "Zephyr" belay is 10 m to the right on the same ledge.

2) 5.10d, 55 m. Climb the superb corner with an excellent wide crack on good gear. At a break continue straight up past a bolt into the shallow corner, sustained climbing to an overhanging slot. Make burly moves up and over and continue up on more excellent and sustained bulging grey rock. The climbing eases then steepens, with hard moves past a bulge to reach the belay.

3) 5.10c, 55 m. From the belay there are two choices. To the left take the obvious finger/hand crack (10a) on good protection or use the stepped blocky ledges to the right (5.7)runout. Take either option to a blocky section, up through this to a shallow left facing corner. Sustained climbing follows the corner past three bolts to an excellent belay ledge.

4) 5.11a, 35 m. Move right to a rounded corner climb this to a ledge clip a bolt and head up the prickled face above. Small seams and excellent rock lead to a v-shaped groove. Enter the groove at the second bolt find the devious sequence to allow you to move right to a bolt, climb a short crack to a good ledge. Belay here or continue over the top past a bolt and belay on top.

Descent: rappel from the top station to "Zephyr" and continue rappelling as for that climb two 55 m ropes required or walk off west to the "Bonanza Descent Gully".

Zephyr*** 5.11a, 200 m, gear standard rack to 4" double ropes recommended
A. Genereux & J. Josephson, July 1995

The first ascent of this route was completed in a single afternoon with rapidly waning battery power. The name was applied two days later as the team used the route as a descent from the first ascent of "Windmills of the Mind." While setting up the top rappel, a violent gust of wind ripped a jet-black jacket out of Josephson's pack. The now-air-borne coat filled with air and took on a humanoid appearance as it briefly hovered 30 m out—taunting the climbers before heading out of sight in the general direction of Calgary. It was just another Ghost climbing experience.

1) 5.8, 50 m. Climb a shallow, intermittent crack in good grey rock to two bolts on a face to the left. Climb the face to avoid the bad rock in the corner to the right. More broken ground passes a ledge with a small tree. Continue up and past a bolt to a large ledge and a bolt belay.

2) 5.11a, 55 m. Move left along the ledge and climb up past two bolts (10b), then continue on excellent rock up and right past a bolt and a fixed piton to gain a shallow corner. Climb the corner (10c) for 10 m and exit left onto the face. Climb up with increasing difficulty past four bolts (11a) with an easier, variation escape to the left at the second bolt (10b). Continue up to easier ground that leads past a bolt to a bolt belay below a large left-facing corner.

3) 5.10d, 45 m. Continue up the corner (5.8) or alternatively climb out right past four bolts on excellent, textured rock (10c). Both options arrive at a large ledge. Overcome a bulge to rib then face climb on awkward moves past three bolts. At the third bolt traverse right (10d) for 3 m and climb past a bolt moving left into shallow corner (10c). Climb the shallow groove with hidden gear placements and after several meters exit right past a bolt to a bolt belay.

4) 5.10a, 50 m. Face climb up and left to avoid a loose block on the right. Continue up and right past a fixed pin to gain a prominent finger crack. Climb the crack (10a) for 30 m to below a shattered block with a bolt at the base. Traverse right for 3 m and climb an awkward corner (10a) to the top and a bolt belay.

Descent: Rappel the route (2/55 m ropes required) or walk off to Bonanza Descent Gully.

Grey Ghost Wall, Left

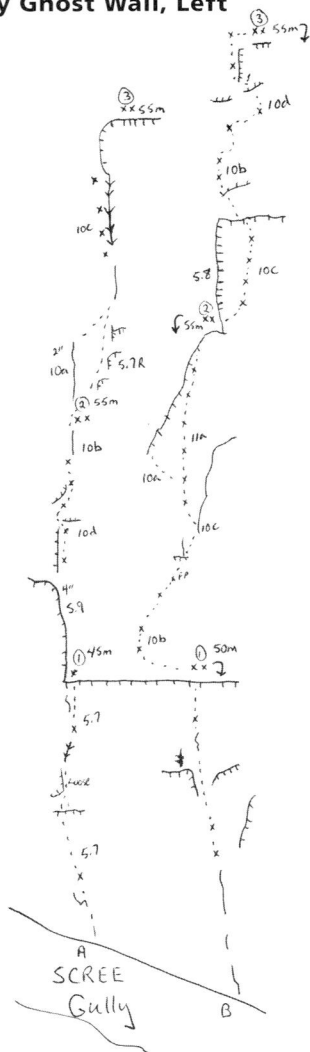

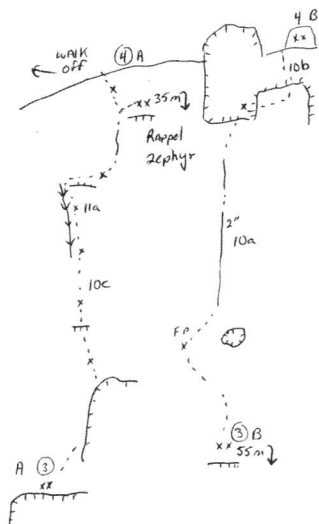

GREY GHOST WALL, LEFT

A The Rookie ***	5.11a, 200 m	gear standard rack to 4"
B Zephyr ***	5.11a, 200 m	gear standard rack to 4"

Banshee* 5.10a, 180 m, gear to 4" and pitons
P. Littlejohn & I. Staples, Sept. 1976

Banshee climbs the well-featured terrain between "Zephyr" and "Grey Ghost." The upper section of the latter route forms the right side of a shallow pinnacle with a well-defined corner system on its left side. "Banshee" climbs this left-side corner system to the top of the pinnacle and then finishes up "Grey Ghost." Pitons would be an excellent idea for this route.

The original route starts left of "Zephyr." Approach as for that route and scramble up the scree gully behind the pinnacles and locate a 4th class ledge system that leads out right. This system crosses "Zephyr" at the first belay (bolts) and extends all the way to "Grey Ghost" (some 5th class). Traverse easily right past "Zephyr" for about 12 m until below and slightly left of the upper corner and then move up to belay on a large ledge. The first pitch of "Zephyr" would make an excellent alternate start.

1) 5.7, 40 m. Climb straight up for 10 m and then use a detached ledge to traverse right to a groove. Climb the left-hand option and continue past a short V-groove to a ledge about 10 m below where the crack steepens.

2) 5.10a, 45 m. Climb up to a piton below the bulge and continue up with difficulty into the corner above. An easy groove leads up and left to a belay behind some big blocks, well left of the main groove line.

3) 5.8, 30 m. Steep climbing bearing right leads to ledges. Climb down to the foot of an easy corner on the right and follow this to a stance beneath the conspicuous left-slanting corner.

4) 5.7, 15 m. Climb the corner to a bolt belay at the top of the pinnacle.

5) 5.10a, 50 m. Climb the slabby groove above and continue up a left-trending corner with a steep move at the top. Finish over an overlap with difficult pro to the top anchor of "Zephyr." Note: you can finish in an easier ramp to the right but there is no anchor on the top.

Descent: Rappel the route (2/55 m ropes required) or walk off to Bonanza Descent Gully.

Silver Ghost*** 5.10a, 225 m, gear standard rack to 3.5"
T. Jones, B. Wyvill & R. Enagonio, Oct. 1998

This climb basically sorts out the best climbing between "Banshee" and "Grey Ghost" then cross "Zephyr" to finish by the "Rookie". You might need a road map for this one. The two sections of (10a) are well protected with the climb going mostly in the 5.8 to 5.9 range on excellent rock. This is a moderate classic and a good introduction to the harder fare on this fantastic wall.

The climb starts as for "Grey Ghost". To start, locate a ramp in the middle of the Grey Wall that rises to the right and is 60 meters left of the trailhead below the route "Southern Exposure". Fourth class along the ledge for twenty meters to reach a two-bolt belay.

1) 5.10a, 35 m. Start up the corner after climbing a few meters traverse left past two bolts. Now head up the face to gain a couple of small ledges. From here continue up past a bolt to a second set of ledges with a piton and bolt belay.

Grey Ghost Wall, Left

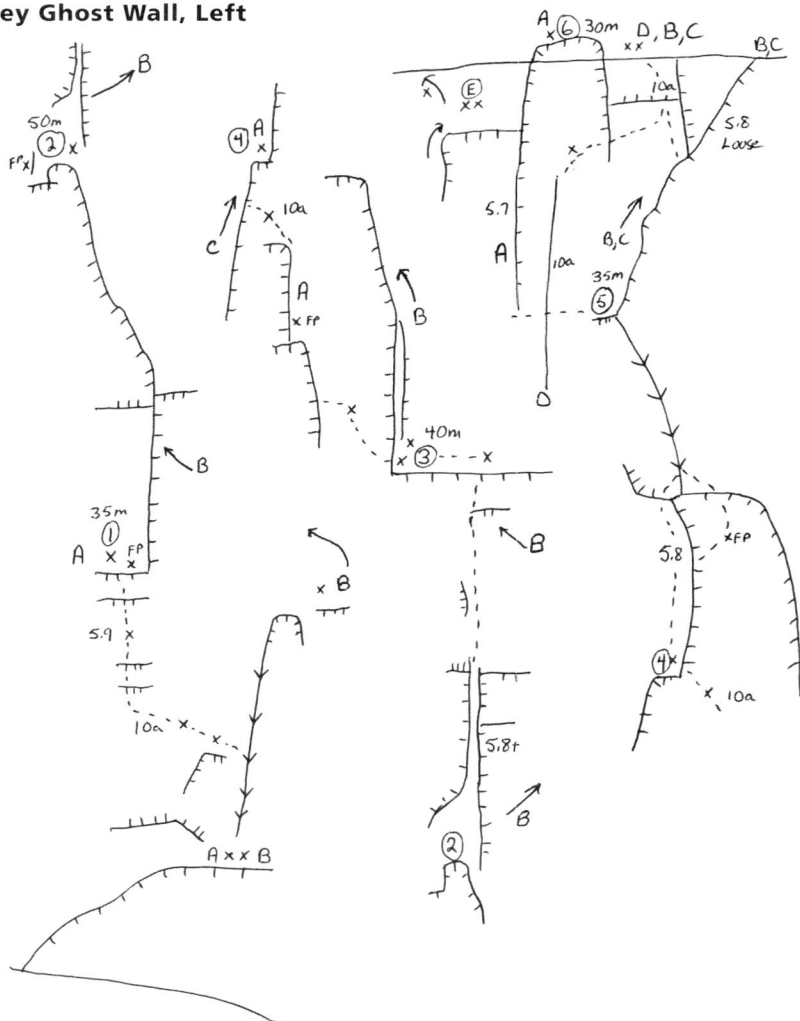

GREY GHOST WALL, LEFT

A	Sliver Ghost ***	5.10a, 225 m	gear standard rack to 3.5"
B	Grey Ghost	5.8, 225 m	gear rack to 4" & pitons
C	Banshee *	5.10a, 180 m	gear rack to 4" & pitons
D	Zephyr ***	5.11a, 200 m	gear standard rack to 4"
E	The Rookie ***	5.11a, 200 m	gear standard rack to 4"

2) 5.6, 50 m. Move right into the left facing corner. Climb the corner as for "Grey Ghost" until you gain a left leaning ramp. Take this to a small pinnacle and a bolt and piton belay.

3) 5.8+, 40 m. Move right to a shallow left facing corner. Take this up to a flare and a steep, wide crack. Climb the crack (5.8+) then continue on easier ground to a ledge and a bolt. Traverse left along the ledge to a two-bolt belay.

4) 5.10a 35 m. Avoid the obvious corner ("Grey Ghost") at the left end of the ledge. Traverse left then up to a bolt then left to a small right facing corner. Climb this up and through a shallow groove to a small ledge. Move up to a bolt, then left into the left facing corner ("Banshee") and up this to a belay ledge with a single bolt and gear.

5) 5.8, 35 m. Take the corner (takes wide gear) to an overlap turn this and enter a grove. Climb the groove to a ledge and a traditional belay.

6) 5.7, 30 m. Traverse left on slabby ground passing below the obvious finger crack of "Zephyr" to a shallow left facing corner. Climb the corner to a ledge with a bolted belay (of The Rookie) pass this and stay with the corner on the right to the top. To belay loop the block with rope and locate a single piton.

Descent: use the rappel as for "Zephyr" just to the east (2/55 m ropes required) or walk west and use the "Bonanza Descent Gully".

Grey Ghost 5.8+, 225 m, standard rack to 4" and pitons
J. Firth & T. Jones, Sept. 1976

This route follows the left-slanting diagonal break in the centre of the cliff. It was originally titled "Rattling Corner." This name should tell you what you're in for. If this route were on Yam, it would undoubtedly clean up and be a classic. To start, locate a ramp in the middle of the Grey Wall that rises to the right and is 60 m left of the trailhead below the route "Southern Exposure". Fourth class along the ledge for twenty meters to reach a two-bolt belay.

1) 5.7,35 m. Climb the corner and then the arête on the right to a single bolt belay.

2 & 3) 5.5, 80 m Continue easily trending left up a series of short steps and corners to a block belay where the climbing steepens (bolt).

4) 5.8+, 45 m. Either climb directly up the corner (5.8+) or traverse right after 6 m past a cracked block to another crack system and follow this until a traverse leads back left to the main corner (5.7). Continue up to the foot of a chimney.

5) 5.8, 50 m. Climb the chimney to the top of the pinnacle.

6) 5.10a, 50 m. Continue as for pitch 5 of Banshee and exit over a difficult overlap with awkward protection to finish at the "Zephyr" belay originally graded 5.8+. Note there is an easier ramp to the right that finishes at this grade but there is no anchor on top.

Descent: either rappel "Zephyr" two 55 m ropes required or walk off west to the "Bonanza Descent Gully."

Mantissa*** 5.10c/d/R, 300 m, standard rack to 4"

double ropes recommended

J. Rollins & C. Young, Oct 1983

"Mantissa" is a testy outing on excellent rock with a couple of really rompy, juggy pitches at an easier grade lower down. The climbing higher up is sustained and bold. This brilliant if not slightly serious route pieces together a natural line, originally without using bolts (they didn't even take any, "Business as usual!" said Yonge)—testimony to a rapidly waning ethic. Originally graded 5.9+ it now goes at the sporting grade of 5.10c/d with several mid 5.10 runout sections.

This classic route has now had some minimal retrofitting and at least two recent ascents.

Due to the vague nature of the description and the certain tendency of the first ascensionist's to under grade their routes, "Mantissa" was not repeated until a couple of years ago. Keith Haberl and Chris Robertson did the second assent. During this accent they added two protection bolts as recommended by John and Chas and also added one or two bolts to all of the belays. Andy Genereux and Jeff Marshal recently undertook the third known assent. They added one protection bolt to the fifth pitch and added bolts to the belays as needed. What follows is an updated description of this excellent but bold route with corrected pitch lengths. This route would be in the same category as the "Maker" in the CMC Valley or "Creamed Cheese" on Epitaph Wall, harder than the former slightly easier than the later.

To start, locate a ramp in the middle of the Grey Ghost Wall that rises to the right and is 60 m left of the route "Southern Exposure". Fourth class right along the ledge for 20 m to reach a two-bolt belay.

1) 5.9, 50 m. Climb the corner directly above the belay for 25 m moving right into a bay, which holds the one bolt belay for "Grey Ghost." From the belay continue up and right climbing a short crack through the steep wall (5.9)   to gain a large ledge to the right, follow the ledge right to a two-bolt belay.

2) 5.8, 50 m. Move back left on the ledge then climb up to a large block 3 m above. Pass the block on the left to gain a shallow groove with some sustained 5.8 moves. Move up and right to gain a shallow right facing corner. Climb this corner to the two-bolt belay.

3) 510b/R, 30 m. Head left on a rising and sustained traverse past a bolt. 10 m past the bolt you reach a shallow groove with some pro! The large corner of "Grey Ghost" is to the left 5 m. Climb the groove on fantastic face holds more or less straight up for the final 10 m to the belay below a right facing corner (2-bolts). Note this pitch is as dangerous for the second as it is for the leader. The potential fall is the same for both, be careful.

4) 5.10a, 50 m. Make hard moves above the belay to enter the corner. Continue on sustained ground, for 10 m. After 15 m move right into a second crack climb this past a fixed pin. Continue up and right to a third crack climb this to a two bolt belay right of a block. Above is a roof, which has a right facing corner on the right.

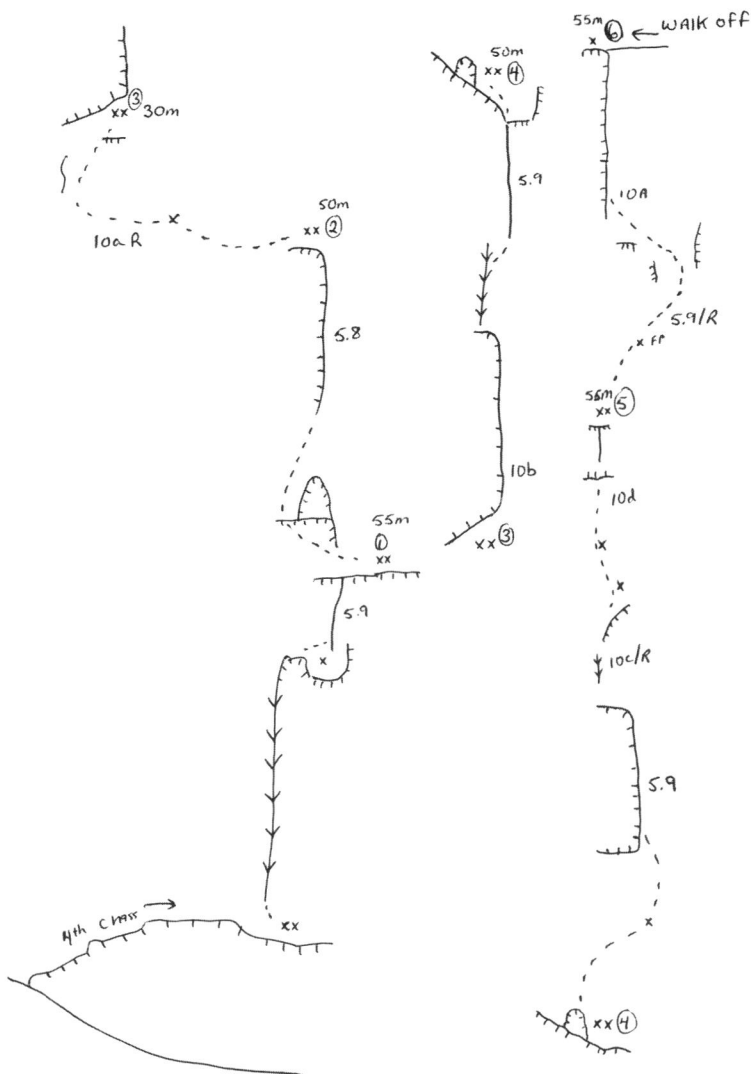

55m ⑥ ← WALK off

50m xx ④

xx ③ 30m

50m xx ②

5.9

5.8

10a R

10A

5.9/R
x fr

56m xx ⑤

10b

10d

55m ① xx

xx ③

5.9

x

10c/R

5.9

4th Class →

xx

5.9

x

xx ④

GREY GHOST WALL, RIGHT

Mantissa ***   5.10d/R, 300 m   gear standard rack to 4"

Ziggurat

5) 5.10c/d/R, 55 m. Climb up and then right to a bolt (former belay bolt) below the corner, move into the corner and climb it to a small ledge. Move left past a block to gain a shallow groove. Climb the groove on sustained ground past a couple of slots, which offer some difficult protection. As the groove ends move right along a short ramp to a bolt. Make hard moves up and left to a second bolt then head straight up on a set of tears sustained to gain a corner crack, which is climbed for 5 m to a two-bolt belay.

6) 5.10b/R, 55 m. Move up and right on good face climbing to a fixed pin at 10 m. Climb up and then right into a shallow corner. Then climb back left, rising climbing leads towards to main right facing corner (this is the corner directly above the belay) climb the line of least resistance. The protection on this section is somewhat difficult and spacious. Climb the corner to the top, locate a single belay bolt back 3 m

Descent: Walk down and to the west to the Bonanza Descent Gully.

Ziggurat** 5.10b, 290 m, gear to 4"pitons recommended
C. Perry & C. Dale, Sept. 1983

"Ziggurat" moves out farther right than "Mantissa" on to the steep grey wall and has a difficult and committing crux section through a compact bulge at about two-thirds height. Another classic in the traditional style. Be sure to include a healthy diet of iron (pitons).

The first ascensionists continued along the "Banshee" traverse to reach "Grey Ghost" and then climbed up to the alternate traverse on pitch 4 of that route. It is recommended, however, to use the first three pitches of "Mantissa." To give a more sustained and technical adventure to the day.

1) 5.9, 50 m. Climb the corner directly above the belay for 25 m moving right into a bay, which holds the one bolt belay for "Grey Ghost." From the belay continue up and right climbing a short crack through the steep wall (5.9) to gain a large ledge to the right, follow the ledge right to a two-bolt belay.

2) 5.8, 50 m. Move back left on the ledge then climb up to a large block 3 m above. Pass the block on the left to gain a shallow groove with some sustained 5.8 moves. Move up and right to gain a shallow right facing corner. Climb this corner to the two-bolt belay.

3) 510b/R, 30 m. Head left on a rising and sustained traverse past a bolt. 10 m past the bolt you reach a shallow groove with some pro! The large corner of "Grey Ghost" is to the left 5 m. Climb the groove on fantastic face holds more or less straight up for the final 10 m to the belay below a right facing corner (2-bolts). Note: this pitch is as dangerous for the second as it is for the leader, the potential fall is the same for both, be careful.

4) 5.10b, 45 m. Climb the corner crack directly above the belay above the bulge move into the second crack to the right climb this into a third crack "Mantissa" heads straight up from here. Ziggurat" continues up and diagonally right on good rock to ledges below a bulge in the wall.

Opposite: Gord Rinke on the fourth pitch of Southern Exposure.
Photo: Andy Genereux.

Southern Exposure

5) 5.8, 10 m. A short pitch leads up left to a belay immediately below the bulge.

6) 5.10a, 40 m. Climb a short corner and move out right past a piton to make a difficult move over an overlap on to the slabby wall above. Continue up and then right to a shallow groove. Climb up the groove to reach a better belay.

7) 5.8, 40 m. Continue up the wall above moving over left near the top to belay in a right-facing corner.

8) 5.7, 20 m. Continue up the corner and move out right to finish.

Descent: Walk off to Bonanza Descent Gully.

Southern Exposure*** 5.11a, 300 m, standard rack to 4"
double ropes recommended
T. Pochay & A. Genereux, Sept. 1993
A. Genereux & G. Rinke August 1998 (Alternate pitches 2 & 5)

This route was completed over two days in somewhat marginal weather. All climbing was established on-lead with the power drill carried by the leader. Several bolts were drilled off hooks and fixed ropes were employed to gain the upper pitches on the second day. As well, Andy was at work earning his wings when he blew a hook to take a 25-footer on the last pitch.

This climb offers some excellent climbing and has become an instant classic. Later climbers found a 5.8 system to the right that avoids the final crux pitch. Why anyone would forsake the final pitch for any reason other than bad weather remains a mystery. The second half of the final pitch presents one of the finest positions imaginable on impeccable rock. It is the most memorable pitch on the climb. The bar was raised a notch with the addition of two variation pitches both done on lead will a power drill no hooks. The pitches add quality and keep the climbing more consistent. It has also become popular to do the first two pitches of "Windmills" in conjunction with the upper pitches of "Southern Exposure" for a superb day out.

"Southern Exposure" is the first route you encounter when the trail meets the base of the wall. It starts in a yellow groove leading to an overhang with a large right-facing corner above. There is a hard-to-see, home-made bolt hanger just below the first roof. There is usually a cairn built on some flat rocks at the base of the route.

1) 5.10c, 50 m. Climb a shallow left-facing corner for several meters and make a move left and then go up past a bolt (10c). Climb the left-leaning corner above and exit right at the roof (10a) and wander up and right to a belay.

2) 5.10a, 45 m. Take the corner directly above the belay for 5 m and then move left onto a face and climb up past a bolt (10a) to broken ground. Take the left of two large corners and climb a steep, wide tower past a bolt to a large ledge and a belay. Note; there are new ringbolts located above the outside lip of the belay platform on the right to aid in rappel do not use these to belay.

2) alt, 5.10c, 40 m. From the broken ground above the bolt move right to a steep rib with three bolts, steep technical face (10c) leads directly to the belay.

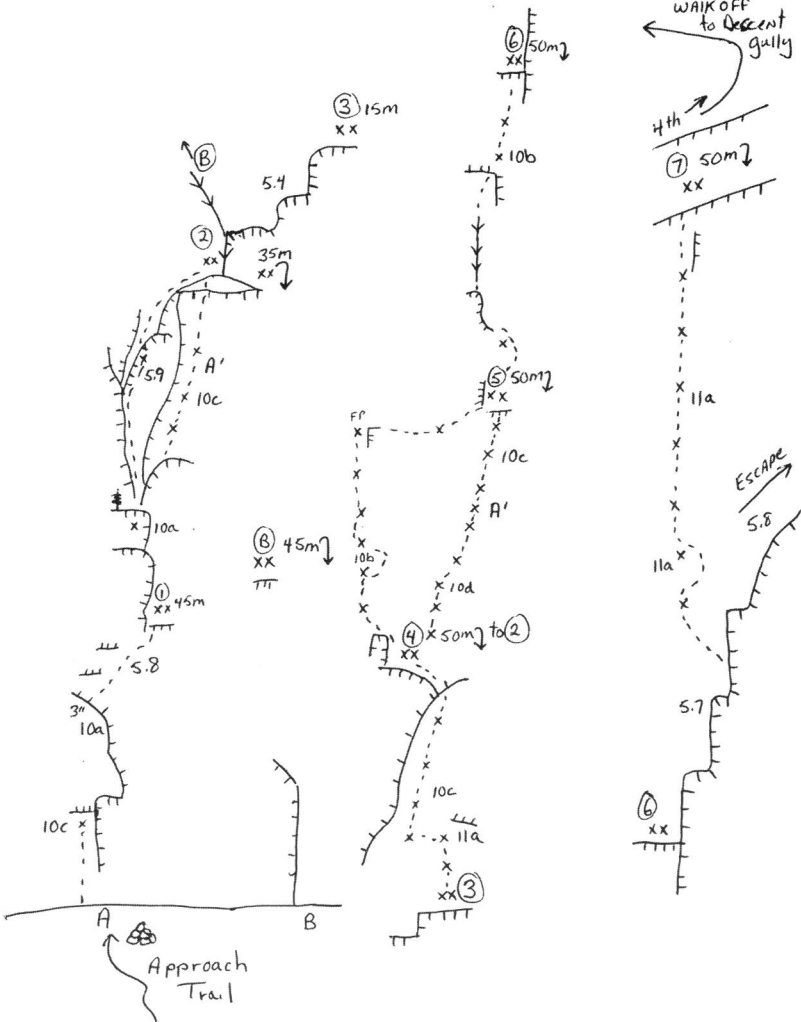

Southern Exposure

GREY GHOST WALL, RIGHT

A Southern Exposure ***	5.11a, 300 m	gear to 4"
A' Southern Exposure variations ***	5.10c, 5.10d	
B Windmills of The Mind ***	5.11b, 300 m	gear to 4"

Windmills of the Mind

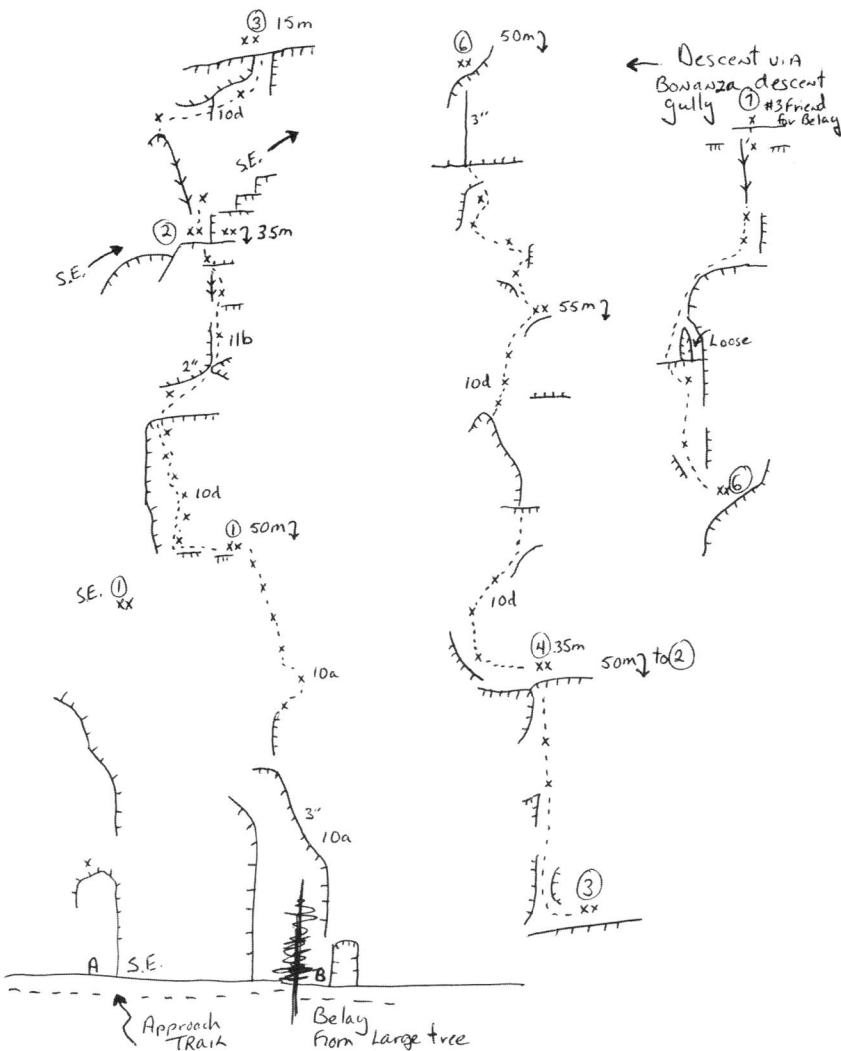

③ 15m
xx
10d

S.E.

② xx xx ↓35m

S.E.

x 11b
2"

10d

① 50m↓
xx

S.E. ①
xx

10a

3"
10a

A S.E.
Approach Trail
B
Belay from Large tree

⑥ 50m↓
xx

3"

xx 55m↓

10d

10d

④ 35m
xx 50m↓ to②

③
xx

← Descent via Bonanza descent gully ⑦ #3 Friend for Belay
x

Loose

xx⑤

GREY GHOST WALL, RIGHT

| A Southern Exposure *** | 5.11a, 300 m | gear to 4" |
| B Windmills of The Mind *** | 5.11b, 300 m | gear to 4" |

3) 5.5, 20 m. Climb the stepped corner up and right to a large ledge and a bolt belay.

4) 5.11a, 35 m. Face climb directly up from the belay past two bolts. Make difficult moves left (11a) to gain a steep and exposed ramp with a shallow right facing corner on the left. Climb the ramp (10c) and exit left over the lip of the corner to a belay.

5) 5.10b, 55 m. Face climb up and left past two bolts. Move out right from the second bolt and go up through an overlap and move back left to a bolt (10b). Climb up and left and into a shallow corner with a fixed pin. From the pin climb a rising slightly run-out traverse right to a belay.

5) alt, 5.10d, 50 m. Climb directly above the belay to an overlap. Make committing but positive moves right then up on exceptional rock past several bolts climbing directly to the belay.

6) 10b, 50 m. Move up and right to gain a ledge. Work back left along the ledge until it is possible to gain a shallow corner. Climb the corner for 30 m and exit up and right (10a) to a belay.

7) 5.11a, 50 m. Climb an obvious left-facing corner for 20 m until it is possible to gain the superb headwall. Face climb up the gently overhanging wall past seven bolts to a belay just below the top.

Descent: It is now possible to rappel the climb on double 55 m ropes. However it is recommended that parties scramble up to the scree and walk off west to the "Bonanza Descent Gully.

Windmills of the Mind*** 5.11b, 300 m, standard rack to 4"
double ropes recommended
A. Genereux & J. Josephson, July 1995

The first pitch of this route was done by Brian Gross and Choc Quinn with only one bolt some eight years earlier just after their ascent of "Creamed Cheese." The pair then traversed left onto what is now the second pitch of "Southern Exposure" and followed that line to their high point near the start of the 5.11 climbing on pitch four. It was an impressive and bold effort as they carried only "five or six bolts."

After his ascent of "Southern Exposure," Andy Genereux climbed the original pitch in its single-bolt, ground-fall state. Obtaining permission to retro bolt the first pitch from Brian Gross, Andy completed the task using a power drill on lead. This opened the way for one of the better and more sustained routes in the area. The climb was established over two days.

"Windmills" is slightly more technical but very similar to its neighbour "Southern Exposure" and has some difficult sections requiring gear. It was done from the ground up except for the second pitch, which was put in on rappel but not top roped. All other bolts were drilled from natural stances without using hooks. The first six belays are equipped for rappel. The top anchor is a single bolt next to a perfect #3 Friend crack.

The route starts directly behind a large tree some 20 m right of "Southern Exposure." It is easily identified by a splitter hand-crack in a right-facing corner.

Windmills of the Mind

1) 5.10a, 55 m. Start up the corner with an excellent hand crack (10a). When the corner peters out, traverse right past a bolt to another older bolt. Climb up and then left to gain a shallow corner. Climb the corner and exit left to the belay.

2) 5.11b, 50 m. Wander up left and climb the steep sustained and devious face past several bolts (10d) to a ledge. Move right to gain a steep corner and climb past a bulge (TCUs to 2") to a bolt (11b). Battle upwards through a bulging overhang that joins the belay platform shared with "Southern Exposure."

3) 5.10d, 15 m. Make several awkward moves to gain a small dihedral directly above the belay. Continue up the dihedral to a bolt and make several exposed moves up and right (10d), traversing to a small corner that is taken up to the belay ledge.

4) 5.10a, 35 m. Move left to gain a shallow right-facing corner and climb the corner (10a) to gain a large ledge and a belay. If you have to retreat pitches 3 and 4 can be rappelled together.

5) 5.10d, 55 m. Traverse left along the ledge for 5 m and climb up. At the second bolt make difficult moves right on slightly crumbly rock and then up to a bolt. Climb up past a small bulge to a ledge and an easy shallow right-facing corner. Climb the corner to gain a pedestal. Thin moves on a bulletproof face, lead up and right to a crack and a belay.

6) 5.11b, 55 m. Climb up and left along a ramp and make several hard moves to a lieback flake on the right (large wire). Move left and delicately climb up on great rock (11b) to gain a rounded ledge below an overlap. A short traverse left leads into a spectacular hand crack. Climb the crack (10c) for 30 m to a belay.

7) 5.10b, 50 m. Face climb left and up to a bolt. Move up and right into a left-facing corner. Climb the corner making hard moves left while below a large detached pinnacle (loose). Climb back into the corner and gently pass the pinnacle to a large ledge. Move right and climb up to a shallow corner that leads to the top (10b) and a single bolt belay with a perfect #3 Friend crack.

Descent: Walk off to the "Bonanza Descent Gully.
Note: Fixed stations allow escape from all but the last pitch. Two 55 m ropes required.

Opposite: Jeff Marshall leading out on Creamed Cheese.
Photo: Andy Genereux.

Epitaph Wall & Phantom Tower

A. The Gods Must be Angry
B. Cream Cheese
C. Prosopopoeia
D. The Wraith

E. SW Ridge
F. Boundary Value Problem
G. South Face

H. Angelus Vicia
I. Phantom Tower
J. Epitaph Wall
K. Border Bluffs

The large stepped corner on the right side of Grey Ghost Wall defines the left edge of this wall; Phantom Tower defines the eastern end. This wall is dedicated to passing friends. May their spirit and dreams stay with us.

Epitaph Wall has large sections of what appears to be rotten, overhanging yellow rock. Subsequently, it is home to fewer routes than its neighbouring Grey Ghost Wall. The four full-length routes found on the wall are however, some of the few routes that compete with the Grey Ghost Wall in quality. All of the multi pitch climbs are of a more traditional vein, however they are superb and highly recommended. Just bring a rack and have fun.

Approach
See page 71 for details getting to the base of the cliff. Follow a trail right (east) from the base of the Grey Ghost Wall to a short scree slope halfway up the scree slope is the obvious chimney for "Creamed Cheese." Below the chimney is a short corner with a bolted line heading out left up excellent grey rock, this is the first pitch for "The Gods Must Be Angry." Near the top of the slope there is a small-detached pillar that marks the left side of the Spirit Pillar area. "The Wraith" is another 80 m right of the detached pillar and 50 m left of the deep gully that separates Epitaph Wall from Phantom Tower. The crag is reached in 45-50 minutes from the car.

Descent
For all multi-pitch routes that reach the top of the wall to descend walk left (west) and use the Bonanza Descent Gully. See page 72 for details. Topo on page 96..

The God's Must Be Angry*** 11d/12a/A0, 320 m, gear standard rack to 4", double ropes recommended
A. Genereux, Aug. 2002

This is an excellent climb dedicated to the memory of Danny Guthrie and Ian Bolt lost in an avalanche in the mid-eighties. This climb has the best of both worlds. It climbs on impeccable, heavily textured, grey rock for half the route with excellent exposed moderate crack climbing to complete the climbing experience. The face pitches are outstanding but you still have fun on several sustained crack sections culminating with the amazing exposed finger crack, which traverses the big roof that dominates the main corner. The climb is located just to the left of Creamed Cheese (photo page 118). It crosses this route at the top of the first pitch and again immediately after the start of the third pitch then it climbs into the massive yellow corner to finish up the Grey Ghost Wall to the right of "Southern Exposure". This is the first major route on Epitaph Wall since Prosoppoeia in 1995 by K. Haberal and S. Steiner. The route was established initially via a ground up rope solo. The first three pitches where put up in this fashion in October 2001 by Genereux. Three sections of aid were used, two of which were later free climbed. Due to several death blocks lodged in the big corner Andy decided to rap, bolt, and clean the upper four pitches. This was accomplished by climbing the descent gully right of Montana

The God's Must Be Angry

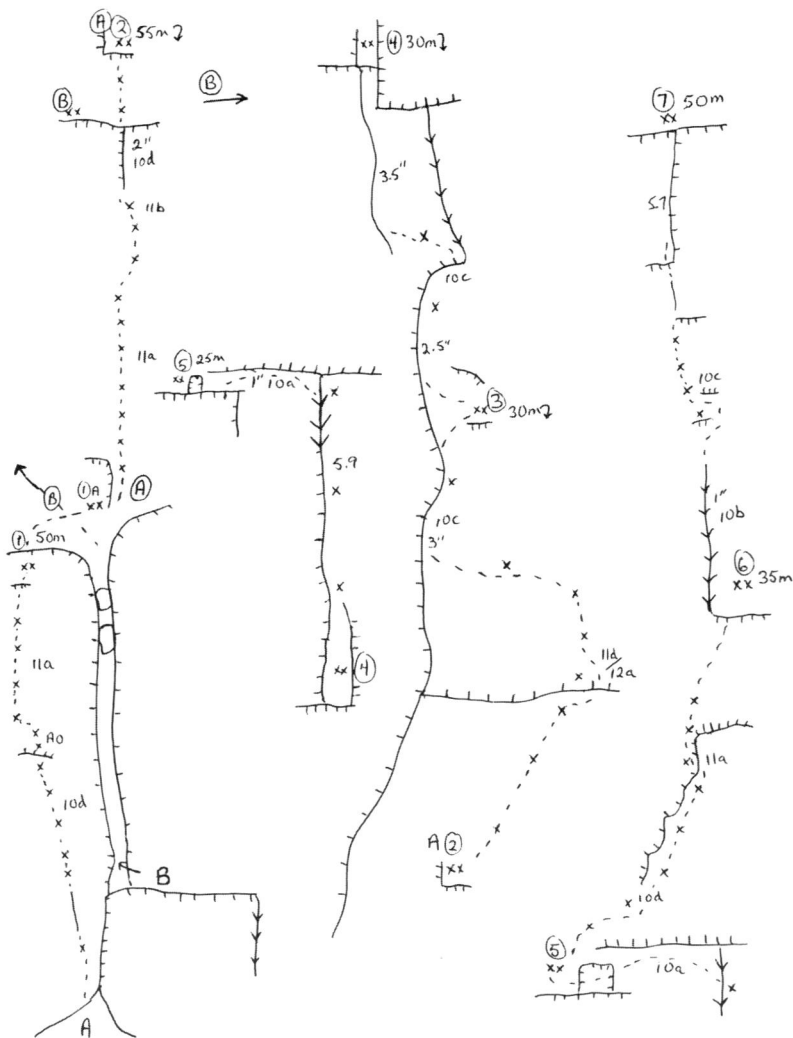

EPITAPH WALL

A The Gods Must Be Angry ***   5.11d/12a, A0, 320 m   gear standard rack to 4"
B Creamed Cheese ***   5.11a, 310 m   gear standard rack to 4"

The God's Must Be Angry

Buttress on North Phantom Crag and traversing around to the top of the wall in "mule like" fashion packing an 80-90 lb. load. Then over 12 hours and surviving a severe electrical storm he rappelled, cleaned, bolted, and rope soloed the four upper pitches in August 2002. The climb is still awaiting a bottom to top continuous assent.

The route climbs the grey face out left of the "Creamed Cheese" chimney. Start in the short corner directly below the chimney, after 3 m angle left on intermittent cracks to gain the prickled grey rock.

1) 5.11a/A0, 55 m. Climb the corner move left to a bolt then follow a thin crack up and left to gain excellent grey rock. Sustained climbing past five bolts leads to a v-shaped groove and a small roof, which is overcome by pulling on two bolts A0 (marked by rap hanger). Continued upward on sustained face climbing past several bolts leading to a small bay with a ringbolt belay. When doing the upper pitches it is better to move up and across the large ledge for 5 m to a second two-bolt belay at a full 60 m.

2) 5.11b, 55 m. Climb the short right facing corner to a bolt. Continued directly up the bulging face on sustained face climbing, find the line of least resistance past 10 bolts. There is a definitive crux at the tenth bolt to gain an open book with an excellent finger crack at the back. Sustained stemming and lie backing for 10 m leads to a ledge, with the "Creamed Cheese" pitch 2 belay located on the left. Skip past this belay and continue straight up on moderate face climbing past 2 bolts for 10 m to a small ledge and ringbolt belay.

3) 5.11d/12a, 30 m. Climb up and slightly right to a bolt, continue up on difficult holds to a roof make hard moves to the right on closely spaced bolts and surmount the roof to gain the face above. Continue up on sustained face holds past two bolts, a thin traverse moves left for 7 m past a bolt to enter the big right facing corner. Climb the corner/crack for 10 m, after passing a bolt move right onto the face to gain the semi hanging ringbolt belay with a small foot rail.

4) 5.10c, 35 m. Continue up the corner past a bolt, as the corner forms a small curving roof after 20 m. Make hard under cling moves out right, then overcome the overlap to regain the corner above. Reach a bolt 2 m higher then move left to gain a hand crack (gear to 3.5") and climb this to a sentry box belay with ringbolts.

5) 5.10a, 20 m. Climb the corner and off-width crack past three bolts to a small ledge under the big roof. Make a long move up to a finger seam at the base of the roof. An amazing and exposed finger traverse leads left for 5 m onto the Grey Ghost Wall to gain a ledge with a large block on the right side. The ringbolt belay is located on the left side of the block.

6) 5.11a, 35 m. Step right onto the block and clip a bolt, make positive moves up to gain a small foot ledge. Traverse right on awkward and exposed moves past a bolt for 2 m Now climb up on sustained face into a small right facing corner. At the fifth bolt make hard moves left to leave the corner. Climb the face up and slightly right on prickly grey rock past three bolts to the bottom of a v-shaped groove with a small ledge and ring bolt belay at the base.

Creamed Cheese

7) 5.10c, 50 m. Climb the groove for 10 m with protection available in the intermittent crack at the back. At the second bolt, climb awkwardly up to the right and with the bolt waist level make hard moves left to a sloping prickled ledge. Climb up and slightly left for three bolts, then move right and up to a ledge above the last bolt. Climb the blocky flake to gain an obvious left facing corner (the escape corner referred to on "Southern Exposure"). Climb the corner to the top of the wall and a ringbolt belay.

Descent: walk off left to the Bonanza Descent Gully. If forced to retreat, every station is equipped with ringbolts to allow a rappel from all pitches on the climb, two ropes required. However, to retreat after the big roof you would have to climb the pitch 5 traverse backward to reach a bolt under the roof, then lower to the station below. Cleaning by the second will require back cleaning to the bolt then lowering off a single bolt. This is very tricky and should only be attempted if the party is in trouble.

Creamed Cheese*** 5.11a, 310 m, gear standard rack to 4",
double ropes recommended
B. Gross & C. Quinn, Aug. 1987

Brian Gross, Choc Quinn and David Cheesmond first started this monumental route. The trio made several attempts, reaching the top of pitch four before David was lost while attempting the Hummingbird Ridge on Mount Logan. The remaining pair, along with Al Pickel, sorted out the fifth pitch on the penultimate attempt. Gross and Quinn returned to polish off the route, which included the spectacular sixth pitch. The pair wanted to name the route the "Dave Cheesmond Memorial" until Gillian, David's widow, christened the route "Creamed Cheese."

The route starts about 20 m left of the detached pillar that identifies the Spirit Pillar area. Look for a large blocky ledge system 10 m off the ground that leads left into the obvious right-facing chimney.

There is a new bolted project out left of the second pitch started by Keith Haberl. Don't be confused by these bolts, you climb the blank face to the right. This new project has resulted in a new two-bolt anchor, which can be used for pitch 1 of "Creamed Cheese". In 1998 Andy Genereux and Jeff Marshall installed a second bolt or double bolts on belays 2, 4, 6, and 7. Now at least the belayer has a fighting chance to survive if the unthinkable happens. Jeff Marshall commented after their ascent "for a couple of engineers those guy's sure build a shitty anchor". The first ascent party rappelled the route from single bolt anchors. Do not attempt to rappel off the route unless in trouble slings would be required and from higher on the climb diagonal rappels would be required. Some back clipping would be advisable to reach lower anchors.

1) 5.6, 60 m. Traverse in from the right on ledge system that leads to the chimney. Several options lead to a blocky ledge system that gains access to a large right-facing chimney. Climb the chimney to a large ledge directly below the big yellow corner. There is a two-bolt belay here but it recommended that you continue left along the ledge, then ascend to a blocky bay gaining a higher ledge with a second two-bolt belay.

Al Pickel sorting out the routefinding crux (pitch 3) of "Creamed Cheese" during the second ascent. Photo: Trevor Jones.

Creamed Cheese

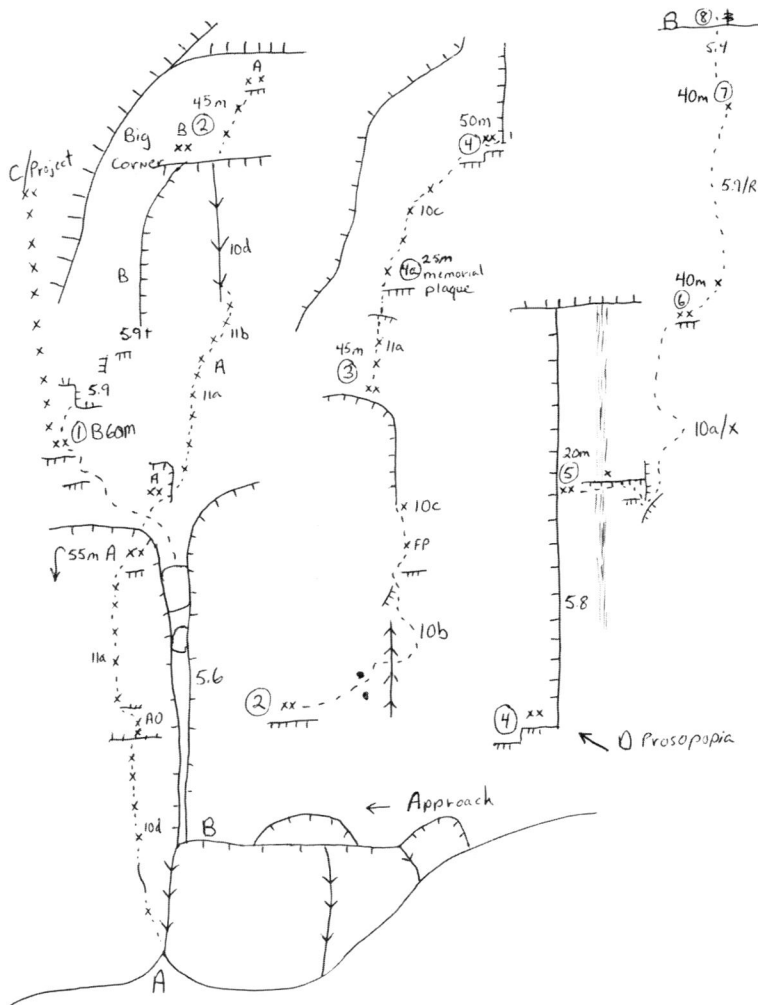

EPITAPH WALL

A The Gods Must Be Angry ***	5.11d/12a/A0, 320 m	gear standard rack to 4"
B Creamed Cheese ***	5.11a, 310 m	gear standard rack to 4"
C Project		
D Prosopopoeia **	5.11c, 310 m	gear standard rack to 4" & pitons

2) 5.10a/R, 45 m. Ignore the bolts heading up and left these are part of Keith's unfinished project. Climb a steep wall up and right (5.9, runout) to a small left-facing corner and roof above the belay. Traverse right to a crack splitting the roof. Climb this (10a/R) to a short wall leading onto a good ledge. Traverse right to the main corner (runout), which is then climbed for 20 m to a good ledge with a bolt belay on the right.

3) 5.10c/R, 45 m. Traverse right from the belay to some pockets (Friends or Tri-cams) near the edge of a broad arête. Climb the arête trending right to gain a short crack on the right-hand side. Climb this up and left to good holds then back right to a small ledge below a steep wall. Launch up the wall to a bolt (hidden from below) then continue to easier ground in a ramp leading up and left to a ledge with a bolt belay.

4) 5.11a, 50 m. Climb the short but "the gently impending wall" above the belay past two bolts. Above the second bolt there are several hard moves with ledge fall potential the belayer must pay close attention. The climbing quickly, however, gets much easier and leads up and right past several ledges to a bolt below a steep brown wall to which is attached is a small plaque commemorating David Cheesmond. Noted as pitch 4a on the topo, it is possible to belay here or continue up (recommend double rope techniques). Climb the steep brown face, then move up and right, sustained 5.10c face past three bolts to a ledge system below the major roofs to a two-bolt belay. Depending on the option taken below you can combine the next pitch with the upper half of pitch 4 if you belayed at the memorial plaque.

5) 5.7, 20 m. Traverse right and make an awkward move into the large right-facing corner capped by an absolutely huge roof some 30 m above Continue up the airy corner to a solid natural gear and bolt belay on a narrow ledge.

6) 5.10a/X, 40 m. Traverse right on the ledge crossing the prominent water streak to a bolt. Continue right on the ledge to where it fades out. Step down and then climb across to a break that leads up to a good but slopping ledge. This is where the fun begins. Climb the unprotected but immaculate wall above on widely spaced holds. The line of least resistance seems to go up from the ledge, trending left, then back right and up to an ill-defined corner. Follow the corner to a small, flat perch with a bolt belay.

7) 5.9/R, 40 m. Climb up and right to a bolt. Continue up and right on excellent rock through corners and bulging rock until a single bad bolt is reached on a good ledge 10 m below the top of the crag.

8) 15 m. A short pitch of easy 5th class leads to the scree and eventually a natural gear or tree belay. If it is possible, it is recommended to combine pitches 7 and 8.

Descent: walk left to the Bonanza Descent Gully.

Prosopopoeia

Prosopopoeia 5.11b/c, 310 m, gear standard rack to 4"
  pitons & double ropes recommended
K. Haberl & S. Steiner, July 1995

"Prosopopoeia" is a fine route that was completed in a single day and in a bold style. The day was quite cold and scattered with rain showers and darkness. Between storms it took several efforts in the morning to establish the serious first pitch after which Keith Haberl and Shep Steiner "just somehow believed" that they would make the top. It is a committing route for the audacious "Hintersteiner Traverse" on pitch three cuts off any convenient means of escape. Except for pitch five, all the belays are off natural gear and are solid. Pins are not necessary but may be helpful for protection. It is recommended that the fixed piton belay on pitch five be replaced with bolts. "Prosopopoeia" is named in memory of Simon Parboosingh who was killed in an avalanche on Mount Athabasca and is Latin for "a voice from the grave."

"The perfect tip of the hat to the enthusiasm and energy we received on this day and others from the spirit of a great man."

The obvious feature of this route is the arching right-facing corner in the middle of the wall. After five-and-a-half pitches the climb joins "Creamed Cheese" at the large corner left of the prominent water streak and finishes as per that route. The rather exact gear descriptions are courtesy of Keith whose original, enthusiastic topo set some sort of record as it ran into four detailed pages. Keith is talking about a retrofit of this route in 2003 after this guide comes out. Give him a call before you climb this imposing route to see if this has been completed.

Twenty meters right of the detached pillar there is an arching overhang just off the ground. The route starts up the crack that splits the left side of the roof (an angle piton is easily visible). There are numerous other cragging routes on either side of the route. See the Spirit Pillar topos on pages 130 & 131 for details.

1) 5.10+/R, 25 m. Climb up and left to the crack through the roof to a "so-so" fixed angle piton (10d). Climb the crack and on to a slab and up to a no-hands rest and the only bolt on the route. Move left around a bulge and go up through a series of difficult "fins" that take "wires in between some of them, but everything flares, so it's all dubious." Continue up and right with increasing difficulty past a good fixed pin to a small ledge and a good natural belay below a right-facing corner.

2) 5.10b, 30 m. Climb the corner with great gear (10b) and eventually break onto the left arête (not steep) and a small stance below a blank wall. Continue up the unprotectable face on perfect rock (5.8) for 12 m to a natural belay around an enormous block on top of the Spirit Pillar formation.

3) 5.11a, 35 m. Move left from the belay past some loose blocks to a large flake with a fixed knifeblade. Continue left along the flake to a second knifeblade at the end of the flake. Back up the pin with a #4 Camalot "stuffed into an obtuse corner at the base of the overhanging wall kind of like it would if you were to try to cam it between your floor and the wall" and traverse left to make the committing Hintersteiner Traverse. This is a blind, dynamic launch leftwards to reach the edge of a left-facing corner.

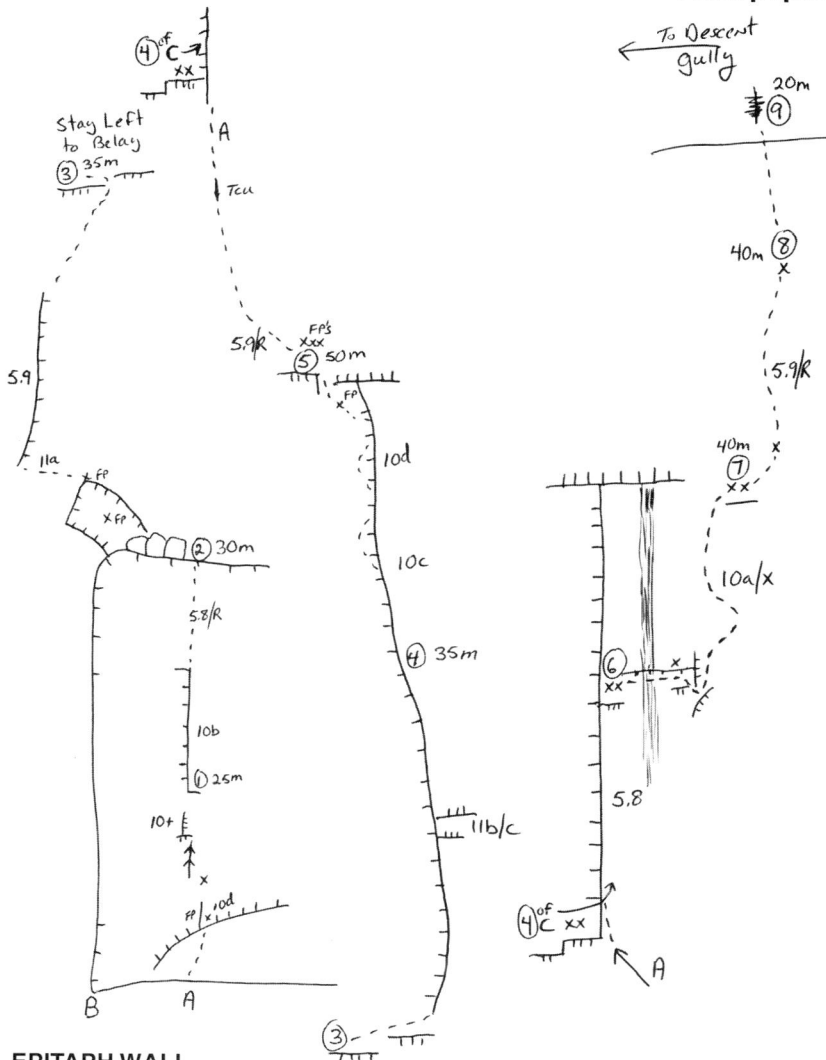

Prosopopoeia

To Descent gully

20m ⑨

40m ⑧

5.9/R

④ of C
xx

Stay Left to Belay
③ 35m

A
Tcu

40m ⑦
xx

10a/x

5.9/R
FP's xxx
⑤ 50m
FP

10d

⑥ xx

10c

④ 35m

5.9

11a
FP
x FP
② 30m

5.8/R

10b
① 25m

10+
x

FP / 10d
x

5.8

④ of C xx

A

B   A

③

EPITAPH WALL

Prosopopoeia **   5.11c, 310 m,

Gear standard rack to 4" long slings multiple mid size cams
Pitons and or bolts to add to belays

Prosopopoeia

Continue up the corner (5.9) on immaculate rock (medium cams) to a slab and bomber natural stance "below the start of the big yellow dihedral." Belay as far left as possible to avoid any rockfall from the next pitch.

4) 5.11b/c, 35 m. Climb the large right-facing corner with good nut protection to a loose, crumbling roof. This is "steep, strenuous and technical" but well protected with small to medium cams. Continue carefully past "the milk crate" on continuously steep and strenuous terrain. Scratch up to an excellent natural anchor and stance with nuts and medium cams.

5) 5.10d, 50 m. Climb up the exceptionally sustained corner "straying out onto the left wall where it seems like that would make easier climbing and back right into the corner for gear when you think you could get it." The corner ends with a short, very strenuous overhanging section that ends at an "airy and scary one-person perch" to the left. Belay off three fixed pitons and a "useless TCU" (This station should have bolts added).

6) 5.9/R, 50 m. Move left from the belay with the unprotected 5.9 crux coming in the first few moves. Continue on excellent rock up and slightly left aiming for the right-facing corner on pitch 6 of "Creamed Cheese." The only gear before the corner is a #1 TCU in a small slot about three-quarters of the way. The first ascensionist belayed on pitons (now bolts) on a ledge at the top of pitch 4 of "Creamed Cheese." It is recommended, however, to climb the "Creamed Cheese" corner (5.7) to a good natural and bolt belay at a small ledge.

7) 5.10a/X, 40 m. Traverse right on the ledge over the prominent water streak to a bolt. Continue right on the ledge to where it fades out. Step down and then climb across to a break that leads up to a good ledge. This is where the fun begins. Climb the unprotected but immaculate wall above on widely spaced holds. The line of least resistance seems to go up from the ledge, trending left, then back right and up to an ill-defined corner. Follow the corner to a small, flat perch with a piton and bolt belay.

8) 5.9/R, 40 m. Climb up and right to a bolt. Continue up and right on excellent rock through corners and ledges until a single bad bolt on a good ledge 10 m below the top of the crag.

9) 15 m. A short pitch of easy 5th class leads to the scree and eventually to a natural gear or tree belay. If it's possible, it's recommended to combine pitches 8 and 9.

Descent: walk off left to the Bonanza Descent Gully.

Between "Creamed Cheese" and "The Wraith" are several tongues of waterworn, grey rock between 20 and 50 meters high. This area is dominated by and named for a large left-facing corner of yellow rock that has been climbed by an unknown party at an unknown grade. There is a fixed piton about 25 m up the corner and on the FFA of "Maya" a piton was found at the top of the formation. The area is unique with a number of quality, pure-crack climbs with several at a moderate grade. Most of the activity to date has been on the natural lines although sport climbs have begun to make an appearance. All of the routes except "Spirit Pillar" and "Prosopopoeia" have bolt anchors but not all are chained and some may need slings replaced.

Dreefree 5.10b, 20 m, gear to 1.5"
J. Josephson & L. Allison, 1994

Starting behind the detached pillar and right of an ugly chimney, this route wanders up some loose rock to a good but short finger crack and finishes through a roof to the top. From the anchor it is possible to top rope the steep arête to the left.

Upspirits* 5.9, 18 m, fixed gear
F. Campbell, J. Josephson & S. Ritchie, Oct. 1993

A fun face climb in the middle of the feature that is a little runout through the easier middle section.

Supernatural*** 5.10a, 18 m, gear to 2"
J. Josephson & T. Jones, June 1992

This is the obvious finger crack in the grey rock left of "Spirit Pillar" and is highly recommended. Finish at the "Up Spirits" belay.

Kobold Crack 5.5, 20 m, OW large gear
B. Spear & M. Talbot, 1995

The first ascensionist, along with Joe Josephson, thought they'd scamper up this route simply as something to do at the end of a long day of cragging. Josephson got lucky when a ledge collapsed and he pitched over backwards only to have his one camming unit stop his head a mere meter from the ground. Needless to say, the others finished the route without him.

Spirit Pillar 50 m
Grade unknown

First ascent unknown. See history section in introduction.
This is perhaps the most obvious feature in the area. This large, left-facing corner of yellow rock looks steep and strenuous. It finishes through a series of overhangs near the second belay on "Prosopopoeia."

Spirit Pillar, Left

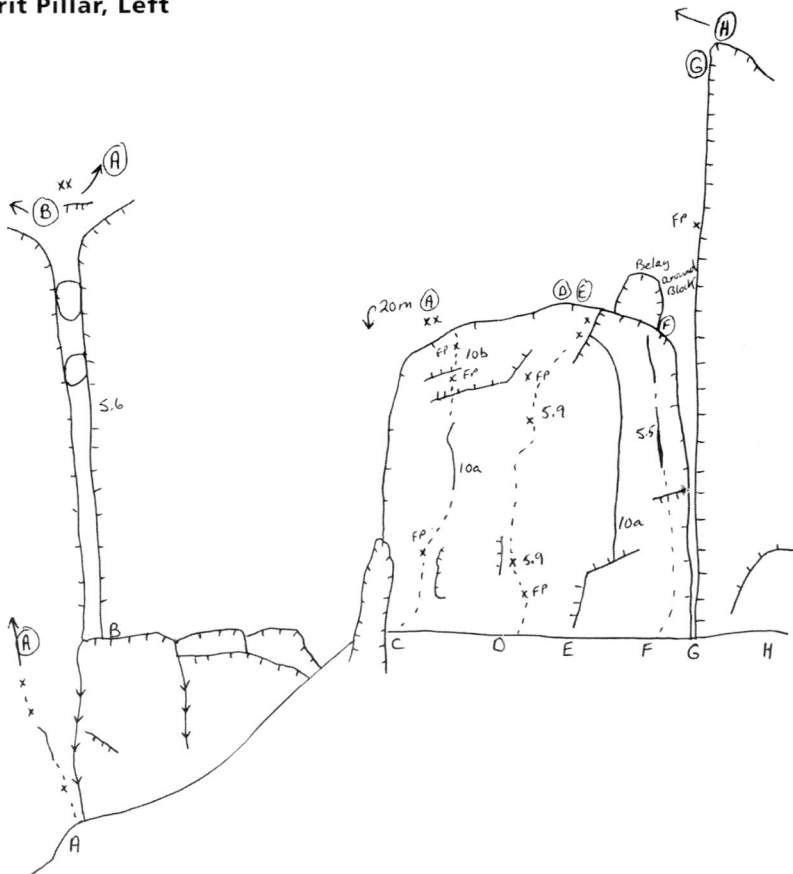

SPIRIT PILLAR, LEFT

A	The Gods Must Be Angry ***	512.a/A0, 320 m	gear standard rack to 4"
B	Creamed Cheese ***	5.11a, 310 m	gear standard rack to 4"
C	Dreefree	5.10b	gear to 1.5"
D	Upspirts *	5.9	
E	Supernatural ***	5.10a	gear to 2"
F	Kobold Crack	5.5	off width, big gear
G	Spirit Pillar	Unknown	
H	Prosopopeia **	5.11c, 310 m	gear to 4" & Pitons

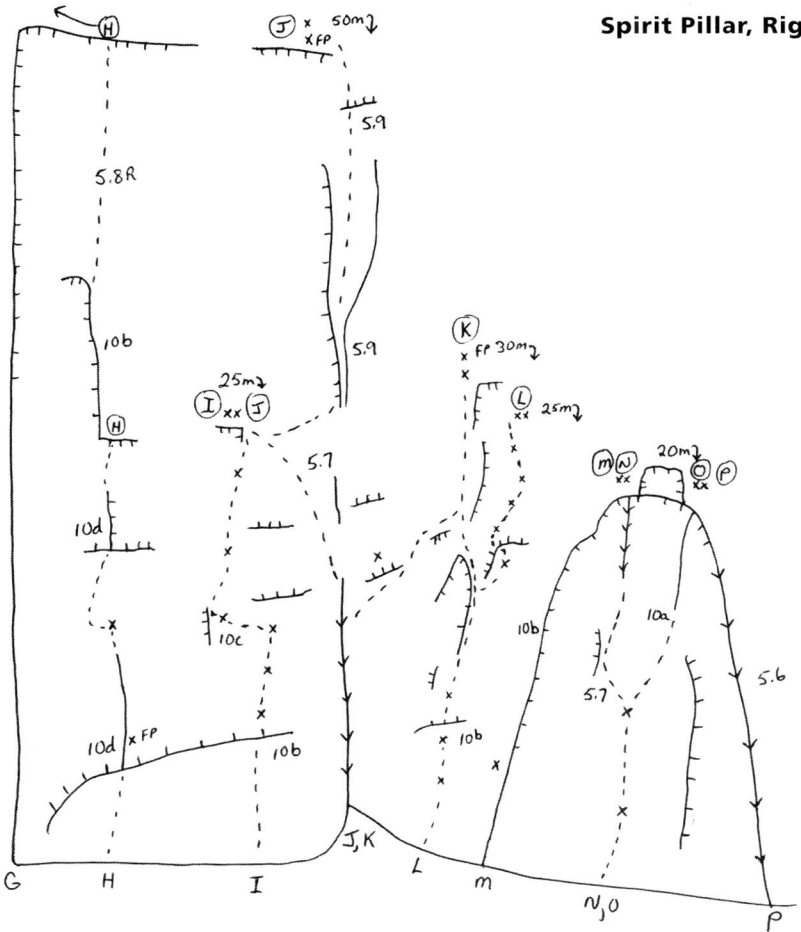

SPIRIT PILLAR, RIGHT

G Spirit Pillar	Unknown	
H Prosopopeia **	5.11c, 310 m	gear standard rack to 4" & pitons
I The Quabalah **	5.10c	
J Maja **	5.9, 50 m	gear to 4" or bigger
K The Place Of Dead Roads	5.10a/R	not recommended
L Project		
M Ghost Buster **	5.10b	gear to 2.5"
N Poltergeist *	5.7	gear to 3"
O Psycokinetic *	5.10a	gear to 1.5"
P Addam's Family	5.6	gear to 4"

Spirit Pillar, Right

The Quabalah** 5.10c, 26 m, fixed gear
J. Josephson, June 1996

Prickly rock and a crux balance move characterizes this sport route. Stick clip the first bolt and finish at the chain belay on the first pitch of "Maya."

Maya** 1) 5.7, 25 m 2) 5.9 OW, 25 m, gear to 4" or bigger
T. Jones & J. Josephson, June 1992

The first pitch is a classic moderate climb with good gear (wires and cams to 2.5 inches). The second pitch sees little traffic despite being quite good. A "Big Bro" or equivalent would be useful for protecting the initial wide crack. The crux pulls through a well-protected (#3 or 3.5 Friend) overhang near the top.

The Place of Dead Roads 5.10a/R, 30 m, not recommended
J. Josephson, 1995

This route branches right from halfway up pitch one of "Maya." Although it climbs a variety of interesting features the rock leaves something to be desired.

Project
At the time of writing it has been impossible to ascertain if this climb has been completed since it was detailed as a project in the last guide.

Ghost Buster** 5.10b, 20 m, gear to 2.5"
J. Josephson & T. Jones, June 1992

This is a fine layback crack that was originally called "Dicky" because the gear at the crux can be awkward to arrange. It was changed later, however, to fit the "spirit" of the area.

Poltergeist* 5.7, 20 m, gear to 3"
T. Jones & J. Josephson, June 1992

Climb the textured face on the left side of the corner past two bolts and into a shallow corner that leads to the same anchor as "Ghost Buster."

Psychokinetic* 5.10a, 20 m, gear to 1.5"
T. Jones & J. Josephson, June 1992

This variation to "Poltergeist" takes a splitter, finger crack in the upper third. It is possible to contrive an almost independent line in the steep corner just right of "Poltergeist." Although it makes the route considerably harder you'd be forced to eliminate the desire to make an easy stem to the left.

Addam's Family 5.6, 20 m, gear to 4"
S. Ritchie & J. Josephson, Oct. 1993

A right-facing corner/crack system named because the whole family can get up it.

The Wraith*** 5.10a, 275 m, gear standard rack to 4" multiples 2"-3"
N. Hellewell & C. Perry, June 1977
Alternate pitches: T. Jones, E. Trouillot & J. Josephson, July 1992

Originally graded 5.8, a major variation was added to pitches two and three in 1992. As perhaps the most sustained 5.9 route in the area I have given it the overall grade of 5.10a, it has since become a popular classic. The original line is somewhat easier but still highly recommended. When you pull the arête near the start of the second pitch, think about doing this without the bolt. A wild position indeed! The new variation above continues more or less straight up to the major corner and is similar to the crux pitch on Yamnuska's "Kahl Wall."

Ten meters to the right of "Addam's Family" there is a large detached block. Continue right for another 10 m to a prominent corner crack that begins on a ledge about 5 m off the ground. There is sometimes a small cairn at the base.

1) 5.9, 45 m. Climb loose rock to the ledge below the corner crack. Excellent climbing with good protection leads to a large ledge with a two-bolt belay.

2) 5.9, 40 m. Step down and traverse left and up to an arête and make a hard move up and round the corner and onto a ledge. Traverse left across a shallow scoop (bolt) and over a cracked pillar to good ledges. (Some parties have gone underneath the cracked pillar.) Continue up to the highest ledge at the base of a steeper section.

3) 5.8+, 40 m. Traverse right across the steep wall to a piton. Make a hard move up and continue up and right to a belay on a slab at the base of the prominent corner.

2) alt. 5.9, 20 m. Step down and traverse left and up to an arête and make a hard move up and round the corner and onto a ledge. Traverse left across a shallow scoop to a bolt. Climb up and back right on excellent rock (5.7 runout) to a corner. Climb the corner to a good ledge and belay off mid-sized camming units. With double ropes, this offers a good top rope for the second on the arête move.

3) alt. 5.10a, 40 m. Climb the short corner above to a ledge (piton). Climb the steep face above up and left past four bolts to good ledge systems. Continue up to a belay located on a slab with a two-bolt anchor at the base of the prominent corner. It is possible with good double rope techniques to run alternate pitches two and three together.

4) 5.8, 45 m. Above the belay, move left around a bulge or alternatively climb directly up the corner (5.9+). Follow the steep hand-crack to a large ledge in the corner.

5) 5.9, 45 m. Continue up the sustained corner past a roof to a ledge. Continue upwards to a smaller ledge below a blocky overhang and establish a natural gear belay. An incredible pitch! **Note**: It was reported that a bolted anchor was added to this pitch but it is located higher than the belay described above on a small foot rail above the overhang mentioned on the next pitch. Using the bolted belay would make for a 55 m pitch.

6) 5.8, 35 m. Climb the overhang (it is not as hard as it looks) and into the corner above to a newer two bolt belay. Traverse up and left across the slab to a bolt. Continue left to a blocky corner. Make an awkward move over this and up into a surprising gully.

The Wraith

EPITAPH WALL

A The Wraith ***   5.10a, 275 m, gear standard rack to 4" multiples 2"-3"
A' Alternate pitches 2&3

Step over the edge and find a belay in a variety of blocks or against the opposite wall.

7 & 8) 5.6, 60 m. Can be combined as one long pitch double rope techniques will help with rope drag. Easier climbing up the gully or on the grey rock to the right leads to the top.

Descent: walk off left, to the "Bonanza Descent Gully" (see page 72, topo page 96).

Grant Statham on The Wraith.
Photo: Dwayne Congdon.

This face is located on the eastern end (right side) of the West Phantom Crag massif. It is separated from Epitaph Wall by a deep, ugly-looking chimney. The tower itself is an attractive form begging to be climbed. It does, however, suffer from rock that is more broken than the well-worn faces of its neighbours to the west. See photo page 118.

Approach

Approach as for West Phantom Crag, see page 71 for details. Hike up to the base of the cliff below Grey Ghost Wall and follow a faint trail right (east) past Grey Ghost Wall and Epitaph Wall to a major scree gully draining the cleft between the tower and Epitaph Wall. Cross the gully to traverse below the south face it takes about 45-60 minutes from the car.

Descent

The original South Face ascent party walked off to the northeast and descended as for South Phantom Crag. Since then, the Bonanza Descent Gully has been established and it is the recommended way. See page 72 for details and page 96 for topo..

Southwest Ridge 5.7, 325 m, gear standard rack to 4", pitons,
double ropes recommended
C. Perry & A. Sole, 1978

The climb follows the left ridge of the tower practically all the way and is loose in places and not sustained. If you enjoy climbing and life, **this route is not recommended**. Start at the loose corner on the right of the ridge and climb this moving left near the top. (A traverse to the edge at about half-height may be worthwhile to avoid the blocky upper section.) Once on the ridge, continue on its left side following the natural line. Higher up, traverses right and up to the large shoulder at about three-quarters height. Climb a short blocky section then traverse to a good crack on the right side of the ridge. Continue up this to the top.

Phantom Cracks

There are two short routes on Phantom Tower that can be included as part of the Devil's Gap cragging routine. Located left of the "South Face Route" is a section of grey rock. At the left end of this there is a deep cleft behind a small blocky pinnacle that leads to an obvious steep off-width crack called "Borderline." At the top of the pinnacle on the right is a steep, yellow jam crack known as the "Boundary Value Problem." Both climbs are approached by climbing a short 5.6 pitch up the cleft and share the same fixed rappel station. See photo on page 118 & topo on page 137.

PHANTOM TOWER, SOUTH FACE

A	SW Ridge Route	5.7	not recommended
B	Borderline Top Rope	5.10d	off width
C	Boundary Value Problem *	5.10c	gear to 2.5"
D	South Face Route **	5.8, 325 m	gear to 4"

Boundary Value Problem* 5.10c, 30 m, gear to 2.5″
B. Durtler & T. Jones, Sept. 1991

Take a collection of small to medium Friends and wires for this fine finger crack.

Borderline 5.10d, 30 m, top rope
Blow the dust off of all of yours and your friends wide gear for this challenging off-width. It has yet to be lead and can be protected by "Big Bro's," extra-large camming units. It has one fixed bolt. To date it has only been top roped after climbing "Boundary Value Problem"

South Face** 5.8, 325 m, gear standard rack to 4″
T. Jones, A. Dunlop, C. Perry & M. White, May 1975

This classic route was the second major climb done in the Ghost River area and marked the beginning of a rapid spate of development in the late seventies. On the first ascent, the team wasn't sure if the formation was detached from the main wall. Expecting a long climb with an epic descent, they carried full bivouac gear. Their climb was made in about seven hours and to their surprise the top is flat with a walk off to the descent gully.

The climb follows a prominent crack line in the centre of the face. The middle portions of route lack interest but the position on the crux overhang of pitch 8 makes it worthwhile. On pitch 5 there are several natural looking lines leading out left. More than one party has followed these to end up on the Southwest Ridge—not a great option but better than the entire ridge.

The route starts to the right of the upper face at a shattered corner leading to the base of a prominent open book. A few meters to the right is a large tree growing close to the cliff and about 30 m farther right is a chimney system leading up to broken ledges on the east face.

1) 5.7, 30 m. Climb the shattered corner moving right and up to a belay at the base of the open book.
2) 5.6, 45 m. Drop down and traverse left around the outside corner. Follow diagonal cracks up and left to the large central ledge.
3) 5.5, 45 m. Move the belay over to the left and then climb a groove system up and left.
4) 5.6, 30 m. Continue following a diagonal line up and left to a ledge below steep grooves.
5) 5.7, 20 m. Climb the grooves and then move right to a slab below a wide corner/crack. Note that the natural line continues up and left to join the Southwest Ridge at the upper shoulder. Care is necessary in locating the proper corner/crack.
6) 5.8, 40 m. Climb the crack and continue up the chimney above until it steepens.
7) 5.7, 30 m. Go up and then move across right to an easier groove system that leads back left to a good ledge below the upper crack. Alternatively, continue directly up the groove (5.9) to the ledge.

8) 5.8, 45 m. Follow the crack that becomes progressively more difficult to an overhang (piton). Pull through the roof (crux), moving right at the top over ledges to the base of the final corner.

9) 5.7, 40 m. Climb the corner and belay well over the top.

Descent: Same as for Angelus Vicia below.

Angelus Vicia** 5.10a, 330 m, gear standard rack to 3.5"
T. Jones, B. Wyvill, A. Pickel, and R. Felber September 1998

The name is Latin for the "Angel of Mercy" the climb starts as for the "South Face" route. Instead of going left up the ramp continue directly up the corner after pitch 1. Pitch 2 was climbed by T. Jones and J. Josephson in 1992 and was described as an alternate second pitch for the south face route in the last guide. This has been eliminated as the pitch works much better and is more in context with this climb. The route climbs a series of corners that can be clearly picked out on the photo on page 118. Topo page 137.

1) 5.7, 30 m. Climb the shattered corner moving right and up to a belay at the base of an open book.

2) 5.9, 45 m. Continue up the open book on sustained (5.9) using several natural chock stones for runners. As the open book meets a sloping ramp locate a fixed piton belay.

3) 5.8, 30 m. Step left across the ramp and climb up the face following several faint features. Start up a shallow corner with a pin. Move out left and up to a bolt and past a piton to gain a small ramp to a fixed piton belay.

4) 5.10a, 45 m. From the belay climb the short corner (5.10a) with a roof to the right wall. From the top of the corner, traverse right to a second corner. Climb this feature sustained 5.9 to a bolt belay.

5) 5.10a, 45 m. Enter the corner above with a bolt on the left wall climb the corner to a stepped ledge, move right to a single bolt belay.

6) 5.8/R, 40 m. Traverse right into the corner, climb up then move left onto the face to a bolt runout face climbing wanders up to a small ledge and bolt belay.

7) 5.10a, 40 m. Take the corner and overcome the roof above, face climb past 2 bolt's (10a) to enter the corner. Either climb the corner 5.8 or wander up the face to the left at 5.6 to the belay marked by a fixed piton. The first ascensionist were out of bolts at this point and feel the belay would be better served if it was lowered to a ledge left of the corner at 30 m. This would require bolts to place an anchor.

8) 5.7, 50 m. Climb the slot chimney above for 25 m then easier blocky ground to the top. There is no real anchor on top get as far back as you can and dig in your heals.

Descent: walk off west to the Bonanza Descent Gully for the complete description see page 72. Topo page 96.

Despite being the home of the Ghost's very first multi pitch rock climb and some fine-looking, waterworn rock, this feature is perhaps one of the more obscure venues recorded in this book. The climbs recorded to date follow natural crack/chimney lines, they were among the earliest routes put up in the mid seventies and have been rarely climbed on since. These were done in an era when Yosemite was considered the Mecca so it was the striking crack lines that attracted the early Ghost River pioneers to this wall.

The East Face of Phantom Tower is considerably wider than it's sister South Face. In fact, from this aspect the formation doesn't look like a tower at all. It is bordered on the left by the rounded southeast buttress of the tower and some 200 m to the right by a very deep, north-facing cleft that separates the tower from South Phantom Crag. See photo on page 141.

Approach & Descent

There are two approaches and descents for the East Face of Phantom Tower.

The first option which is recommended over the second option is via the standard West Phantom Crag approach, see page 71. This entails hiking past the Epitaph Wall, the South Face of Phantom Tower and continuing around the corner and up to the East Face. Because your car will be in Devil's Gap it is recommended you descend by walking west along the top of West Phantom Crag to the Bonanza Descent Gully, see page 72 for details and page 96 for topo..

The second option is to approach as for South Phantom Crags and then continue south past Montana Buttress to the East Face this option has almost no trail for the last third of the approach which undulates along the base requiring more of a bushwhack to arrive at your destination. See page 179 for details. If you come this way, you will need to return to your car at the old CMC campsite. Use the South Phantom Crag descent to the right (north) of Montana Buttress which can be hard to find and has a short section of 5.6 down climbing, see photo page 178.

The times for either approach are approximately the same, about 60-75 minutes. The West Phantom Crag approach and descent are better established and have easier travelling both along the base of the cliffs and along the top. Therefore, it seems the preferred way although the South Phantom Crag option was used for most of the first ascents.

Texas Peapod 5.8, 200 m, standard rack to 4" and pitons
D. Vockeroth & P. Robbins, Aug. 1971

The route was named after its more diminutive British equivalent by Chris Perry and Alan Burgess after their second ascent in 1977. Thinking they were on a new route, they found an old soft-metal piton on the last pitch. It was nearly 20 years later before Chris discovered Don Vockeroth as the culprit.

This route is roughly in the middle of the East Face and is easily distinguished as a deep, pod-shaped chimney that closes near the top. It is the farthest left of the obvious cracks that split the face. Start directly below the line at the right-hand of two short chimneys. Several pitches of easy climbing lead to a steep section below the upper

Phantom Tower, East

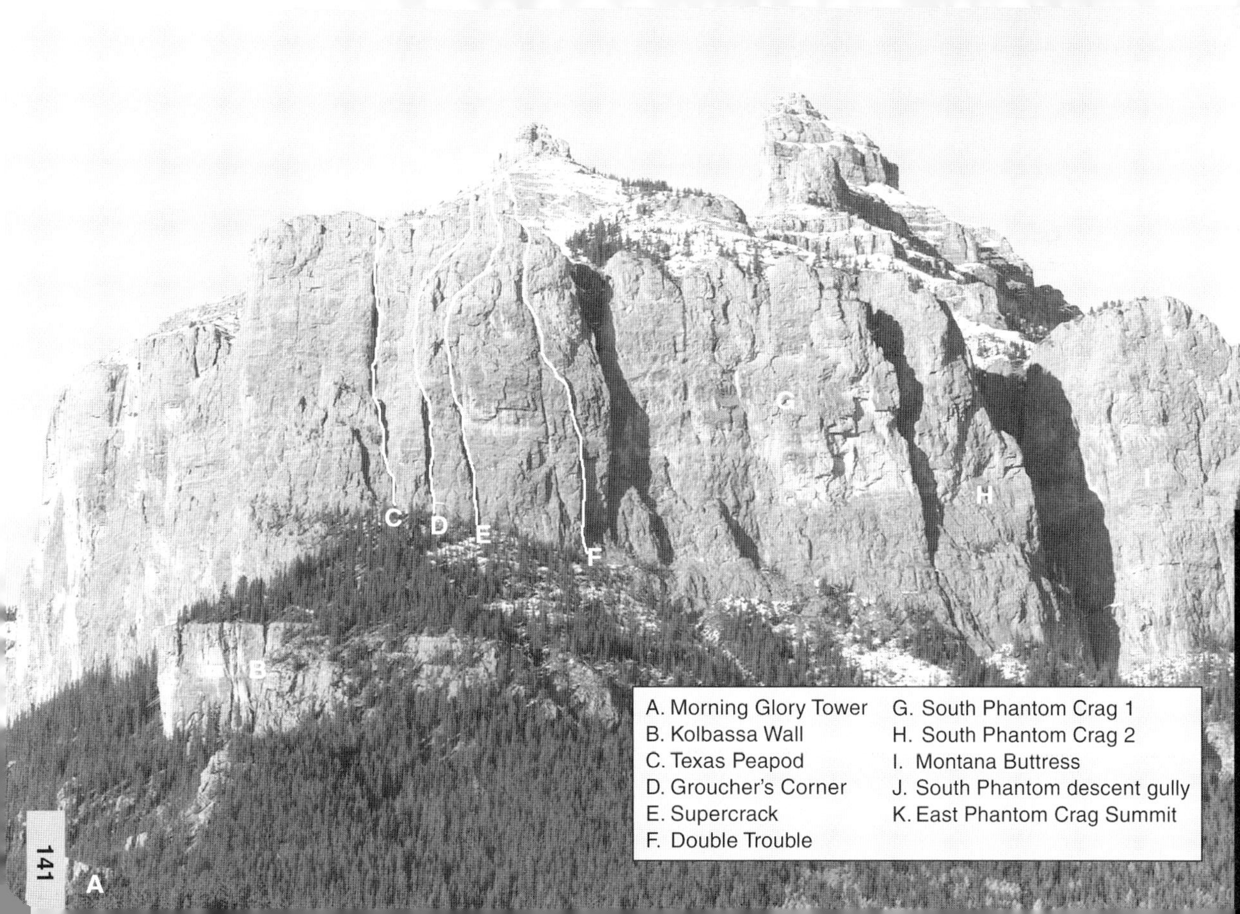
A
B
C
D
E
F
G
H
I
A. Morning Glory Tower
B. Kolbassa Wall
C. Texas Peapod
D. Groucher's Corner
E. Supercrack
F. Double Trouble
G. South Phantom Crag 1
H. South Phantom Crag 2
I. Montana Buttress
J. South Phantom descent gully
K. East Phantom Crag Summit

chimney. Climb the right wall (5.8) and belay in the chimney beneath the overhanging section. Two 5.8 pitches directly up the chimney lead to the top. Above the easier-angled lower section it is possible to exit to the right up a steep chimney/crack that faces south. This was climbed by the same first ascensionist at a similar grade but no detailed information is available.

Groucher's Corner 5.8, 190 m, gear standard rack to 4" and pitons
A. Sole & R. Nelson, June 1978

To the right of the "Texas Peapod" on the protruding front face are two chimneys. The left-hand one peters out after two pitches (on the left skyline when viewed from below). "Groucher's Corner" climbs this chimney and then exits up the right-hand side of a large bowl.

1) 5.7, 40 m. Climb the right-facing chimney to belay on a ledge below the right of two cracks.
2) 5.8, 45 m. Climb the loose crack above, trending left near the top leading to ledges.
3) 5.7, 40 m. Climb up 10 m then left to a loose corner. Climb this traversing left at the top and up to ledges.
4) 5.8, 25 m. Climb the solid 15 m corner on the right.
5) 5.7, 40 m. Continue up slabs to the top.

Supercrack* 5.8, 190 m, gear standard rack to 4"and pitons
C. Perry & P. Morrow, Aug. 1975

This chimney, immediately right of "Groucher's Corner," goes up to a large stepped roof at just over one-half height and turns into a groove above. It is the most attractive of the crack lines when viewed from the Big Hill and may be the best route on the face.
Climb the chimney trending left where it steepens. Traverse back in above the steep section and "back and foot" up to a small belay below the stepped roof. Stem out right and climb over the final bulge to the crack above. Steep climbing leads to a belay about 15 m higher. Two easier pitches lead to the top.

Double Trouble* 5.9, 210 m, gear standard rack to 4" and pitons
C. Perry & N. Hellewell, June 1976

This interesting climb begins up the right hand of two crack lines at the north end of the face. It starts well right of the previous climbs in a steep, right-facing corner some 25 m left of the gully marking the edge of the East Face. Scramble up to a ledge on the right.

1) 5.7, 20 m. Climb the crack at the left end of the ledge for a few meters then traverse diagonally left over blocks to the main corner. Follow this to a small ledge above.
2) 5.9, 20 m. Climb the steep left wall (hard) to gain the groove on the left. Follow this past a large overhang to a belay at the foot of a chimney.
3 & 4) 5.8, 85 m. Follow this chimney-crack system for two pitches past several 5.8 sections and traverse left to large ledges.

5˘& 6) 5.9, 85 m. Climb the crack above (5.8) trending right past an overhang and up a steep wall (crux) to the top. A memorable pitch that is "forever etched in my mind," claims Chris.

Bill Rennie on Super Heroes Top Rope, Border Bluffs. Photo: Andy Genereux.

"Ju-Jube" used to be the only climb on the lower band of cliffs west of the main West Phantom Crag approach trail. Not much has changed but there are now two new routes added to the area to make the trip more of a "day outing." "Ju-Jube" is located near a large, right-facing corner about 250 m west of the waterfall/seepage that forms the ice climb "Malignant Mushroom." The waterfall is in the lower part of the Bonanza Descent Gully drainage. When viewed from the park boundary, the right-facing corner is below and slightly to the right of the Kemp Shield. "Ju-Jube" climbs the wall immediately right of the large corner and finishes up a clean, left-facing corner/crack.

The crack pitch is excellent and makes the climb well worth the walk. This was put up in July 1982 and was Andy Genereux's first, first ascent. Considering the number of classics he has scored and the different venues he has opened up, this makes the route historically noteworthy. Back in those days there were little or no available updates on Ghost River climbing so "Ju-Jube" was the scene of several "first ascents."

It is unfortunate that little development has occurred on the western end of Phantom Bluffs. There are several patches of excellent quality rock awaiting a keen party. The southern exposure and 40 minute access would make this part of the "Bluffs" a popular venue with more development.

Approach Details

No trail has been established to the base of "Ju-Jube" but the best approach seems to be via the creekbed that leads up to the "Malignant Mushroom" waterfall. From the park boundary, go west along the riverbed until directly below the drainage and then follow the creekbed up through fairly open trees until it begins to narrow and the hillsides steepen. At this point, traverse left and climb out the steep west bank and then go

Ju-Jube

diagonally up left through an open pine forest to a scree slope that leads up to the base of the climb. A suggested day is to combine this route with climbs at the Kemp Shield or Wild West Wall.

If the river level is high and precludes getting to the "Malignant Mushroom" drainage, it is possible to contour low along the north bank from the start of the standard West Phantom Crag trail to enter the drainage.

Descent

Rappel from the large tree at the top (55 m) or scramble down a diagonal break in the cliffs to the east. The break could also be used to access Kemp Shield via the "Ju-Jube" approach or as a more direct means of descent from the upper cliffs. However, no trail has been established and the break is difficult to find from above. It is located directly below the edge of the buttress left of "Bonanza" and runs down from east to west.

Ju-Jube** 5.9, 55 m, gear to 3.5"
A. Genereux, R. Lanthier & W. Rennie, July 1982

Begin a few metres right of the large, right-facing corner, directly below the upper crack. Take small wires and gear to 3.5".

1) 5.9, 35 m. Climb the slabby wall for 10 m and make a difficult move (5.9) right to follow a weakness to a ledge just left of the upper corner/crack. Move right to a single bolt belay. This pitch was a sandbag from the past. It now goes at the stiffer 5.9 grade after Andy re-climbed the route nearly 20 years after the first ascent and decided 5.7 wasn't appropriate.

2) 5.8, 20 m. Climb the excellent and classic corner and crack to a large tree at the top.

Bon Bon* 5.9+, 55 m, gear to 4"
G. Fletcher 2000

Locate a bolt about 10 m right of "Ju-Jube" at roughly mid height on the wall. The traditional climb trends slightly left following a series of weakness past this bolt to the top of the cliff.

Project
Located on the wall to the immediately left of the waterfall "Malignant Mushroom" the duo of Greg Fletcher and JC Debeau are up one pitch on this steep and juggy wall. The climbing to date is reported to be very good.

Project
Located 20 m right of the waterfall the same pair mentioned above have climbed a scrappy corner at 5.8 for a 55 m pitch. They think it might clean up with a lot of work but for now is best avoided.

The "true" first ascent of "Ju-Jube."
Photo: Andy Genereux collection.

BORDER BLUFFS

The highest concentration of short, "user-friendly" routes along with one of the quicker approaches make this one of the most developed and understandably one of the more-often visited venue in the Ghost River area.

Border Bluffs were developed principally by Andy Genereux and Jon Jones and have everything from prickly slabs, open books and arêtes to overhanging jug hauls. The earliest routes were done in a bold, ground-up style and some have slowly evolved to be reborn as fully equipped sport climbs. Some of the bold yet moderate climbs of the early years have been retrofitted to make them more accessible to climbers whose leading potential is at the stated grade but are more in line with traditional bolting practices. While other climbs have been intentionally left in their original state to reflect the ethic of a lost era. The end result is a great crag with something for everyone.

Approach
Leave your car at the Banff Park boundary. See page 4 for details to this point. Take the west Phantom Crag Trail. Walk down stream 100 m (west) from the park boundary (identified by yellow pickets) until opposite a ravine on the north shore, just downstream from a prominent dirt scar in the far bank. Wade the river and take a game trail on the other side up the ravine. A good trail leads across a flat bench then switchbacks up a steep slope to an open rounded shoulder. As the shoulder enters the trees there is a cairn marking a fork in the trail. The left fork is the West Phantom Crag trail. Take the right fork to the Border Bluffs. It traverses east for 200 m along a bench to arrive back at the Banff Park Boundary marked by a cut line. Head uphill (left) on the cut line and take several switchbacks up the scree slope to arrive at the right end of the "Borderline Buttress" below the right most climb on the cliff "Rackless". You should arrive here in about 20-25 min. Gumbie Rock, Super Heroes Tower and The Haystack are to the right 10 m, 30 m and 70 m respectively.

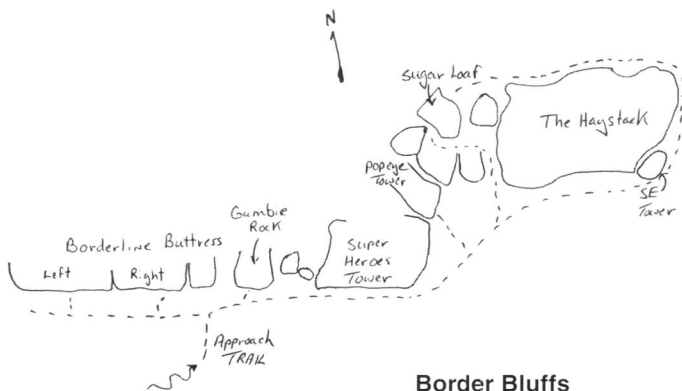

Border Bluffs

Borderline Buttress

This crag is the farthest left of the established Border Bluffs. It faces due south and is characterized by steep slab climbing on excellent grey rock. The area was originally a challenging ground-up venue but some what recent drilling has produced some modern sport routes and saw some of the older climbs retrofitted.

Borderline Buttress extends left from where the park boundary intersects the cliff (prominent cut line on the hillside below) to a vertical break and well-defined edge, beyond which the cliffs become more broken and less interesting. Most of the climbs end at a long, treed break at about two-thirds height and descent is by rappel. A prominent feature near the left end of the cliff is a long overlap about 12 m above the base.

Travellin' Light* 5.10b, 45 m, gear to 2"
D. Morgan & B. Huseby, June 1984 pitch 1
A. Genereux, J. Jones, and W. Rennie 1985 pitch 2

This early Dave Morgan route is characteristic of the time. It was established ground up, is runout and has a minimum number of bolts due to the hand drilling practiced. The original climb exited left as shown on the topo and the finishing pitch, which is also runout, was added a year later. Descent: from the top of pitch two traverse right 10 m on the scree covered ledge to the fixed tree rappel of "On the Border".

Achilles** 5.10b, 20 m, fixed gear
J. Jones, W. Rennie & A. Genereux, Aug. 1985

This route climbs a small pillar to the left of the overlap and was established ground-up. The crux section is sustained and the climb originally was a bold lead but has since been retrofitted. It ends about halfway up to the break at a fixed rappel station.

Old Style* 5.10b, 20 m, gear medium wires
J. Jones, 1985

Climb a shallow depression to the left end of the overlap and continue up the wall above to the fixed station of "Achilles."

Strongbow* 5.11a, 20 m, fixed gear
J. Jones, 1994

A modern, but squeezed in, sport route that gives good technical climbing up to the station on "Achilles."

On the Border** 5.10b/R or 5.10d, 40 m, gear wires
A. Genereux & R. Lanthier, May 1984

This is one of the early ground-up routes that have since been retrofitted. However it still has a very traditional feel to it. It climbs through the middle of the overlap, past a bolt, up the face to a second overlap. There are two options straight up at 10+ or out right, then back left, on more reasonable ground to a shallow groove that leads to the top.

BORDERLINE BUTTRESS, LEFT

A	Travellin' Light, original	5.10b/R	wires
A'	Travellin' Light Direct	5.10b/R	gear to 2"
B	Acillies ***	5.10b	
C	Old Style *	5.10b	med. wires
D	Strong Bow *	5.11a	
E	On The Border **	5.10b/R or 5.10d	wires
F	Revelations ***	5.10a	gear to 2.5"
G	Shimera ***	5.10c/R	wires, TCU's
H	Diawl **	5.11b	
I	Rhydd **	5.10b	
J	Check Point	5.6	gear to 4"

Revelations*** 5.10a, 40 m, gear to 2.5"
A. Genereux & W. Rennie, May 1984

This excellent route breaks through the right-hand end of the overlap. It was the first route to be climbed on this section of Phantom Bluffs and marked the beginning of a stage of rapid development. It was established ground-up and two bolts have since been added to the upper section, which was originally led in a spring snowstorm.

The Chimera*** 5.10c/R, 40 m, gear TCU's & wires
A. Genereux & J. Jones, May 1985

"The Chimera" is one of the finer sustained climbs on the Bluffs. The route begins on the right side of a small arête just to the right of "Revelations." It moves over left to gain a shallow groove and continues up past a second groove with widely spaced protection to anchors just below the top. Best to avoid this friction climb on hot days.

Diawl** 5.11b, 40 m, fixed gear
J. Jones, 1994

An excellent sport route on the blank wall just right of "The Chimera" that provides a marked contrast to the early rap bolted "traditional feeling" route to the left.

Rhydd** 5.10b, 40 m, fixed gear
J. Jones & A. Genereux, Aug. 1987

The route begins as per "Diawl" at the top of a large shattered block and climbs through a lower bulge via an obvious, left-facing corner. This is another retro bolted climb from an earlier time.

Border Bluffs

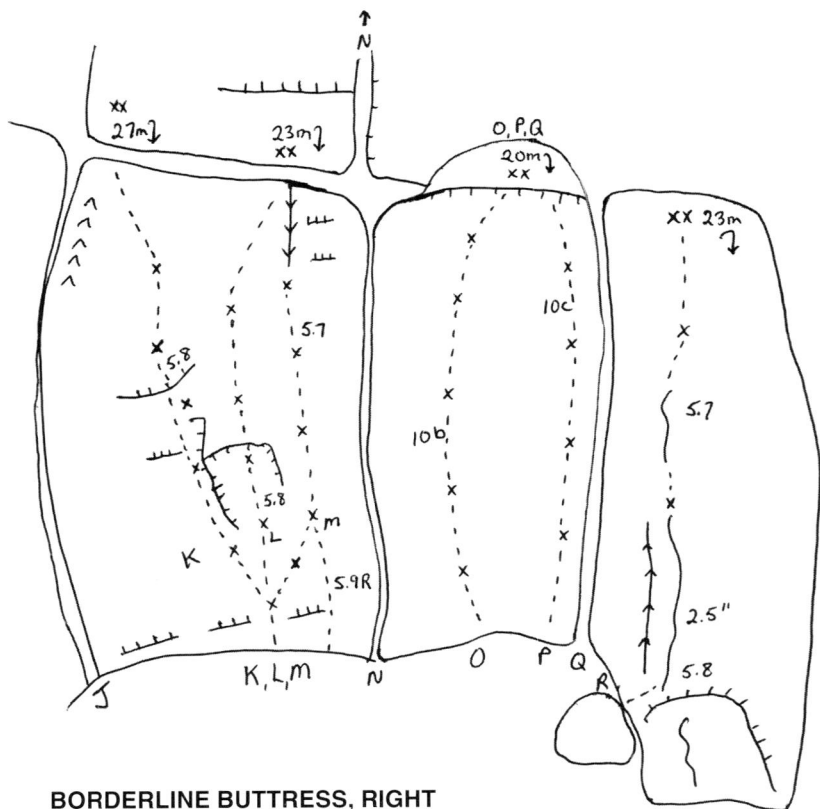

BORDERLINE BUTTRESS, RIGHT

J	Check Point	5.6	gear to 4"
K	Cathedral Steps ***	5.8	
L	Tuesday Afternon*	5.8	
M	Border Rat **	5.7	
N	Bandidos	5.6	75 m, gear to 4"
O	Legal Alien**	5.10b	
P	Border Sweep **	5.10c	
Q	Rat Patrol	5.7	gear to 4" not recommended
R	Rackless *	5.8	gear to 2.5"

Checkpoint 5.6, 35 m, gear to 4"
R. Lanthier & M. Parr, May 1986

Climb the obvious wide crack to a tree on the ledge above. Descent via the "Cathedral Steps". Anchor to the right.

Cathedral Steps*** 5.8, 35 m, fixed gear
J. Jones, July 1987

Traverse up and left to a bolt and then climb an intermittent crack. Hard moves lead past bolts to the top on excellent grey rock. Retro fitted this is now a moderate sport route!

Tuesday Afternoon* 5.8, 35 m, fixed gear
J. Jones, 1994

Another moderate clip-up that offers a somewhat contrived right-handed variation to "Cathedral Steps." You can finish to the anchor for either "Cathedral Steps" or "Border Rat" the later being slightly better.

Border Rat** 5.7, 30 m, fixed gear
A. Genereux & P. Farrar, Aug. 1990

This route, originally done with a 5.9 direct boulder start and given a gear list of "bolt, wires, TCU's and Friends to #2" has since been bolted and the start rerouted to be more consistent with the rest of the route. Start as for "Cathedral Steps" and climb up to the first bolt then move right and climb a shallow groove on good rock to a bolt belay.

Bandidos 5.6, 75 m, gear to 4"
First ascent unknown

A gear route that climbs an obvious gully/crack and continues above the lower section of the cliff. This is possibly an old Don Vockeroth route or one of his contemporaries, a vintage piton was found at 30 m (see history section page 23).

Legal Alien** 5.10b, 20 m, fixed gear
A. Genereux & G. Rinke June 1999

Established ground up it takes the excellent steep grey face right of the wide crack of "Bandidos". Sustained climbing past 5 bolts to a ring bolt anchor.

Border Sweep** 5.10c, 20 m, fixed gear
A. Genereux & G. Rinke June 1999

This is a slightly contrived climb. It climbs the steep prickled face just to the left of the wide crack "Rat Patrol". One has to work to not use the wide stems into "rat Patrol" and to confine your climbing to the face only. It shares the anchor with "Legal Alien".

Borderline Buttress, Right

Rat Patrol 5.7, 20 m, gear to 4" or larger, not recommended
A. Genereux & G. Rinke June 1999

Climbs the wide crack, which has some loose rock. Not very inspiring, use the bolt anchor of "Border Sweep" to the left to descend.

Rackless* 5.8, 23 m, gear to 2.5"
A. Genereux & G. Rinke June 1999

Step right off a boulder to gain a crack in the slabby face. The crack takes excellent gear, which the first ascent party didn't have, thus the name. Climb the crack until it ends, move past a bolt to a second short crack. Face climbing passing a second bolt leads to a ring bolt belay.

Gumbie Rock

As the approach trail meets the bluffs Gumbie Rock is located a few meters to the right with a large spruce tree at the base. This blob of rock divides the Borderline Buttress on the left from Super Heroes Tower to the right. There are two new routes here that climb the better bits of rock on the formation.

The Gumbies Go Bolting** 5.10c, 25 m,
fixed gear
D. Kenefick & L. Rotter May 2002

From stepped blocks on the left side of the formation climb onto the face passing an overlap at the third bolt with difficulty. Continue up generally slabby ground to a bolted belay.

Half Man, Half Biscuit* 5.9, 25 m,
fixed gear
L. Rotter & D. Kenefick May 2002

Starts just to the right of the large spruce tree, it cruises past seven bolts with the crux coming just before the anchor. This is a welcome addition to the "Bluffs" expanding the range for more moderate climbs.

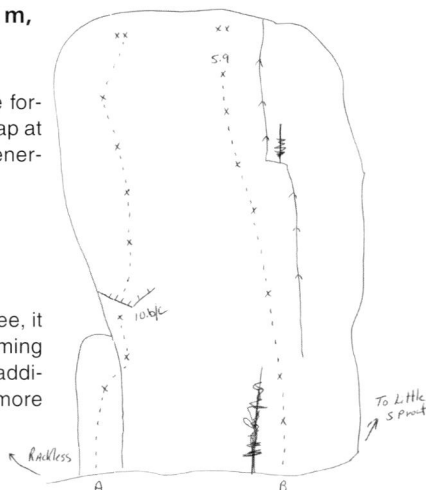

GUMBIE ROCK

A Gumbies Go Bolting **	5.10b/c
B Half-Man, Half Biscuit *	5.9

SUPER HEROES TOWER

This steep formation is home to a high concentration of harder but excellent climbs on three sides. The east, south, and west faces all provide great climbing on the Ghost's famous prickled limestone. The Ghost River's first 5.12 was established on this formation. The west face requires some tricky route finding to access the scree ledge part way up the tower. Climb the easy chimney between the "Borderline Buttress" and the tower and traverse behind the small pedestal of "Little Sprout" then drop down to the ledge. See the topo for a visual. The south and east faces are reached from the approach trail which passes directly in front of the south face.

Andy Genereux on the first ascent of Boy Wonder. Photo: Jon Jones.

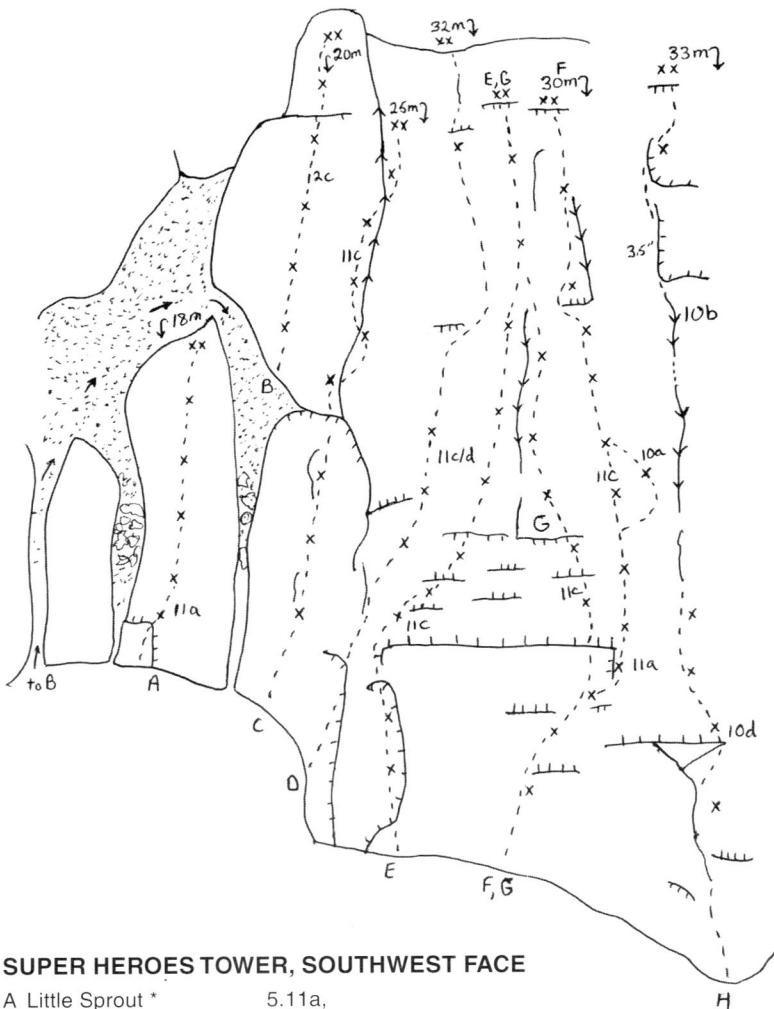

SUPER HEROES TOWER, SOUTHWEST FACE

A Little Sprout *   5.11a,
B Super Heroes ***   5.12c   top rope
C Boy Wonder ***   5.11c
D Batman Kicks Ass *   5.11c/d   gear to 3"
E Catwoman *   5.11c
F Incredible Hulk ***   5.11c or 5.11a
G Super Hulk ***   5.11b/c
H Captain Canada **   5.10d   gear to 4"

Little Sprout* 5.11a, 18 m, fixed gear
A. Genereux July 1999

Climbs the small independent pedestal immediately west of "Super Heroes Tower". The route was rap-bolted then rope soloed. The crux is making the hard move to get by an overlap at the first bolt. Steady 5.10 climbing past four bolts to the anchor.

Super Heroes Tower, West Face

The gently overhanging face with heavily prickled rock. There is limited scope but the two routes found here are both excellent.

Super Heroes Top Rope*** 5.12b/c, 20 m, fixed gear
Originally discovered by Andy Genereux in 1991, he established an anchor and top-roped the line. With his blessing the line was first bolted and climbed on top rope by Keith Pike of Colorado the red point was foiled by rain and Keith returning south. Andy later relocated the top anchor and moved the top two bolts to make for a more aesthetic line. The climbing is notoriously steep and technical with continuous 5.11+ climbing leading to a temperature-dependent, friction crux. To date all known attempts at a clean redpoint ascent have fallen short.

Boy Wonder*** 5.11c, 25 m, fixed gear
A. Genereux August 1991, direct start July 1999

Immortalized on the cover of the 1995 edition of Sport Climbs in the Canadian Rockies, this route takes the short technical classic arête to the right of "Super Heroes Top Rope". In 1999 Andy added a direct start that goes at 5.10. It avoids the loose scramble up and around to the original start, from a loose ledge. This direct option greatly improves the line of this fun route.

Super Heroes Tower, South Face

Marked by a big roof for two thirds its length the south face used to have only two routes. In 1999 Andy Genereux fully developed this steep ground uncovering several very good climbs. The access trail traverses directly below the base of the wall. Under the big roof can be a good place to stay dry and avoid afternoon thundershowers.

Batman Kicks Ass* 5.11c/d, 30 m, gear to 3"
A. Genereux & J. Jones August 1991

This route was originally graded 5.11b. After returning several years later and admitting to a bad memory for detail, Andy reluctantly upped the grade to represent the short but stiff crux moves. The route offers mostly 5.10 face and crack climbing with an out-of-context, devious bolt protected crux.

Super Heroes Tower, South Face

Cat Woman* 5.11c, 30 m, fixed gear
A. Genereux, July 1999

Climbs a small pillar to the left end of the big roof. Hard thin moves to overcome the roof and then leads up right to some excellent 5.10 face climbing above.

Incredible Hulk*** 5.11a or 5.11c, 30 m, fixed gear
A. Genereux, July 1999

Climbs steep overhanging ground to turn the big roof on the right end. Continue direct over the bulge (11c) or alternatively traverse right to a groove then up and back left to avoid the bulge to give an overall grade of 5.11a.

Super Hulk*** 5.11b/c, 30 m, fixed gear
A. Genereux, July 1999

The direct arm numbing finish through the big roof for "Incredible Hulk." From the third bolt climb directly through the roof, after the steep section continued 5.10 climbing leads up prickled rock to the anchor.

Captain Canada** 5.10d, 32 m, gear to 4"
A. Genereux ,July 1999

An excellent companion route for "Cling of the Spiderman" to the right. Surfing past the triangular shaped roof low on the climb is the crux. Sustained mid 5.10 crack climbing and stemming leads to a bolted anchor. **Note:** be very careful when lowering from the station, it is over 30 m and a real rope stretcher. Make sure to tie a knot on the end of your rope.

Super Heroes Tower, Southeast Face

Cling of the Spiderman** 5.10c, 30 m, gear to 4"
A. Genereux, C. Yonge & S. Dougherty, 1989

Start on the southeast corner of the tower. From the east side of the tower climb a rising traverse onto the south face to a bolt above the prominent overhang. Steep and sustained climbing with a hard crack to finish give this climb a bit of everything to challenge the well-rounded climber. Yonge and Dougherty were in the right place at the right time when they showed up. Andy had just finished cleaning the route and needed a belay. New hangers and ringbolt anchor were added 1999.

Super Heroes Tower, East Face

Undercut at the bottom on the left side, this narrow but taller aspect of the tower holds three excellent routes on the heavily textured face.

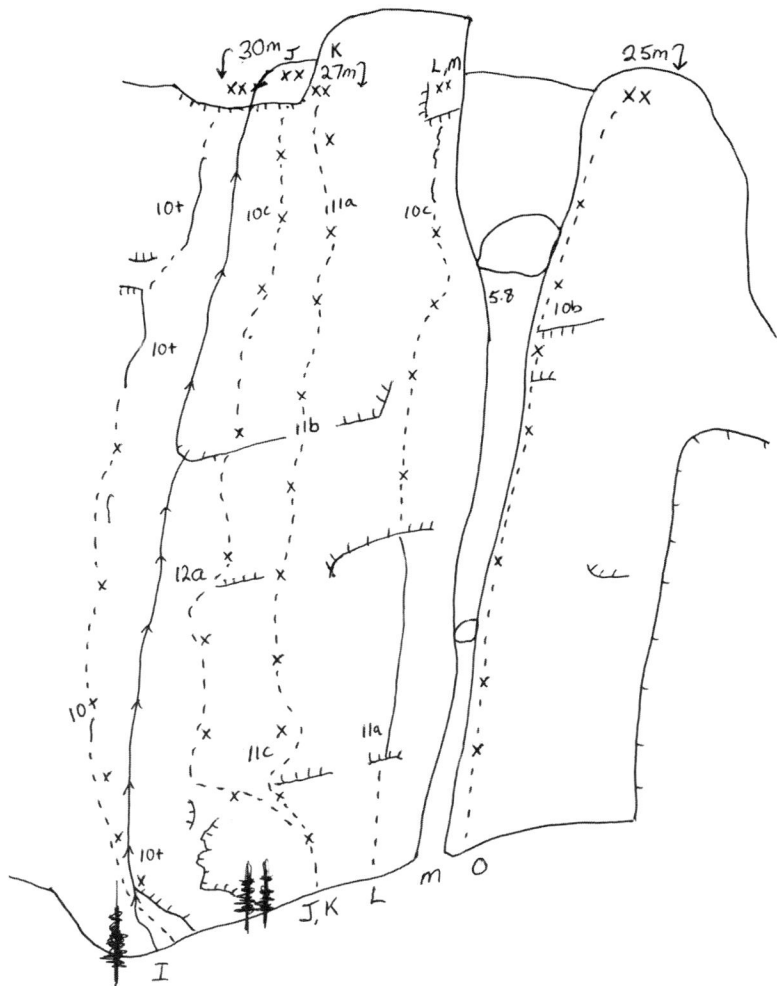

SUPER HEROES TOWER, SOUTHEAST & POPEYE TOWER

I Cling of The Spiderman **	5.10c	gear to 3.5"
J Superwoman's Wildest Dream **	5.12a	
K Flash Gordon ***	5.11c/d	
L Wanna Fly Like Superman ***	5.11a	gear to 2.5"
M Eat your Spinach	5.8	gear to 4"
O Popeye **	5.10b	

Superwoman's Wildest Dream** 5.12a, 30 m, fixed gear
A. Genereux & J. Jones, Aug. 1989

A sustained bottom section is reached by traversing left diagonally on a slabby start to the left of "Wanna Fly...." Continued hard technical climbing leads through a bulge to pleasant 5.10 face for the upper half.

Flash Gordon*** 5.11c/d, 30 m, fixed gear
A. Genereux, July 1999

Start as for "Super Woman's Wildest Dream" at the first bolt climb straight up then right on sustained ground. The crux is a funky mantel at the third bolt. Excellent and sustained face climbing past multiple 11- cruxes make this climb "good till the last drop".

Wanna Fly Like Superman*** 5.11a, 25 m, gear to 2.5"
A. Genereux, 1987

Andy was spurred on by Dave Morgan to attempt the free ascent of this line, which was originally a practice aid ladder established by Mike Blenkharn. It was clearly established that the route must be attempted from the ground up. Andy used wires over the existing rivets and arrived at the original station at two-thirds height a quivering mass (which is substantial). On rappel to clean the line, Andy popped all the rivets with his nut tool, which left an even sicker feeling in his stomach. The climb was re-bolted and later extended to the top of the tower.

Eat Your Spinach 5.8, 30 m, gear to 3.5"
A. Genereux, 1987

Free soloed to gain access to the towers, the line takes the slot separating the Super Heroes Tower east face from the Popeye Tower. Climb the slot/chimney, to an overhang bulge (large block) near the top move left onto a ledge to belay using the "Superman " anchor to the left.

Popeye Tower

This somewhat independent tower lies immediately north the east face of Super Heroes Tower and is home to one classic route.

Popeye** 5.10b, 25 m, fixed gear
J. Jones & R. Lanthier, 1987

"Popeye" climbs the slabby arête immediately north of the Super Heroes Tower. Originally a combo route with gear and bolts, it has suffered two separate retrofits, the latest one replacing the self-drives with Hilti bolts and a chain anchor.

Sometimes called the Short but Sweet Tower, this small feature is tucked in behind the Super Heroes Tower and The Haystack. To access the base of The Sugar Loaf scramble up a gully immediately left of the south face of The Haystack. It is possible to reach the top of the feature by walking around The Haystack to the north side. The wall is hard to see from this vantage and is not recommended to go this way on the first visit.

Short but Sweet*** 5.8, 25 m, fixed gear
J. Jones & A. Genereux, June 1990

A sport route up the left side of the wall on excellent face climbing. It begins off a scree ledge below a corner with a single bolt belay.

Sugar and Spice** 5.8, 30 m, gear to 2"
A. Genereux & C. Genereux, June 1990

Climb the lower face on mixed gear, mostly wires are used to reach the bolted arête on the right side of the wall.

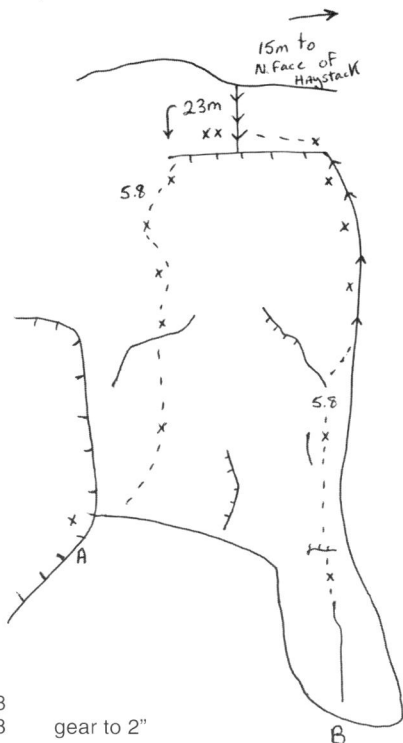

THE SUGAR LOAF

A Short But Sweet ***   5.8
B Sugar and Spice **   5.8   gear to 2"

THE HAYSTACK

This aptly named feature is the right-most formation of the Border Bluffs. (There are a couple of small rock piles in the trees to the right but there are no significant cliffs until one reaches Morning Glory Spire, well to the east.) The Haystack is a large flat-topped block of rock that offers a wide variety of climbing. It has everything from the slabby south face to the steeper, scarier traditional routes of the east side, to the overhanging sport routes on the north & west faces.

Descent
A number of the routes have their own anchors that can be used for rappelling but due to their length require two ropes to descend. If you have only one rope or your climb has an inadequate rappel anchor. There is a common descent anchor on the northwest corner above the route "Rapture." This is a three-bolt, cabled anchor requiring 15 meter's to reach the ground.

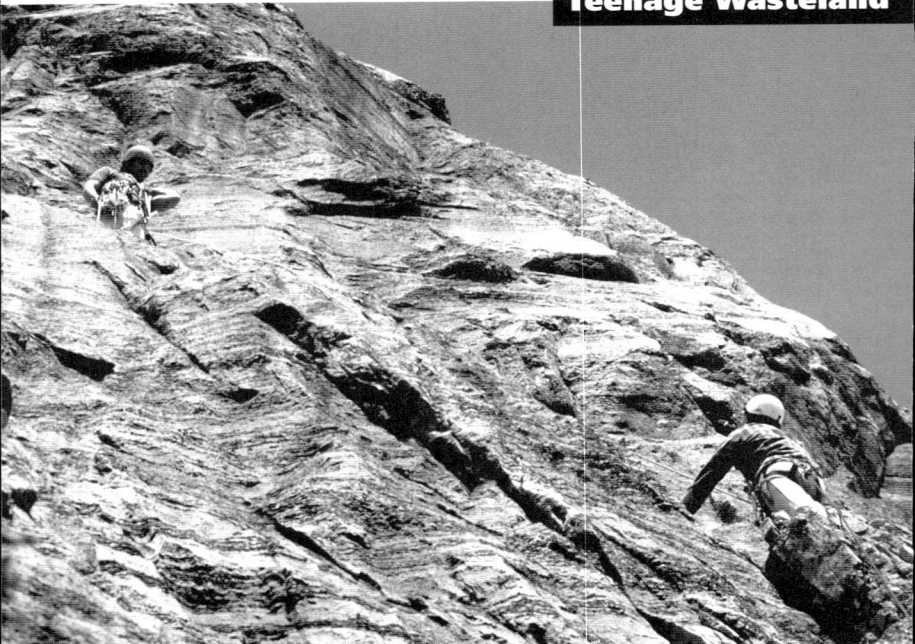

Teenage Wasteland

The second ascent of the original "Teenage Wasteland". Photo: Andy Genereux collection.

Solitaire** 5.10b, 30 m, gear to 1.5"
A. Genereux, 1989

This route was established as an on-sight, roped solo using a dubious self-belay system. Even with a proper belay the route still requires some traditional leading skills.

The Grooves* 5.7, 35 m, gear to 2.5"
First ascent unknown. See history, starting page 23.

Start behind large trees and follow the shallow groove that angles up and left. At the top move left to the fixed anchor of "Solitaire." A single 60 m rope accommodates a 30 m rappel from this anchor.

Midlife Crisis* 5.10d, 40 m, gear wires & RP's
J. Jones & A. Genereux, Aug. 1989

Hard moves surmount a steep face that leads to pleasant climbing above on a faint rib. This leads to the anchor.

Teenage Wasteland*** 5.9/R, 70 m, gear small wires & friends to 2"
Original route: J. Marshall & partner(s), 1981
Variation: A. Genereux & J. Jones, 1990

This route starts at the lowest point on the south face. From a flat area behind trees start up a rib with a couple of hidden wire placements. The crux is getting to the first bolt. Above the bolt the original line traversed right to a loose corner and climbed up to a single bolt anchor (as for "Waste of Time" on topo). The route then went up and left to a bolt (now a two-bolt station) on a small pedestal. Above here the route went up a short distance and then left across a slab onto the left edge of the formation (marked on topo).

The more direct variation was added on lead and is now the preferred and highly recommended route. From the first bolt continue straight up past bolts and small wires to the two-bolt anchor at the pedestal. The second pitch goes up and then left as before but stops short of exiting off the left edge of the formation. It follows a hand crack up after a few meters leaves the crack to climb good rock on a bulging face past two bolts to finish out right on top of the cliff at a single bolt anchor. Descend via the common rappel on the NW corner of the crag.

Wasted** 5.10b, 70 m, gear wires & RP's
C. Yonge & A. Genereux, 1984
This direct finish to "Teenage Wasteland" follows a shallow groove with a difficult overlap. Like the original route, this was first put up in traditional style with sketchy gear. The final piton has been replaced with a bolt and several small wire placements have been cleaned out to make this a fun and now a well protected outing. There is a single bolt belay on top. **Descent:** rappel via the common NW corner rappel.

The Haystack, South Face

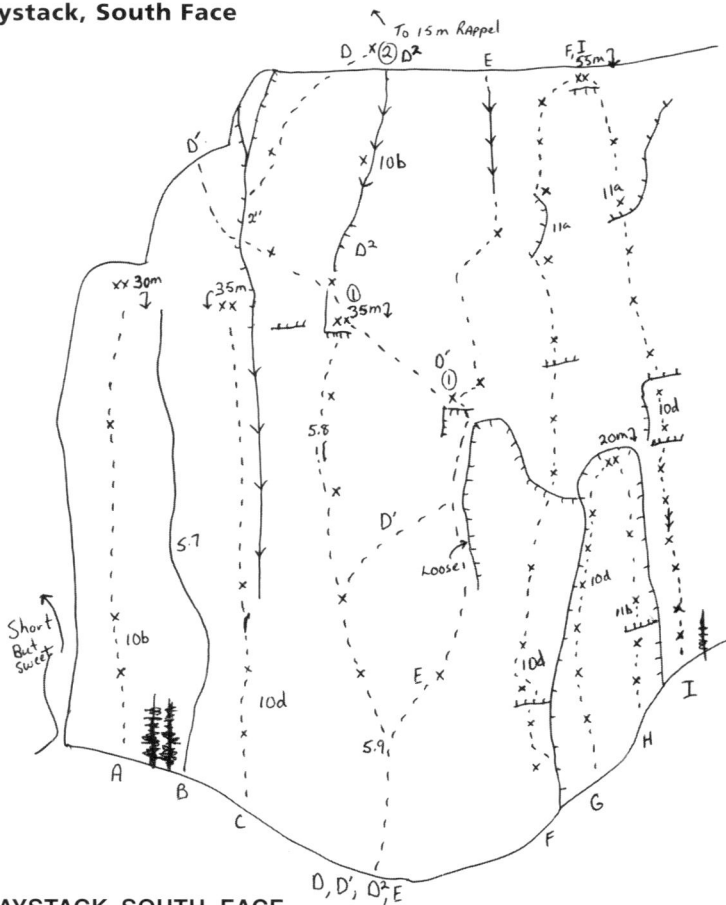

THE HAYSTACK, SOUTH FACE

A Solitaire **	5.10b	gear to 1.5"
B The Groves *	5.7	gear to 2.5"
C Midlife Crisis *	5.10d	wires , RP's
D Teenage Wasteland ***	5.9/R	gear to 2"
D' Teenage Wasteland, original	5.9/R	gear to 2"
D2 Wasted **	5.10b	wires
E Waste Of Time	5.10c/R	wires
F Heart Stopper **	5.11a	
G Tower Power **	5.10d	
H Quick Fling *	5.11b	
I Lord of The Flies ***	5.11a	

Waste of Time 5.10b/R, 70 m, gear to 2"
C. Yonge, S. Carr & J. Rollins, 1989

This meandering route climbs part of the original "Teenage Wasteland" and then heads up and right to the top of the face. There are several bits of good rock but the runout nature and grovelling for marginal gear usually leaves it off the to do list. A retrofit and some rerouting of this climb might yet make it worthwhile.

Heartstopper** 5.11a, 55 m, fixed gear
A. Genereux, August 1999

Start left of a small tower located on the southeast corner of the south face. This long pitch climbs on excellent grey stone with two technical cruxes. The first crux comes overcoming a bulge at the third bolt. The second comes at two-thirds height requiring thin friction and body language to over come a right leaning groove. This climb is dedicated to Owen Hart a friend who was tragically killed in a "High Wire" stunt for professional wrestling. The climb was put up the day of his funeral. It was rappel bolted and then rope soloed.

The Haystack, Southeast Tower

A small tower located on the southeast corner of The Haystack. There are two sport climbs that ascent the SE face to share a common anchor.

Tower Power** 5.10d, 23 m, fixed gear
A. Genereux, August 1999

A fun little climb that starts up the face onto the left arête takes it to the top of the tower, six bolts.

Quick Fling* 5.11b, 20 m, fixed gear (optional gear to 2")
A. Genereux, August 1999

The route is a bit of a one-move wonder, the "quick fling" might be easier if you are taller. Climbs the right side of the tower past four bolts.

Lord of the Flies*** 5.11a, 50 m, fixed gear
J. Jones, 1989

Starts immediately to the right of the Southeast Tower. Sustained face climbing leads up to a series of overlaps which had sustained technical climbing and used to be the crux. The climb was retrofitted and the upper portion moved. Now the climbing is more sustained but much better protected and you now have to deal with an additional crux at a bulge, higher on the route. This good route was made better by the retrofit.

Little Bo-Peep* 5.10c, 25 m, gear to 2.5"
A. Genereux & J. Jones, 1991

This is the left hand of two routes on the east face. An interesting traditional line that starts by moving left to overcome a tricky overlap. The line of least resistance winds up the face eking out gear to go along with the minimal bolting. The climb was originally done to the top of the formation but it is now recommended to finish right at the same anchor as "The Needle."

The Needle** 5.11a, 25 m, gear wires & TCU"s
A. Genereux, 1988

Start with hard 5.10+ climbing on natural gear in a shallow corner. After the corner peters out, hard moves through a bulging face past two bolts lead up to the bolted belay.

THE HAYSTACK, EAST FACE

G Little Bo-Peep *	5.10c	gear to 2.5"
H The Needle **	5.11a	wires, TCU's
I Italian Stallion **	5.10b	optional wires

Bill Rennie on an early ascent of Imbroglio. Photo: Andy Genereux.

The Haystack, North Face

Italian Stallion** 5.10b, 30 m, fixed gear (optional wires)
A. Genereux & R. Lanthier, 1987

This route was done on-sight in traditional style. In 1999 Andy returned and retrofitted the climb to modern sport standards. Step off a block and traverse left to a bolt. Hard moves lead past a bulge into a groove. Then up the face to a bolt belay.

Phantom** 5.11b, 23 m, fixed gear
A. Genereux, August 1999

The bolted line on the face left of the "Imbroglio" groove. This route has devious and sustained climbing to a tree belay. Descent: use the common rappel on the NW corner of The Haystack.

Imbroglio*** 5.10d, 30 m, gear to 3"
A. Genereux & C. Yonge, 1984
"Imbroglio" is the first route on the imposing north face of The Haystack and remains one of the best. It was first done from the ground up using a couple of points of aid and then free climbed the following season. It follows an obvious and very steep groove line. Climb an easy open book on gear to bolts which lead a through a difficult stem crux. Continue up a corner on sustained climbing past new bolts to a ringbolt belay.

Lethal Weapon** 5.12a, 20 m, fixed gear
A. Genereux & J. Jones, July 1990

A pumpy, thin line to the right of "Imbroglio." The crux comes at the forth bolt then the climbing eases up the groove. The upper groove makes for an alternate finish for "Imbroglio" after the stem crux move right and climb the corner. There is a new ring-bolt belay on top.

Arms Race*** 5.12a, 23 m, fixed gear
A. Genereux & J. Jones, July 1990

This is the alternative right hand finish to "Lethal Weapon". After the 5.12 crux it moves right to take the v-groove and overhangs for an even more strenuous finish to a bolted anchor just below the top.

Mental Physics** 5.10c, 20 m, fixed gear
A. Genereux & J. Jones, June 1990

A fine technical route, which makes for a good warm-up for those to either side. Sustained climbing to a cruxy reach move in the middle leads to a difficult sustained shallow corner near the top.

THE HAYSTACK, NORTH FACE

I Italian Stallion **	5.10b	optional wires
J Phantom **	5.11b	
K Imbroglio ***	5.10d	gear to 3"
L Leathal Weapon **	5.12a	
M Arms Race ***	5.12a	
N Mental Physics **	5.10c	
O Rapture **	5.11b	
P Edge Clinger ***	5.11b	
Q Winds of Time **	5.11d	

Rapture** 5.11b, 15 m, fixed gear
A. Genereux August & G. Rinke August 1999

Climbs the short steep pumpy face to the left of "Edge Clinger" directly to the common rappel anchor on the NW corner.

Edge Clinger*** 5.11b, 18 m, fixed gear
A. Genereux, June 1990

A devious arête that winds it's way up the boundary of the steep north face and the even steeper west face.

The Haystack, West Face

There is only one route on this short overhanging face, the previous guide referred to an abandoned project called the" Hourglass" this was finally completed in 1999.

Winds of Time** 5.11d, 12 m, fixed gear
A. Genereux, August 1999

Located a couple of meter's right of "Edge Clinger" it climbs the hour glass formation on powerful sequential holds to a rap bolt anchor.

Doug Heinrich warming up on "Edge Clinger." Photo: Joe Josephson.

Is situated immediately to the east of The Haystack and higher up the hillside. It is the largest of the cliffs in the lower tier and has three distinct faces. The most prominent of these is the South Face. The cliff then turns 90 degrees into an east-facing wall that extends over to a second, smaller and scruffier, south-facing wing. The cliff received little attention until the mid-ninety's development has recently stalled and the cliff seems long overdue for some new activity.

Approach

Kolbassa Wall can be reached quite easily from The Haystack although presently there is no definitive trail. The best method of approach seems to be from the path below The Haystack, traverse right through fairly open trees, rising only slightly, until an open slope is reached and the South Face of Kolbassa Wall comes into view. Climb directly up the centre of the slope and then cut over to the crag near the top.

When going directly to the crag, the best approach is probably to follow the main West Phantom Crags trail to the base of the upper cliffs. Then traverse right beneath Phantom Tower to reach the top of the cliff at its west end this will take approximately 55 to 65 minutes.

Kolbassa Wall, South Face

This part of the cliff consists of predominantly yellow rock and is split, towards its left end, by several prominent crack lines. All the climbs completed to date were done in one day by a group of motivated youth. The climbs are gear routes and are described briefly below and shown in the accompanying topo. There remains large expanses of steep, small-featured terrain that have not been attempted.

Big Ass* 5.8, 15 m, gear bigger the better
D. Bartrom & B. Firth, July 1995

This route climbs a short and strenuous off-width, set in a left-facing corner, at the extreme left end of the cliff. Big Bro's or equivalent are useful for protection.

Allahu Akbar* 5.9, 35 m, gear rack to 3"
B. Firth & D. Bartrom, July 1995

"Allahu Akbar" begins just right of two large trees growing close to the face and starts up thin cracks to gain a prominent left-slanting ramp.

Ockham's Razor 5.8, 40 m, gear standard rack emphasis on large sizes
D. Bretsloff & D. Crosley, July 1995

"Ockham's Razor" goes up the left side of a large block that forms an overhang near the ground and then follows a prominent wide crack to the top in one pitch.

Kolbassa Wall, South Face

Yo' Mama** 5.10a, 40 m, gear standard rack to 4"
D. Crosley, D. Bretsloff, B. Firth & D. Bartrom, July 1995

Begin as for "Ockham's Razor" and above the initial block move down and make difficult moves across right to gain a right-trending break and corner system. The second pitch climbs up a striking hand crack and then up good corners to the top.

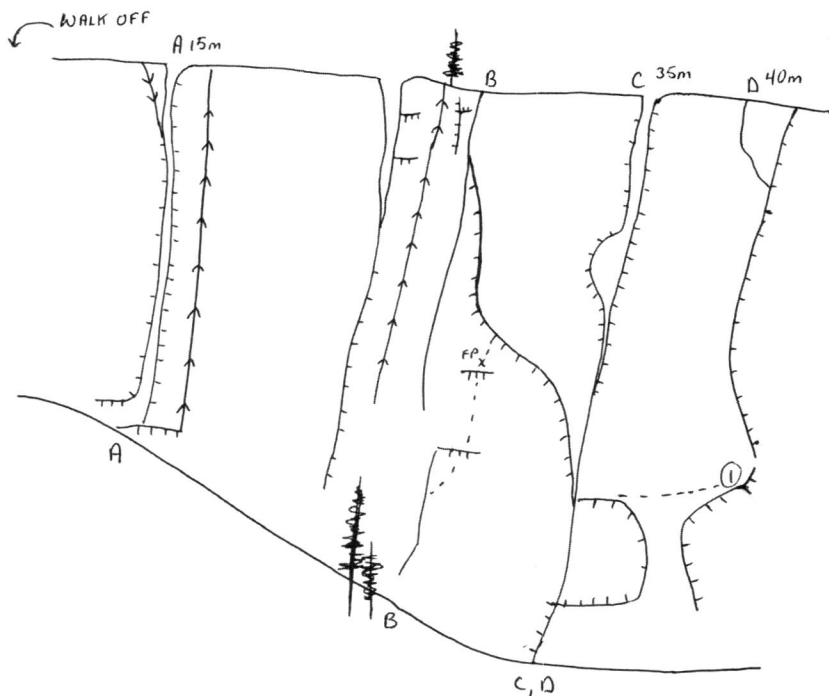

KOLBASSA WALL, SOUTH FACE

A Big Ass *	5.8	off width big gear
B Allaha Akbar *	5.9	gear to 4"
C Ockham's Razor	5.8	gear to 4"
D Yo Mama **	5.10a	gear to 4"

East Bay
A. If You Love Her, Buy Her A Gun
B. When You're This Big, They Call You Horse
C. The Freshest Sausages In the West

South Face
A. Allahu Akbar
B. Ockham's Razor
C. Yo' Mama

Kolbassa Wall, East Bay

To reach the East Bay walk downhill along the south face and turn the corner to the east face. A large block forming a squat pinnacle sits at the base near the edge. Walk through some trees and around the pinnacle to arrive at the East Bay, which is formed by the 50-60 m long east facing wall and a smaller, perpendicular south facing wing that runs downhill to the east toward Morning Glory Tower.

To date, three quality routes have been done in the East Bay although there is at least one project several good face lines and a number of scrappy crack lines await the adventurous.

If You Love Her, Buy Her A Gun** 5.11a, 55 m, gear to 3"
J. Fehrman & L. Rotter, Aug. 1996

This fine two-pitch route was raided by a couple of visiting Americans. The first 11a pitch is 25 m while the second pitch to the top goes at 5.9. Because the pitches are so different, they thought they could get away with giving each pitch a label and thus get their name in the book twice. I disagreed! But seriously, if you're not up to 5.11 you could rappel in and do only the top pitch. It would, however, be very difficult to find from above unless you scope it out previously from the bottom. The route is located in the good grey rock near the left edge of the east face and begins from the top of a large block that sits at the base.

When You're This Big, They Call You Horse* 5.9, 55 m, standard rack to 4"
J. Josephson & D. Crosley, May 1997

If you enjoy steep, 5.8-5.9 corner cracks on Yamnuska, this is the route for you. "Mr. Big" takes the left hand of two closely set crack lines in the middle of the east face. Despite being a predominately off-width-sized crack, you need not do any off-width climbing nor do you need any particularly wide gear, although a #4 Camalot or equivalent nicely protects the exit. Four bolts and a fixed pin, a variety of face holds, stemming, thin cracks and lay backing make for a sustained and engaging route.

project
An anchor at the top of the wall and several directional bolts marks this project on the fine grey wall found right of the two prominent crack lines and left of the crack/chimney line that marks the right-hand edge of the true east face.

The Freshest Sausages In the Valley** 5.11a, 30 m fixed gear
D. Crosley, May 1997

"Sausages" is sandwiched on the narrow, grey wall between the corner/crack at the back of the bay and a prominent left-facing corner on the south wing. Being somewhat under equipped, the first ascensionist came without enough bolt hangers and so the route was first led with knifeblade pitons used for hangers on the bolts. It has since been outfitted with proper hangers. Technical and sustained moves with a crux mantle move are enhanced with exciting, but safe, left-handed clips.

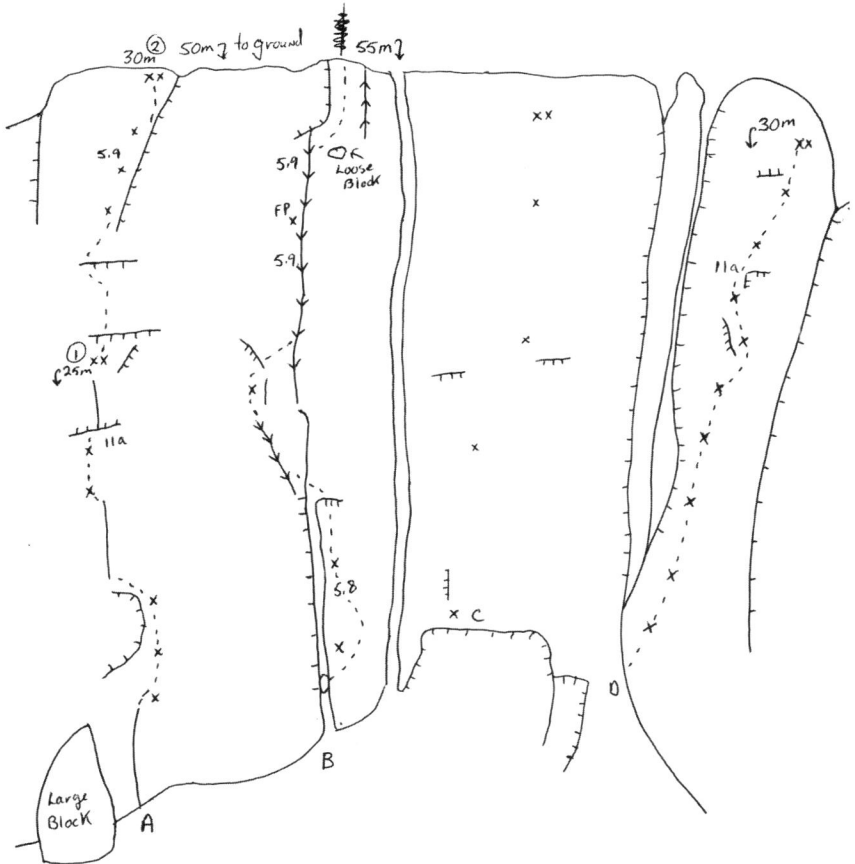

KOLBASSA WALL, EAST BAY

A If You Love her Bur Her a Gun **	5.11a, 55 m	gear to 3"
B When Your This Big They Call You Horse *	5.9, 55 m	gear to 4"
C Project		
D The Freshest Sausages In the Valley **	5.11a	

MORNING GLORY TOWER

This small outcrop of steep grey rock faces east and has three short but interesting sport climbs. The crag itself is quite difficult to reach and tends to blend into the hillside from many viewpoints. When viewed from the south on the valley floor, it is situated down and east of Kolbassa Wall, beyond a broken south-facing crag, and appears only as a small, shattered pinnacle. Its clean, square-cut east face is best seen from the Big Hill. From here, it lies below and slightly east of the east face of Kolbassa Wall. See photos on pages 65 & 141.

Approach

This crag would most likely be visited in combination with Border Bluffs or Kolbassa Wall. However, there is no established trail to the tower. From the trail below the Haystack at Border Bluffs, traverse across through fairly open trees as for Kolbassa Wall, but instead of climbing up, drop down slightly below a small, shattered crag consisting of two towers. Continue traversing across a treed slope for some distance to a shallow bowl in the hillside and then to open slopes beyond. There should now be a fairly large broken crag directly above and the backside of Morning Glory Tower should be visible below and farther east. This same point may be reached from Kolbassa Wall by descending a fairly open hillside below a band of broken crags that angle down to the east. The backside of Morning Glory Tower, however, is not easy to identify. From this direction, the cliff has a flat top, which blends into the hillside.

The three climbs are on the east face and are shown in the accompanying topo. They are all bolt protected face climbs on good rock. The short yet overwhelming south face of this tower is super steep and could perhaps be home to a truly hard sport project.

Yellow Jacket Special* 5.12a, 18 m, fixed gear
A. Genereux, July 1999

Named for a hornet's nest that was painfully disturbed on the first foray to this formation. The first bolt is meant as a belay, the second bolt should be stick clipped to avoid the ledge. The climbing is sustained and technical on somewhat friable rock. Most holds have had the official dumpling test and should stay put.

Early Morning Light** 5.10c, 17 m, fixed gear
A. Genereux, 1994

Climb to the first bolt and climb the bolt line to the left up good rock to a belay at the lip. Established ground up, on-sight rope solo.

Rise and Shine** 5.10a, 17 m, fixed gear
A. Genereux, 1994

Shares the first bolt with "Early Morning Light" but goes straight up the right hand bolt line. Established ground up, on-sight rope solo.

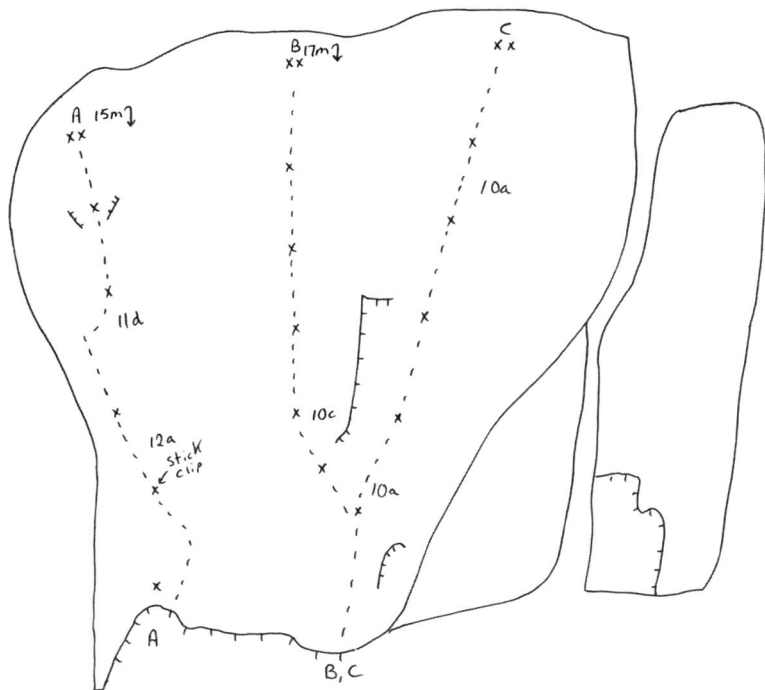

MORNING GLORY TOWER

A Yellow Jacket Special *	5.12a
B Early Morning Light **	5.10c
C Rise and Shine **	5.10a

Ghost River Valley

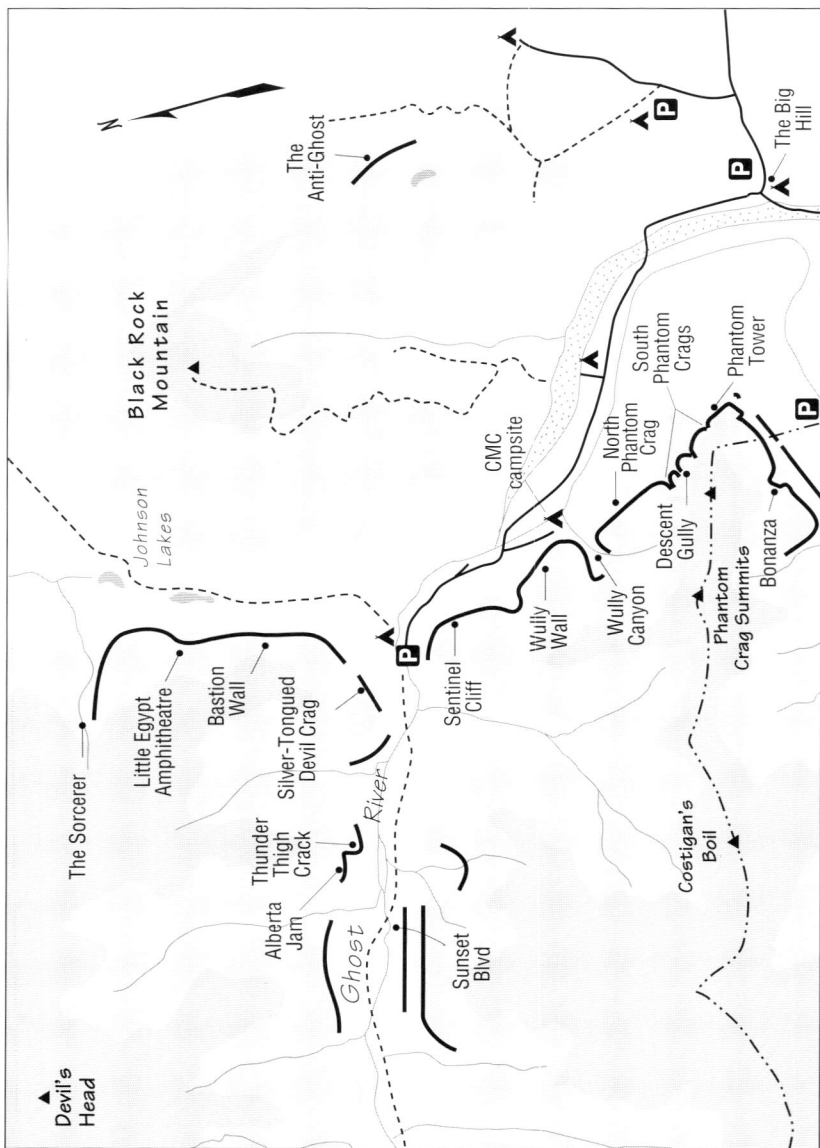

The Ghost River Valley lies at the bottom of the Big Hill and runs north-south perpendicular to the Minnewanka Valley and Devil's Gap. Way back when, the local utility company diverted the Ghost River so that it would flow west over a height of land through the Devil's Gap to enlarge Lake Minnewanka, which had been dammed to produce hydroelectric power. This is the main reason the access road to the Ghost exists. There are over four kilometres of east-facing cliffs rising above the diversion canals. They can be seen from the top of the Big Hill and extend out of sight to the right (north). Because of the diversion canal, which is very dangerous to cross at any time of the year, you must approach the cliffs from the bridge that crosses the canal some 5 km north of the Big Hill.

The crags are, from south to north, the East Face of Phantom Tower (described under Devil's Gap, see pages 71 & 140), South Phantom Crag, North Phantom Crag, Wully Canyon, Wully Wall and Sentinel Cliff. After Sentinel Cliff the Ghost River takes a 90-degree turn to the west and is then referred to as the "North Ghost." Overall, the Ghost River Valley cliffs are shorter than the ones found in Devil's Gap and have a considerably shorter season owing to their eastern or northern aspect. They have numerous outstanding natural features and were popular in the seventies and early eighties. More recent activity has begun to unearth some of the older climbs and opened up previously uncharted terrain, of which there is still plenty.

CMC Campsite

Back in the mid-to, late seventies, when rock climbing in the Ghost was first being developed, the Calgary Mountain Club had a regular campsite below Wully Wall. This remains a fine area to camp and a good starting point for all the Ghost River Valley climbs with maybe the exception of Sentinel Cliff, which is reached by continuing north past the bridge for just over a kilometre. See the Sentinel Cliff section on page 242 for details.

Parking Access

From the bottom of the Big Hill, turn right and follow a good road north for about 1 km until it turns left (west) to cross the riverbed. This can be a difficult crossing depending on time of year and the clearance of your vehicle. Take care to choose the best spot then take the good road on the other side and continue north. After about 1 kilometre you will pass a road heading off right, this is for the "Black Rock Mountain" hiking trail and is marked by a large cairn. Stay on the main road to reach a small bridge over the diversion canal, 4.3 km from the Big Hill.

Just past the bridge turn sharply left on to a road paralleling the canal. If you are climbing on the "Consolation" area of Wully Wall, park after 250 m directly below the route. For Wully Canyon, North Phantom Crag or Montana Buttress continues for another 200 m to where the road becomes impassable and the general area of the **old CMC campsite**.

Montana Buttress

A. Original Start
B. Tough Trip Through Paradise
C. South Phantom Descent Gully

South Phantom Crag is the section of cliff that extends from the East Face of Phantom Tower northward to a deep drainage separating it from The Streaker Wall on North Phantom Crag. South Phantom Crag consists of four very distinct buttresses or walls separated by deep gullies. They are identified from south to north (left to right) as South Phantom crags 1, 2, 3 and 4. To date, only buttress 3 has been climbed and is called "Montana Buttress." The others await more creative names by those who manage to first climb them.

South Phantom Crag 1
This is the broad wall immediately right of the East Face of Phantom Tower. There is a series of grey water streaks pretty much in the middle of the face and this area looks to have the best potential for new routes. Right of the grey streaks, the wall holds large overhangs near the centre.

South Phantom Crag 2
This is the most buttress-like formation of the four cliffs. A very steep and narrow slot separates it from Crag 1 on the left. On the right edge by, much wider and lower angled drainage, which separates it from Montana Buttress.

Montana Buttress
A tower-like wall, Montana Buttress is one of the most impressive formations in the valley. It also has the most consistent grey rock of any of the South Phantom crags. Subsequently, it appears to be the most climbable, although to date only the obvious line up the middle of the wall has been done.

South Phantom Crag 4
This wall is separated from Montana Buttress by the Descent Gully. It faces mostly north and is wider than it is tall. On its right end, it curves into a deep gully that separates South Phantom Crag from North Phantom Crag.

East Gully Approach
The previous guide recommended the most logical approach from the CMC campsite to access the South Phantom Crags and the south end of North Phantom Crag was to use the East Gully approach. From the campsite, walk south along the gravel flats to the base of a major gully that splits the hillside below South and North Phantom crags (cairn). This is called the "East Gully." The trail in the gully is presently not well defined and is only marked intermittently by cairns. A second option is now available with a much-improved trail that traverses the entire North Phantom Crag from Wully Canyon to South Phantom Crag. Of the two options the later seams to be the method of choice to arrive at these venues. Another popular option is to reach the south end of these cliffs is to come from Devils Gap by traversing north from "Phantom Tower" (page 140) Whether travelling from the CMC Campsite or devils Gap the approach from either direction will require about hour and twenty minutes to reach "Montana Buttress." See the Parking Access details for the CMC Campsite on page 177.

South Phantom Crag

South Phantom Descent Gully

This along with the Bonanza Descent Gully are the major descent avenues for the Phantom Crags. Down climb and or rappel the gully (possibly 5.6 for a short section previously reported as 4th class if you found the easiest way) immediately north of Montana Buttress. See photo below and on page 178 and the map on page 176. The "South Phantom Descent Gully is the best descent for all climbs in the area including South Phantom Crag and the left side of North Phantom Crag. It is possible to traverse around the top the crag on sloping scree slopes south to "Phantom Tower" then west to the "Bonanza Descent Gully" (page 72) if you approached from devils Gap this would be preferred option. Allow 40 minutes to an hour to complete the traverse. Unless you like rappel epics do not attempt to descend the next large gully (Upper East Gully) to the north between South Phantom Crag 4 and North Phantom Crag.

Care is required in locating the South Phantom Descent Gully from above, although some cairns are in place. From a small ridge that splits a bowl above the two gullies drop off to the right and follow the drainage keeping Montana Buttress immediately to your right as you descend. The descent involves reasonable down climbing if the easiest line of descent is located. The gully can be wet and slippery and has loose rocks on several ledges. Do not count on rappel slings or fixed anchors. Anchors may be hard to locate if they exist at all. Be prepared you may have to be install your own anchors if you have limited down climbing ability. Take care and exercise caution when descending on this little used gully. From the base of the gully it is recommended to travel north and traverse along the base of the cliffs following an increasingly better trail to Wully Canyon.

South Phantom Crag

A. Phantom Tower
B. South Phantom Crag 1
C. South Phantom Crag 2
D. Montana Buttress
E. South Phantom Descent Gully
F. South Phantom Crag 4

Original Start* 5.10a, 100 m, gear to 4"
F. Campbell & R. Banard, 1990

This is the scene of several original attempts that stalled at the overhanging headwall on pitch 4. It begins about 30 m left of "Tough Trip" below a major groove system in the centre of the face. It joins "Tough Trip" at some treed ledges part way up the face and is likely to become the preferred way of doing the climb. See photo page 178.

1) 5.9, 35 m. Climb up to a shallow groove and continue up this to a ledge on the right. Alternatively, climb an easier (5.7) line on the left moving across right higher up past a piton to join the main groove system.

2) 5.10a, 20 m. Continue up the groove past a bolt to an overhanging section. Go over this with difficulty to a bolt belay just above at a small ledge.

3) 5.10a, 35 m. Climb the groove above past a small, awkward overhang (bolt) and continue up to a large ledge with trees at the base of a right-facing corner system and the junction with "Tough Trip" near the beginning of pitch 3.

Tough Trip Through Paradise* 5.10a/b, 290 m,
gear standard rack to 4" & Pitons
J. Josephson & B. Hendricks, July 1993

A good climb with interesting routefinding and in many places excellent rock. There are some moderately loose sections (pitches two and three) that should clean up with use and opportunities exist for several top-notch variations. The first ascent party completed the route in a day and well before darkness. They then, however, made the mistake of descending the wrong gully to the north of the normal descent. Half a rack and two chopped ropes later they made it back to the car by 1:00 am.

Begin about 40 m left of the edge of the Descent Gully at a right-slanting chimney system leading up to a group of small trees. See photo page 178.

1) 5.10a, 50 m. Start in a clean left-facing corner just left of the right-slanting chimney system and after about 20 m, step left onto a clean slab. Traverse left below an overlap to its end and climb up thin flakes (knifeblades) until moves right can be made to a small ledge with a bolt. Climb a steep face above the bolt to a horizontal crack and then handrail left to a corner. Climb up a short distance to a ledge and belay below a loose bulge.

2) 5.8, 55 m. Climb over the bulge and continue up the corner to where it steepens. Step right and continue up a faint groove (runout) just right of the corner for 10 m until you can traverse across the corner above a roof. Climb up broken terrain to a ledge system and belay in a small corner.

3) 5.8, 50 m. Traverse left on the ledge system to a large corner. Climb up the corner on loose rock to a bolt, or alternatively climb clean rock to the right of the corner for about 10 m before stepping back into the corner. Climb steeply past a bolt toward a triangular, white overhang. Step right into a right-facing corner and climb up to a fixed belay on a slab below a large, white rock scar.

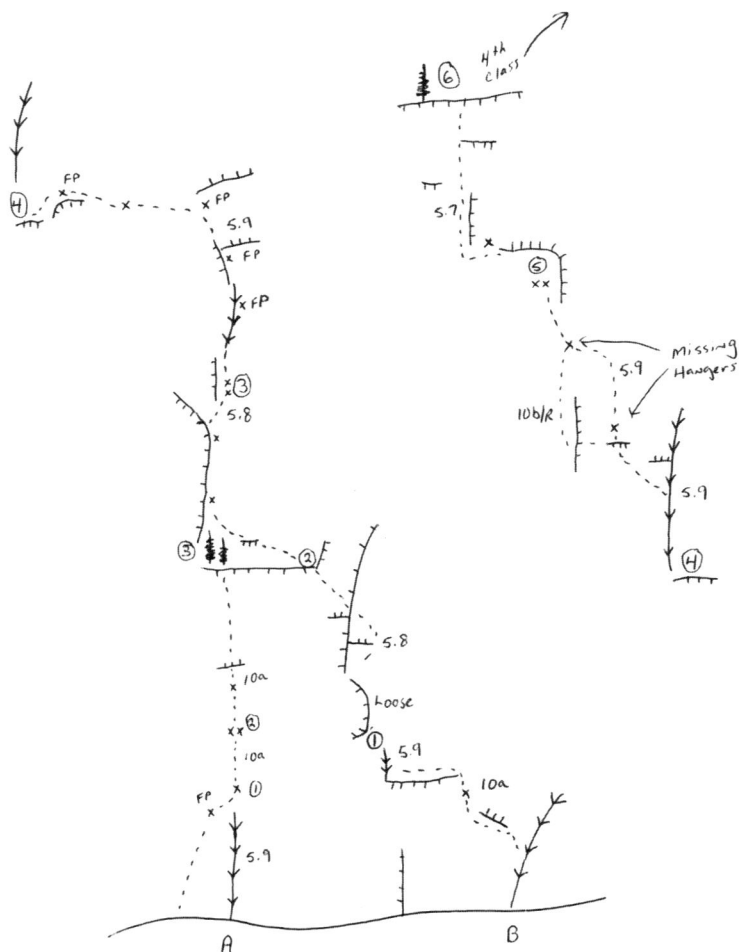

MONTANA BUTTRESS

A Original Start*   100 m, 10a
B Tough Trip Through Paradise*   290 m, 10a/b

Opposite: From left to right: Dave Reid, Garry Jennings, Mike Sawyer, Anda Rogan, Gerry Rogen, Jack Firth and Chris Perry. Photo: S. Climpson.

4) 5.8+, 45 m. Climb up a steep corner past two fixed pins to a third pin below a large overhanging headwall. Traverse straight left on good grey rock past a bolt to a fixed pin. Step down and then go left to a semi-hanging belay in a shallow corner.

5) 5.9+ or 5.10b, 50 m. Climb a groove above the belay (runout) for 15 m. Traverse easily left under a large roof and across some blocks to a steep wall. Move up to a bolt (no hanger), climb straight up for 5 m (5.9+), then step left to a rest and a second bolt (no hanger). Alternatively, traverse left at the first bolt and climb steep flakes (5.10b) directly to the second bolt. From the second bolt, step up and then left into a short corner and climb it to a bolt/piton belay below a large roof. Note; bring a wrench and a couple of hangers for 5/16 cap screw to replace these missing hangers.

6) 5.7, 40 m. Traverse left past a bolt to the edge of the overhang. Step down and traverse left into a corner system and climb up steep rock for 10 m. Step left again below a roof and onto easier ground. Follow it up to the first large tree.

7) Fourth class terrain traverses around the corner toward the backside of the buttress.

CMC Campsite, 1981

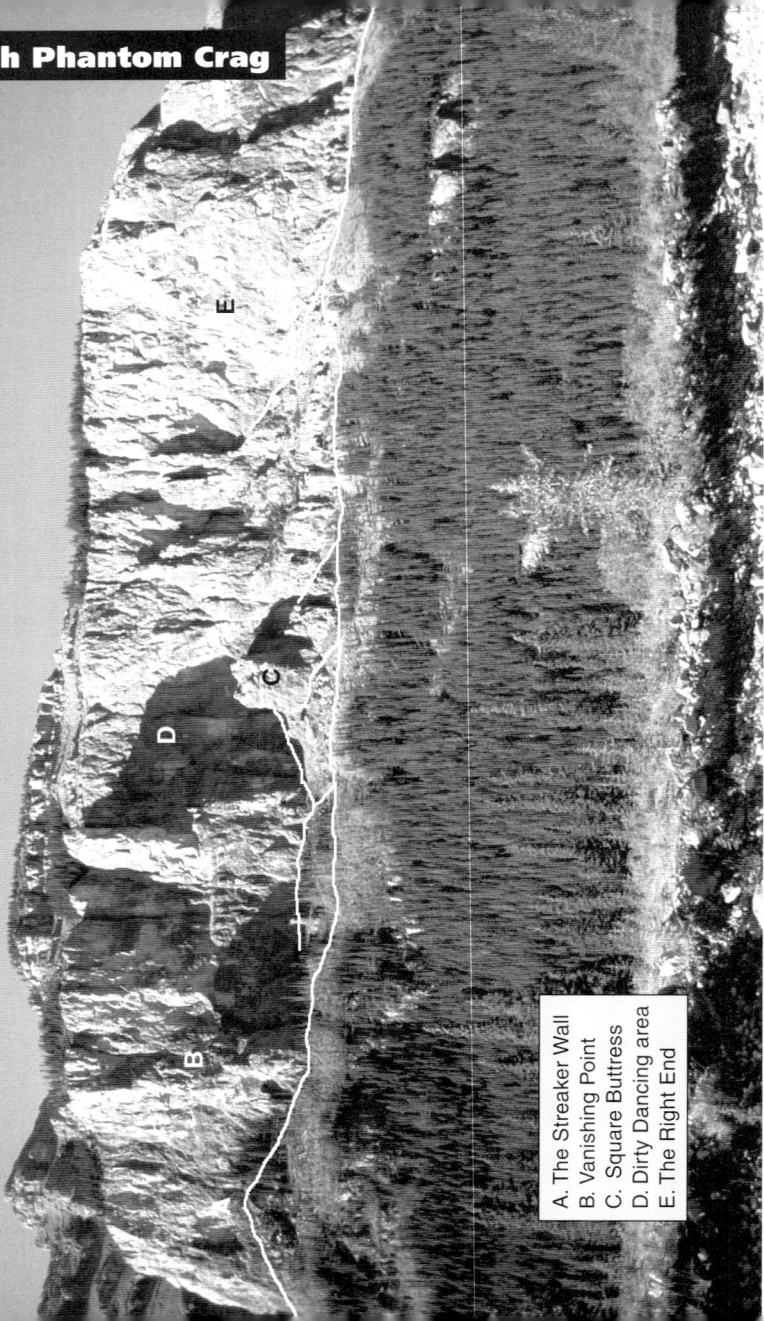

A. The Streaker Wall
B. Vanishing Point
C. Square Buttress
D. Dirty Dancing area
E. The Right End

An impressive cliff close to a kilometre long, North Phantom Crag is graced by some of the best routes in the Ghost, while other climbs have been totally forgotten, a few are among the worst and maybe should be forgotten. Until recently all the routes followed obvious natural features. It is the home of "Dirty Dancing", the first top down multi pitch route established in the Ghost. In the last few years there have been two excellent multi pitch sport routes established to the right of "Dirty Dancing". The small "Square Buttress" in front of the main wall sports several good short routes. The crag has sections of somewhat disappointing rock but several areas abound with quality compact rock for new route development. Starting with the "Dirty Dancing" area, which still has lots of potential for short crack and bolted face climbs. Several moderate multi pitch possibilities exist on the right side particularly right of the "Bowl" and on the north end of the cliff as the wall turns west. These would be mostly bolted affairs as this part of the cliff has only a few natural lines remaining. The crag's relatively moderate height, between 150 and 200 meters and a walk to the top make this a likely scene for more routes using rappel tactics. For the purposes of this guide the wall has been broken into four parts: "The Streaker Wall," the unique "Vanishing Point" and the excellent "Dirty Dancing" area and the much wider "Right End," which includes everything north (right) of "Pinnacle Chimney".

Approach Details

The entire cliff is best approached from the stream bed to the north known as "Wully Canyon". Park at the CMC campsite. See pages 177 & 210 for details. At this point a washed-out road heads up the hill and into an old gravel pit. Walk across the pit and into the small stream coming from Wully Canyon. Continue up the canyon through a tiny gorge (Lower Wully Canyon) for 150 m to where a faint trail on the left comes down the scree from the north end of the crag. Follow the trail up to a good path that leads back south across an open scree slope along the base of the crag. Enjoy—it is one of the easiest approaches in the Ghost. An easy 20 minutes will put you at the north end of the cliff with its north facing rolling grey rock. See photo page 184.

The following is a quick rundown of the features that are encountered when traversing south along the base of the cliff. The climbs are then described from left to right in the normal fashion. After the path reaches the base of the cliff, it goes past a small cave and then passes below a black, overhanging chimney in the upper part of the face. This is the line of "Snake's Tongue," which avoids the upper chimney on the right. After rounding the corner, the pinnacle of "Vanishing Point" comes into view and the trail moves out to a small, rocky rib (cairns). The prominent orange overhang of "The Bowl" is now directly above. The large leaning pillar to the left is the home of the "Black Hole" and defines the left edge of The Right End. Drop over the rocky rib and scramble across a tricky section and follow a good trail through large scree. After a few minutes you will be below the amazing distinctive crack of "Crack-A-Jack" and a scree slope leads up left to the base and left again to the start of "Pinnacle Chimney." Allow about 30 minutes to get to this point. To continue south stay on the main trail traversing left through a blocky boulder field (again cairns). Staying low below The Square Buttress a 60 m high blob of grey rock that sits in front of the main wall. On the main cliff slightly to the left is "Dirty

Looks like granite! Dave Crosley and Ben Firth attempting "Dirty Dancing." Photo: Paul Valiulis.

Dancing" the incredible right facing corner line that defines this area. The trail moves to cross a loose scree gully below the obvious left leaning diagonal break of "Spooks." Once on the more stable ground at the edge of trees two options are available. The first option is used to approach the "Dirty Dancing "area and routes to the right of Vanishing Point. Climb the open slope to the right of the trees for 30 m to the base of the main wall, then scramble right up along the base overcoming loose scree for 40 m to reach "Dirty Dancing." Follow the base of the wall left to reach the climbs "Whispering Smith " and "Moondance" two obvious corner crack lines on the main wall. Option two takes you to the base of Vanishing Point and then onward to the Streaker Wall. From the scree gully continue traversing left through the trees through an old burn on a good trail directly to the base of Vanishing Point. From here the trail rises to the south to meet a shoulder directly below the pinky purple streaks of the Streaker Wall. Allow about 50 minutes to arrive at this point on the trail. Drop over the shoulder and take a good trail down along the wall to meet the drainage between North Phantom Crags and the South Phantom Crags. This is the same spot where the East Gully approach would arrive at the base of the wall. A faint trail continues across the scree slope south to Montana Buttress.

Walk-Off Descent

For most routes, the quickest walk-off descent is to travel north into Wully Canyon. From the top of your climb, walk right and continue downhill until it starts getting very steep and cliffy. At this point, bear left and go into the creek bed running down from the East Phantom Crag Summit (aka Devil's Fang). Follow the stream down, easily passing the first small waterfall on the right. Above the second, larger waterfall cross over to the left (west) side of the creek and pick up a trail that descends easily into the main Wully Creek. Plan on 30-45 minutes depending upon which of the routes you're coming from.

Rappel Descent

Only four full-length routes have fixed stations suitable for rappel. These are "Dirty Dancing," Smoking In The Boys Room," "Don't Forget to Dance" and "Separated Reality." Either could be used but only "Dirty Dancing" and "Smoking In The Boys Room" and "Don't Forget to Dance" may be considered suitably set up for mass use and for using a single 60 m rope to descend. However, they can be tricky to locate from above for the first time user. To locate the **"Dirty Dancing" rappel,** traverse over to a depression forming a drainage groove in the scree slope above the route. About 10 m north of the drainage and 20 m above the main face there is a small cliff with a tree at the base. Rappel from the tree into the drainage (15 m) and locate fixed cable anchor on the lower cliff at the top of the main face. This first rappel has the potential for loose scree to be pulled off be careful. Some of the anchors are fixed with rappel slings, not chains, and slings may need replacing. Three 50 m rappels or six 25 m rappels from fixed stations lead to the base of the cliff—see the accompanying topo on page 195 and the photo on page 193.

North Phantom Crag

The **"Smoking" rappel** is 15 m to the north of the "Dirty Dancing" drainage. From the upper cliff locate a larger tree just in front of the cliff. From the tree rappel 20 m down the scree and over the edge to a good ledge, 3 m below the lip with a ring bolt belay. Five 30 m rappels to the ground all on ringbolt stations make this the preferred rappel.

The third option is to locate the **"Don't Forget to Dance"** rappel station at the lip, 35 m north of the "Dirty Dancing" drainage. Although easier to find **caution** is required on the second rappel (fourth pitch). You must back-clip several bolts to reach the next station. Failure to do this will leave you stranded in space on totally overhanging ground out of options. Five 30 m rappels on ringbolts to the ground. See photo on page 193.

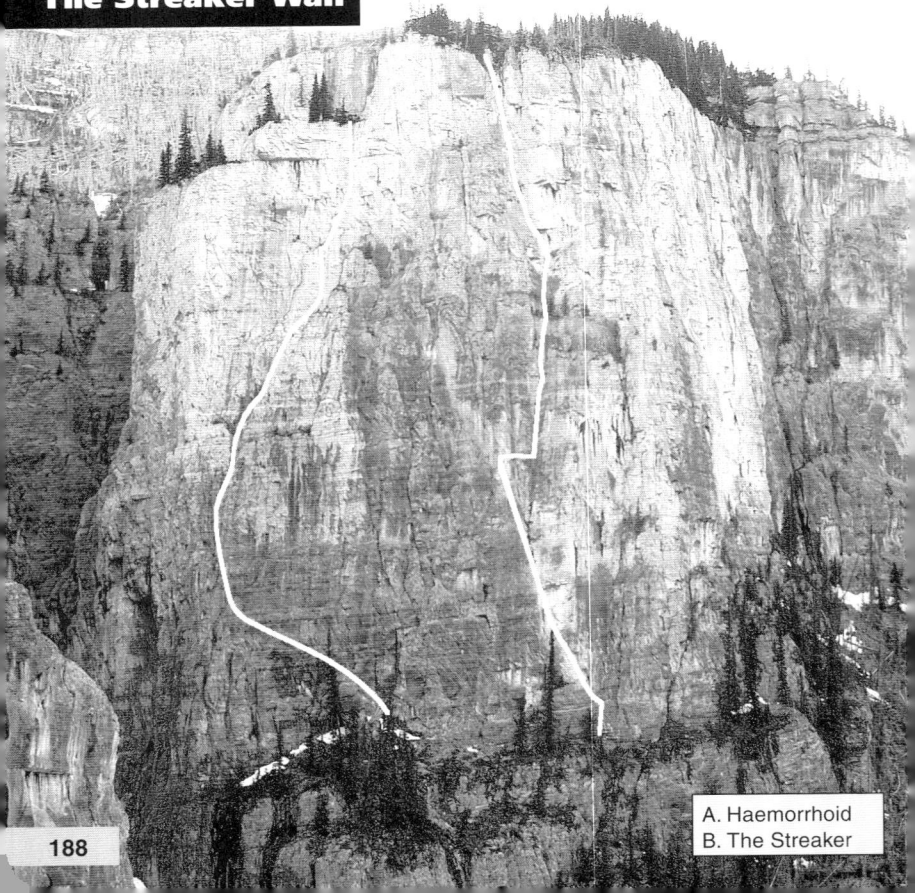

The Streaker Wall

A. Haemorrhoid
B. The Streaker

The Streaker Wall

The left end of North Phantom Crag has a most bizarre history. Sometime in the 1960s there was a forest fire raging above and below the cliff. The Alberta Forest Service called in air support to drop fire retardant. Most of it, however, hit the cliff and permanently stained it red. The deep pinky purple color has started to fade over the years but the right hand of two prominent streaks can still be readily seen. Only two climbs ascend The Streaker Wall both are appropriately named. There is scope for many climbs to the south on this part of the wall. With the improved trail we will hopefully see this cliff bear some fruit in the future.

Approach
The easiest approach used to be recommended via the stream bed known as the East Gully. With a recently improved trail it is now a better option to take the more popular traversing trail left from "Wully Canyon", it requires about 50 minutes to approach the cliff using this trail. When immediately below "The Streaker Wall" the two climbs are easily seen. They start off a large treed ledge about 40 m above the trail, which is reached by scrambling up easy ground to the right. See photo page 184.

Descent
For The Streaker Wall, it is recommended to use the descent gully for South Phantom Crag, see page 180 for details. Photo on page 178.

Haemorrhoid 5.11a, 150 m, gear to 4"
G. Powter & B. Wyvill, Sept. 1981

From the far left end of the large ledge, climb lower-angled slabs and a corner above for two pitches aiming for an obvious crack system that diagonals up and right. Once in the crack system, follow it to an obvious, left-facing exit corner that is climbed with difficulty and marginal protection to ledges at the top. Up to this corner the route maintains an average grade of 5.7. The exit corner, however, is very difficult and radically unprotected. Thus the reason for the route name, "The climb is bright red and a pain in the ass."

The Streaker** 5.9/R, 145 m, gear to 4"
C. Perry, J. Firth & M. White, July 1975

From the approach, the line of "The Streaker" is obvious and quite striking. A lower crack system, which curves slightly to the left, connects via an undercut groove to a ledge in the centre of the face on the right. Above this, a large corner leads to the top. The first pitch is not well protected and overall, the route is quite difficult for its grade. However, the addition of bolted rappels a bolt runner at the crux and increased traffic could make the route a classic.

   Begin at the right-hand end of the large ledge at the base of the lower crack, below and slightly left of the central ledge.
1) 5.9/R, 35 m. Follow the groove easily for about 6 m, then move left onto the wall. Climb this for about 8 m (runout—needs a bolt) until a rightward traverse leads back

The Streaker

into the groove just above an overhang. Follow the groove to small ledges level with the only possible-looking traverse right.

2) 5.9, 5 m. Traverse up and right across the steep wall to a small ledge just around the corner.

3) 5.7+, 30 m. Follow a groove exiting right and up to a tree on the central ledge.

4) 5.7, 35 m. Continue up corners to an alcove immediately below a perched block.

5) 5.8, 40 m. Step down and left, then climb up paralleling the main groove and rejoin it higher up. Move up over an awkward roof and continue up trending left at the top.

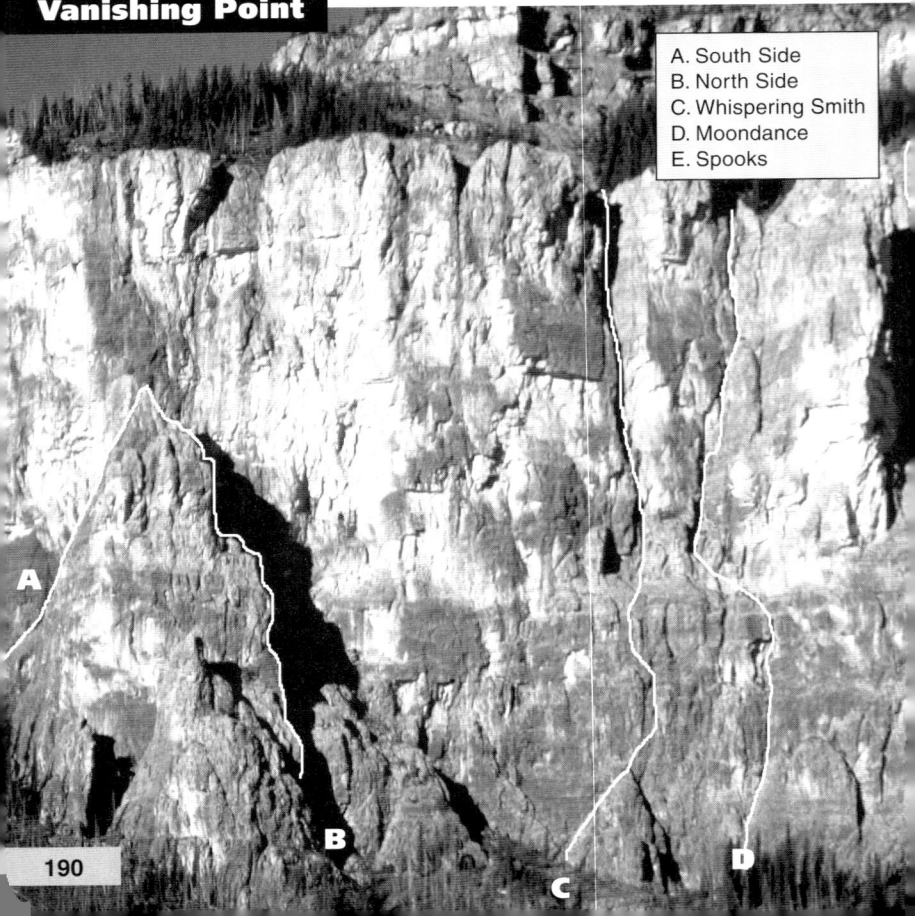

Vanishing Point

A. South Side
B. North Side
C. Whispering Smith
D. Moondance
E. Spooks

This is a large pinnacle completely separated from the main face, in certain light it is impossible to see from the river flats. The top of the Point is about 100 m right of The Streaker Wall. See photo on the opposite page and on page 184. This section will cover all climbs including the pinnacle and the main wall for a hundred meters to the right to a large yellow pillar on the upper half of the wall that defines the left edge of the bay housing the "Dirty Dancing" area.

Approach Details

It takes about 40 minutes to reach the base of " Vanishing Point" from Wully Canyon. See pages 177 & 210 for details.

Descent

Scramble down from the top of the "Point" at the top of the pinnacle to rappel bolts at the top of pitch one of the South Side route. Rappel for 50 m, then scramble down the south gully.

South Side* 5.7, 55 m, gear to 4"

C. Perry & I. Staples, Aug. 1975

This is the better of the two routes up the pinnacle. Scramble up the gully on the south side to ledges on the right, about 10 m below the notch attaching the point to the main wall.

1) 5.7, 45 m. Traverse right onto the face and go up to a slabby ramp that, diagonals up leftwards to the inside edge of the pinnacle. Follow this around on to the face overlooking the notch and climb up a groove to a small ledge with two rappel bolts about 10 m below the top of the pinnacle.

2) Scramble to the top.

North Side 5.6, 85 m, gear to 4"

C. Perry & P. Morrow, July 1975

Beginning well to the right of the pinnacle, scramble up over easy ledges to gain the gully on its north side. Go up the gully until about 12 m below the notch and level with a slabby ledge that leads out left to ledges on the arête.

1) 25 m. Traverse to the arête.

2) 5.6, 40 m. Diagonal up rightwards to an awkward right-facing corner. Climb this and continue more easily back up to the arête.

3) Scramble up to the top.

Vanishing Point

Whispering Smith 5.8, 170 m, gear to 4" pitons
J. Firth, T. Jones & C. Perry, July 1975

Between "Vanishing Point" and the diagonal break of "Spooks" are two large, open book corners in the upper part of the face. "Whispering Smith" climbs the left hand of these. See photo page 190. Of all the forgotten routes on the crag, this may be the most worth checking out.

Scramble up from the left to the top of a subsidiary buttress directly below the upper, prominent open book.

1) 5.7, 35 m. Traverse diagonally right across the wall, then up and a long way back left to a good ledge.

2) 5.8, 35 m. Climb the steep, shallow crack at the left end of the ledge and belay high on the ledges above.

3 & 4) 5.7+. Climb the corners above to the upper chimney and go up this belaying below a bulge just short of the top.

5) Move left over the bulge and continue up to the top.

Moondance 5.8+, 190 m, gear to 4" pitons
T. Jones & C. Perry, Sept. 1975

This interesting route, which may be closer to 5.9 in difficulty, follows the upper corner system to the right of "Whispering Smith." See photo page 190. It is named after an extremely long move right on the fifth pitch, which for a tall leader is "one small step" but for others may be a "giant leap." Begin about 10 m right of the subsidiary buttress of "Whispering Smith" at a small cave with a shattered yellow wall above.

1) 5.8, 30 m. Climb the wall to the right of the cave and make a hard move left to a shallow groove. Climb this to a ledge and continue up the easier groove above to a small belay ledge below a wide crack.

2 & 3) 40 m. Climb the crack and the chimney above to the large central ledges.

4) 30 m. Traverse left to a groove and climb this to the second of two ledges.

5) 5.8+, 45 m. Climb the left-hand corner until it steepens (18 m), then make the "one small step" right to a ledge on the slab. Move right again round the corner and up the groove to a tree.

6) 45 m. A groove and chimney lead to the top.

A. Spooks
B. Dirty Dancing
C. Smoking in the Boys Room
D. Don't Forget to Dance

E. Separated Reality
F. Pinnacle Chimney
G. Crack-A-Jack
H. More Dirty Dancing
I. Square Buttress

Dirty Dancing Area

Located in the middle of the North Phantom Crag. The area is bounded on the left by a large yellow pillar on the upper wall and on the right by the right leaning "Pinnacle Chimney". The large pillar forms a shaded bay, which houses an abundance of excellent climbs. It is located by the classic right facing corner of " Dirty Dancing" on the lower half of the main face to the left of the "Square Buttress" a slabby formation sitting in front of the main wall. There are six multi pitch routes on the wall of which four are excellent. These along with the collection of shorter routes along the base of the main wall and on Square Buttress give this area good variety and excellent climbing. The climbs vary from pure sport climbs to the more traditional styled routes and range in grade from 5.6 to 5.12. The east and northern exposure make this is a great destination for the hot days of summer.

Spooks 5.7, 190 m, gear to 4"
J. Palmer & J. Carmichael, Sept. 1978

"Spooks" climbs a deep, left leaning chimney that diagonals up through a more broken section in the middle of the cliff. It lies to the right of a large yellow pillar on the upper half of the wall that defines the left side of the shadowed bay. See photo pages 184 & 190. The route begins with a classic deep chimney (5.6) that is unprotected but probably more secure than it feels. Two long easy pitches lead to the upper section where the route moves out on to the left wall above a large chockstone. The next pitch gives enjoyable 5.7 climbing and a final 5.6 pitch leads to the top.

More Dirty Dancing** 5.11c, 25 m, fixed gear
A. Genereux Sept. 1995

Two sport routes have been established on the small buttress of excellent grey rock immediately left of the first pitch of "Spooks." Both climbs end at the fixed stations below the beginning of the magnificent corner line of "Dirty Dancing." Details of the "Dirty Dancing" access routes are given below and in the accompanying topo. See photo page 193.

"More Dirty Dancing" was rap bolted & roped solo. The rock is good after an overlap the upper third of the pitch is very sustained to the final slab finish. This interesting climb could be used as a variation start to "Dirty Dancing." This would give five pitches of sustained 5.11 climbing—a must for those that would enjoy that many!

Another Dirty Dance*** 5.12a/b, 25 m, fixed gear
A. Genereux August 1998

This very technical pitch, has sustained sequential climbing that bear hugs the outside wall of the "Spooks" chimney this is an excellent alternative start for "Dirty Dancing".

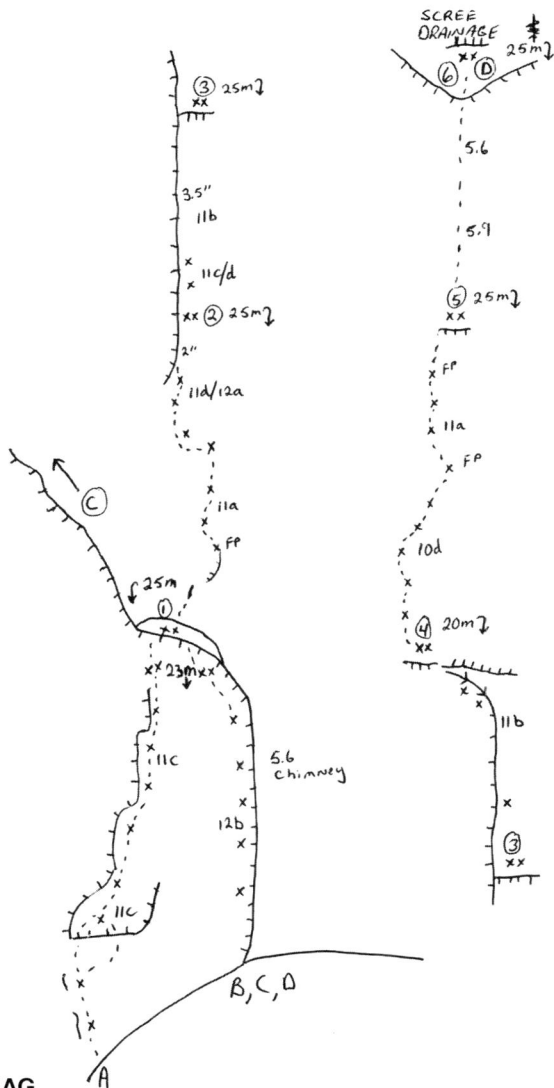

NORTH PHANTOM CRAG

A More Dirty dancing **   5.11c, 25 m
B Another Dirty Dance***   5.12a/b, 25 m
C Spooks   5.6, 190 m, gear to 4"
D Dirty Dancing ***   5.11d/12a, 145 m, gear standard rack to 4" multiples 2"-2.5"

Dirty Dancing

Dirty Dancing*** 5.11d/12a, 145 m,
gear standard rack to 4" multiples 2"& 2.5"
A. Genereux & J. Jones, Aug. 1991

This superb route is one of the best natural lines in the Ghost River Valley with sustained climbing and excellent rock. It follows a clean-cut, and very impressive, right-facing corner system directly above the first pitch of "Spooks." The first pitch, which is also the hardest, was put up on-lead, hand drilled off hooks over several hours. However, dirt deposited by drainage in the upper corner required cleaning from above. The remainder of the climb was then cleaned and bolted on rappel. Genereux gained access to the top by soloing "Spooks" with a 30 kilogram pack! He then went on to rappel, clean and hand-drill the route in a total of eight hours—an effort that helped inspire one of his nicknames, "The Human Hilti." Several 3/8" bolts were added on the first ascent to allow for 25 m rappels. This test piece only received the second and third known ascents in 2002.

Gear: Friends to #4 with doubles of #2 and #2.5, a full set of TCUs and #4 to #7 Rocks for the first two pitches. Above this, wires and TCUs will suffice, so the rest of the gear can be left and retrieved on the descent.

1) 5.6, 25 m. Ascend the chimney of "Spooks" for 25 m until above and behind two large chockstones. Traverse across the left wall of the chimney to a large patio ledge and bolt belay. Or alternatively, climb "Another Dirty Dance" or "More Dirty Dancing" directly to the patio belay bypassing their lower hanging anchors.

2) 5.11d/12a, 25 m. Step back across the chimney and onto the wall. Climb up to a small hole (large Friend) and then move right and up to a piton. Make hard moves left to a bolt. Sustained climbing past the next bolt leads to a small ledge. From here make difficult moves left to gain a shallow corner that is the start of the main open book. Hard, sustained climbing past a friction bulge then finger and hand crack leads to a hanging bolted belay.

3) 5.11c/d, 25 m. Continue up the classic dihedral. Hard, sustained stemming past two bolts (11c/d) leads to a superb continuous, steep, finger/hand crack (11a/b) up the corner to reach a pedestal ledge and bolt belay.

4) 5.11b, 20 m. Climb the corner above with continuously difficult moves. Below a roof, make moves left onto the face to finish up on a large ledge and bolt belay.

5) 5.11a, 25 m. From the left side of the ledge make difficult moves up to a bolt. Continue up the face with sustained climbing on excellent grey rock. At the fourth bolt make an awkward move right to gain a ramp that leads to a shallow corner. Climb the corner moving onto the left wall at the top to a small ledge with a cable and bolt belay. This pitch is completely fixed and is the end of the major difficulties.

6) 5.9, 25 m. Climb the face directly above the stance past some wire placements to gain a slabby groove. Easier but runout climbing leads up to a bolt and cable belay at the top.

Descent: Rappel the route. Six 25 m rsppels (see page 187).

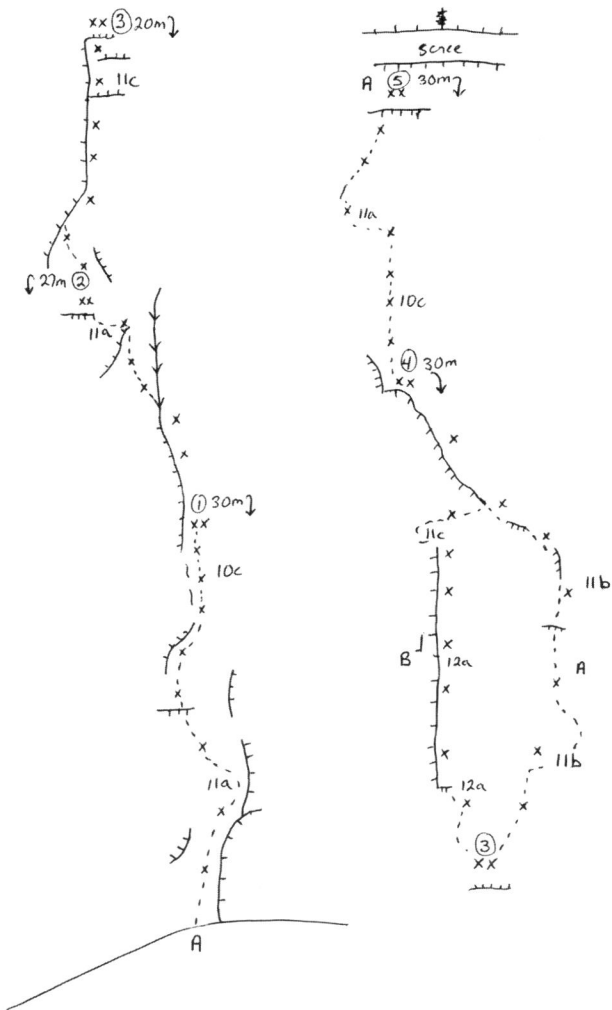

NORTH PHANTOM CRAG

A Smoking In The Boys Room ***   5.11c, 140 m
B Ghost Dance ***   5.12a/b

Smoking In The Boys Room

Smoking In The Boys Room*** 5.11c, 140 m, fixed gear
A. Genereux & G. Rinke, Aug. 1998

This route was established top down with exception of the first pitch, which was put in on lead from free drilling stances. This big solo rap bolting effort over two days was accomplished by packing a huge load over from the Wully creek drainage. The first day was cut short in the middle of the overhanging wall by a malfunctioning battery on the drill. Trapped in the middle of nowhere led to some interesting rappels using knotted slings and scary equalized marginal horns of rock. Andy intending to establish a multi-pitch sport route had only brought the essentials, bolts and draws and what he thought was enough battery power to bolt the entire route in a day, wrong!

This is an outstanding route and can be done using a single 60 m rope. It is located 30 m right from the start of "Dirty Dancing". It climbs up the centre of the wall on excellent dark rock. The optional fourth pitch "Ghost Dance" was originally the fourth pitch. The right variation now considered the regular fourth pitch was added a few weeks later and is more in line with the rest of the route grade wise. It took several efforts to redpoint the sustained "Ghost Dance" thus resulting in the search for an easier and more consistent pitch out to the right. On the fifth try the route was redpointed to the top in a single push.

1) 5.11a, 30 m. Start up a shallow left facing corner. Above the second bolt a hard move left leads onto a rippled face, climb up to a ledge. From here climb the bulging face to a small right facing arch. Pass this on the right and head up on juggy holds to a bolt belay.

2) 5.11a, 27 m Take the groove/corner above, for 15 m. Now move left to a shallow right facing corner. At the top of the corner make a difficult move left then up to a ledge with bolt belay.

3) 5.11c, 20 m. Climb directly above the belay past a bolt and move left to the over-hanging corner. Move up the corner on increasingly steeper and more challenging ground. At an overlap make several burly moves up and left then back right to reach an exposed hanging belay.

4) 5.11b, 30 m. Take the line of bolts to the right. From the second bolt make a difficult set of face moves to the right. Now head up to a small foot ledge with a bolt above. Make a committing move to gain shallow edge that faces away. Climb the steep ground to a leaning ramp. Take this left up to the belay.

5) 5.11b, 30 m. Sustained 5.10 face climbing leads past 5 bolts. From the fifth bolt move left on devious holds and climb through a technical bulge, sustained up to a good ledge with a bolt belay a few meters from the top.

Descent: rappel the route. One 60 m rope required. **Note:** three of the rappels are a full 30 m make sure to tie knots on the ends of your rope.

Ghost Dance*** 5.12a/b, 30 m, fixed gear
A. Genereux, Aug. 1998
The superb optional fourth pitch to "Smoking in the Boys Room". Take the line of bolts to the left of the belay. Clip the bolt directly above the belay make hard, thin friction moves

up and left to an awkward mantel into the corner. Climb the steep corner on sustained 5.11+ ground to a shark fin type feature. Continue up the corner sustained and move left as it ends. Make difficult and blind moves back right through a scoop to join the ramp leading left up to the belay.

Don't Forget to Dance** 5.11d, 135 m, fixed gear
A. Genereux, Aug. 1998

The second major route established by Andy on this wall in the summer of 1998. It was rap bolted and rope soloed over three days. To start the route, squeeze through a hole between the main wall where the back of the "Square Buttress" butts up against the main wall, 15 m right of "Smoking in the Boy's Room". The climb starts just on the other side of this hole.

1) 5.10a, 25 m. Climb the face to the right of the short corner created by the "Square Buttress". Step onto the top the corner and launch off onto the main face following a shallow groove then trend up and right to a belay.

2) 5.11c/d, 20 m. From the belay climbs a rib of steep rock left of a leaning right facing corner. Continuously sustained technical ground lead up the rib and left to a rest. Move right and fight up a series of thin technical holds and pull into the hidden right facing corner. Move up the corner to a hanging belay.

3) 5.11a, 30 m. Climb up and angle left up the face to a short roof hidden juggy holds lead over and up the steep face to a ledge with a huge block. Leave the left edge of the ledge, the belayer should take care a ledge-fall is possible here. Continue on sustained fingery climbing which angles up and right to a ledge and bolt belay.

4) 5.11b/c, 30 m. The climbing is immediately steep and sustained off the belay through a bulge and slightly right into a shallow groove. Take the left leaning groove for 20 m sustained 5.10, then up the bulging face to gain crack through a slab to the belay.

5) 5.10c, 30 m. Go into a short left facing corner above the belay move right above this then up into a larger left facing corner. Climb the corner to the top. The bolted belay is located just over the top.

Descent: Note this route can be rappelled using a single 60 m rope. **Caution:** you must back-clip bolts on the forth pitch when rappelling or you will find yourself stranded in the middle of overhanging ground to the left of the belay. Another option is to go left to rappel either "Dirty Dancing" or "Smoking in the Boy's Room". See page 187.

Be My Partner** 5.10c, 25 m, fixed gear
A. Genereux, Aug. 1998
A more difficult optional first pitch for "Don't Forget to Dance". Which can be done on it's own or with the pitches above. It starts at the same place but heads out right after the first bolt and then up on a bulging face, sustained 5.10 ground to the same anchor as "Don't Forget to Dance"

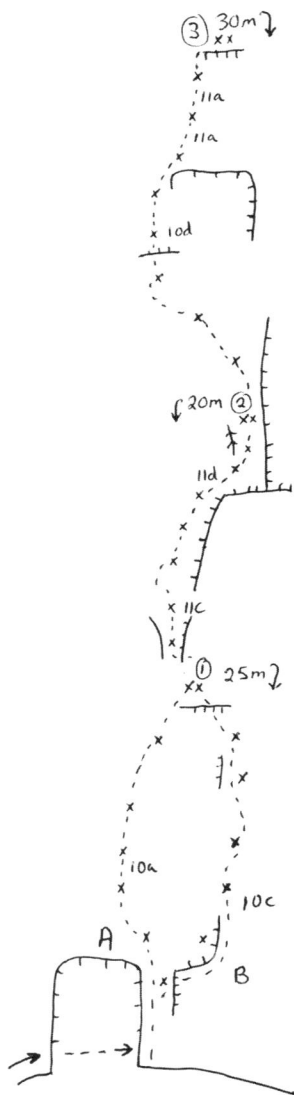

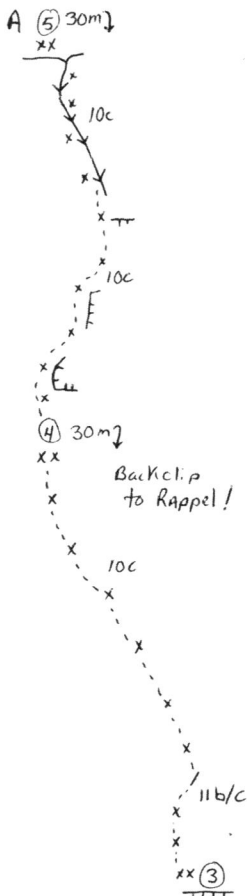

NORTH PHANTOM CRAG

A Don't Forget to Dance **   5.11d, 135 m
B Be My Partner **   5.10c, 25 m

Square Buttress

An appropriate name for this slabby squared off block of grey limestone. Located to the right and in front off the main wall below the climb "Dirty Dancing" and can be clearly seen in the photo on page 193. Its eastern aspect and the fact that it stands out front of the main wall allows it to enjoy early morning sun and can make it a lot warmer than routes on the main wall behind. This allows for a few pitches early in the morning while the temperature comes up on the more difficult routes behind. Take the normal approach trail as for "Dirty Dancing" and trend up to the buttress from the north end. This is an excellent place for the 5.10 climber who would like to consolidate their leading ability. There are a variety of climbs all on excellent rock. All climbs on this buttress where established by Andy Genereux about half were established ground up using rope soloing techniques and a power drill. The other half of the routes were rap bolted, then rope soloed. The first two climbs were done in 2000 and six others put up in a single day effort in 2002.

Square Dance** 5.11b, 50 m, gear medium wires
A. Genereux, July 2000

Starts on the left side of Square Buttress, sustained 5.10 climbing leads to an overlap near the top of the wall. Hard moves up and left to overcome the overlap is the crux. Continue to a bolt belay.

Descent: walk off over the top or rappel the route.

Hoe Down** 5.10c, 50 m, gear to 2.5" TCU'S
A. Genereux, July 2000

Similar to the previous route but its at a slightly easier grade. Face climb past bolts to a crack and shallow corner. When you arrive at the over lap contrived climbing avoids the easy corner to the right. You must make hard moves left onto the face to a bolt and continue sustained past two more bolts to the belay.

Descent: the same as Square Dance.

Thinking Little Thing** 5.10d, 27 m, fixed gear
A. Genereux, August 2002

Climbs the rounded arête right of the Hoe Down corner. The crux is overcoming a bulge, four bolts up. Continue to a bolted belay on a good ledge.

No Dance Partner* 5.9, 22 m, medium wires
A. Genereux, Aug. 2002

Located at the middle of the buttress, a bolt leads up to a short crack. Continue up to a second crack with a shallow left facing corner above a ledge. Climb past three bolts to the top of a pedestal with a bolt belay.

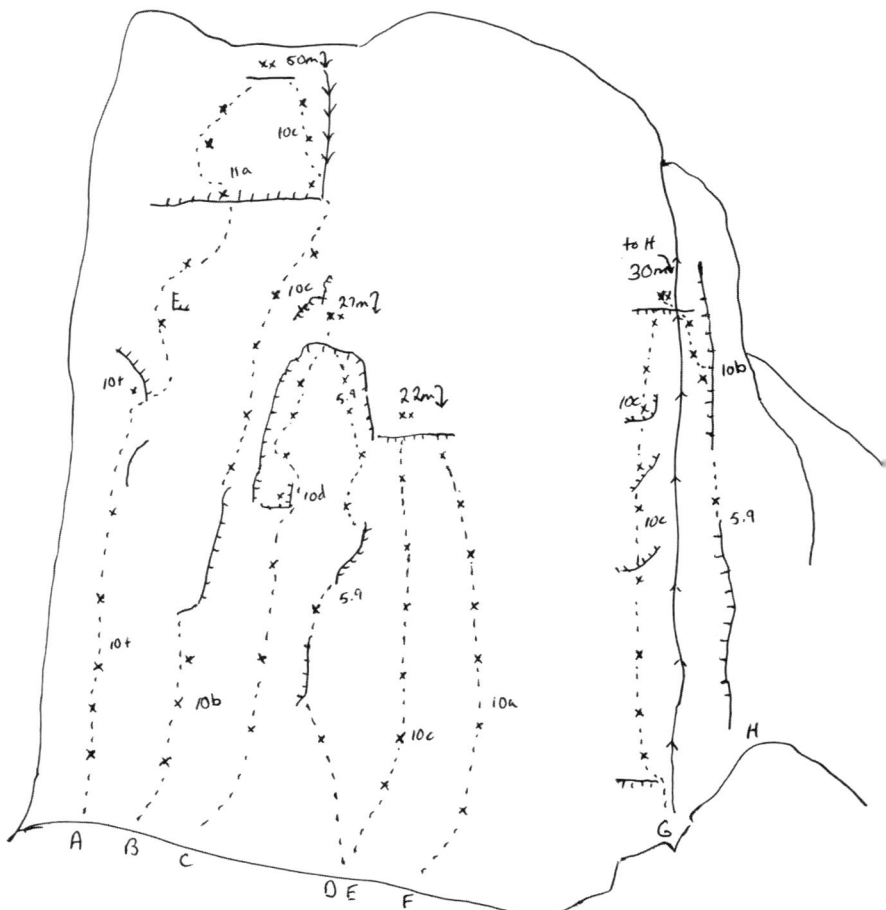

SQUARE BUTTRESS

A	Square Dance **	5.11a/b, 50 m	med. wires
B	Hoe Down **	5.10c, 50 m	gear to 2.5" & TCU's
C	Thinky Little Thing **	5.10d	
D	No Dance Partner *	5.9	med. wires
E	Slow Dance **	5.10c	
F	Where is my Dog **	5.10a	
G	Nose Job ***	5.10c	
H	Shady Lady*	5.10b	gear to 4"

Slow Dance** 5.10c, 22 m, fixed
A. Genereux, Aug, 2002

Climb up and right to bolt, sustained climbing past the next two bolts, leads to easier ground and a bolt belay on a ledge.

Where Is My Dog** 5.10a, 22 m, fixed
A. Genereux, Aug. 2002

This is a nice climb on quality rock. Hard moves up and right to the first bolt. Steady climbing past five more bolts to share the same anchor as Slow Dance.

Nose Job*** 5.10c, 32 m, fixed
A. Genereux, Aug. 2002

Climbs the rounded prow, which forms the right side of Square Buttress. Climb up to an obvious ledge. Continuous face climbing over several hard overlaps. Follow the rounded prow to a bolt belay. Note: **Caution** when rappelling or lowering one needs to be careful to angle right to the start of "Shady Lady" to have enough rope, make sure to tie a knot in the end of your rope.

Shady Lady* 5.10b, 30 m, gear to 4"
A. Genereux, Aug. 2002

Scramble up to a ledge below a right facing corner with an obvious hand crack. Located on the north face just right of the prow that forms the right edge of the buttress. Climb the obvious crack. When the crack ends, face climb past a bolt to regain the crack. Stay with the crack until a bolt is reached on the left wall. Make hard moves at the bolt left to gain the east face. Two more bolts on sustained ground lead to the bolted belay.

Pinnacle Chimney 5.6, 170 m, standard rack to 4"
J. Firth & T. Watson, 1976

"Pinnacle Chimney" is a right-slanting chimney that forms the left side of a wide, shallow pinnacle that defines the right side of the "Dirty Dancing " area. It is even more difficult to see than "Vanishing Point." The pinnacle is separated from the main face in its upper section and can be readily located from the trail by the obvious crack line of "Crack-A-Jack" towards its bottom on the left side. Photos pages 184 and 193, topo page 205.

1) 5.6, 40 m. Follow the chimney on the left side of the pinnacle to below a difficult section.
2) 5.5, 35 m. Continue past the fixed rappel point of "Crack-A-Jack" and up ledges to some small trees.
3) 5.5, 20 m. Scramble up behind the pinnacle to its top.
4) 5.6, 40 m. Traverse up diagonally leftwards across the face above the pinnacle to a ledge.
5) 5.5, 35 m. Climbs a short wall then goes up and left to the top.

Mike Sawyer on Crack Attack
Photo: Chris Jones

NORTH PHANTOM CRAG

A	Crack A Jack ***	5.10b, 75 m	gear standard rack to 4" or bigger
B	Pinnacle Chimney	5.6, 170 m	gear to 4"
C	Seperated Reality **	5.10c, 230 m	gear standard rack to 4"

North Phantom Crag

Crack-A-Jack*** 5.10b, 75 m, gear standard rack to 4" or bigger
J. Firth, J. Horne & M. Sawyer, 1976

This excellent crack climb, which was originally called a 5.9 hand crack, follows an obvious line leading to the left shoulder of the pinnacle.

1) 5.10b, 40 m. Follow the crack with increasing difficulty past an awkward off-width section through an overhang to a ledge with a single bolt.

2) 5.8, 35 m. Continue up the crack to ledges in the Pinnacle Chimney.

3) 5.5 Downclimb the chimney to the left easily for 10 m to a fixed rappel point just above the first belay of "Pinnacle Chimney" (usually pitches 2 & 3 are done together). Or, from this station continue to the top of the cliff via "Separated Reality" which is an excellent option.

Descent: One 55 m rappel.

Separated Reality** 5.10c, 230 m, gear standard rack to 4"
B. Wyvill & T. Jones, June 1990

A well-protected, sustained climb on good rock throughout. When combined with "Crack-A-Jack" this route constitutes an exacting and enjoyable three-star traditional outing. The route name makes no illusions to the famous Yosemite test piece but rather suggests marital problems being suffered at the time.

1 & 2) 5.10b, 80 m. As for "Crack-A-Jack," descend to the bolts at the rappel station.

1) alt, 5.6, 55 m. Climbs the first pitch of "Pinnacle Chimney" to the fixed station.

3) 5.10b, 50 m. Traverse left and climbs the ever-steepening groove (piton) until the crack closes (piton). Some interesting moves lead to a wider crack that is followed to a crevasse stance and a traditional belay.

4) 5.10a, 25 m. Step out right passing a two-bolt rappel station, go right again around the arête and climb up to a bolt. Climb up and step back left, turning a small overhang on the right. Climb up easier ground to several pitons. Traverse left above to a good stance in a corner with a good wire and single bolt belay.

5) 5.10a, 30 m. Traverse left and climb the groove to where it steepens unreasonably. Make a delicate traverse right under an overhang to reach a more accommodating groove (piton). Follow this to an exposed ledge on the left with a two-bolt belay.

6) 5.10a, 35 m. Continue up the steep groove to the top. There are two fixed pitons in a scruffy cliff some distance back from the edge.

Descent: It is possible to rappel the route with double ropes from fixed anchors (no chains) atop pitches 6, 5 & 3 and the final rappel from the "Crack-A-Jack" station in "Pinnacle Chimney." An alternative is to use the "Smoking" rappel (details page 187 & photo page 193) to the left.

A. The Black Hole
B. Caspar
C. The Bowl
D. The Snake's Tongue

The Right End constitutes the northern third of the cliff. Shown in the photo on the previous page. The quality of the rock varies widely from compact corners and prickly slabs to overhanging choss. In some places where the rock looks suspect the climbing is actually rather good. I suggest you get out and explore, this part of the cliff only has four established routes and is a good bet for more than a few new routes. Particularly to the right of "The Bowl" and on the rolling north end of the cliff which should cough up some excellent but moderate classics.

Approach

For the routes "The Bowl," "Caspar" and "The Black Hole." Take the standard traversing approach trail until the trail meets a rocky rib, where the trail drops slightly down left. From the rocky rib scramble up the scree slope above and follow the main wall left to your objective. The Black Hole is a dark chimney that climbs the right side of a large leaning pillar that defines the left boundary of the Right End. For "The Bowl" locate on obvious orange overhang at mid height on the face directly above the trail. The route starts slightly left of this and finishes up a crack to its right. Caspar is the right leaning chimney starting roughly halfway between these two features.

The Black Hole 5.7, 150 m, gear to 4"
N. Hellewell & C. Perry, June 1976

This forgettable route climbs a very unappealing chimney on the right side of a large pillar that leans against the face near the right end of the cliff. It is situated opposite "Caspar" at the top of the scree slope, now continue up and left in a gully to the base of the chimney.

1) 5.7, 30 m. Avoid the initial off-width section by climbing a cracked wall on the left and then hand traversing back right into the chimney (crux). Move up to a belay, deep inside the chimney.
2) 5.6, 45 m. Climb a steep crack in the outer wall of the chimney to a ledge on the outside, near the top of the leaning buttress that forms the chimney.
3) 5.6, 35 m. Move up and onto the main face then continue up into the shallow groove above.
4) 5.5, 40 m. Climb the groove to the top.

Caspar* 5.6, 160 m, gear to 4"
J. Firth & C. Perry, 1976

This route climbs the obvious diagonal chimney at the right end of the cliff. It is probably the easiest climb in the Ghost and as such is a worthwhile beginner's route. The climbing is varied and the rock is reasonably solid. The route follows the wall to the right of the chimney for most of the way and exits to the right at the top.

The Bowl 5.8+, 165 m, gear to 4" multiple 3" to 4"
J. Firth, J. Horne & M. Sawyer June 1976.

On the buttress to the right of "Caspar" there is a large overhang at just over half height with a left-facing corner above and to its right. The overhang is directly above the small, rocky rib noted in the trail description. "The Bowl" climbs the face below and left of the overhang, it then traverses to the right below it and then follows a corner to the top. Some large gear is needed for the top crack, which is the crux. From the trail, scramble up to below and slightly left of the overhang. Then follow easy ledges out right for about 10 m onto the face.

1) 5.7, 20 m. Move up and right, then go up past an awkward bulge to a ledge.
2) 5.7, 35 m. Climb the wall on the left to a slab that trends up and right. At the top of the slab, traverse left past a block and go up to a higher ledge below and left of the large overhang.
3) 5.6, 30 m. Traverse right on the ledge and climb an easy crack system leading past the right side of the overhang.
4) 5.7, 35 m. Follow the crack until it steepens, about 6 m below a jammed block.
5) 5.8+, 45 m. Continue with the crack, which is difficult at first (crux), to the top.

The Snake's Tongue 5.6, 140 m, gear to 4"
O. Fluehler & J. Carmichael, 1978

"The Snake's Tongue" climbs the prominent crack system with a black overhanging chimney near the top at the north end of the cliff. Photo page 207. The upper chimney is avoided by traversing to a hidden crack on the right wall.

Follow the crack system for two pitches to a belay ledge on the left, about 6 m below an obvious fork in the chimney. Climb up to a good ledge, about 5 m higher, which leads out right for about 12 m to a flake crack. Climb this to the top.

WULLY CANYON

The Wully Canyon climbing area lies in the upper part of the stream bed between North Phantom Crag and Wully Wall. The climbing includes the south facing Wully Wall from where it bends west to meet the Upper Wully Canyon creek drainage and includes a smaller cliff below in the middle of the canyon. It has a very short approach of 15 to 20 minutes and many of the routes have a southern exposure and are generally away from the wind. Making this yet another good venue to extend the climbing season. The last guide listed three routes here. The past few years have seen a great deal of development mostly of a mixed traditional nature. Several projects are still under way but there is still some untapped potential for new routes.

Approach

Park at the CMC campsite. See page 177 for details. At this point a washed-out road heads up the hill and into an old gravel pit. Walk across the pit and into the small stream coming from Wully Canyon. Continue up the creek to the "Lower Canyon," located in a tiny gorge, which is reached after 10 minutes. To date there are four short climbs located in the "Lower Canyon." The trail continues up the creek to where the canyon opens up. This is where the trail for North Phantom Crag takes off to the left. On the north side of the creek a thin grove of spruce trees climbs the hill to the main wall just left of the Climb "The Bat and The Raven." By continuing upstream staying to the right you arrive in "The Middle Canyon" (there is a fork to the left that leads up south toward the Phantom Crag Summits). The short waterfall known as "Wully Falls" blocks the stream bed. The small wall on the right of the falls is "Bulky Boy's Wall". "Rodents' Arête" lies on the main cliff directly above this small wall. The south facing extension of Wully Wall travels west to form a box canyon at a second set of waterfalls. This main south facing wall and the areas to the west will all be covered under the section referred to as the "Upper Wully Canyon."

To reach the Upper Wully Canyon there are two choices. Climb through the trees below the climb "The Bat and The Raven" then traverse left or right to access your climb. The other option is to climb the scree slope to the right of Bulky Boys wall to the base of the main wall. Arriving at the left edge of a bowl with a black water streak to the right. The grey prow line just to the left is "Rodent's Arête." To access the 4-Play Wall and upper box canyon, now scramble left across the base of a buttress below "Rodents' Arête" to cross in front of a pinnacle of rock that spans a deep gully on the main wall behind. This pinnacle is referred to as the "4-Play Wall" and the deep gully behind is called the "Female Gully." Continue left down a short slope into the upper gorge. "Womb With A View" climbs the right wall of the upper canyon starting below the second falls. A small buttress to the left of the second falls gives the line of "Priapism." The crack to the left of the buttress has also been climbed at 5.8. Above the second fall there is a narrow canyon and an interesting waterspout. Note that the upper gorge by "Womb With A View" is only in condition later in the year when the creek level is low or not flowing.

Descent

For the three multi-pitch routes that ascend the main wall it is recommended that you go left from "Rodents' Arête" traverse into the Female Gully to a 55 m rappel. Followed by two shorter single rope rappels the second to a tree with a chain, then to the base of the wall.

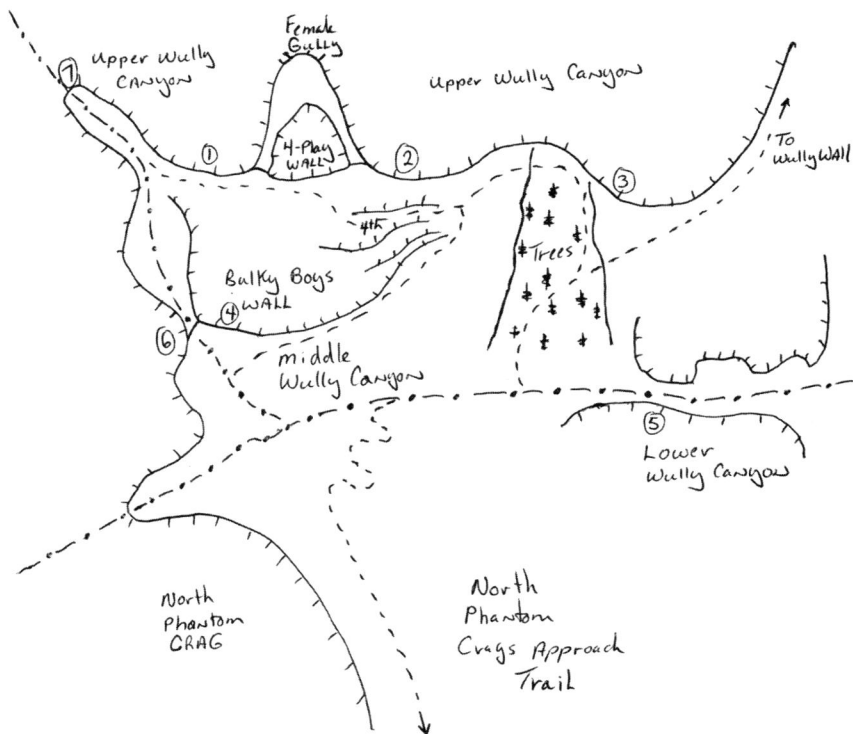

WULLY CANYON OVERVIEW

1 Womb With A View
2 Rodent's Arête
3 Bat and The Raven
4 Chalka Lotapus
5 Wouldn't You Know it
6 First Waterfall
7 Second Waterfall

Lower Wully Canyon

The cliffs run for just over a hundred meters in length, range in height from 15 to 25 m, they face north and south. With the creek running most of the year it's a bit reminiscent of canyon areas in the Bow Valley. The 10 minute approach makes it one of the quickest destinations in the Ghost. There are four climbs established so far. Three climbs on the right, and one on the left. There is scope to establish some short sport routes on the compact left (north facing) wall. With lesser quality rock on the south facing right side, however there is still room to unearth a few more traditional lines along this sunny aspect.

Lower Wully Canyon, Left Side

Wouldn't You Know It* 5.8, 12 m, fixed gear
R. Felber & C. Smith, 1999

Located on the slabby (north facing) wall is a four bolt route 10 m before you break out into the wider creek basin beyond.

Lower Wully Canyon, Right Side

The Dirty Dike 5.9, 20 m, gear to 4"
T. Jones & G. Fletcher, 1999

Climbs the corner to the right side of a boxy bay, just before the gorge narrows. Climb the corner passing a bolt.

Crew Cut Corner 5.6, 20 m, gear to 4"
T Jones & J. Billings, 1999
Climb a scrappy left facing corner just right of the bay.

Lynn's Route 5.5/X, 20 m, no gear to chains on a tree
R. Felber & Lynn, 1999

Climbs the lower angled face to the left of an obvious corner to a tree with a rappel chain.

1. Wouldn't You Know It
2. The Dirty Dike
3. Crew Cut Corner
4. Lynn's Route

Is reached in about 20 minutes, stay to the right at the first fork in the creek. Follow the creek until blocked by a short waterfall with a steep wall to the right.

Bulky Boys Wall

Is a small steep cliff, which forms the right wing of the first waterfall directly below "Rodents Arête" on the main wall above.

Slippery When Wet 5.6, 30 m, gear to 3" pitons
T. Jones and R. Felber, 1998

Not really on the wall proper it climbs the waterfall chute/stream bed when it's not flowing from the upper canyon.

Northern Solar 5.8 A1, 25 m, gear to 3"
G. Cornell & G. Fletcher, Feb 2001

1) Scramble the finger crack past two pitons as for "Slippery when Wet" to the upper pool (avoid in spring) and belay.
2) Climb the steep crack on the left wall for 20 m on mixed aid and free moves. Enter into a chute, then stem right and up past two bolts to gain the corner crack and a fixed pin, a few feet more to a two bolt belay.

Descent: rappel 25 m to the base of the Bulky Boys Wall.

Project/Rope chopper
Has an anchor and has been top-roped at 5.10+/11-, it climbs the face immediately right of the waterfall.

Chalka Lotapus** 5.11c, 25 m, fixed gear
J.C. Debeau & G. Fletcher, 1999

The first bolted route 5 m to the right the waterfall. The crux comes low in this technical climb. Steady face climbing continues all the way to the top.

Jelly Belly** 5.10a, 25 m, gear to 2"
T. Jones, 1999

This is a mostly bolted climb but still requires some small gear to get to the top and a bolted anchor.

Thin Man's Groove* 5.9, 22 m, gear to 3.5"
F. Campbell, 1999

Starts halfway up the right side of the cliff. Climb a series of shallow corners to finish up a groove to a fixed anchor.

Bulky Boys Wall

Fat Boy Dream* 5.7, 20 m, gear to 4"
R. Felber, 1999

The original "Bulky Boy" finally gets to have his own climb. Start left of a scrawny tree climb up past a bolt to an overlap turn this past two bolts to climb a groove up to a chained anchor.

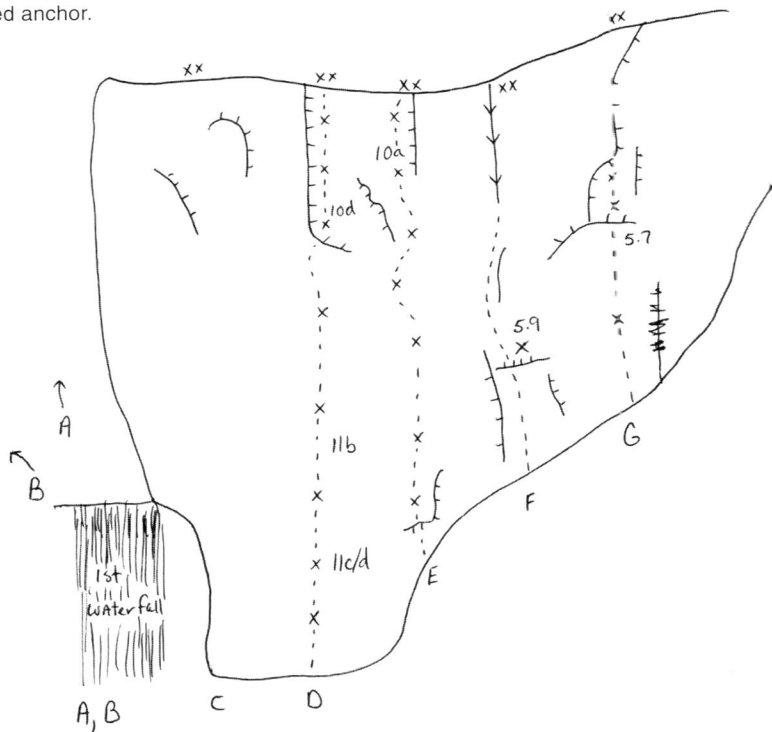

BULKY BOYS WALL

A	Slippery When Wet	5.6	gear to 4' & pitons
B	Northern Solar	5.8/A1	gear to 3"
C	Project Rope Chopper		
D	Chalka Lotapus **	5.11c/d	
E	Jelly Belly **	5.10a	wires, gear to 2"
F	Thin Mans Groove *	5.9	gear to 3.5"
G	Fat Boys Dream *	5.7	gear to 4"

Traverse left below "Rodent's Arête" scramble across on broken ledges to better ground below the 4-Play wall a short pinnacle that blocks the deep hidden Female Gully. Drop down a short scree slope to enter Upper Wully Canyon a tight box canyon with a waterfall at the west end. It is also possible to access the upper canyon via the climb "Slippery When Wet" which ascends the creek from the lower waterfall this is only possible if the creek is dry usually late summer.

Priapism 5.10b, 30 m, fixed gear
G. Powter, B. Wyvill, E. Trouillot & E. Niemy, July 1990

Located on the left wall of the slot canyon left of the second waterfall. Climb the bulge and continue up the wall above to a fixed station.

Womb With A View* 5.10c, 40 m, gear to 4"
B. Wyvill, G. Powter, E. Trouillot & E. Niemy, July 1990

Climb the wall (bolt) and arête to the right of the second waterfall and continue past a bolt until it is possible to swing left into a bottomless, bulge-capped groove (the Womb). Climb the Womb and exit diagonally left to where the route steepens. Climb the steep wall on the left (bolt) and exit left via an exciting mantle shelf move. The climbing is sustained and on good rock. Protection is partly on bolts but a selection of small nuts and two Friends (#3 and #4) are also required. It is recommended that an additional bolt be placed in the lower part of the climb where adequate protection is difficult to arrange.

Spider in a Bowl 5.10c TR, 45 m
Located below the top rappel in the Female Gully this only becomes available if you are descending off one of the multi-pitch climbs on Wully Wall out to the right. It is hoped this project will soon be bolted to allow bottom access from climbs on the 4-Play Wall.

Frank Campbell on The Bat and The Raven. Photo: Trevor Jones.

4-PLAY WALL

This is the small pinnacle that plugs the deep and hidden Female Gully left of "Rodents Arête". The formation is home to three traditional lines. For descent it is best to go off the back and scramble over to the short rappels on the left which exit by the project "Smells Like A Fish" to the left side of the 4-Play wall. The top rappel is off a bolted anchor the second off a tree with a chain.

(project) Smells Like a Fish
Located where the left side of the 4-Play pinnacle spans the wall left to join the upper canyon. "Smells Like A Fish" is the short project that attempts to enter the Female Gully via a short left facing corner. The third of three bolts has a knifeblade piton for a hanger.

Rolling Thunder* 5.7, 35 m, gear to 4"
R. Felber & J. Billings, 1999

Climbs up to a bolt then enters a groove, climb the groove and continue up intermittent cracks to the summit of the pinnacle.

The Sphinx* 5.7, 35 m, gear to 4"
G. Fletcher & R. Felber, 1999

Climbs an obvious corner up to the Sphinx shaped nipple at the top of the pinnacle it exits to the right of this feature.

Holy Thundrin Jesus* 5.7, 35 m, gear to 4" pitons
R. Felber & J. Billings, 1999

Climb the right side of the tower bypassing a large boulder stuck between the pinnacle and the main wall. Climb intermittent cracks to the top and locate a single bolt belay.

Rodents' Arête 5.6, 105 m, gear to 4" pitons
A. Watts (Mouse), C. Aspill (Rabbit) & K. Manning (Mrs. Mouse), 1978

Near the west end of Wully Wall (the main upper wall directly above the lower waterfall), is a prow like buttress. This is the line of "Rodents' Arête." This looks to be a good line maybe a good cleaning and some solid anchors might yet turn it into a classic.

The climb begins near the top of a scree slope to the right of the buttress. You then scramble left to start the climb. Despite its good line, the climb is reported to be quite scrappy.
1) 5.5, 35 m. Traverse easily left across the buttress to a crack in a groove. Ascend this to a small stance.
2) 5.6, 30 m. Climb diagonally up and right onto the arête proper and go straight up on compact but slightly friable rock to a ledge.
3) 5.6, 40 m. Traverse right for about 2 m and then go straight up the steep wall above to the top (not well protected).

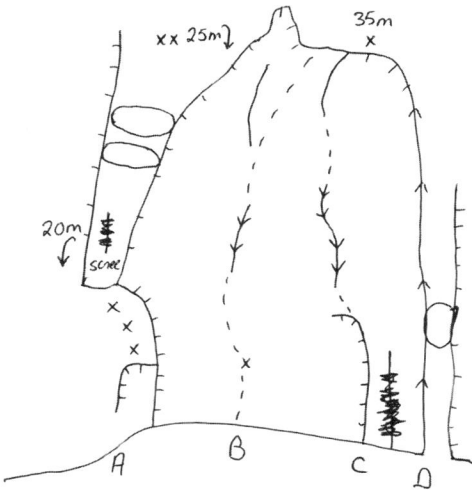

4-PLAY WALL

A Project Smells Like A Fish		
B The Sphinx *	5.7	gear to 4"
C Rolling Thunder *	5.7	gear to 4"
D Holly T'underin Jesus *	5.7	gear to 4"

Sounds Like A Rodent** 5.9, 120 m, gear to 2.5"

T. Jones, R. Felber, G. Fletcher and C. Fletcher, May 1999

Start as for "Rodents Arête" from near the top of the scree start by traversing left on easy ground across the base of the buttress. Climb to a crack in a groove. Climb the groove until a railway pin (Bulky Boy piton) is reached, now the route diverges out to the right.

1) 5.7, 45 m. Climbs to the railway pin then move right to a short left facing corner with a fixed pin at the base. Climb this to a bolt on the face above, from here move up and left to a pair of short cracks now move up and right to a fixed belay.

2) 5.7, 45 m. From the belay head up and left passing a bolt, traverse left past a left facing corner. Climb up to a small roof leading to a short right facing corner. Climb this to a bolt and then make a rising traverse up and right to a fixed piton. Ascend a set of weakness left then right to a good ledge and bolted belay.

3) 5.9, 30 m. Climb to a bolt up and right. Make a rising traverse left past two more bolts on sustained ground. The climbing eases to a single bolt station on top.

Upper Wully Canyon

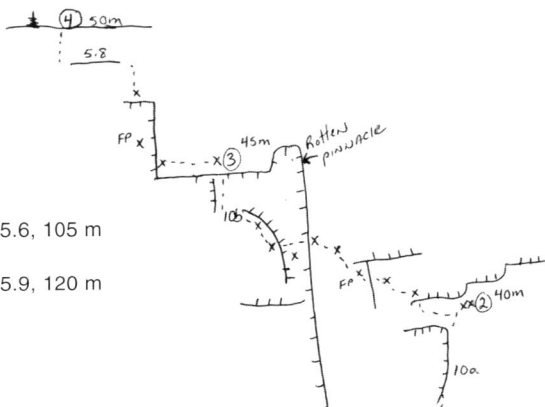

below
A Rodent's Arête   5.6, 105 m
   gear to 4"

B Sounds Like A Rodent **   5.9, 120 m
   gear to 4"

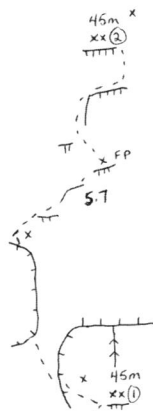

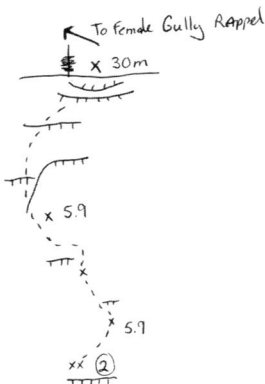

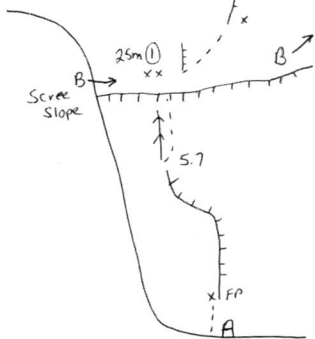

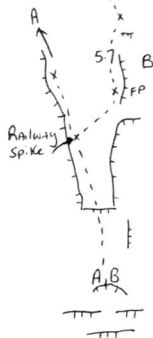

above
A The Bat And The Raven ***   5.10b, 170 m
   gear standard rack to 2.5"

B Wind In The Wullies *   5.8, 200 m
   gear standard rack to 4"

Hooky 5.8 A1, 30 m, gear (project)
G. Fletcher & T. Jones, 2001

Located halfway to the black water streak in the bowl to the right of "Rodents Arête." This climb was commemorated by snow flurries, several thin hook moves, a collapsing ledge and other fun bits of horrid rock to a single bolt anchor. Sounds like a ghost classic in the making. It is hoped that this will clean up and get free climbed and be extended up the wall in the near future.

The Douche A2, 30 m (project)
Climbs the black water streak located in the middle of the bowl right of "Rodents Arête" several bolts and pitons lead to a sling belay on this ongoing project.

The Bat and The Raven*** 5.10b, 170 m, gear to 2.5"
several long slings and double ropes
T. Jones, F. Campbell & A. Pickel, Aug. 1997

This excellent climb can be reached by following the base of the rock bowl right from "Rodents Arête" onto a sidewalk like ledge at its right edge. There is an optional 5.7 pitch that starts below the ledge. To reach this lower pitch drop down the scree for 25 m to the base of some good grey slabby rock.

1) 5.7, 25 m. Climb the slabby face to a left leaning shallow corner. Climb the corner to a groove to arrive at the sidewalk ledge and a bolt belay.

2) 5.10a, 40 m. Move up and out right to a bolt, climb a small pedestal on the left side up to a bolt. Continue up past bolts to a two-bolt stance. Keep moving past this to climb the right facing corner above to a hanging belay below a roof. The belay should be moved to the ledge on the left now that a huge block has been removed.

3) 5.10b, 45 m. Two bolts move left to a seam climb this to a small ledge then left to the large right facing corner, avoid climbing the corner up to the frail pinnacle. Instead make a blind traverse left from the corner to gain an arching corner. Climb this, strenuous to a ledge and single bolt and gear belay.

4) 5.8, 50 m. Move left along the ledge to a bolt. Climb the short corner above to reach a second bolt, move up and take the 5.8 handrail left. Easier ground leads to the top and a tree belay.

Wind In The Wullies* 5.8, 200 m and growing, gear standard rack to 4"
T. Jones & R. Felber

Start off the sidewalk like ledge as for pitch two of the "The Bat and The Raven". Continue along the sidewalk to the right then take a series of right leaning ramping corners to the Tree Island on Wully Wall. The first pitch is 5.8 the remaining three are 5.6. The team has a dream for this route to eventually form a complete girdle traverse of the entire east facing Wully Wall.

Andy Generoux leading the third pitch of Heavy Weight Contender. Photo: Fay Wilkinson.

Wully Wall is a relatively large cliff situated immediately to the north of North Phantom Crag and separated from it by the deep drainage of Wully Canyon. Because of its proximity to the CMC campsite, the relatively short approach the cliff received a fair amount of attention in the early years of Ghost River development. The name was given to the cliff by Bugs McKeith and reflects his professed affinity for sheep. In recent years Wully Wall has undergone a rejuvenation of sorts. One new multi-pitch sport route and several new multi-pitch mixed traditional lines have been recently added. These climbs complement some of the forgotten classics like "The Gateway" a good climb with some interesting moves and the memorable "Big Willy" the exposed roof capping a corner at the south end of the Tree Island. As well the runout crux of "Countdown" has been retro bolted to make for a fine outing. With it's eastern aspect, the much-improved trail, and the expanded range of good climbs both in style and grade the crag now has something to offer everybody. This has become a great place to hang on those hot summer days. A small selection of pitons is required for several of the older climbs; it will be noted in the gear selection.

Wully Wall

Wully Wall

The most prominent feature on the cliff is a large, treed ledge referred to as Tree Island. It is situated toward the left side at about two-thirds height. At present six routes reach the Tree Island directly and three separate finishes have been climbed. Three other full-length routes lie to the right of Tree Island. The rest of the routes on Wully Wall focus around the "Consolation" area. Wully Wall will include all climbs contained on the east and northern aspects of the cliff. This wall does continue around to the west from the south end, however all routes on the south facing exposure will be covered under "Wully Canyon." The climbs will be described from left to right, as is the norm for this guide.

Tree Island Approach
This used to be recommended by approaching from the middle of "Wully Canyon". Due to an improved trail along the base of the cliff, it's now recommended to traverse the cliff left from the consolation approach trail. Allow 20 to 25 minutes to reach the wall below the "Tree Island".

Consolation Approach
To reach the "Consolation" area, turn left toward the CMC campsite and locate a small side road on the right, about 250 m south of the canal bridge, that leads to a small clearing in the trees (campsite). Starting from here, flagging leads right to an overgrown gully/drainage that leads up to the main wall to the right of a scree cone. The scree cone is immediately to the right of the start for the route "Consolation".
Just after entering the drainage cross the gully to the right and take a good winding trail up the slope. Near the top, the trail traverses back left across the drainage gully and arrives at the main wall below and 5 m right of the route "Trace." A good trail traverses left below Wully Wall to the south end and is used for all climbs left of "Consolation" Including the Tree Island.

Tree Island Descent
If you climb a route to the Tree Island and forego the top of the wall, it is possible to rappel off "Jeff's Route" at the north (right) end of Tree Island. Two 55 m ropes are required to reach easy ground in one rappel from a tree with a rappel chain.

Scramble Descent (from the top of Wully Wall)
The normal walk off descent is to the north, although no good trail has yet to be established. This can involve slippery down climbing and can be difficult to find the best way. One means of descent is to cut down the steep, wooded hillside immediately north of the cliff and follow a vague trail, flagged initially by intermittent seismic tape. However, the trail peters out lower down and a descent in this direction always seems to end in swinging off tree branches and downclimbing small cliffs. Probably the best descent route is to follow the top of the cliff some distance north and pick up a small game trail that leads to a major drainage. Bypass a large cliff near the top of the descent, by some easy down climbing to the right (south). Take fairly open slopes down that lead back to the road. The south end of the crag extends a long way back (west) beyond "Wully Canyon" and a descent in this direction is not recommended.

A. Big Willy
B. Chicken on the Way
C. Hangover
D. Jeff's Route
E. Sellout
F. Countdown
G. Chicken Heart
H. Runner Up
I. Heavy Weight Contender
J. Ratty The Rope Eater
K. Consolation Direct
L. Consolation
M. Wullywatchers
N. Trace
O. Snake Bit
P. Prize Fight
Q. Wully Sport

Wully Wall

Rappel Descent (from the top of Wully Wall)

Recently, a new rappel route has been established from the top of "Consolation". The **Consolation Rappel** requires two ropes and descends on fixed ringbolt stations in 4 rappels. See the topo on page 234. The climbs "Wully Sport," "Runner Up" and "Sellout" all have fixed rappel stations that can be used to descend the wall, each has five rappels requiring two ropes to descend. The "Sellout" rappel line can be difficult to find from above due to the top anchor being located below a sub cliff from the top of the main crag. For the rappel options see the Consolidation topos on pages 234 and 235 and photo on page 237. The new "Consolation rappel should become the method of choice when descending from most climbs on Wully Wall it is described under the climb "Heavy Weight Contender" page 231.

The Gateway* 5.8+, 105 m, gear to 4"
C. Perry & M. White, 1978

Take the trail to where the east face starts to turn west into Wully Canyon. The most prominent feature is a wide corner with an impressive, and as yet unclimbed, crack on its left wall. Immediately right of this is a smaller, right-facing corner with a square-cut roof near its base. "The Gateway" climbs the corner and continues up to the south end of Tree Island. The second and third pitches are good and the grade of the route may be closer to 5.9.

1) 5.7, 40 m. Climb a loose, easy pitch up from the left to the base of the crack.
2) 5.8+, 40 m. Layback the crack and go round the roof to a good foothold at the lip. Follow the crack more easily moving slightly right to the higher of two ledges.
3) 5.8+, 45 m. Climb the chimney on the left bridging out left round the overhang and then following an easier crack system to Tree Island.

Big Willy 5.9, 150 m, gear to 4" pitons
B. McKeith & Alan Burgess, May 1978

Below the southernmost end of Tree Island are two deep corners. "Big Willy" climbs the left one, which begins halfway up the face at a large, right-facing overhang. Start left of the obvious, grassy groove of "Chicken on the Way."

Two short pitches left of the groove (5.6-5.7) lead to a belay 6 m below the roof. Traverse beneath the roof and layback the rib on the right to gain the groove above (5.9). Follow the crack to a belay on a large ledge. Scramble up to the highest point of Tree Island and climb the wall above for about 6 m to gain a fault line leading diagonally rightwards to the top.

Chicken on the Way 5.8, 150 m, gear to 4" pitons
P. Morrow & W. Frifz, 1976

"Chicken on the Way" is named for a still popular, if not slightly controversial, fast-food joint in Calgary. This route climbs the more obvious corner to the right of "Big Willy" and starts below the shallow, grassy groove. The groove begins at the highest point reached by the trail where it starts to drop into Wully Canyon. Two pitches of good 5.7 climbing lead to the south (left) end of Tree Island. Scramble up to the highest point as for "Big Willy." Climb the wall above for about 5 m and then make a long poorly protected diagonal traverse to a bay on the left (5.8, 45 m). From here a short, loose pitch leads to the top.

Hangover 5.8, 150 m, gear to 4" pitons
A. Sole & N. Hellewell, June 1978

Start a few meters right of "Chicken on the Way" below a left-facing crack.
1) Climb the crack, which ends after about 10 m. Avoid the steep, continuation crack by moving right for about 2 m to a corner that leads up to a tree belay.
2) Climb a crack on the right to a right-trending, yellow layback crack. Go around the roof to good jams above. Dynamic bridging leads up to Tree Island (surprisingly solid). Finish as for "Big Willy."

Jeff's Route 5.7, 55 m, gear to 4"
J. Upton & E. Brooke, June 1976

"Jeff's Route" follows the obvious, large right-facing corner leading to the north (right) end of Tree Island. It can be used as a convenient means of descent by rappel from a large tree with a chained rappel. From the bay of "Sellout" climb the trail left for 40 m, and then scramble up and right to a large tree at the base of the corner. Climb the corner in one pitch, exiting either slightly to the left or by traversing right just before the top.

Sellout** 5.11b, 200 m, gear to 2" double ropes recommended
B. Wyvill & T. Jones, summer 2001

Takes a line 20 m to the left of "Countdown." Locate a large open book corner with a line of bolts 6 m to the right. The bottom two pitches are a little contrived, but the climbing above follows a more natural line for the final three. The rock is good to excellent on all pitches. Unfortunately the broken ledges off the Tree Island take away from the climb somewhat.
1) 5.10c, 30 m. Climb the steep slab moving left after 15 m to a crack. Climb the crack then move right to a belay at a two-bolt station.
2) 5.10c, 25 m. Hard moves past two bolts lead up and left. The climbing then eases up to a large rubbly ledge. Climb another short wall to reach a second large ledge and a bolt belay.
3) 5.11b, 30 m. A series of holds connect to form an unlikely line up the wall above

Sellout

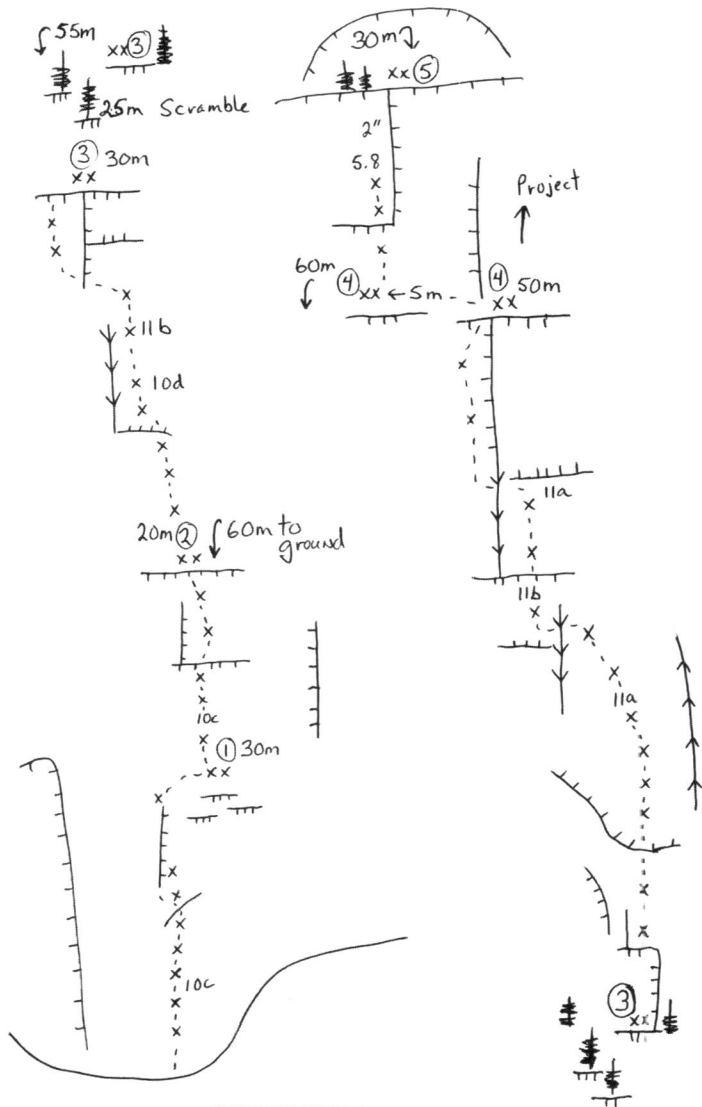

WULLY WALL

Sellout ** 5.11b, 175 m, gear to 2"

trending slightly leftwards on lovely rock. The difficulty steadily increases until the crux. After the crux, climb up to an overhang. Step left and up past two bolts to a bolt belay. There are 9 bolts on the pitch. Belay here or continue up and scramble 30 m over treed broken ledges to a bolted anchor at the base of the upper wall.

4) 5.11b, 50 m. Directly above the belay is large tree at the base of a right facing corner beneath an overhang. Climb the corner and step left onto a ledge with a bolt. Climb the slab past a bolt to reach the over hang. Make difficult moves rightward past a bolt to overcome the overhang. Climb the wall above with increasing difficulty past four bolts. Step left to a shattered groove, climb up and traverse leftwards beneath a bulge. Move up more easily for a few feet then climb over a small overlap to gain a short groove, up this and left to reach a bolt belay. From this point there is a planned direct continuation of this route. For now traverse left for 5 m to a second belay below an easier finishing pitch.

5) 5.8, 30 m. Climb the wall and groove past three bolts to the top and a bolt belay.

Descent: Rappel the route two 60 m ropes required and possibly slings see topo on opposite page.

Countdown* 5.9, 195 m, gear to 4"
B. Keller & C. Perry, June 1978

This route climbs up to the prominent right-facing corner that is level with, and about 60 m right of, "Jeff's Route." It continues directly up the slabby wall above to the top of the cliff. The slab on pitch 5 is was poorly protected it has now received a retro fit by Trevor Jones and Brian Wyvill increasing the star value of this climb. The name of the route was inspired by this pitch and refers to the depletion of Bruce Keller's "nine lives." Fortunately for Bruce, sport climbing was invented soon after this lead.

From the lowest point of the trail where "Sellout" starts, move up and right along the wall for 15 m to a prominent right-facing corner formed by a huge block. Beginning about 12 m right of the corner, scramble up and right via an easy groove to a tree-covered ledge about 12 m above the ground. Belay immediately below two short corners, the right hand corner is capped by a small roof and has yellow rock on its right-hand wall.

1) 5.7, 20 m. Traverse across yellow rock from the right to a shallow groove below the right-hand corner. Move up to a ledge and traverse left to the left-hand corner, which leads to more broken ground above.

2) 45 m. Scramble up rightwards to the base of the main corner.

3) 5.7, 40 m. Climb the corner to ledges on the left.

4) 15 m. Scramble up to a ledge below the upper wall and belay to the right of a steep slab below a small overlap. At the top of the slab there is an overhang with a crack on each side.

5) 5.9, 35 m. Traverse diagonally left onto the slab and go up to a small ledge on the left side. Climb up moving back right slightly and then go up to small ledges beneath the overhang (bolt protected). Continue via an awkward crack on the right side of the overhang.

6) 40 m. There is an easy crack system, which leads to the top.

Paul Stoliker negotiates the traverse of "Consolation." Photo: Maria Bikaitis.

Chicken Heart 5.10b, 230 m, gear to 4" pitons

A. Sole & N. Hellewell, June 1978

FFA: unknown, well Chris knows! He remembers the details, he just can't remember who told him.

Immediately to the right of the corner of "Countdown," part way up the cliff, are three short grooves set close together. The route climbs the left-hand groove and then wanders over to the right to exit near but left of the final pitch of "Consolation." There are bits of OK climbing but overall the route is a substandard adventure for Ghost River climbing.

Begin about 30 m to the right of "Countdown," at a short, cracked corner that leads up to broken ground. A recent repeat of this climb has not done much to raise its stock. The short aid section was free climbed. Other than that, it was described as having good bits of rock but wanders around too much with a lot of ledges and loose rock.

1) 5.8, 30 m. Climb the corner and continue up past a tree to a second larger tree below and right of a right-facing corner. Move up and then across right to a yellow groove. Climb the groove and traverse right again to a ledge.

2) 5.7, 45 m. Climb the earthy groove on the right and then go diagonally rightwards to a tree beneath the left-hand groove noted above.

3) 5.10b, 45 m. Climb the groove, the first ascent used one nut for aid, this has been recently freed, continue to ledges at the top.

4) 5.6, 45 m. Move up and across right to a chimney (note there is a ring bolt belay several meters before the chimney for the climb "Runner Up") and climb this to a tree belay.

5) 5.8, 45 m. Move up for about 3 m and then go diagonally across to an easier groove, which is followed to beneath a steeper section near the top of the cliff.

6) 5.6, 20 m. Move left to a second corner and exit up this.

Runner Up** 5.10d, 200 m, gear standard rack to 4"
double ropes recommended

A. Genereux & J. Jones, Aug. 2002

This climb is located 50 m left of the start for "Heavy Weight Contender." Locate a major stepped right facing corner with an easy ramp leading up to the base of corner. There is a bolt on the face at the top of the ramp. The lower pitches are good but still a bit scruffy, however the upper portion of the route is excellent, particularly the outstanding fourth pitch.

1) 5.10a, 50 m. Climb the ramp to enter the corner past a bolt, follow the stepped corner passing a second bolt for 5 m. As a ledge leads left to the bigger right facing corner a hand crack splits the right wall. Climb the hand crack for 5 m then face climb past three bolts to a large ledge with a tree and a ringbolt belay.

2) 5.10d, 35 m. Climb up easy to a ledge, From here three bolts lead up the bulging face to a shallow right facing corner. Hard moves over an overlap to enter the corner are somewhat height dependent. Continue up the corner, sustained climbing leads past a bolt. The climbing eases at this point into a bay past a bolt to a ringbolt belay.

3) 5.7, 35 m. Climb the shallow right facing corner until it peters out. Easy fourth class up and right to a ring bolt belay.

Runner Up

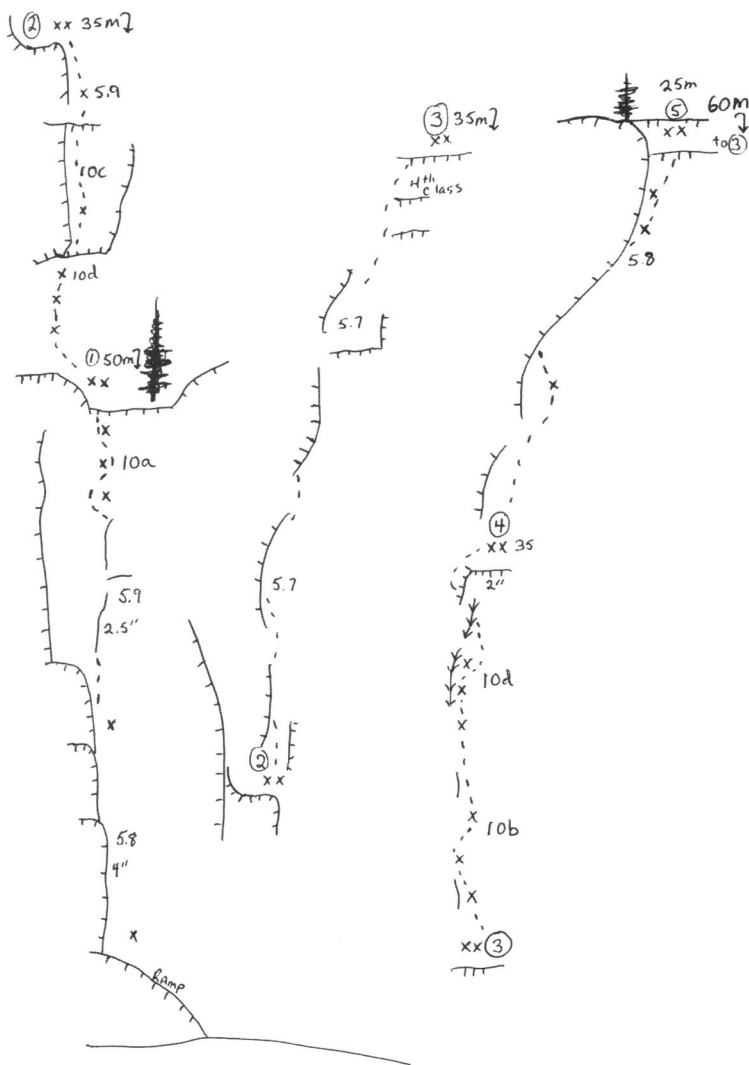

WULLY WALL

Runner Up ** 5.10d, 200 m gear standard rack to 4"

4) 5.10d, 35 m. Face climbs the groove above on impeccable rock. Hard stemming and face holds lead to a small roof, which is turned on the left. The climbing is excellent and sustained. Several wires and gear to 2" required for this mostly fixed pitch.

5) 5.8, 25 m. Head up the slab, aiming for the leaning right facing corner. Climb the corner passing bolts to a ringbolt belay.

Descent: Rappel the route, two ropes required. Pitches 4&5 can be combined as a full 60 m rappel.

Brain of Wull 5.10a, 120 m, gear to 4" (Project)
Greg Fletcher is at work on a climb to the left of "Heavy Weight Contender". Locate a right facing corner in a bay 25 m south of the above-mentioned route. There is a bolt on the face to the right of the corner. So far the climb is established up about two and a half pitches. Hopefully Greg will complete this project in the near future.

Heavy Weight Contender** 5.10b, 190 m, standard rack gear to 4"
A. Genereux & F. Wilkinson, July 2002

Locate this climb to the left of the variation "Direct start for Consolation on page 236. From this corner go down hill and start left of a prominent arête Climb the obvious crack with a moss-covered ledge at the bottom. Both Trevor's route "Rattie the Rope Eater" and "Heavy Weight Contender" start here.

1) 5.8, 50 m. Climb the obvious 5.7 crack for 20 m moving left below an overlap to easier ground. Climb up and slightly left to a bolt right of a tall skinny tree. Passing the tree move left into a small right facing corner climb this for 3 m and exit left up to a groove with two bolts. Climb the groove 5.8 to a good ledge and a ringbolt belay.

2) 5.9, 35 m. Thin moves leave the belay on the right, then climb up and slightly left passing a bolt into a shallow left facing corner. Climb the corner, sustained past a jog then follow ramping holds up and right to a ring bolt belay on the left end of an obvious ledge with a second bolted station to the right for "Rattie the Rope Eater".

3) 5.10b, 15 m. From the ledge traverse left onto the face using thin holds for a meter then up to a bolt, Sustained climbing follows the incipient crack past two bolts (crux). Continue up into a shallow corner to reach a large ledge and ringbolt belay.

4) 5.10a, 35 m. Climb the shallow right leaning corner past five bolts and several gear placements. At the fifth bolt move left and up into a bay with a ring bolt belay.

5) 5.8, 25 m. Move left onto a ramp of grey rock. Awkwardly climb up to a short corner with a bolt on the left wall. Move onto the face past a second bolt. A series of intermittent cracks head up and left on excellent rock to a semi hanging ringbolt belay.

6) 5.10a, 30 m. Climb to the overlap above the belay. Make a hard move up and past a bolt to gain the right facing corner. Layback and stem the corner to the roof that caps it. Make hard moves left onto the face past a bolt, into a shallow corner (the finishing corner of "Consolation') climb this to the top. Locate the ring bolt belay on the right.

Jon Jones leading the crux pitch of Runner Up. Photo: Andy Genereux.

Descent: The Consolation Rappel uses the ringbolt belays of this route to descend on pitches: 6-30 m, 5-57 m, 3-50 m, and 1-50 m. Two 60 m ropes are required, this should become the standard rappel route for many of the climbs in this part of Wully Wall.

Rattie the Rope Eater 5.10c/d, 200 m, gear standard rack to 4"
double ropes recommended
T Jones & R Felber, 2001

This climb starts as for Heavy Weight Contender they share the first pitch until the tall skinny tree is reached at 30 m. The routes cross each other a couple more times to the top of the wall.

The lads had their hands full trying to keep enough rope from the rats so they could actually descend in the gloom before total darkness set in.

1) 5.7, 50 m. Climb the crack 5.7 then move left after 20 m to easier ground. Climb up to a bolt then climb the corner out right of a tall skinny spruce tree. From the corner head right to a leaning groove, up the face then move right to a ledge with a bolt belay below and right of a shallow right facing corner.

2) 5.10b/c, 47 m. Move left past a bolt into the shallow corner. Stay with the corner passing a couple of small overlaps with bolt protection. Above the second overlap there is a difficult section passing two fixed pitons to gain a ledge. Belay at either of two fixed stations on this ledge. The left one is for "Heavyweight Contender" which arrives from the left.

3) 5.8, 50 m. From the left end of the ledge climb the right leaning wide crack for 15 m. Below a bulge traverse left 10 m to a large ledge passing a ringbolt belay to enter the flaring corner at the left end of the ledge. Climb the right facing corner crack. A bolt on the right wall below the bulge protects the crux and eliminates rope drag. Continue up the corner for 5 m, large gear required. Move left onto a slab then up to a two-bolt belay 2 m higher.

4) 5.10a, 45 m. Climb the to a bolt then enter the corner above. Sustained 5.9 climbing up the corner. At the top of the corner is a shattered ledge out left with a bolt belay. It is recommended to avoid this belay and clip the bolt out right on the face. Make a hard traverse right for 2 m. Then climb up intermittent tears, moderate but excellent face climbing past several seams leads to a semi-hanging ringbolt belay. This last bit of climbing below the belay crosses the famous "Consolation" traverse at its left end.

5) 5.10c/d, 30 m. Move left off the belay to an overlap. Climb up past a bolt and make hard face moves right to a line of bolts on the face left of a shallow right facing corner. Sustained climbing leads up to a roof. At the roof move right and climb a short crack to enter the grove above. Climb the groove for 2 m the moves up and right over the bulging face to the top.

Descent: use the new **Consolation Rappel** ringbolts located 2 m left as described under Heavy weight Contender (above).

Consolation Area, Left

CONSOLATION AREA, LEFT

A Project Brain of Wull
B Heavyweight Contender **   5.10b, 190 m   gear standard rack to 4"
C Ratty the Rope Eater **   5.10d, 200 m   gear standard rack to 4"
D Consolation Direct Start *   5.8   gear to 4"
E Consolation ***   5.8, 250 m   gear standard rack to 4"

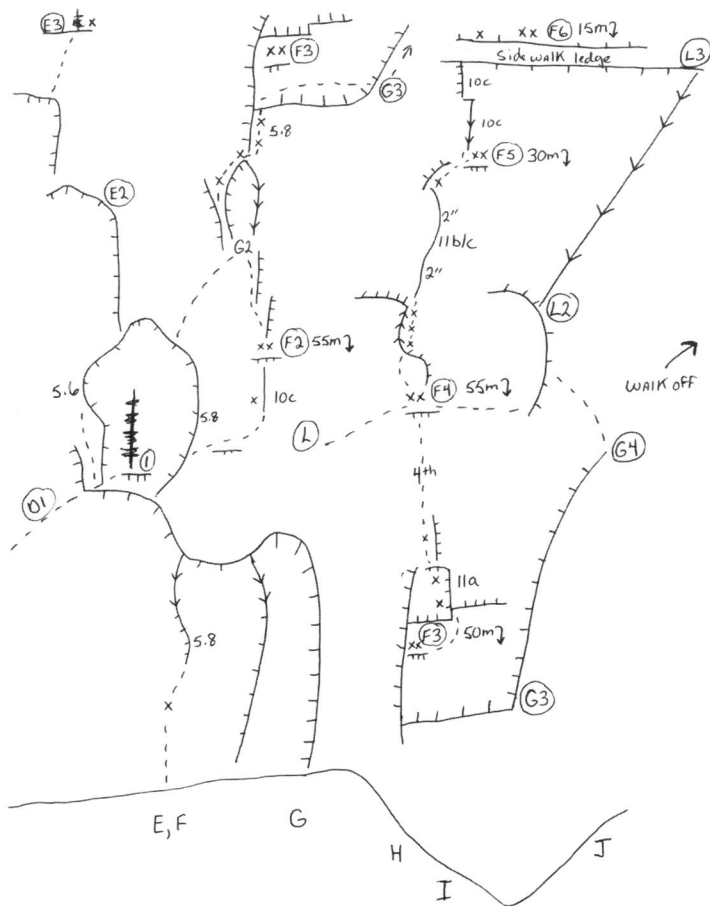

CONSOLATION AREA, RIGHT

E Consolation ***	5.8, 250 m	gear standard rack to 4"
F Wully Sport**	5.11c, 205 m	gear standard rack to 4" multiple 2"
G Wully Watchers *	5.8, 150 m	gear standard rack to 4"
H Project		
I Trace **		5.10d, 145 m
J Snake Bit *	5.9, 145 m	gear standard rack to 4"
K Prize Fight ***	5.11a	optional gear to 3"
L Consolation Direct Finish	5.8	gear to 4"

Consolation

Prize Fight*** 5.11a, 40 m, fixed gear, optional pro to 3"
A. Genereux, Aug. 2002

Climbs the overhangs through the stellar prow directly to the top from the belay at the start of the famed "Consolation" traverse on the sixth pitch. (page 238) To arrive at the belay ledge climb as for either "Consolation" or Heavy Weight Contender." For the later route, climb right up an easy groove from the second bolt on pitch five to the belay ledge of "Consolation." From the belay climb directly up to a small pedestal to enter an open book, with a bolt on the right wall. Sustained climbing leads up and right past 10 bolts (optional gear: wires and a 2.5" & 3" cams could be useful) on very steep and sustained ground. There are at least 4 crux sections in the 10+, 11- range, with sustained 5.10 climbing between. After reaching the top scramble up the scree for 4 m to reach two bolts for the belay.

Descent: use the new Consolation Rappel route 10 m to the left (south).

Consolation Direct start* 5.8+, 60 m, gear to 4"
First ascent unknown

Not really, it climbs the dirty corner 15 m to the left of the regular "Consolation" start. The mossy corner would be quite good if it where cleaned, in its present state is quite challenging for the grade. Belay on gear above the corner then make a rising traverse back right to belay in a corner left of a large tree. Climb the corner to join the regular version of "Consolation." There is potential to push this pitch straight up the wall to make it a truly direct start.

Consolation*** 5.8, 250 m, gear to 4" double ropes recommended
C. Perry & M. White, July 1977

Perhaps the outstanding feature of Wully Wall is the spectacular prow of overhanging rock in the upper portion of the middle of the cliff. The original line of "Consolation" follows a prominent, open book below and right of the prow and, in the finest of limestone traditions, traverses underneath it to exit up slabs on the left. To cate, all of the climbing on this part of the wall has centred around the first few pitches of this classic. As a result, there are numerous variations to any of the seven multi-pitch routes in the area and over the years, a number of alternate pitches and belay options have been developed. The descriptions given below may differ slightly from the more recent preferences indicated on the topo.

The original "Consolation" route is remarkably sustained and has interesting climbing on almost every pitch. Approach via the gully, below and slightly to the right of the climb, as described in the introduction. Start about 10 m left of the top of the scree cone below

A. Brain of Wull	E. Consolation	I. Trace
B. Heavy Weight Contender	F. Wully Sport	J. Snake Bit
C. Ratty the Rope Eater	G. Wully Watchers	K. Prize Fight
D. Consolation Direct Start	H. project	L. Consolation Direct Finish

Consolation

a shallow groove leading to a ledge with a large tree. On the face below the groove is a bolt with an orange hanger about 10 m above the ground.

1) 5.8, 35 m. Climb into the groove past an orange bolt and belay at the tree below a short right-facing corner.

2) 5.7, 40 m. Climb the corner and continue more easily to ledges at the foot of the open book. A belay can be taken here or after moving up and left into the main corner and then out to a ledge on the left wall by a small pinnacle.

2) alt. 5.7, 40 m. Move left over blocks for about 3 m and climb an easier corner up to the open book.

3) 5.6, 45 m. Move up into the open book and then go diagonally left across the wall past a blocky section until almost at a gully. Move up and back right to a small ledge with a flake. Either belay here or make awkward moves up and right to reach easier ground.

4) 15 m. Scramble up to a below a lower band of overhangs.

5) 5.7, 35 m. Follow the slabs up and left beneath the overhangs past a piton to ledges that lead left round the edge of the buttress immediately below yellow roofs. Descend slightly to a bolt belay.

4 & 5) alt. 5.7. From a piton belay by a small tree on the left at the top of pitch 3, move steeply left and climb a diagonal break up and left to reach the top of the fifth pitch to a bolted belay.

6) 5.8, 30 m. Climb up to a horizontal break in the slab and make a delicate foot traverse left to easier ground. Continue up and left to a small, exposed ledge. Climb up a short distance to clip a new ringbolt belay ("Heavyweight Contender" & "Ratty the Rope Eater") and continue to traverse down and left around a steep arête to a ledge with a bolt belay.

7) 5.8, 35 m. Move up right with difficulty to regain the arête. Continue up a corner and then either move left slightly to climb a shallow groove or go directly up, past a piton and a small roof with a second piton, to the top.

Descent: Rappel from new ringbolt stations (the **"Consolation Rappel"**) directly down the face from the completion of this climb. Two 60 m ropes required, rappel lengths are 30 m, 57 m, 50 m and 50 m from top to bottom. See page 233.

Consolation Direct Finish 5.8, gear to 4"
T. Higgins, R. Hoare & M. White, 1979

This is hardly a direct finish as it simply traverses in the opposite direction from the normal route. The "Direct Finish" is somewhat more obvious than the normal route but was originally avoided because Chris wanted to add a few more pitches of "real" climbing. The true direct is up the amazing prow that both routes convenient y avoid, now climbed by the fantastic "Prize Fight". From the top of pitch 4 (verbal description) on "Consolation," move up to the right and cross "Wully Sport" to a corner/crack system that trends up right to the top. A wide section higher up can be either climbed directly or by traversing onto the right wall for a few moves.

Wullywatchers* 5.8, 150 m, gear to 4"
N. Hellewell & B. McKeith, May 1978

"Wullywatchers" is a similar butt shorter less desirable sister route to "Consolation" it shares the same second pitch with "Consolation," which begins just to the left. It then heads out right to head directly up the excellent open book before exiting out right up easy slabs. One could then move left to join up with the finish of "Consolation Direct." The climb is worth doing for its third pitch up the open book.

1) 5.7, 45 m. Climb the right-facing corner at the top of an obvious scree cone about 10 m right of "Consolation." Move across left and up to the tree belay on that route.

2) 5.7, 40 m. Continue as for "Consolation," then move right to the foot of an open book.

3) 5.8, 35 m. Climb a shallow, the left right-facing corner to the top of a small pillar in the open book (avoid the corner on the right that is loose). Move up right past a piton into the corner, and continue up with difficulty past an overhang (2 bolts) into the corner above. Ignore the fixed station of "Wully Sport" near the top of the open book 10 m above. Instead, traverse right 5 m to a ledge at the base of an exit groove with a natural gear belay.

4) 5.6, 30 m. Climb the right leaning groove that leads to easy slabs above. Scramble up to the top of the cliff.

Wully Sport** 205 m, 5.11b/c, 205 m, gear standard rack to 4' multiple 2"
A. Genereux & G. Rinke, Sept. 1995

"Wully Sport" is a longer much harder and more direct version of "Wullywatchers" that finishes up a very impressive hand crack (the crack will eat up to four # 2 friends) that ascends the steep headwall above the main open-book corner.

1) 5.8, 35 m. Climb the first pitch of "Consolation" to the tree belay.

2) 5.10c, 20 m. Move right and up across the face to a bolt. Move right again and then make difficult moves up to gain a shallow seam. Climb this to a bolt belay at a small ledge (Pitches 1 and 2 may be done as one 50 m lead using double rope techniques).

3) 5.9, 50 m. Climb up and slightly left following several seams to gain the bottom of the open book of "Wullywatchers." The pitch may be split here. Continue as for "Wullywatchers" past the overhang and up to a fixed station below the large roof at the top of the open-book corner.

4) 5.11a, 50 m. Move right from the belay for about 3 m and climb up past two bolts on the right side of the overhang (short but strenuous) to gain a ledge above on the left. Continue up a shallow corner above past a bolt and then wander up easy ground (crossing "Consolation Direct") for about 25 m to a bolt belay below the exit crack in the headwall.

5) 5.11b/c, 35 m. Traverse left for about 3 m and climb up past a left-facing corner and three bolts to a bay below an overhang. Move right under the overhang until it is possible to climb up past a bolt into a superb, curving crack in the headwall. Climb

the crack with sustained moves for 25 m to a roof and then traverse right to a bolt belay. This great pitch offers full value for its grade.

6) 5.10c, 15 m. Continue up a shallow corner to a ledge and then climb a crack and layback flake to a wide ledge just below the top. From a bolt move right along the ledge to a bolted chain belay.

Descent: Rappel the route, or take the good ledge left to the top of the cliff then continue left for another 20 m to the ring bolts for the preferred **"Consolation Rappel"** (see page 233).

Project 45 m
Mostly bolted two-pitch sport climb to the left of "Trace." Has been left unfinished for a few years by Anthony Nielson.

Trace** 5.10d, 145 m, fixed gear
A. Nielson & S. Huisman, Aug. 1998

The only true sport route on the wall. It starts just left of the drainage gully where the "Consolation" approach trail arrives at the main wall.

1) 5.10d, 45 m. After two bolts make hard moves up and left to continue clipping closely spaced bolts to a dipping ledge and the belay.

2) 5.9, 40 m. Several bolts diagonal up and left across the face then climb to the base of a groove the belay is on a small ledge to the left.

3) 5.6, 15 m. Climb the groove to stepped tears to a ledge and belay.

4) 5.10b, 45 m. Climb a short corner above the belay then move up and right to gain a second corner. Sustained but excellent stemming ascends the corner to a bolted belay.

Descent: Rappel the route, with double 60 m ropes this can be done in two rappels from the top of pitches four and two.

Snake Bit* 5.8,145 m, gear to 4"
T. Jones & R. Felber, 2001

Climbs the corner system to the right of "Trace". Start 5 m up and right from the bottom of the drainage gully. The climb could use a bit of straightening out and would benefit from having its own bolted belays. The first part of the climb was first climbed in 1998 by Anthony Nielson, Karen McNiel and Nancy Hanson and was used to establish "Trace" to the left. The name for this route comes from the fact Rick was bitten by his pet snake earlier in the day.

1) 5.7, 35 m. Climb the corner into a bay to a natural stance.

2) 5.7, 40 m. Continue up the corner to belay below a slabby section.

3) 5.8, 35 m. Climb the slab past two bolts to reach a left leaning corner. Climb the corner to join the route "Trace" bolt belay.

4) 5.8 or 5.10a, 45 m. Angle up and right to gain a stepped right facing corner. Either climb the lower arching corner (5.10a) or stay out right on the face to enter the corner higher up (5.8). Continue up the corner to a ledge on top, move left along the ledge to a bolted belay for the route "Trace."

Descend by rappelling "Trace".

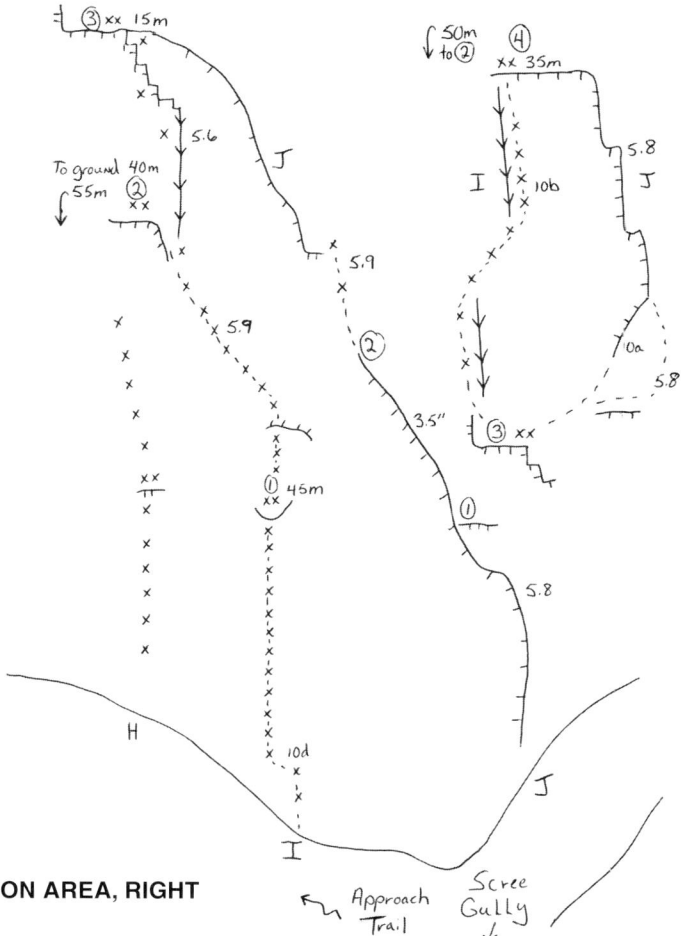

CONSOLATION AREA, RIGHT

H Project
I Trace **   5.10d,145 m
J Snake Bit *   5.9, 145 m,   gear standard rack to 4"

SENTINEL CLIFF

This is the last cliff on the south (west) side of the valley before the river bends around to the west. It is almost 2 kilometres long with rock that varies from exceptional to very bad. The main cliff faces east, but the northern end of it rises virtually right out of the Ghost River where it makes the 90 degree turn. This north-facing section is very steep with large overhangs. The crag's namesake was an Inukshuk built by Bugs McKeith, which once stood at the base of the cliff. Considerably longer than it is tall, Sentinel Cliff has several pockets of excellent rock that have seen some development. The cliff is described in three sections: "The South End," "Sentinel Bluffs," which is a pseudo-sport climbing area, and "Sentinel Crag." The obvious feature of the cliff is the large, open bay just left of centre. This is the home to the two-pitch crack known as "Cyclops" (5.10b), one of the better traditional routes in the Ghost. Sentinel Bluffs lies below and about 200 m to the left.

Despite the existence of some modern sport climbs, there are several routes on Sentinel Bluffs from the early pseudo sport-climbing era. Some of these routes have run-outs on easier ground exceeding 10 m!

There is extensive potential for moderate two and three pitch routes both bolted and traditional styled climbs available. As well there are several pockets of exceptional stone, which are still untapped that should produce some excellent harder sport routes.

Approach

Cross the bridge over the diversion canal near Wully Wall. Continue north along the main road through the trees until it opens up and a secondary road comes in from behind on the right (about 0.9 km from the bridge). A cairn marks an indistinct trail 50 m further on that heads uphill just to the left of a large scree slope that is hidden from the road by timber. About 30 minutes of steep uphill slogging should put you near the top of a scree cone on the right side of the Bluffs near the route "The Surprise."

Approach as for Sentinel Bluffs. The "South End" is located about 200 m south of the Sentinel Bluffs. With more development it would be worthwhile to establish a trail up from the drainage separating Sentinel Crag from Wully Wall. For now you need to traverse left from the "Bluffs" crossing two drainage gullies separated by a small lateral moraine. After the second drainage continue 50 m to an obvious right facing corner with a grassy ramp leading up to it. This is the line of "Stretcher Case" to the left on the rolling face is "Ambulance Chaser." Note you will require small profile carabiners to clip into the vintage Dave Morgan bolts. There is a bolted belay with aluminum hangers to the left of the corner. Dave couldn't remember much about these climbs or even the fact that there were actually two climbs. It was Trevor Jones who rediscovered these lost routes several years later. He then promptly forgot about them until recently. The rock is very good on this part of the cliff. The wall should relinquish several more excellent climbs in a wide range of grades.

Ambulance Chaser* 5.9, 50 m, gear to 2"
D. Morgan & T. Friesen, 1987

Climbs up a shallow groove through a rolling grey face with a few spacious bolts to a bolted anchor.

Stretcher Case** 5.10a, 50 m, gear to 4"
D. Morgan & T. Friesen, 1987

Scramble up easy grass covered ledges to a bolt belay left of the corner. Climb the corner with increasing difficulty to a belay.

SENTINEL BLUFFS

Sentinel Bluffs has many routes of a more moderate grade and the rock is above-average quality. The best routes are the face/friction climbs with the obvious breaks having the poorest rock. Gear recommendations are listed. Most of the routes were established from the ground-up, some with very little gear. Many of the bolts have home-made hangers and may require small profile carabiners to clip. It is a fine destination in itself or can easily be combined with one or more routes on Sentinel Crag to the right. This area still holds plenty of potential for new routes. The possibilities for moderate face climbs on impeccable rock are excellent.

Descent
All of the Sentinel Bluff routes are descended via fixed anchors. Double ropes required for most climbs

Project
A bolted belay is found up an easy left leaning corner from the top of the scree cone that marks the south end of the Sentinel Bluffs before you descend the next drainage gully to the south. Not much is known about this climb other than the first pitch is 5.4. The second pitch possibly takes a wide crack up and right.

Minou* 5.10a, 35 m, fixed gear
A. Skuce & A. Geoffry, 1987

"Minou" is a fun face-climbing route with the hard climbing well protected.

Centrefold** 10a, 25 m, fixed gear
A. Skuce & A. Geoffry, 1987

A very good route which starts from a short crack. Climb the crack to gain the first of two bolts that protect the crux and then the climbing eases toward the belay.

Pinup* 5.8, 30 m, gear to 2.5"
A. Skuce & A. Geoffry, 1986

This is a mixed-gear route that was rap bolted with natural gear placements left intact.

Black Mango 5.8, 35 m, gear wires
A. Skuce & A. Geoffry, 1985

This route was done in order to access the top of the previous three routes. Climb the left-facing, shallow corner to a bolt belay to the right. Originally the route went left and continued toward the top of the crag—not recommended.

Creeping Senility* 5.9, 35 m, gear wires
D. Morgan, D. Kemp & B. Huseby, 1986

This route was named by the late Dennis Kemp who was 60 at the time of the first ascent, he thought the name appropriate.

Softly, Softly*** 5.10b/R, 35 m, gear wires
D. Morgan, 1986

This is an outstanding face climb that requires the leader to be steady at the stated grade.

Twinkle Toes*** 5.10b, 40 m, gear to 2.5"
A. Genereux & C. Genereux, 1990

"Twinkle Toes" offers excellent face climbing similar to "Softly, Softly." It was the first route in the area to be bolted on-sight, on-lead with a power drill. As a result it has more reasonable protection than "Softly, Softly."

Feeling Groovy* 5.9, 50 m, gear to 2.5"
D. Morgan & B. Huseby, 1985

This good traditional climb with spacious gear, it climbs the corner just right of "Twinkle Toes."

Diagonal* 5.8, 75 m, gear to 2"
D. Morgan & B. Huseby, 1985

Pitch one follows an arch moving right over the steep headwall of "Prickly Fear." The second pitch is more run out on face climbing.

Prickly Fear* 5.11b, 30 m, fixed gear
D. Morgan & D. Kemp, 1986

Climb a short, steep headwall past three bolts to gain runout 5.8 ground. Most people don't bother with the second pitch of 5.8.

Last Mango in Paradise** 5.10c/R, 45 m, gear wires & RP'S
D. Morgan & B. Huseby, 1985

This Morgan classic was done in the finest British fashion of meager gear on good rock. Face climb to a corner crack to finish.

Dog's Life 5.7, 45 m, gear to 4"
D. Morgan & B. Huseby, 1985

This is a scrappy corner crack with some loose sections.

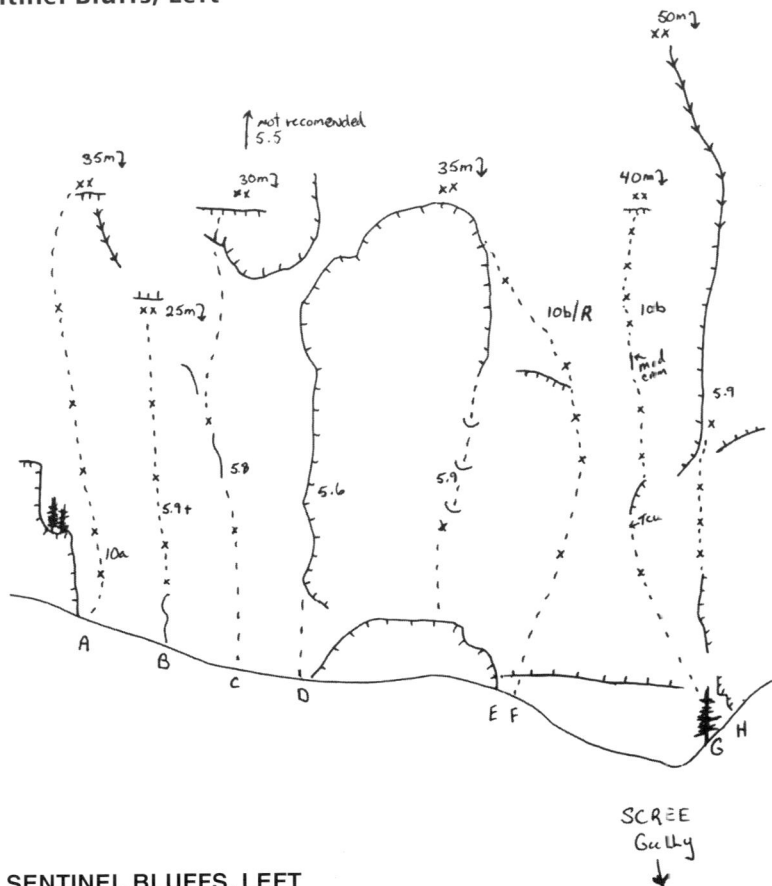

SENTINEL BLUFFS, LEFT

A	Minou *	5.10a	
B	Centrefold**	5.10a	
C	Pin-Up *	5.8	wires, RP's, med. cams
D	Black Mango	5.8	wires
E	Creeping Senility *	5.9	wires
F	Softly, Softly ***	5.10b/R	wires
G	Twinkle Toes ***	5.10b	wires, TCU's, med. Cam
H	Feeling Groovy *	5.9	wires, TCU's

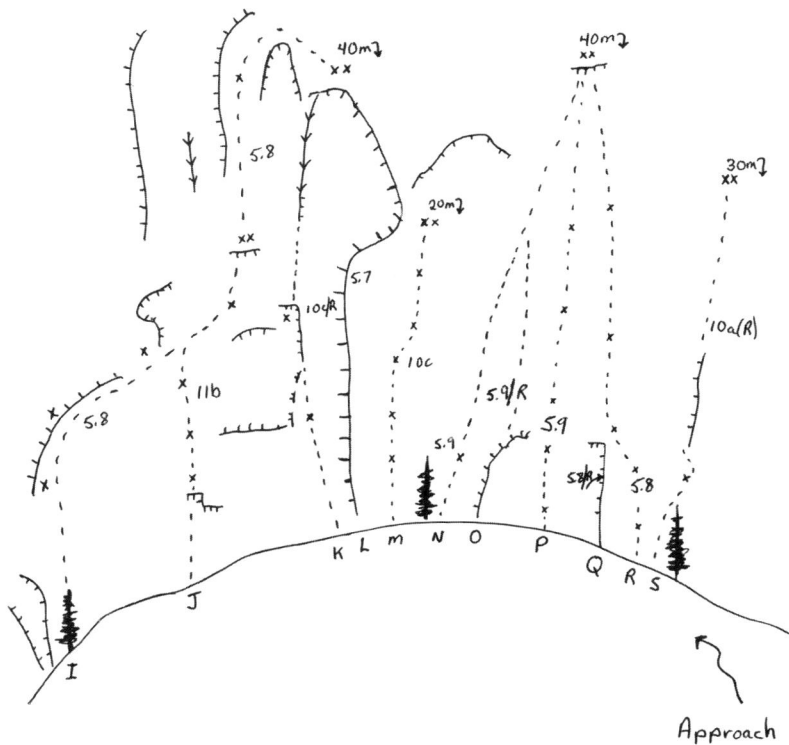

SENTINEL BLUFFS, RIGHT

I	Diagonal *	5.8	wires
J	Prickly Fear *	5.11a	
K	Last Mango In Paradise **	5.10c/R	wires, RP's
L	Dog's Life	5.7	gear to 4"
M	Buddha Belly **	5.10c	
N	Static Cling *	5.9/R	wires
O	Skylark	5.9/R	gear to 3.5"
P	Menagerie ***	5.9	wires
Q	Little Gem **	5.8/R	wires
R	Koala Springs *	5.8	wires
S	The Surprise	5.10a/R	wires

Buddha Belly** 5.10c, 20 m, fixed gear

A. Genereux & C. Genereux, 1990

"Buddha Belly" was done the same day as "Twinkle Toes" and also established from the ground up with the Hilti. It is a fun little face climb and the name describes the leader's "third lung."

Static Cling* 5.9/R, 40 m, gear wires

A. Skuce & D. Morgan, 1985

Climb the flake left of "Menagerie" to its top and make delicate moves out left to continue up the face. This route would be more fun with some protection; it is basically soloing at the stated grade with some protection for the crux sections.

Skylark 5.9/R, 40 m, gear to 3.5"

D. Morgan (solo), 1985

Read the comments in the previous route description for an idea about the character of "Skylark." For the faint of heart, both routes can be top roped from the fixed station of "Menagerie."

Menagerie*** 5.9, 40 m, gear wires

D. Morgan, B. Huseby & A. Geoffry, 1985

This is one of the best routes at the Bluffs and fortunately it has some decent protection. Climb the centre of the wall to the left of "Little Gem" to a bolt at 6 m Steep climbing on big holds leads to a large scoop that is climbed to the belay of "Little Gem."

Little Gem** 5.8/R, 40 m, gear wires

D. Morgan, 1985

Hard, unprotectable moves off the ground lead to a groove and a bolt some distance above. Climb the low-angled rib above to easier ground.

Koala Springs** 5.8, 40 m, gear wires

I. Freeman, B. Huseby, A. Geoffry, 1985

This route was bolted on rappel by Dave Morgan and then led, on-sight, by the all-women's team of Isobel, Bev and Annick. It is a fun direct start to "Little Gem" that leads up a steep face past three bolts to the lower-angled face above.

The Surprise 5.10a/R, 30 m, gear wires

D. Morgan, 1985

This is one of the more serious routes at the Bluffs and to date may not be repeated. Climb to a bolt and then up left with difficulty into a corner. Easier climbing leads to a bolt belay left of the corner.

SENTINEL CRAG

Two hundred meters right of the Bluffs near the route "Déja-Vu," Sentinel Cliff takes a dramatic shift in steepness. As the cliff heads north it becomes steeper and has more well-defined features. It culminates in the large blocky overhangs on its north face directly above the North Ghost parking area. This entire area right of the Bluffs is called Sentinel Crag. Only the area around the "Cyclops" bay has been explored even though the north end is easily the Ghost's most accessible rock.

Approach

Hike up to the base of the cliff as per the Bluffs area, see page 242 for details. Once at the base of the cliff head right in a short while you'll be headed down the right side of a scree cone. Go to the bottom of the cone and up and over another slightly larger scree cone. At the bottom of this second scree cone is a left-facing corner that is the start to "Déja-Vu."

Continue traversing 20 m further right to three climbs that start from the base of the lower wall. To continue up to the "Cyclops" bay and access for the rest of the routes on the crag. Climb up a steep slope to a short scruffy cliff below the bay. Continue north past the bay for 20-30 m until it is possible to easily scramble up to a large-ledge system below the route "Cyclops".

Descent

"Duveinafees" has its own rappel bolts while all other multi-pitch routes in this area descend via "Cyclops." Some of the trees at the very edge of the "Cyclops" finish are eroding away and are not suitable for anchors. There is a large, forked tree up and right of the bay that presents a fine anchor. Rappel 30 m to the bolt belay as for pitch one of "Cyclops." Another 40 m rappel leads to the ground.

Déja-Vu 5.8, 135 m, gear to 4" & pitons
N. Hellewell, B. McKeith & D. Knaak, Sept. 1975

The climb follows a system of corners in the stepped buttress just left of "Cyclops." From the right end of the Sentinel Bluffs follow the crag to the right and go over the top of the next scree cone to an obvious large corner system.

1) 5.6, 45 m. Climb the open corner at the base of the buttress to a large ledge system. Scramble up and right to belay off the largest tree (20 cm diameter) directly below a steep hand crack.

2) 5.7, 50 m. About 5 m right of the steep crack you now follow a broken groove up to a large ledge. From the ledge, climb up and right over a steep slab, overcome a small overhang (5.7) to easier ground and a small ledge. Traverse left to belay off a large tree.

3) 5.8, 40 m. Above the belay there is a flared corner with a snag hanging out over the top. Follow this to the top of the crag.

Descent Make a somewhat exposed traverse right (45 m) through steep trees to the top of the "Cyclops" bay and rappel as for that route.

Vuja-Dé* 5.9, 140 m, gear to 4"
First ascent unknown.

This climb consists essentially of variations on pitches 2 and 3 of "Déja-Vu," which were established at various times in the last 20 years.

1) 5.6, 45 m. Climb the first pitch of "Déja-Vu."

2) 5.9, 50 m. From the tree climb the steep hand crack directly above (5.9) to a large ledge. Either traverse right into the corner of "Déja-Vu" or climb an easy break that leads slightly right to the base of a good grey slab. Move back left on big holds to a cam placement, then continue up the unprotectable slab (5.6) to belay off a large tree.

3) 5.8+, 45 m. Traverse under the flaring corner of "Déja-Vu" to a right-facing corner capped by a roof. Climb up the corner, then face climb up to the edge of the roof (fixed pitons) and continue into a prominent flake on the upper slab. Follow this to the top and the first treed ledge. Climb another short rock band to belay off trees.

Descent Make a somewhat exposed traverse right (40 m) through steep trees to the top of the "Cyclops" bay and rappel as for that route.

Fromage** 5.8, 32 m, gear to 4"
S. Midwinter & L. Nichols, Oct. 2002

Start as for "Suffrage" to the first bolt then angle up and left behind the spruce tree, on steep textured rock to a small roof. Traverse left along the roof for 2 m then climb up on several horizontal pockets to gain a small arête to the bolted anchor. There is some thought that this route might be sport bolted depending on the quality of natural protection that would be a shame.

Suffrage** 5.10a, 25 m, fixed gear
L. Nichols and S. Midwinter, 2002

Located just right of a large spruce tree it climbs past several bolts then right at the top to share an ringbolt anchor with the route to the right.

Slack Jawed Blondage* 5.8, 25 m, gear to 2"
L. Nichols and S. Midwinter, 2002

Located 2 m right of "Suffrage" it climbs a shallow groove past a couple of bolts then climbs the prickled grey face to a ring bolt Anchor.

Monster Mash 5.9, 60 m, gear to 3"
D. Morgan & T. Friesen, 1982

According to Dave's rapidly waning memory, this climbs the wall just to the right of the arête that defines the left edge of the "Cyclops" bay. The details are lost but it "might have a crack to start and probably joins the arête higher up." Put some adventure back into your climbing and have a look, the rock looks great.

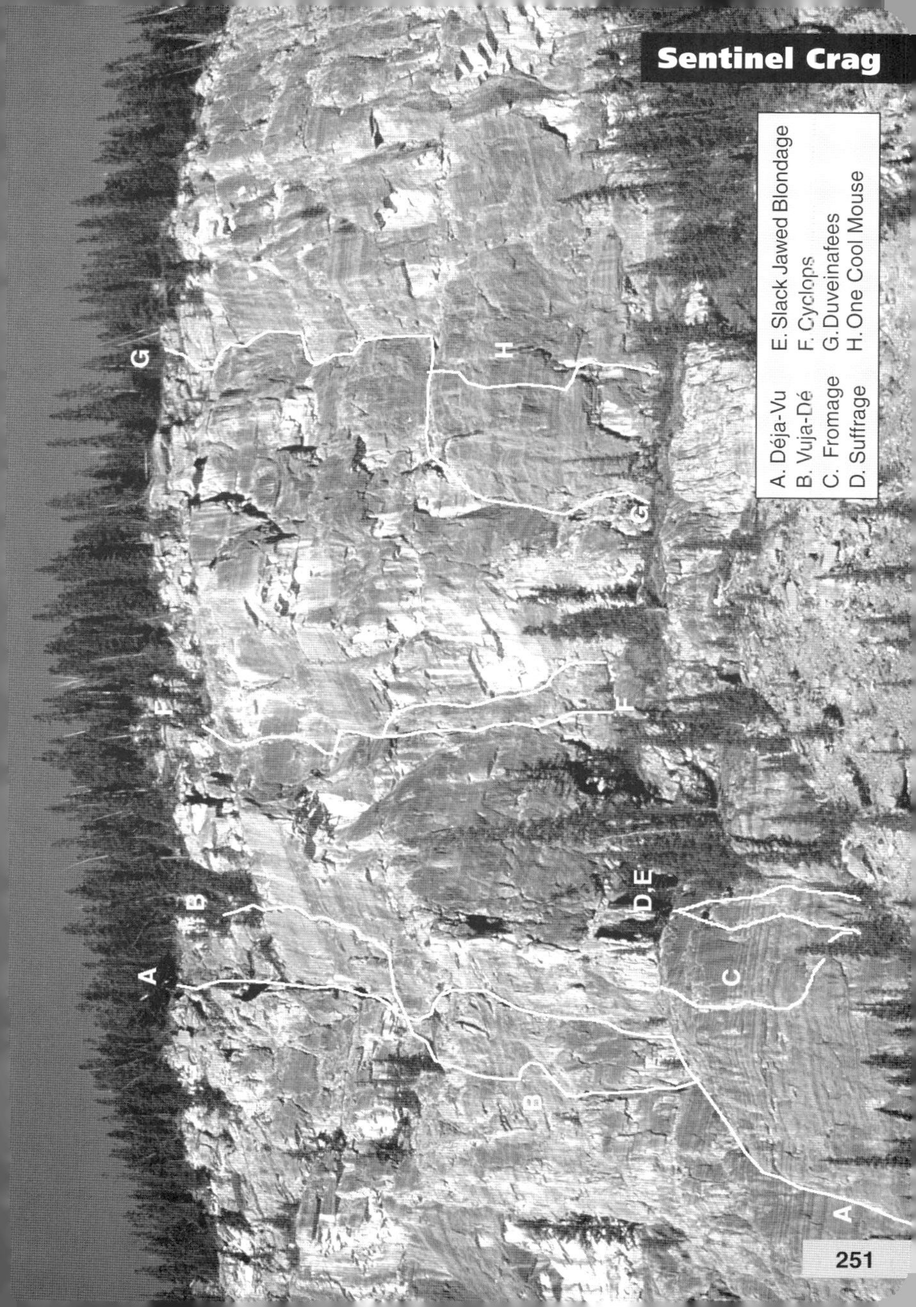

Sentinel Crag

A. Déja-Vu
B. Vuja-Dé
C. Fromage
D. Suffrage
E. Slack Jawed Blondage
F. Cyclops
G. Duveinafees
H. One Cool Mouse

Sentinel Crag, Left

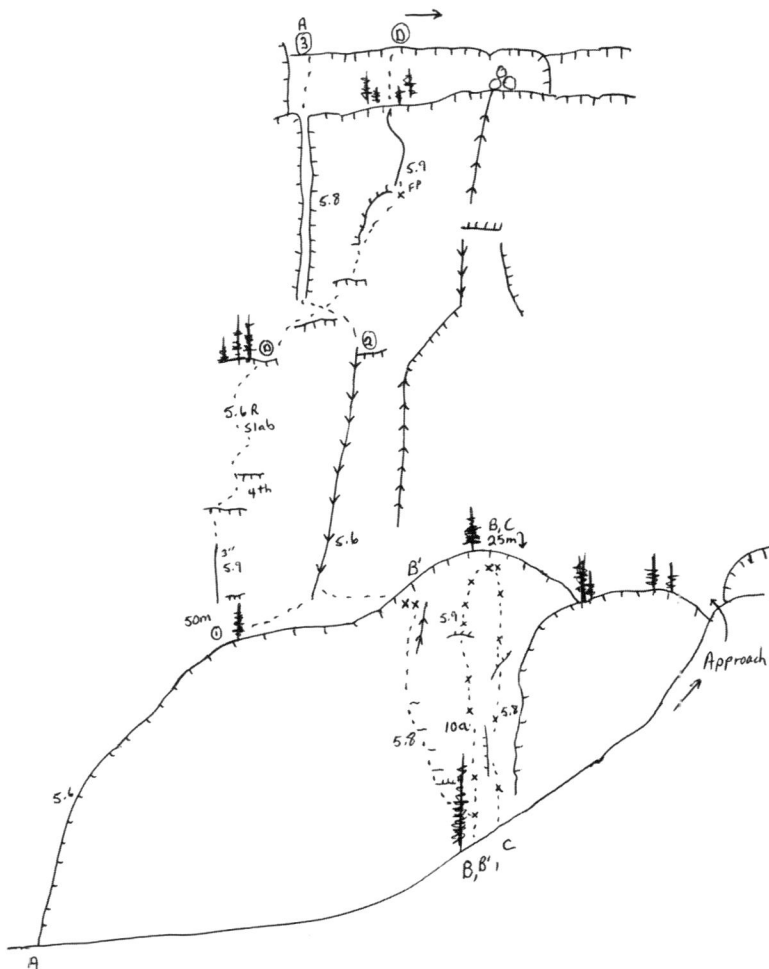

SENTINEL CRAG, LEFT

A	De'ja-Vu		5.8 gear standard rack to 4" & pitons
B	Suffrage **	5.10a	
B'	Fromage **	5.8	gear to 4"
C	Slack Jawed Blondage *	5.8	gear to 2 "
D	Vuja-De' *	5.9	gear standard rack to 4"

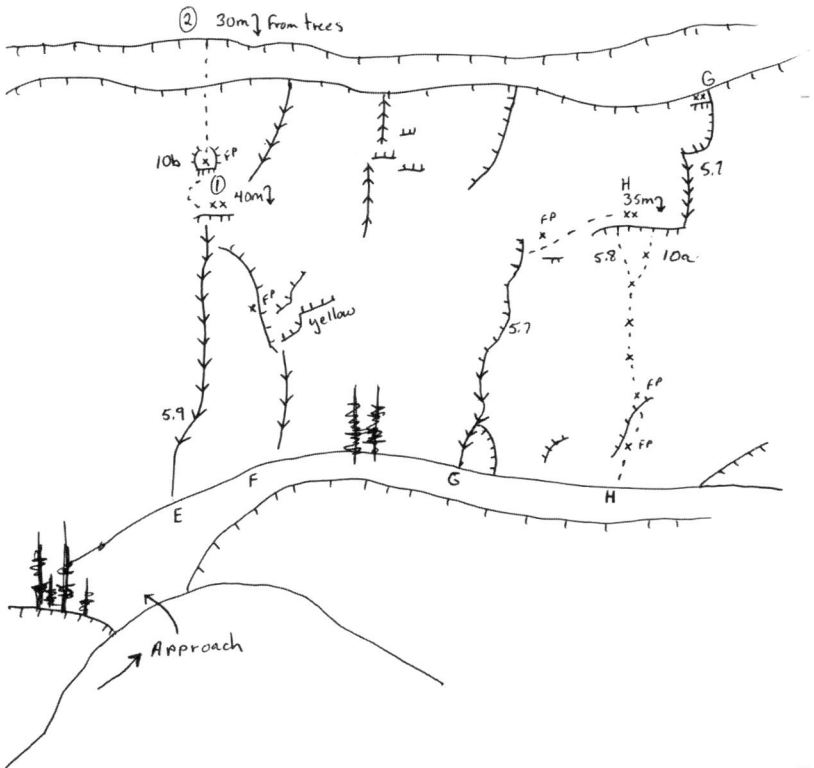

SENTINEL CRAG, RIGHT

E	Cyclops ***	5.10b	gear standard rack to 4" multiples 2"-3"
E	Cyclops Variation Start ***	5.10b	gear standard rack to 4" multiples 2"-3"
G	Duveinafees **	5.7	gear to 4"
H	One Cool Mouse **	5.10a	

Sentinel Crag, Right

Cyclops*** 5.10b, 70 m, gear to 4"
A. Sole & G. Spohr, June 1978
Alternate first pitch: Adrian Burgess & E. Brooke

This is an original Ghost River classic that remains near the top of the heap for quality and character. Two different variations are available for the first pitch. Both are recommended and converge on the same belay. The climb finishes up a crack in the centre of a beautiful slab. The alternate first pitch was originally done as a mistake while looking for the route "Duveinafees." In a fit of poor memory, Nigel Hellewell was convinced that it climbed this crack, joined "Cyclops" at the belay, and finished out right. Thus, the original Chris Perry guide showed it as such. When Burgess and Brooke came to repeat "Duveinafees," a 5.7 route, and found hard 5.9 climbing, they realized something was amiss.

1) 5.10a, 40 m. The original route climbs the obvious crack on the left side of the bay. It has several overhanging sections that lead to a bolt belay on a small stance below the upper slab on the right side.

1) alt. 5.9, 40 m. A slightly easier variation that climbs the corner crack right of the original route. It traverses left under a blocky, yellow overhang after about 15 m.

2) 5.10b, 30 m. Traverse left from the belay and then up to the horizontal edge. Traverse out to the edge to the obvious square ledge in the middle of the slab. Make a difficult mantle to a bolt (crux) and continue up the crack (awkward at first) to the top and a suitable belay tree some ways back from the lip. It is also possible to bridge up the groove directly above the belay and then move left to the crux mantle.

Duveinafees** 5.7, 80 m, gear to 4"
A. Sole & N. Hellewell, June 1978

For years, this climb suffered from confusion over its location (see "Cyclops" story above). Recent unearthing (literally) has rediscovered this very fine two-pitch crack climb. It begins in the major corner system just around right from" Cyclops."

1) 5.7, 40 m. Climb the corner (loose at first) to a fine layback crack that leads to a large overhang. Traverse right under the overhang to a mossy ledge. Scramble up to a higher ledge (piton) and traverse easily right for 5 m to a two-bolt belay.

2) 5.7, 40 m. Traverse right past a tree to a corner. Follow the nice corner to a large overhang and traverse right under the overhang into a splitter layback crack (recently unearthed). Follow this to a two-bolt belay on a ledge to the left.

Opposite: Albi Sole on the first ascent of Cyclops. Photo: Greg Spohr.

One Cool Mouse** 5.10a, 35 m, fixed gear
B. Spear & J. Josephson, July 1996

This is a friction climb up the wall of excellent black rock to the left of "Duveinafees." Begin just left of a small cave 20 m right of the "Duveinafees" start. Climb up large jugs past a piton to a second piton (needs replacing with a bolt). Traverse left around an exposed arête to a stance and a bolt. Climb up past three more bolts with the crux mantle coming at the last bolt. Finish up an easy groove to the first bolt belay of "Duveinafees." From the third bolt it is possible to climb an unprotectable groove (5.8) to the left, bypassing the final bolt.

The Sentinel Triangle

Considering the vast amount of memory loss that has surrounded the routes of this crag, the author couldn't help but ponder the existence of some ephemeral, magnetic field or substance that leads to chronic forgetfulness. It appears to be just like the "Bermuda Triangle," only different. Beware! As well as the "Duveinafees" story and the routes "Stretcher Case," "Ambulance Chaser" and "Monster Mash" mentioned above, there are the following vague reports.

From Dave Morgan: Right of "Cyclops" and "Duveinafees" with Albi Sole, probably '82 or '83 called "Frosties."

From Peter Charkiw: A difficult roof above a large boulder that has 'God is Love' scrawled on it (the inscription is now difficult to read).

From Bill Stark: A couple of lines where the cliff meets the river; but no recollection of what, where or when they were climbed.

Or the climb described below; a more recent addition to this phenomenon.

If only I could Remember 5.8, 80 m, gear to 4″
G. Fletcher, J.C. Debeau & G McNmauh, about five years ago?

Climb somewhere left of the big roofs where the river meets the north end of the wall. The first pitch goes at 5.8 to a bolted anchor. "The second pitch was about 5.7 to the top of the crag but it's better forgotten: well that's what I remember." "Oh ya! we found part of an old stopper on the first pitch so it might have been climbed before." The author spent a half-hour trying to spot the line or anchor to this vague climb with no luck. Maybe you will have more success.

Opposite: A view of the North Ghost and Mount Aylmer with
STD Crag in the foreground: Photo Andy Genereux.

NORTH GHOST VALLEY

The north face of Sentinel Cliff (see map on page 176), Silver-Tongued Devil, Bastion Wall, Alberta Jam and Sunset Boulevard all lie at or beyond where the Ghost River makes a 90 degree turn to the west. Being farthest away from the Big Hill, in the past it they were the least visited cliffs in the area.

This has certainly has changed since the last guide. Silver Tongued Devil Crag has turned into one of the premium moderate sport cliffs in the Ghost growing from three early traditional lines to explode to almost forty climbs. Many of which are multi pitch sport climbs. Bastion wall has seen a doubling of climbs. As well a few new lines surround Alberta Jam including the hardest technical climb to date in the Ghost "Dionysus" 12d/13a/R. Early forays into the region tended to pluck the best lines closest to the car. "Thor," "Alberta Jam" and "Sunset Boulevard" in particular might be three of the top five traditional routes in the Ghost. The trend has continued with the "storming of the Bastion" that saw several new climbs all follow predominantly traditional lines. Seemingly endless untouched cliffs extend west up the Ghost River and to the north along Johnson Creek and into the Waiparous region, as well as up most every side drainage and canyon that flow into the Ghost River. Several explorations have been made into the Malamute Valley with a couple of projects underway. Other than a few tentative forays much of this area beyond the cliffs mentioned above remains untouched.

Parking Access

From the diversion canal bridge, continue north through some trees for 0.9 km to where a smaller road comes in from behind on the right. The east-facing Sentinel Cliff is directly above you at this point. To reach the crags continue for 500 m or so to where the river turns west and the road merges onto the rocky flood plain. Park here unless you are feeling particularly macho. Silver-Tongued Devil Crag is directly above you on the right across the river.

Sunset Boulevard crag lies on the south side of the river just over two km west of the North Ghost parking access at the 90 degree bend in the river. It is a large north-facing cliff consisting of a lower tier 40-80 m high and almost a kilometre long. This alone would be impressive if it weren't for the fact that the upper tier is just as long and closer to 200 m high!

There are only three established routes on the lower tier and the upper cliff is unclimbed. "Sunset Boulevard" lies on the eastern end of the lower cliff band and its elegant arching dihedral (right-facing) cannot be missed. The other two routes are found right of the centre of the crag and both are mixed ice climbs called "Burning in Water, Drowning in Flame" and "The Sliver."

Dave Morgan was the first person to find and start on the unmistakable line of "Sunset Boulevard". He rappelled and cleaned the upper pitch and placed one bolt. However, he refused to top rope the pitch and set about establishing the climb from the ground up. Shortly after this, Andy Genereux spied the line and established the first pitch left of where Dave was working. On rappel he discovered Morgan's bolts. The two then embarked on a joint effort in which they were to take turns at establishing the upper pitch. Morgan refused to allow either one of them to do any "hanging or dogging."

The first day saw several attempts fail at the first crux. On the second day Andy finally overcame the technical difficulty of the lower crux and arrived at the second crux only to find he didn't have a carabiner to fit the home-made hanger Dave had previously fixed. This resulted in Andy launching into a 10 meter upside down fall and he relinquished the lead. Dave made it through the first crux but was unable to solve the second one. Andy had another turn, this time armed with the proper quick draw.

Approach

Park at the bend in the river below Silver-Tongued Devil Crag. If you have a good 4WD with clearance you can often make it closer to the crag or even park at its base. Be forewarned that spring floods have been changing the track/road on a regular basis and the river crossings can be rather deep.

When on foot there is a river crossing right after the parking area that can usually be avoided on the left (south) bank. Pick up a faint trail below the north facing Sentinel Crag and continue upstream along the south bank to the old road. When you have travelled almost to the end of a long straight section of road, (about 30 min) there is a fork that crosses the river to the right. From this point looking north across the river is "Alberta Jam". Located above a 30 minute scree bash is a spectacular, vertically-tilted bedding plane. Photo page 262. "Sunset Boulevard" is up stream 500 m on the south bank and lies on the bottom tier of a layered north-facing cliff. To reach "Alberta Jam" wade the river and continue uphill picking the line of least resistance to deposit you below the routes.

Opposite: Dave Morgan attempting the crux pitch
of Sunset Boulevard. Photo Andy Genereux.

Sunset Boulevard

Sunset Boulevard*** 5.11c/d, 70 m, gear standard rack to 3.5"
RP's & TCU's recommended

A. Genereux & D. Morgan, 1987

The original Dave Morgan start was never completed and is not currently used but it might be a better option as it would avoid the loose first half of pitch one.

1) 5.10d, 25 m. Climb a loose corner for 7 m and exit onto the face to a bolt. Good face climbing with the crux at the last bolt leads to a single bolt and gear belay below the right-facing arch.

2) 5.11c/d, 45 m. At this point it is pretty obvious what to do next. Climb the superb dihedral with sustained cracks and stemming. Pull through a roof at the top and follow a short hand crack to a bolt belay.

Descent: walk off left and back around to the start or rappel the route double ropes required.

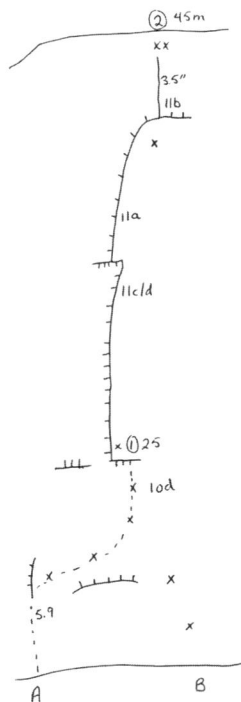

SUNSET BOULEVARD

A Sunset Boulevard ***   5.11c/d, 70 m
    gear standard rack to 3.5", RP's & TCU's

B Project Direct Start

Opposite: Dave Morgan on the first ascent of Alberta Jam. Photo: Greg Spohr.

Like "Sunset Boulevard," if this route were in Yosemite, it would see hundreds of assents every year. As it sits in the backwaters of the Ghost it might see several attempts on a good year. This baby is a classic not to be missed by any serious crack-climbing addict. It used to sit by itself and as result saw few people willing to make the effort to get there but in recent years a few other routes have been added to increase the scope of this area and this will hopefully increase the traffic to this worthwhile spot.

Avoid this area in extremely hot weather. Due to its southwest exposure, it tends to be a suntrap (a big solar oven). On the other hand this makes for a great early and late season venue when the sun is out making it possible to enjoy a cold marginal day.

Recky Route** 5.9, 25 m,
gear standard rack to 4"
G. Spohr & C. Yonge, 1982

This climbs the obvious corner that forms at the left side of the bedding plane. Originally the climb climbed the corner then trended left onto some very marginal ground for a total of 55 m and wasn't recommended. In Oct 98 a mid belay was installed at 25 m and this climb now makes for a fine warm up, with crack and stemming moves to get ready for the harder routes above and to the right.

Fat City** 5.11a, 25 m,
gear standard rack to 4"
A. Genereux, Oct.1998

This is an extension of Recky Route that heads out right from the mid point anchor to a bolt (crux) and climbs the finger crack which gradually widens to an off width crack protected by two bolts to a bolt anchor. Rappel the climb to descend.

October Finger Fest** 5.11a, 25 m, gear standard rack to 4"
A. Genereux, Oct. 1998

This starts as for Fat City after the bolt the climb heads out the right fork of the crack, on continuous 5.10+ finger and hand crack to a bolt belay.

Alberta Jam*** 5.11b/c, 50 m, gear standard rack to 4"
D. Morgan, 1982

The obvious diagonal finger & hand crack that starts from the left side of the wall and angles up and right to the top of the tipped bedding plane. Greg Spohr first discovered "Alberta Jam". Recognizing a classic when he saw one, Greg made an effort to climb it. He soon realized that he needed bigger guns and brought in Dave Morgan and Chas Younge. The route was originally aided in order to clean the crack and remove loose blocks. All efforts at free climbing were done on lead. It was Morgan who managed the first redpoint, after several efforts. This climb has repelled many on-sight attempts and should not be taken lightly. An extensive rack is required for this seemingly endless pitch.

The technical crux of the route is in the first 10 meters but it is very strenuous and sustained while you figure out the gear you want to place. If you reach the pod milk the rest, for the remaining two thirds is sustained finger and hand crack at the 5.10 range with a taxing 10+ crux just before the bolt belay. Rappel the route using double 50 m ropes or climb up the edge of the bedding plane 5.5 to the belay anchor for October Finger Fest if you have only one rope and complete two 25 m rappels.

Dionysus** 5.12d/13a/R, 50 m, gear to 4" extra RP's
Ben Firth, 1999

This is probably the hardest technical climbing to date in the Ghost. It's a direct start for "Alberta Jam" and climbs a series of thin cracks on marginal small gear directly to the pod and finishes as for Alberta Jam. Look to see more of these mind blowing finger numbing projects from Ben in the future. Starting with the one to the right of this route.

Project
Ben has an anchor and is at work on another test piece. Ben stated "The initial top rope kicked my ass." Might this be the first solid 5.13 in the Ghost when it's completed?

Alberta Jam

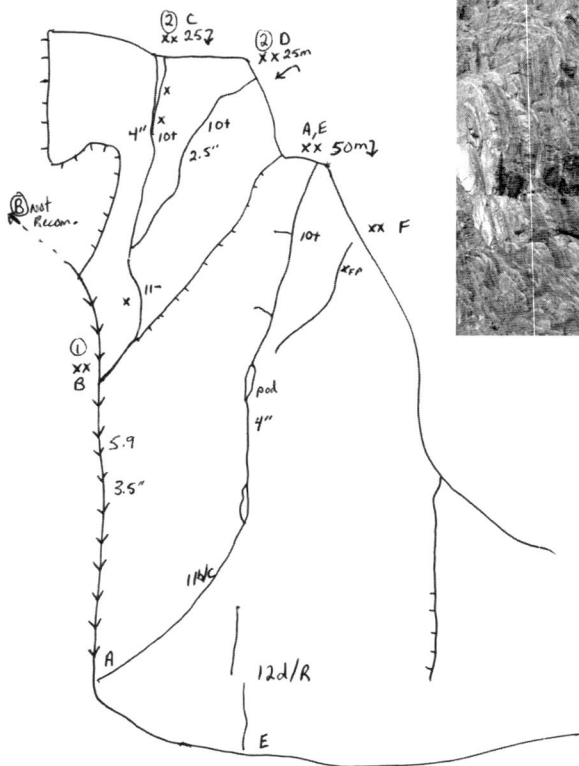

A Alberta Jam ***   5.11b/c, 50 m gear standard rack to 4"
B Recky Route **   5.9   gear standard rack to 4"
C Fat City **   5.11-   gear standard rack to 4"
D October Finger fest ** 5.11-   gear standard rack to 4"
E Dionysus **   5.12d/R   gear standard rack to 4" & multiple RP's
F Project

Thunder Thigh Crack 5.9, 125 m, gear standard rack to 4"
    or bigger the better
K. Nagy, F. Campbell & J. A. Owen, Sept. 1986

This route faces due south and is found out on the prow like buttress before the cliff disintegrates into the Valley of the Birds. Although considerably larger than the Alberta Jam formation, the west-facing, inverted bedding plane to the left of "Thunder Thigh Crack" remains unexplored.

Approach

The top of the route can be easily identified by a 30 m-long, left-facing dihedral. Climb a short scree slope immediately above the creek past a massive boulder to the base of the route. The first three pitches have the occasional 5.6 move. The team performed a lot of cleaning but still expect to find occasional loose sections. Several #11 Hexes or tube chocks are useful for off-width.

1) 5.6, 35 m. Start immediately above the big boulder. Climb the steep blocky wall trending slightly left to a good ledge with a boulder and small shrub.

2) 5.6, 30 m. Climb diagonally up and right for 6 m moving past a short wall to an easy groove that is followed for 12 m to an easy gully. Go up the gully trending left to a big ledge below a steep wall.

3) 5.6, 30 m. Pass the steep wall by going right up a groove to a small ledge. Traversing left along the ledge then climb the blocky face to another good ledge below the obvious corner crack.

4) 5.9, 30 m. Climb the crack that goes from hand to fist to off-width and gets progressively steeper and harder. Near the top, step around left to a loose ledge and go across easy slabs for 7 m to an old tree.

Descent: Walk right over to a treed ridge heading east toward the Valley of the Birds and go diagonally down toward the main valley staying in the trees all the way.

Climber on third pitch of Talk + Action = 0
Photo Jamie McVicar.

This is an attractive south-facing cliff above the Ghost River where it makes a 90-degree turn to the west. It is named after the first route established on the cliff, a waterfall ice climb. Silver-Tongued Devil (STD) Comes from a distinct cave halfway up the cliff on the left end. All of the early rock routes were established in this area. Due to its southern exposure short approach and a tendency to be out of the wind this crag tends to have one of the longest seasons of any cliff in the Ghost. Rock climbers have been seen here as early as March and as late as mid December on the right days. All you need is a few degrees on the plus side of zero for temperature and a sunny day, the dark rock will take care of the rest.

For these reasons the cliff has been significantly developed in the past few years mostly on its right side. There were no climbs here when the last guidebook was written, only a photo stating the unclimbed right side. Well not any more! Thanks to Shawn Huisman & his wife Shelley, Jamie McVicar, Bonnie Hamilton, and Brian Talbot and their herculean effort. They have established a total of eleven three & four pitch sport routes as well as a dozen more one & two pitch climbs. A couple of traditional lines have also crept into the mix. This has resulted in the cliff becoming a very popular venue due to the excellent rock, short approach, and the abundance of bolts. There has been a lot of heated discussion on the abundantly bolted nature of the climbing and some of the pitches being over graded. The grades have sorted out with time, and I for one would agree that there are few too many bolts. My personal solution is to skip the odd bolt, and to lead the longer climbs two pitches (50 m) at a time, to get my adrenaline fix. It is my view that the Ghost has always been about having a little adventure. These climbs are very safe and round out the Ghost climbing experience but I wouldn't like to see all of Ghost bolted in this fashion. I feel the climbing is fantastic and the over-bolted nature has been popular as demonstrated by the steady flow of people. I am sure some folks feel some of the other routes in the Ghost River are somewhat under protected and I certainly wouldn't want them changed. It all boils down to ones personal taste. The Ghost has always been about respect for other peoples views and many climbing styles have coexisted here for years.

Trevor Jones even stated "the cliff (STD) is great when your getting started in the spring, I don't mind the bolts being close together then". This from a long-standing traditionalist speaks loads for the quality of this cliff. What this area does is give a venue for those who want a safe leading environment on great rock with which to enjoy themselves. One has to agree other than the bolting issue the routes are great and the popularity of the area attests to this. In the fall of 2002 Andy Genereux established three new climbs on this wall. The bolt spacing on these routes is slightly further apart and is more in line with the normal bolting practices in the Ghost and should provide a bit more flavour and balance to the area. With the addition of this new wall the Ghost now has a little something for everybody. So get out there to climb and enjoy.

STD the cliff takes a slight turn to the east and becomes very grey and rippled. It is a fine-looking cliff with numerous corners in the upper half. Kelly Tobey and Frank Campbell have both done routes on this well bolted section but neither of them remembers much about them. Frank did one short route that ends in a cave about 30 m right of STD and

Silver-Tongued Devil Crag

he and Orvil Miskiw did a two-pitch route that climbs 5.9 face with a 5.3 groove above. Kelly remembers nothing of the route(s) he did. Unfortunately, this is the only information that remains.

Chas Yonge and partner followed a route just to the left of the Silver-Tongued Devil smear in order to reach the cave and check on spelunking opportunities. Rappelling off "Hoods in the Woods" you might see some fixed pitons (see topo STD, left on page 272) from this route but it is not recommended. By the way, despite having a nearly flat floor, the cave is nothing more than a frost pocket and extends only a few meters into the cliff. There is a fixed station on the left wall of the cave that is used to rappel from the waterfall ice climb.

The modern development of the cliff resulted from the compelling photo published in the last guide it spurred the activists to establish their first climb on the right side. From the outset they set out to build well protected sport routes, and hopefully in the moderate range, a low commitment crag to complement the scarier climbs found on other Ghost River venues. This cliff fit the bill. They wanted to find a cliff with no ex sting lines for their development so they wouldn't raise the hackle's of staunch traditionalists. They still received some flack mostly from Allan Pickel, who claimed the routes where way over-bolted and over-graded. Al threatened to steal hangers to create a new runout route called "Repo Man." They where surprised one day "to find Al hanging like a sack of potatoes all over the third pitch of Grindstone 5.10d." What they now refer to as "pullin' a Pickel" when someone is seen taking a hang. This confrontation also lead to the route called "Jerkin' a Gherkin" which now has an alternate traditional gear top pitch.

In keeping with traditional roots of the area the trio of Shawn Huisman, Brain Talbot and Jamie McVicar felt the first line up the crag should be ground up. The line they established was the forgettable "Pandora's Box" a runout crappy gear route followed by the top two pitches of "Talk-Action=0" which where established on lead using aid. The two excellent lower pitches where then rap bolted but not before a large detached block almost wiped out the ropes and one of them. Due to having only one battery and the number of bolts installed they returned over three days to get the route in place. On the redpoint day the trio where blindsided by a heavy thunderstorm. It left Shawn trying to complete the last pitch while turning blue and hypothermic. Meanwhile Brian and Jamie where pinned down at the third belay trying not to drown in the onslaught of hail and the ensuing rivers of slush. Needless to say they went home to Canmore to lick their wounds and consume some liquid courage to return and continue the fight another day.

In the early days of development there wasn't any trail and it took over an hour thrashing through wind fallen trees to reach the cliff. It was a huge effort that saw the trail established resulting in today's mere twenty minutes to reach the cliff. They also wrecked a transmission and beat the crap out of their vehicles so this area could come to life. When your out there clipping bolts and enjoying the sun at this great venue or you run into one of the first ascensionist give them some thanks, without their effort and tenacity you couldn't enjoy the many fine climbs they created.

Approach

Park in the cobblestone flats where the river turns west. This is referred to as the North Ghost Parking Access, (see page 257 for details). From here wade the river or drive across and locate an old road heading west into the trees. Follow the road for 120 m to a pullout with a flagged trail on the right (north side of the road). Take the trail through large timber until it starts to climb, then take the more travelled left fork, 20 minutes should put you below the small Tree Island in the middle of the right side. Al climbs to the Right of the tree Island are detailed on the topo STD, right on page 278. Climbs to the left of the tree island are detailed on the topo STD, centre on page 275 and covers all climbs to roughly the mid point of the crag. There the cliff base becomes a series of loosely treed blocky/ledges. This broken lower section travels left to the west end of the cliff to diminish to the right of Silver-Tongued Devil. The climbs located on this part of the cliff are referred to on the topo STD, left on page 272. The climb "Unrepentant" starts above the right end of this broken section and climbs between two distinctive roofs at mid height. To reach all the other climbs on STD Left traverse to the left (west) on a thin trail that undulates along the base of the cliff for 5 to 7 minutes until below and slightly left of the cave and wet streak for the waterfall ice climb Silver-Tongued Devil.

Descent

The climbs established at the west end of STD Left Side will require slings to rappel and double 50 m ropes or walk off to the west and down through the trees to return to the base. Descend "Rabid Crack" by walking off left.

   "Hoods in the Woods" and "Devil's Eye" are descended via two 50 m rappels. The top anchor is a single bolt backed up by a good natural thread. It is required to carry replacement rappel sling because the rats will undoubtedly take care of any that were left before.

   For "Unrepentant" and all climbs on STD Centre and STD Right they all have fixed rappel anchors and a single 60 m rope will get you off all the recommended routes.

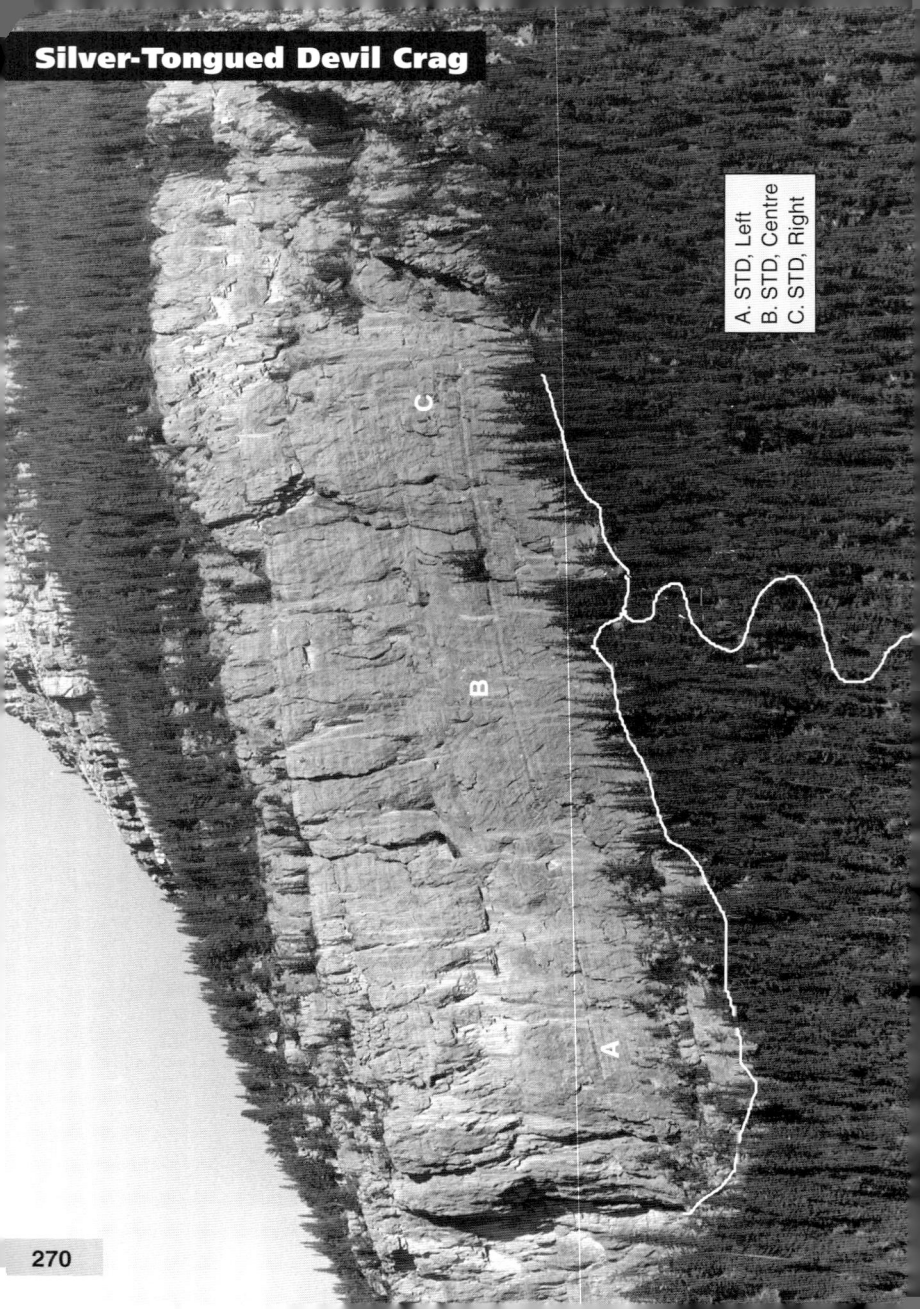

A. STD, Left
B. STD, Centre
C. STD, Right

Rabid Crack** 5.8,100 m, gear to4"

First ascent unknown.

This could be one of the Kelly Tobey routes that he no longer remembers. The name was applied later by Joe Josephson after his finger was bitten by a bat that had taken residence in the crack on the second pitch. A fine route with good crack climbing. Start about 10 m left of the Silver-Tongued Devil.

1) 5.7, 55 m. Climb up an easy slab to a large ledge below a nice corner. If you have short ropes it may be wise to belay here. Climb the corner up and left to a fixed piton in the crack just before the corner turns more sharply to the left. Traverse right across a steep grey wall and climb up a short wall to a small ledge with a large block. Follow the top edge of a huge flake left and up to a small ledge with a two-bolt belay.

2) 5.8, 45 m. Move left from the belay going up a short slab until you can make a difficult step right on to a small ledge below the upper corner and about 5 m above the belay. Climb up the corner and around the "bat bulge" (5.8) and continue up the corner to a small roof. Either climb the roof directly (5.8) or traverse onto an unprotectable slab of good rock to the left (5.6). Either route takes you to a large ledge with some small trees and a possible belay. If you don't mind some rope drag, traverse left for 10 m or so to a tree below a loose corner. Climb the corner to the top.

Hoods in the Woods** 5.10b, 90 m, gear standard rack to 4"

F. Campbell & L. Terras, June 1988

This takes the intimidating yellow wall between "Rabid Crack" and the Silver-Tongued Devil. The second pitch traverses right into the obvious corner crack directly above the STD cave. The first pitch is 5.9 and rates as one of the finer pitches of that grade. The second, crux pitch is also good despite being awkward in the upper corner.

1) 5.9, 50 m. A few meters right of the Silver-Tongued Devil climb up easy broken ground to a slab with a horizontal break. Continue up the slab to an old bolt. Either climb straight up from the bolt to the edge of a left-facing corner or alternatively, move left immediately from the bolt and then go straight up (5.8, small wires or RPs) to the corner, which is followed (fixed pitons) to a small ledge at the top. Climb the steep yellow wall above (5.9) past a bolt and into a right-facing corner. Struggle up the corner until easier ledges lead right to a fixed cable anchor.

2) 5.10b, 40 m. Step right from the belay and then up a large yellow scoop to a bolt. Continue up and right (10a) past two more bolts that lead onto grey rock and a large corner. Climb the increasingly and surprisingly difficult corner (10b, large cams helpful) for 25 m to a large ledge on the right. Belay off a bolt and a good natural thread to the right.

Silver-Tongued Devil Crag, Left

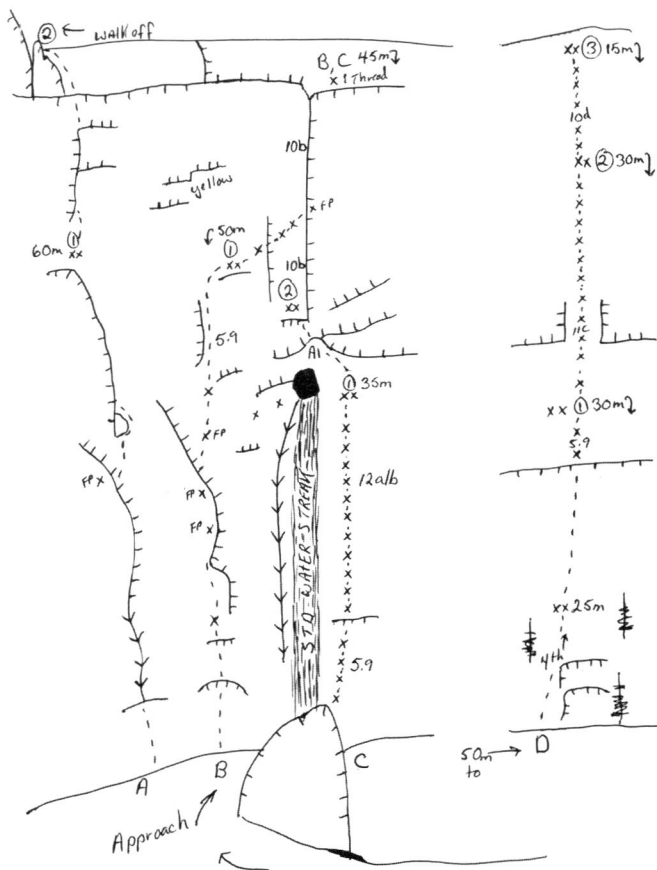

SILVER-TONGUED DEVIL CRAG, LEFT

A Rabid Crack **	5.8	gear to 4"
B Hoods In The Woods **	5.9	gear to 4"
C Devils Eye *	5.12a/b or 5.8/A1	gear to 4"
D Unrepentant **	5.11c	gear to 3"

Devil's Eye* 5.10b/A1, or 5.12a/b, 90 m, gear standard rack to 4"

F. Campbell & R. Banard, June 1991
FFA G. Dickey 2001

Directly above the STD cave there is a large roof with a crack splitting it. Wishing to check it out, Frank Campbell began a bolt ladder up the water streak right of the STD waterfall. Frank made many efforts to establish the bolt ladder, which was drilled by hand and often at times solo when he couldn't find partners for other projects. More natural aid pulled the roof above the cave and led into the upper corner taken by "Hoods in the Woods." The roof has a bunch of fixed gear and would likely go free. The position on the roof over the cave is unbeatable. Although not as steep, the bolt ladder now goes free although it requires considerable retro bolting to make it a worthwhile sport climb. Greg feels there would be a better, more consistent finish out to the right over overlaps. This to would require extensive bolting. However, the immaculate, compact rock looks like it might be worth the effort. Good luck! Begin immediately right of Silver-Tongued Devil.

1) 5.9/A0 or 5.12a/b, 35 m. Excellent climbing (5.9) up a steep slab leads past four bolts to a silver streak just right of the water smear. Climb the bolt ladder for 20 m to a bolt belay below a large overhang and about level with the cave.

2) 5.10/A1 or 11a, 15 m. Climb a left-leaning crack in the overhangs above. Free and aid moves along the crack lead to the big roof directly over the cave. Aid the roof and continue free to a small ledge on the left with a two-bolt belay. It is possible to combine pitches 1 & 2.

3) 5.10b, 45 m. Climb the corner (10b) to a small ledge where "Hoods in the Woods" traverses in from the left. Continue up the corner (10b) to the belay ledge on the right.

Unrepentant** 5.9, 11c, 10d, 75 m, gear to 3"

S. Huisman & S. Huisman, Sept. 2002

This climb starts from an open treed shelf just left of the centre of the cliff. Located 20 m above the trail 20 m left of the bolted route "Essence". An easy scramble leads up the path of least resistance over ledges and small bands of rock to belay at a bolt with a hammer link. This line climbs a series of easy cracks to gain the silver streak, which splits the two roofs above. The natural pro on this route is on the first and third pitches the second pitch is totally fixed. **NOTE:** When rappelling with a single 60 m rope make sure to tie knots in the ends of the rope. Two of the rappels are a full 30 m.

Essence** 10a, 10d, 11a, 92 m, fixed gear
S. Huisman & S. Huisman July 2001

There is a distinctive tree growing out of a dihedral 20 m above the base of the wall. The route climbs the face to the left. There is a rap station 10 m down from the top of the second pitch to allow rappelling with a single 60 m rope on this 40 m pitch. **NOTE:** two of the rappels are a full 30 m and care should be taken to tie knots on the ends of the rope.

Seducin' Medusa*** 11a, 10c, 10c, 11a, 95 m, fixed gear
S. Huisman & S. Huisman, Jamie McVicar, Aug. 2001

This is an excellent face climb on superb rock with sustained 5.10 climbing and a couple of short 5.11a cruxes.

Southern Lines*** 10d, 10b, 10b, 10b, 93 m, fixed gear
S. Huisman & S. Huisman, July 2000

This is an outstanding climb, one of the best on the cliff. It's slightly easier than the climb "Seducin' Medusa" to the left. Make sure you figure out which line of bolts your on. This is the middle of three climbs that all start close together.

Nightshift Guru** 10c, 10b, 58 m, fixed gear
S. Huisman & S. Huisman, Sept. 2002

This is the right of three climbs that start close together. This two-pitch route climbs to the base of a large orange overhanging dihedral on the upper wall. (This dihedral might make for a good trad pitch if anyone is game.)

Grind Stone** 5.8, 10a, 10d, 10a, 93 m, fixed gear
S. Huisman, B. Talbot, and J. McVicar, Sept. 1999

This route climbs to an obvious tree at two-thirds height that marks the base of a stunning arête on the upper wall. The climb avoids the arête to follow a set of breaks on the face to the right then moving back left to the arête at the top of the last pitch.

Mental Health Day** 10c, 25 m, fixed gear
A. Genereux & D. Dunbar, Nov. 2002

This is the first pitch of an ongoing project there are two bolts established on the second pitch. The spacing of the bolts is a little further apart than other routes on this wall.

Baylie's Trail*** 5.9, 10c, 10c, 85 m, fixed gear
A. Genereux & D. Dunbar, Nov. 2002

Locate a single belay bolt on the left end of a small ledge left of the climb "Summerteeth". Climb up to a ledge with a small tree. The belays are marked with red rap hangers.

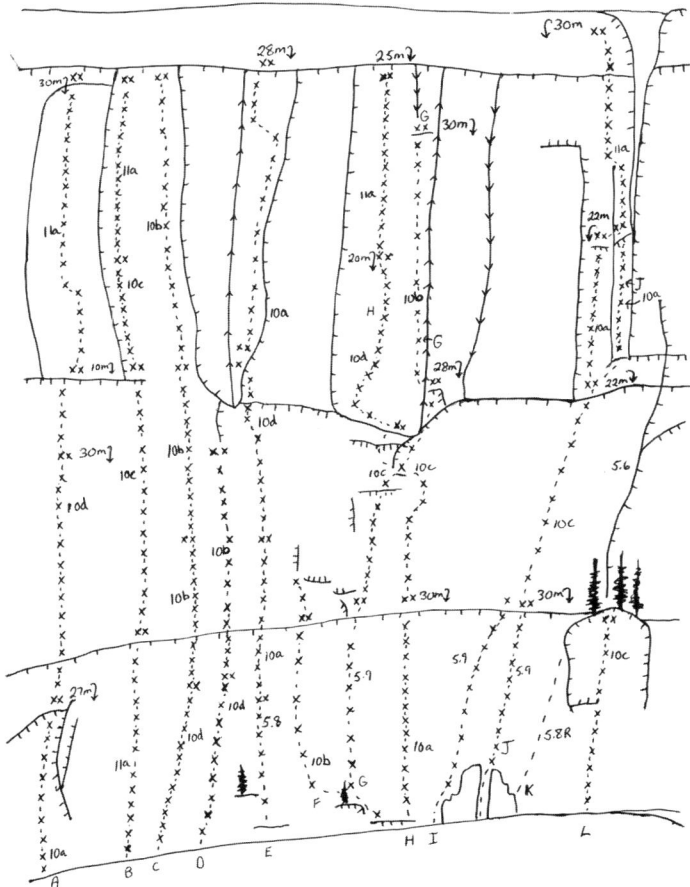

SILVER-TONGUED DEVIL CRAG, CENTRE

A	Essence **	10a, 10d, 11a,
B	Seducin' Medusa ***	11a, 10c, 10c, 11a
C	Southern Lines ***	10d, 10b, 10c, 10b
D	Nightshift Guru **	10c, 10b
E	Grind stone **	5.8, 10a, 10d, 10a
F	Mental Health Day **	10c
G	Baylie's Trail ***	5.9, 10c,10c
H	Summerteeth ***	10a, 10c, 10d, 11a
I	Talk-Action=0 **	5.9, 10c, 10a, 11a
J	Talk-Action=0 *	9, 10a right variations
K	Pandora's Box	5.8R, 5.6 gear to 3.5" not recommended
L	In One Ear Out Your Mother *	10c

The second pitch crosses "Summerteeth" at the crux on the second pitch, the routes share a bolt then the climb moves out right to the arête. The last pitch climbs the rounded arête and it is an outstanding pitch. Andy established the first two pitches and part of the third before the battery ran out, via rope solo ground up. The remainder of the third pitch was also put in ground up with Daren Dunbar. **NOTE:** the rappel on pitch 3 is a full 30 m, make sure to tie knots in the end of your rope when using a single 60 m rope to rappel.

Summerteeth*** 10a, 10c, 10d, 11a, 95 m, fixed gear
S. Huisman & S. Huisman, Jamie McVicar, Aug. 1999

Starts directly above the trail as you arrive at the crag. There is a small ledge with a single belay bolt at the left end. The climb starts from the right side of the ledge. This climb just gets better the higher you go. Pitches 3 & 4 are excellent. All belays are on ringbolts.

Talk-Action=0** 5.9, 10c, 10a, 11a, 95 m, fixed gear
S. Huisman & S. Huisman, Jamie McVicar, July 1999

The first multi pitch sport route established on the cliff. Start on the left side of a blocky pedestal at the base of the wall. The route has good to excellent climbing but is marred by a ledge and having to deal with a couple of trees that want to snag the rope moving from the third to the forth pitch. The first ascensionist's are talking about putting up a direct forth pitch to eliminate this problem, which in my mind would up the star quality of this climb.

Talk-Action=0** Right variations 5.9, 10a, fixed gear
S. Huisman & S. Huisman, Jamie McVicar, July 2000

Start by climbing the groove that splits the blocky pedestal at the base of the wall. Pitch one makes for a good alternate warm up pitch and is often done as a single pitch. Pitch 3 was the original pitch for the climb and is OK but the pitch to the left is superior.

Pandora's Box 5.8R, 5.6, 60 m gear to 3.5" not recommended
S. Huisman & Jamie McVicar

This was the first climb established on the cliff its only purpose was to access the better climbing on either side of it. It is included for historical purposes only. It is quite scrappy and is not recommended.

In one ear out your Mother* 10c, 28 m, fixed gear
D. Kennefick & L. Rotter, Aug. 2002

Start from the right side of the blocky pedestal and climbs directly to the Tree Island.

Jerkin'a Gherkin** 10b, 10b, 10d, 10a, 110 m, fixed gear
J. McVicar & B. Talbot, Sept. 2001

Starts off the "lunch ledge" the first of two climbs that depart from the right end of the ledge. It climbs a left leaning shallow dihedral for four bolts then heads out right on the face. This climb was named after a vocal opponent of the bolting practices being employed on the cliff. The climb had three pitches added in 2002 and is a very good multi pitch sport climb.

This bolts Not for You** 10a, 30 m, gear to 3"
B. Hamilton, Oct. 2002

This is an alternate fourth pitch to "Jerkin'a Gherkin and is a further response to the criticism over the bolting practices. The climb follows a series of good cracks to a bolted anchor. **Note:** Be careful. The rappel is a full 30 m, make sure to tie knots in the end of your rope when using a single 60 m rope to descend.

Seams Easy*** 10c, 30 m, fixed gear
S. Huisman & S. Huisman, J. McVicar, July 1999

The second route to leave the right end of the lunch ledge. It climbs up for four bolts then jogs to the right before continuing to the top on excellent rock with steady climbing.

Report a Poacher* 10c, 30 m, fixed gear
S. Huisman & S. Huisman, J. McVicar, July 1999

Starts from the centre of the shield, after four bolts you have to decide to finish on the line to the right or to go on the one on the left.

Slabulous** 10a, 30 m, fixed gear
S. Huisman & S. Huisman, J. McVicar, July 2000

The route climbs the right side of the shield and makes for a good warm up for some of the longer routes on the cliff.

Beeline*** 10d, 10d, 10d, 85 m, fixed gear
A. Genereux, Oct. 2002

This excellent climb was rap bolted and rope soloed. It starts behind a large spruce tree on the wall just to the right of the corner that marks the right side of the shield. It finishes up the bulging arête to a large ledge below an overhanging corner. Red rap hangers mark the belays of this route. All three pitches have a technical crux at 10c/d with the remaining climbing sustained in the low 10's.

Up In Arms*** 10b, 10a, 10c, 85 m, fixed gear
J. McVicar & B. Talbot, July 2000

Yet another fine climb up impeccable grey stone it finishes on the same ledge as "Beeline" to the right of the overhanging corner. The third pitch has a tricky technical crux

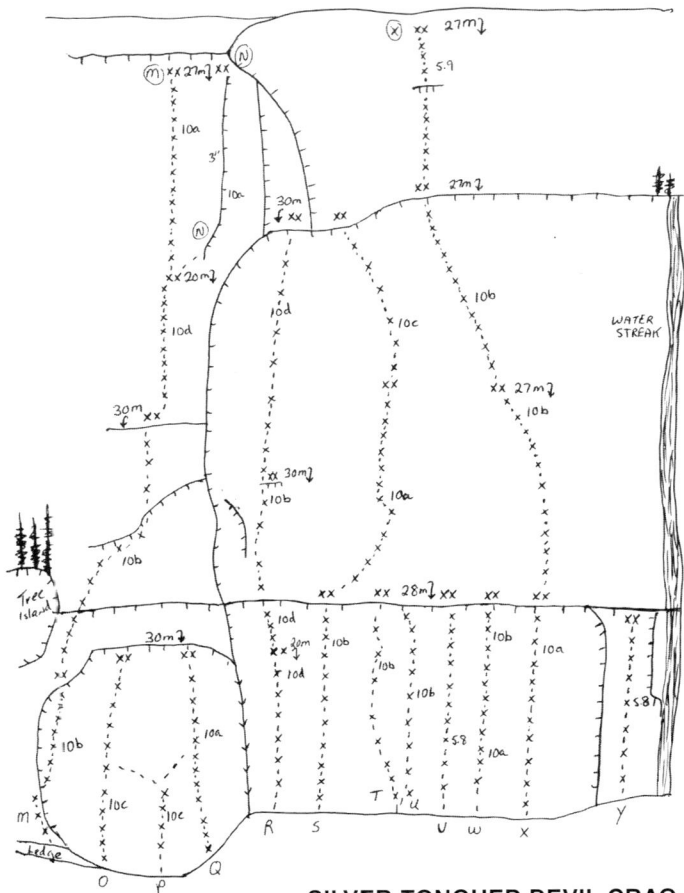

SILVER-TONGUED DEVIL CRAG, RIGHT

M Jerkin'a Gherkin**	10b, 10b, 10d, 10a
N This bolts Not for You**	10a gear to 3"
O Seams Easy***	10c
P Report a Poacher *	10c
Q Slabulous**	10a
R Beeline***	10d, 10d 10d
S Up In Arms***	10b, 10a, 10c
T Charmed Life **	10b/c
U Mom's Time Out**	10b
V Ghosts of Phyl and George***	5.8
W This Bolt's For You**	10b
X Heidies with Hilties**	10a, 10b, 10b, 5.9
Y Weird Tales**	5.8

section which has had the grade bumped up a notch since the first ascent.

Charmed Life** 10b/c, 28 m, fixed gear

A. Genereux, Oct. 2002

This slightly squeezed in climb was rope soloed ground up just as a snow flurry started. This fact and the fact that Andy survived the ugly munge corner on the right side of the wall, which was climbed to access "Beeline" made for this appropriate name. The climb shares the anchor with the route to the right "Mom's Time Out".

Mom's Time Out** 10b, 28 m, fixed gear

B. Hamilton, Oct. 2001

Another good 5.10 face route. Good to see a lady out strutting her stuff and packing a drill.

Ghosts of Phyl and George*** 5.8, 28 m, fixed gear

P. Rondina & B. Hamilton, Sept. 2001

Just what the crag needed a moderate warm up climb. This route climbs the wall to the left of an obvious tree on the belay ledge above. Climb the solid grey rock past bolts to a bolt anchor.

This Bolt's For You** 10b, 28 m, fixed gear

S. Huisman & J. McVicar, Aug. 1999

This climbs the wall to the right of the tree located on the belay ledge that runs across the wall.

Heidies with Hilties** 10a, 10b, 10b, 5.9, 109 m, fixed gear

S. Huisman & B. Hamilton, Sept. 2000

This all women's team established this excellent moderate multi pitch sport route. This is the only Climb to go all way to the top on this part of the right side. It is the second climb left of the water streak that marks the right edge of the wall.

Weird Tales** 5.8, 25 m, fixed gear

S. Huisman, Aug. 1999

This is an excellent route that climbs the face between the shallow right facing dihedral and the water streak that marks the end of technical climbing on the wall.

Munge Corner 5.8, 125 m, gear to 4" not recommended

A. Genereux, Oct. 2002 November

Originally used to access the top of the wall by Andy. It climbs the slot canyon to the right of the main wall. Mostly 5.4 with two technical loose dirty steps, it is characterized as vegetated and choked by deadfall. Don't go here!

Also in this area were two smaller cliffs that were developed in 1999 called the Curbside Crags, Sheep Head Buttress and The Monolith. The top of these cliffs can be spotted at the base of the hill below and slightly left of STD cliff from the south side of the river before you cross over. There are eight one-pitch sport routes four on each cliff. To reach this area, continue (west) past the trailhead for STD page 269 for 65 m through a section of overgrown track to a flagged trial. Follow the winding trail and flagging for several minutes to reach a small cliff the Sheep Head Buttress. These cliffs face south and have the shortest approach in the Ghost. Be wary of a yellow band, which has loose rock at the top of these routes. Follow the base of the cliff west (left) for a 100 m to reach the Monolith.

Sheepshead Buttress

Sheepish 5.9, 15 m, fixed gear
S. Huisman & S. Huisman, 1999

Located left of a large spruce tree it climbs the left edge of the wall.

Sheep for Brains** 5.9, 20 m, fixed gear
S. Huisman & B. Talbot, 1999

Climbs a line of bolts to the right of a large spruce tree.

Screw Ewe* 5.8, 25 m, fixed gear
S. Huisman & B. Talbot, 1999

Climb past a bolt to gain a dipping ledge then take the left line of bolts to a fixed anchor.

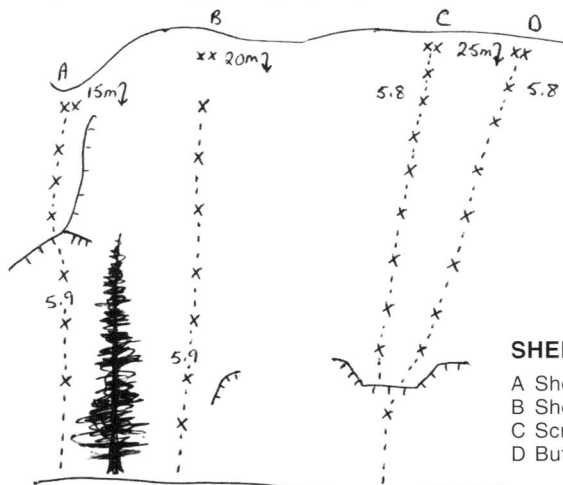

SHEEPSHEAD BUTTRESS

A Sheepish *   5.9
B Sheep For Brains **   5.9
C Screw Ewe *   5.8
D Buthead Sheepstress * 5.8

Butthead Sheepstress* 5.8, 25 m, fixed gear
S. Huisman & B. Talbot, 1999

Climb past a bolt to gain a dipping ledge, then take the right line of bolts.

The Monolith

Eyes Wide Shut* 5.10c, 15 m, fixed gear
S. Huisman & S. Huisman 1999

The left most climb on this small crag. Go over a crumbly ledge to gain the line of bolts above.

Full Metal Jacket* 5.10a, 15 m, fixed gear
S. Huisman & S. Huisman, 1999

Climbs past five bolts straight up the middle of the face.

Dr. Strange Glove 5.10a, 15 m, fixed gear
S. Huisman & S. Huisman, 1999

After the first bolt on the climb "Full Metal Jacket," head out right an up a three-bolt variation.

Paths of Glory* 5.9, 15 m, fixed gear
S. Huisman & S. Huisman, 1999
A leaning line of bolts just left of the right side of the cliff.

THE MONOLITH

A Eyes Wide Shut *   5.10c
B Full Metal Jacket *   5.10a
C Dr. Strangelove   5.10a
D Paths of Glory *   5.9

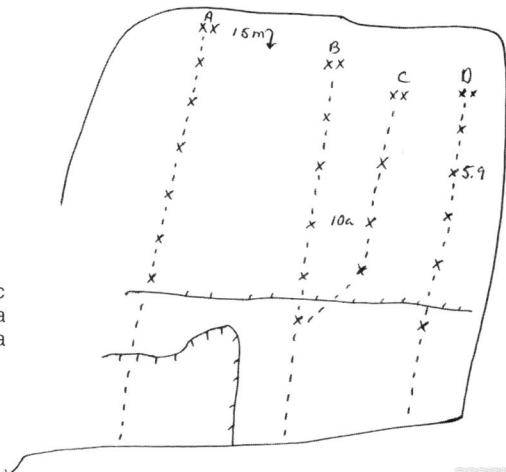

BASTION WALL

This aptly named cliff begins just north of Silver-Tongued Devil Crag and extends a considerable distance (almost 7 km!) to the north around the base of Devil's Head Mountain (see maps pages 176 & 302). The rock is among some of the best in the Ghost. The West End of the cliff faces due south up to the climb "Thor" where the wall bends to face east. A major cleft 200 m after this bend is the climb "Satan". The early routes concentrated on the few natural lines and only seven routes had been climbed when the last guide was published in 1997. Of these, only "Thor" had a significant number of ascents to warrant a star rating.

The number of climbs has doubled in resent years. Thanks to the efforts of Keith Haberl, Brian Spear, Ken Wylie and several of their friends. Several styles where employed from a ground up traditional ethic to rappel bolting and cleaning to something in between. "The storming of the Bastion" in resent years has only touched the potential on this fantastic wall. Some of the early routes still have very few ascents and not enough is known about them to warrant stars, although some of them look very good. All are located on the south end within the first kilometre of cliff line. Ian Bolt and Dan Guthrie were reported to have done two routes somewhere left of "Thor," however details were lost when the pair perished in an avalanche in Alaska.

Brian Spear and partners have pushed three moderate routes in a previously unexplored Little Egypt Amphitheatre on the north end of the wall before it rounds the corner to the drainage for the ice climb the "Sorcerer". Farther north near the waterfall routes "Sorcerer" and "Hydrophobia," the cliff contains massive towers and sweeping, blank faces with several sections of excellent rock. Several rumours abound that climbs have been completed here, to date none have been confirmed. A French climber who once saw the cliffs refused to believe there were no rock climbs on these walls. He declared that in France there would be over a thousand routes. Well, this ain't France and there they sit, *sain et sauf* (virtually untouched).

Approach

Park in the cobblestone flats where the Ghost River turns west. This is referred to as the North Ghost Parking Access, see page 257 and map page 176 for details. It may be possible to drive across the river and park near a meadow that marks the start of the approach trail. The trail (actually an old road) begins steeply as it heads north between Bastion Wall to the left and Black Rock Mountain to the right. Please walk from the start of the road. Do not attempt to drive this narrow track. There is no parking and it is nearly impossible to pass oncoming vehicles, it is a rough 4X4 track that might trash your vehicle if you loose it on several steep side hills and it only saves about 15 minutes to Johnson Lakes.

Climbs near the west end can be reached by leaving the road just before the top of the final steep section and heading up a ridge that is partially open at first and then more treed higher with sections of wind fall. This comes out above and left of "Thor."

The traditional and better approach, however, is to continue up the road to the gully below "Satan," which can then be followed to the base of the cliff with a minimum of bushwhacking. From the base of this climb most climbs can be reached in 5 to 10 minutes going right or left. It is possible to reach "Little Egypt Amphitheatre" from this approach but the traverse has no defined trail so it is better to approach from the Johnson lakes see a description on page 296.

Descent

Since the cliff extends a long way to the north, the only feasible general descent route is located at the West End. A bench at the top of the cliff can be followed past "Thor" and "Lucky for Some" to a good tree at the edge. See photo below. Two 50 m ropes are required to reach the base of the cliff. Alternatively, traverse at a higher level farther west and scramble down the **Treed Descent**, which follows the treed, break in the cliff bands between Bastion Wall and Silver-Tongued Devil Crag. Several climbs can also be descended using fixed anchors but many can be hard to locate from above when coming off other climbs. The individual descriptions for each climb will indicate your options with each description.

At the West End of the wall, to the left of "Thor," there are a number of short crack and corner lines. The farthest right of these, at the beginning of the main wall, is "Lucky for Some," a prominent, right-facing crack and chimney system. Immediately left of this is a groove that begins at a ledge part way up the cliff and is climbed by "Lugey's Copter." To the left again, also starting from the ledge, is the steep, flaring corner/crack of "Larry, Curly and Mo." Descent for all three routes use the 50 m tree rappel just to the west or walk off above the higher band to the Treed Descent.

Bastion Wall

A. Thor
B. **O** Tree rappel
C. Treed Descent
D. ridge approach
E. Satan approach
F. Little Egypt approach

A. Larry, Curly & Mo
B. Lugey's Copter
C. Lucky for Some
D. Thor
E. Men of Fashion
F. The Curio Emporium
G. Barbarella Psychedella
H. Forbidden Planet
I. Satan

Larry, Curly and Mo 5.9, 65 m, gear to 4″
S. Dougherty, C. Quinn & D. Cheesmond, 1985

Begin as for "Lugey's Copter" at the short, left-facing chimney.
1) 5.6, 25 m. Go up the chimney and then move up and left to belay below the flaring corner/crack.
2) 5.9, 40 m. Climb the corner to ledges at the top.

Lugey's Copter* 5.8, 70 m, gear to 4″
A. Pickel & T. Back, July 1982

Begin to the left of the upper groove noted above, below a short, left-facing chimney. Pitch 2 is sustained and on good rock.
1) 5.6, 25 m. Climb the chimney to a large ledge. Move right along the ledge for about 6 m and then step down to belay below the groove.
2) 5.8, 45 m. Climb the steep groove above for about 12 m and then move left and continue up the face. After about 6 m, make moves back to the right into the groove and follow it to the top of the cliff.

Lucky for Some 5.6, 100 m, gear to 4″
A. Sole & N. Hellewell, 1978

Follow the crack and chimney system described above for three pitches of 5.6 climbing. The name is derived from an incident on the first ascent when Nigel Hellewell fell off while climbing solo. Fortunately, he landed on Albi Sole who was directly below and who managed to hold both of them!

Thor*** 5.10a, 145 m, gear standard rack to 4″
N. Hellewell & J. Upton, July 1977

"Thor" follows the obvious shallow corner near the south end of the main cliff. It is one of the best climbs in the area and a number of repeat ascents have confirmed its quality. The climbing is sustained and on excellent rock but good protection is somet mes diffi-cult to arrange, notably on the first pitch and the beginning of the second. Take a good selection of gear for the long pitches.
1) 5.10a, 45 m. Follow the groove with continuous interest and awkward protection to a small stance and bolt belay.
2) 5.10a, 35 m. Make a few moves left and up to gain a short ramp that leads back right. The ramp ends in a shallow, steepening scoop, above which difficult bridging past old, dubious pitons leads to a steep chimney. Continue up to a small ledge about 5 m below a blank-looking bulge.
3) 5.9, 45 m. Climb the groove to a bolt on the right and continue up over the bulge. Hard, sustained climbing leads to a ledge near the top of the cliff.
4) 5.3, 20 m. Continue to the top and belay at a tree higher up.

Descent: walk southwest to the tree rappel or the Treed Descent.

Bastion Wall

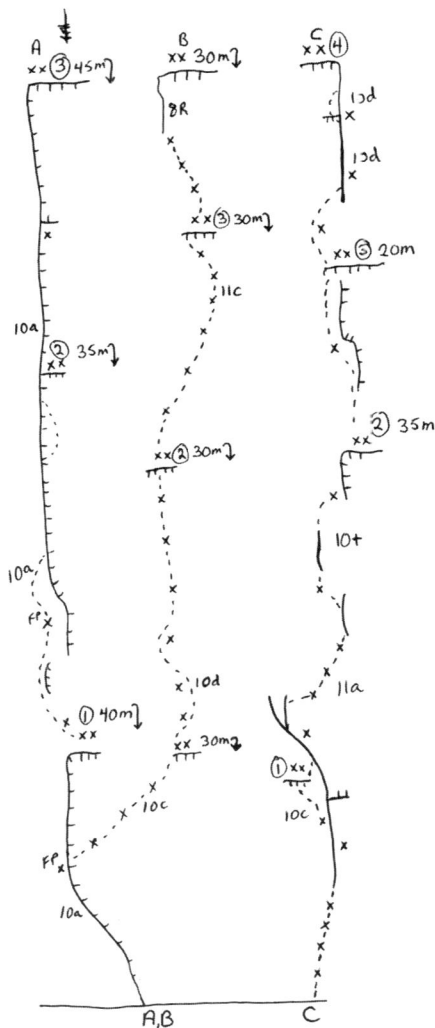

BASTION WALL

A Thor ***	5.10a, 145 m	gear standard rack to 4"
B Men Of Fashion ***	5.11b/c,125 m	gear to 3"
C The Curio Emporium***	5.11a, 120 m	gear to 3.5"

Men Of Fashion*** 5.11b/c, 125 m, gear to 3"
K. Haberl, J. Haigh, J. Nazarchuk, A. Yamada, Sept. 1999

Uses part of the first pitch of "Thor" to gain access for this excellent climb.

1) 5.10c, 35 m, Start up the corner groove of "Thor" at a fixed piton (skip or back clean because of rope drag) traverse up and right past three bolts (10c) to a bolted station.

2) 5.10d, 35 m, Climb the brilliant steep water grooved limestone past 6 bolts to a bolt belay.

3) 5.11b/c, 30 m, Technical-climbing leads diagonally up right to a small blunt dihedral. Climb the short dihedral then make a thin traverse left to a bolted station.

4) 5.10-, 30 m, Climb the face past three bolts to gain a crack climb this to the top and a bolt belay.

Descent: Rappel the route with a single 60 m rope (be careful some of the rappels are a full 30 m) or walk of to the southwest to the Treed Descent.

The Curio Emporium*** 5.11a, 120 m, gear standard rack to 3.5"
long slings & double ropes
K. Haberl, R. Jagger, K. Wylie, summer 2000

This climb starts 20 m meters right of "Thor". It is a fantastic route with lots of sustained 5.10 climbing on superb rock.

1) 5.10c, 30 m, Climb past four bolts to enter a crack. Continue up the crack, passing two more bolts. Overcoming a small roof is the crux of the pitch. Finish up the crack stepping left to a ledge and a fixed belay.

2) 5.11a, 35 m, Climb the crack to a main break (yellow chimney) climb high in the chimney passing bolts on the right wall to big holds. Hand traverse right on some funky moves into a crack. Step left into a slabby dish to a bolt climb up into the burly slot, which uses large gear to gain a slab. Clip the bolt on the slab and step down and right to traverse into a corner, climb the corner to a chained belay. Double rope techniques recommended for pitch two.

3) 5.10a, 20 m. Climb a crack to below a small roof. A rising traverse left past a bolt then up to a ledge and a bolt belay.

4) 5.10d, 35 m. Climb the slab to a bolt then traverse right to a crack. Follow the crack difficult to pass a bolt. The natural protection is challenging but when you reach the second bolt there is a good rest out left on a pedestal ledge. Finish up by climbing sustained crack moves to the top and a belay.

Descent: To try and rappel this route using a single 60 m rope is extremely dangerous unless you have two ropes traverse left to "Men Of Fashion" to rappel or walk off to the southwest as for the Treed Descent.

Bastion Wall

Barbarella Psychedella** 5.11c, 145 m, gear standard rack pro to 3"
K. Haberl, B. Spear, K. Wylie, Aug. 1998

This is a high quality route on solid rock with mostly natural protection. After the last bolt on pitch two the only bolts to be found are on the fixed belay/rappel stations. This route is located halfway between "Thor" and "Satan". Either the "Thor" or "Satan" approaches will work to get to this route and its neighbour to the right "Forbidder Planet". By approaching from "Satan" there is a little less elevation to overcome. Look for two crack systems that descend from near the top of the cliff and blanking out about two-thirds the way down the wall. (See photo on page 284),

1) 5.8, 30 m. Climb cracks to an obvious left facing corner, then onto a ledge with a small tree to a two-bolt belay. Alternatively climb the slope for 25 m to the left and take the fourth class ramp back right to reach the same point.

2) 5.11c, 35 m. Climb over a loose arch and up steep rock past three bolts to a small roof. Step left and climbs up past 4 spaced bolts to below a corner. Move left and arc up and back right to gain the corner (an awkward crux). Climb the corner past 2 more bolts then several gear placements to reach the bolted belay.

3) 5.10+, 20 m. Climb the crack jamming and stemming into a left facing corner, climb the corner to a two-bolt belay.

4) 5.10-, 35 m. Stem the corner above until it blanks out, move right into a thin crack and climb a few meters until it is possible to move left back into the corner. Continue in the corner to a fist crack to a roof below a flared chimney and a fixed piton the climbing eases as you gain a small ledge and a bolt belay.

5) 5.9, 25 m. Climb up and left on thin moves to gain the corner. Follow the corner until below a roof. Make a long move left to gain a ledge. Easier climbing leads up and right to regain the corner with a bolt belay at the top.

Descent: rappel the route two ropes required or walk off to the southwest to the Treed Descent.

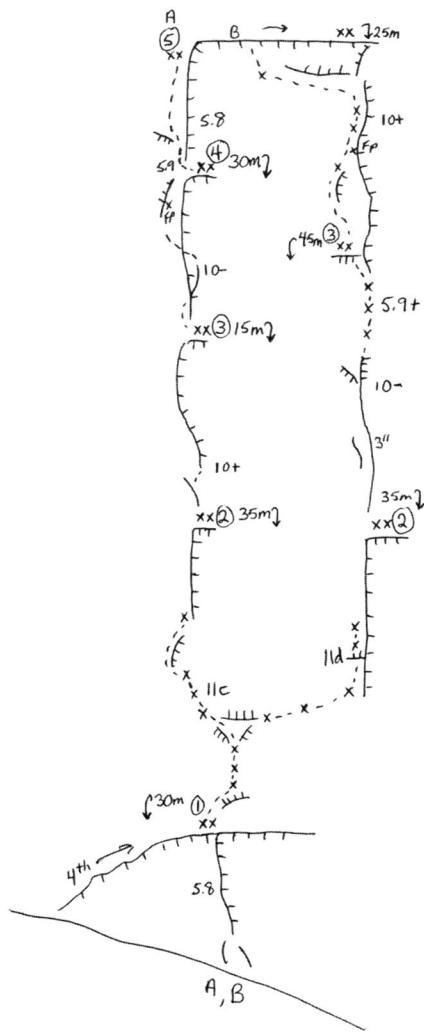

BASTION WALL

A Barberela Psychadella **   5.11c, 145 m   gear to 3"
B Forbidden Planet **   5.11d, 145 m   gear to 3"

Ken Wiley on Rave. Photo: Brian Spear.

Forbidden Planet** 5.11d, 145 m, standard rack to 3"
K. Haberl, C. Robertson, B. Spear, Sept. 1998

This is the more difficult sister route to "Barbarella Psychedella" They share the same start only after you climb the first three bolts on the second pitch you traverse out right to gain the right of the two crack and corner systems. This route goes on mostly natural protection and climbs on very good rock. The climbing is excellent, steep, and safe.

1) 5.8, 30 m. Start as for Barbarella Psychedella by climbing the left facing corner to gain a ledge and a bolt belay.

2) 5.11d, 35 m. Climb the steep arch past 3 bolt's (11b) to a small roof. Step right and traverse out right past 2 more widely spaced bolts to below a corner. Physical climbing up and over the roof past a bolt to reach the corner and continue upward on steep sustained 5.11 laybacking and stemming. The corner is protected naturally. At the top of the corner is a bolt belay with chains.

3) 5.10-, 45 m. Climb the crack into a slot. Continue up into a straight in crack that is bulging above and narrows to thin hands. Pull into a sentry box then past three bolts to a ramp leading up and left to a belay with chains.

4) 5.10+, 35 m, Pro to 3" Climb up and left on the ramp until you can traverse back right on thin holds past two bolts to a fixed piton (10+). Climb straight up to gain a chimney/slot. Move up this feature until a few meters below a roof (the exit slot on the right is choked with several death blocks; avoid at all cost) Traverse hard left under the roof then move up to a bolt. Continue left angling up to reach the top and a belay.

Descent: rappel down the route by using a station a few meters to the north, two ropes required or alternatively walk off to the southwest to the Treed Descent.

Satan* 5.10b, 200 m, gear standard rack to 4", double ropes recommended
N. Hellewell & F. O'Sullivan, July 1977

When walking north along the road, the first really prominent line is a huge corner above a shallow gully in the hillside. "Satan" goes up the corner and has some interesting climbing in its lower section particularly on the pitch leading to the upper corner. It should be noted that this was one of the first climbs to be graded 5.10 in the Ghost and this may be a sandbag if some of Nigel's other routes are to be considered. To date there has been little traffic to confirm the grade or quality.

There is a new bolt 10 m up the corner this might be part of a retrofit of this climb information is still lacking at this time. Climb the right side of the bowl beneath the corner moving left near the top to a bolt belay beneath overhangs (5.8). Traverse right to a crack through the overhangs and climb this (5.9) and the groove above to a ledge beneath an overhanging chimney. Climb the overhanging chimney and the steep groove above (5.10b). Several pitches of less difficult climbing (up to 5.8) lead to the top of the cliff.

Descent: Walk off to the southwest to the Treed Descent or tree rappel.

Bastion Wall

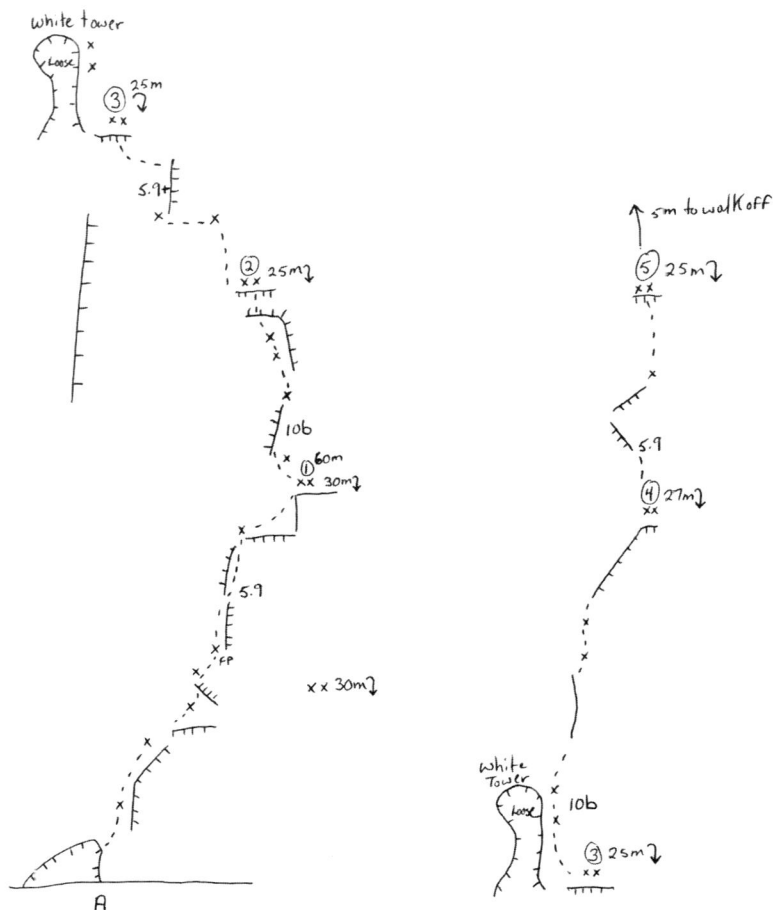

BASTION WALL

Rave*** 5.10b, 185 m, gear standard rack to 4" & long slings

Rave*** 5.10b, 185 m, gear standard rack to 4" several long slings
B. Spear & K. Wylie, June 2000

Approach as for "Satan". The route climbs the steep grey headwall around the corner to the right of "Satan". The route starts from a rock tooth about 100 m right of "Satan", and angles right up the overhanging grey wall and then left to a yellow/white pillar at half height. The climb then follows the obvious crack to the top.

Bruce Keller & Chris Perry originally attempted this climb in early 1980 they succeeded in climbing the first three pitches but the climb was never finished. There was a photo of Bruce Keller leading the overhanging first pitch on the original Ghost Rock Guide by Chris Perry. This picture was used in the last guide as well to entice someone to finish this route off. Brian and Ken finally took the bait. The 2000 ascent team led the original pitches in their original condition, due to several serious runout sections and 20+ year old fixed pitons they decided to do some retrofitting of these pitches to make them more reasonable for parties that were to follow.

1) 5.9, 60 m. Climb up angling right over some loose rock to a corner. Climb the corner (on poor protection) to a bolt. Continue up past a ledge with a bolt and continue up past two more bolts to the base of a steep corner (fixed piton). Climb this corner to a ledge and into a second corner to a better ledge with a bolt (this is a possible belay to avoid rope drag). Hand traverse right and climb a final corner to an excellent belay ledge with two bolts.

2) 10b, 30 m. Clip the bolt above the belay and make difficult boulder moves to gain the crack above. Tricky layback moves lead to a bolt where the crack ends. Climb past two more bolts to an overhang. Overcome this on good holds and gear to a ledge climb to a higher ledge and a bolt belay.

3) 5.9+, 30 m. Climb the wall above to an old rappel station (where the Keller/Perry party traversed in from the right) now move left to a slabby corner with a bolt. Lay back this corner to the top and cross a slab to a right facing corner then to a ledge and a two-bolt belay.

4) 5.10b, 30 m. Move left to the white tower (do not attempt to climb it!) and a bolt on the right side. Climb the thin face right of the tower (10a) to a second bolt by the towers top. Climb the crack/face past a small ledge with a bolt. Climb higher to a second ledge with a bolt. Move right to a corner and follow this to a two-bolt belay.

5) 5.9, 35 m. This pitch is lacking a little quality. Step right and climb fins of rock past a piton to a ledge. Rubble ramps lead up left then right to a clean slab with a bolt. Climb the slab to a rappel station.

Descent: The route can be rappelled with a single 60 m rope. There has been a rappel station added right of the first pitch to facilitate this or walk off to the southwest as for the Treed Descent.

Bastion Wall

Leprechaun 5.9/A0, 210 m, gear to 4"
J. Firth & T. Jones, July 1977

"Leprechaun" climbs a discontinuous corner system in the upper part of the buttress to the right of "Satan" and left of a large bay. The climb can be seen on the approach at the break in the trees by a distinctive stump some 6 m high and 30 m from the highest elevation of the road. On the grey wall directly ahead are three yellow patches; "Leprechaun" ascends a lower corner system below the central yellow patch and traverses across right to gain the second of two upper corners, which is then followed to the top. It has some excellent climbing especially on the last two pitches.

1 -3) Three pitches of 5.6-5.7 climbing lead to a ledge on the left near the base of the lower corner.

4) 5.9. Climb the corner past the first roof. Move left to avoid a steep section and traverse back into the corner on the ramp above. Belay beneath a second open book.

5) 5.7, 50 m. Climb the corner and the wall above.

6) 5.9, A0, 50 m. Climb progressively steepening rock up and right to the base of a groove capped by an overhang. Move right across a slabby wall and up to a prominent corner. Climb this to a nut (in place) and tension right to a crack below a second corner. Follow this, using three pitons for aid near the top to a good ledge. The pitch will likely go free at about 5.10c.

7) 5.7. Climb up the overhanging crack to the top.

Descent: walk off to the southwest as for the Treed Descent.

Loki 5.6, 150 m, gear to 4" or bigger
N. Hellewell & M. Talbot, May 1980

Located on the right wall of the shallow bay to the north of "Leprechaun' is a left facing chimney line which jogs left at about one-third height. The climb follows the obvious line all the way except for an optional detour onto slabs on the left at about half height. This climb appears to be more difficult than the stated grade. Noting the first ascent team it probably is.

Descent: walk off to the southwest as for the Treed Descent.

Opposite: Photo from the cover of the original 1980 "Ghost River Rock" guide. Bruce Keller attempting a new route on Bastion Wall; now the completed route, "Rave." Photo: Chris Perry.

This is a big basin shaped area just to the north of the climb "Loki." Before the wall turns to head west into the major drainage for the ice climb the "Sorcerer" At present there are three climbs located in this area. To **approach** it is best to park as for Eastion Wall and follow the 4WD road north as if going to "Thor" but continue on the road until you reach the first of the Johnson Lakes (approximately 30 mins). Leave the road and head west through the trees and follow the drainage up to the "little Egypt" amphitheatre (see photo pages 283 & 298 and map page 302). Allow about 50 minutes to an hour for the approach.

Uller* 5.8, 220 m, gear to 4" pitons
K. Haberl & B. Spear, Dec, 2002

This moderate route climbs the low angled ridgeline/face north (right) of "Loki" as the cliff turns west to become north facing as you enter the "Little Egypt Amphitheatre". Due to their mid December ascent it was named for "Uller" the "Norse god of Winter". It ascends a system of cracks connected by slabby sections, climbs an amazing right facing corner to low angled ramps leading to a prominent buttress.

1) 5.8, 55 m. Start just left of a raised platform and climb up and left to a crack. Climb this (bolt) past difficulties to ledges. Continue up past a bolt to a bolted belay down and right from an obvious right facing corner.

2) 5.6, 60 m. Diagonal up and left to enter a steep crack, just right of the corner. Stay with the crack until it peters out (30 m). Climb the path of least resistance to a bolt and piton belay on a small stance between two small gullies below a small shrub.

3) 5.2, 55 m Climb easy ground straight up to a bolt and piton belay below an overhang below the top of the wall.

4) 5.7, 50 m. Ascend up and right on compact clean rock to a corner below the overhang (thin piton protection). Climb the corner to until about 8 m below the overhangs. Now traverse out left to where an easy step onto an arête leads to excellent but run out climbing to a two-bolt belay just below the top.

Descent: rappel the route two 60 m ropes required or walk off southwest towards "Thor" for the Treed descent.

Anubis** 5.10a, 140 m, standard rack to 4"
B. Spear & K. Wylie, Sept. 2002

Anubis is a traditionally protected line with only three bolts protecting the climbing. The climb is located on the right side of the wall that forms the left side of a big basin like amphitheatre known as the "Little Egypt Amphitheatre." The climbing is sustained 5.8 to 5.9 with an occasional 5.10 move. Anubis climbs an obvious crack system the northeast-facing wall left of a steep seepage on the left side of the amphitheatre. Scramble 20 m up to a platform just right of a major right facing corner system to a single bolt belay.

Opposite: Brian Spear hand drilling while "Storming the Bastion"on "Bastion Wall." Brian Spear collection.

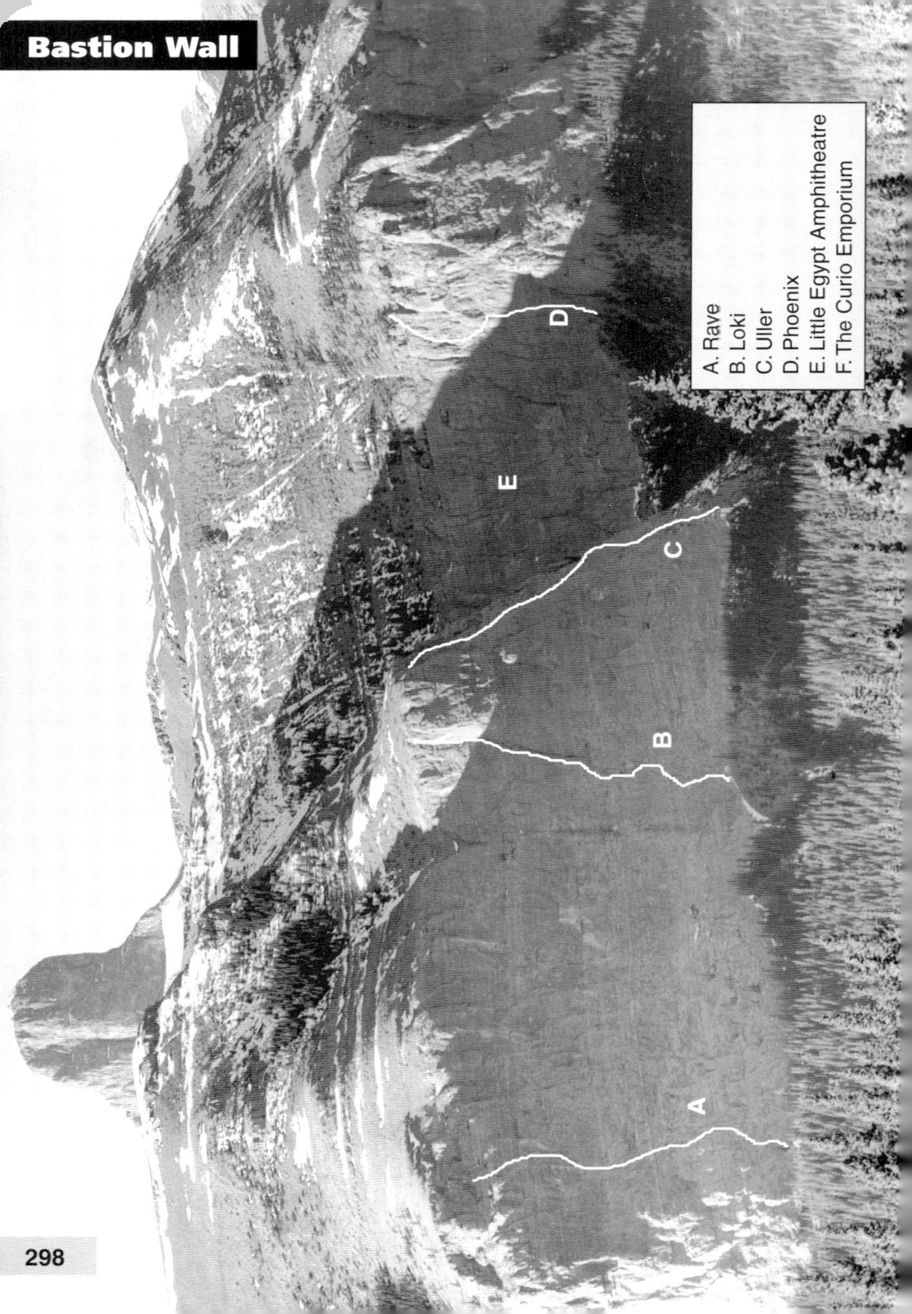
A. Rave
B. Loki
C. Uller
D. Phoenix
E. Little Egypt Amphitheatre
F. The Curio Emporium
A
B
C
D
E

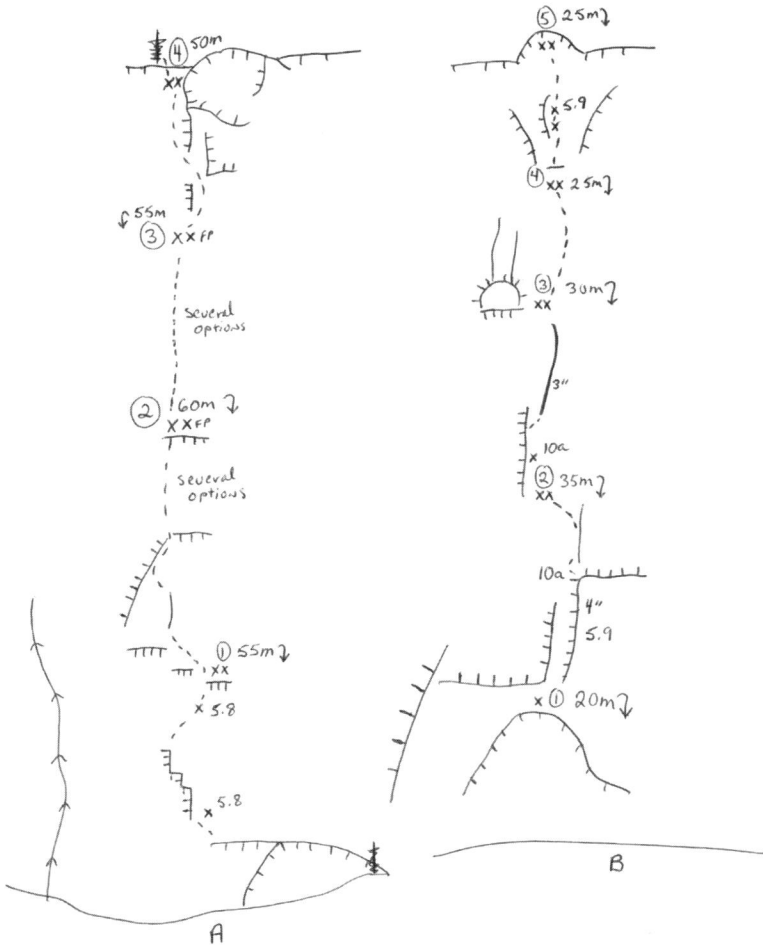

"LITTLE EGYPT " AMPHITHEATRE

A Uller*   5.8, 220 m, gear rack to 4" & pitons
B Anubis**   5.10a, 140 m, gear rack to 4"

Phoenix

1) 5.10a, 45 m. Angle up and right to gain a steep crack that leads into a right facing corner. Climb the corner passing a small roof at it's top (10a) now ascend the steep crack until easy climbing leads up and left to a two bolt belay in a clean corner.
2) 5.10a, 35 m. Make hard moves by a bolt that lead to a ledge. From the ledge step right to gain a wide crack and climb this to a two bolt belay right of a big ledge.
3) 5.6, 30 m. Climb the slabs above to a grassy ledge and a two-bolt belay.
4) 5.9, 30 m. Ascend clean slabs past a horizontal crack to gain a pedestal and a bolt. Challenging moves lead up and past a second bolt (5.9) leads to an easy slab and the top of the wall with a bolted belay.

Descent: rappel the route two ropes will be required.

Phoenix* 5.7, 135 m, standard rack to 3"
N. Hansen, B. Spear, Sept. 2002

This is the third climb located in the "Little Egypt" amphitheatre. "Phoenix" is the most northern rock climb known to be established on Bastion wall at this time. It climbs the obvious crack system left of a deep gully/chimney on the right side of the amphitheatre. The climb traverses left near the top to a mushroom shaped buttress. The route is barely visible from the road and the deep gully cannot be seen from the road. It is best to locate the climb once you have arrived at the "Little Egypt" amphitheatre. Then scramble up 5 m to a platform just left of the big gully.

1) 5.5, 25 m. From the platform follow the shallow corner system to a natural stance below the right side of a small roof.
2) 5.7, 35 m. Climb the roof above and traverse left to continue up the left facing corner past a piton to gain a wide crack. The climbing eases to a ledge and a bolt belay (one bolt is missing the hanger and cap screw 10 m).
3) 5.6, 40 m. Angle left following the crack system past a ledge, then follow a clean crack line to the ridge and a small tree. Walk left on a scree covered ledge to a belay (one bolt requires a hanger and a 10 mm cap screw).
4) 5.6, 35 m. Climb the corner to the right side of the mushroom shaped, yellow buttress. Easy ground up to a tree belay.

Descent: Due to a lack of gear the first ascent team had to rappel the deep gully to the right. They rappelled on slings from natural chock stones. Bring fresh slings or better yet bring a bolt kit and rig two bolt stances to rappel the climb.

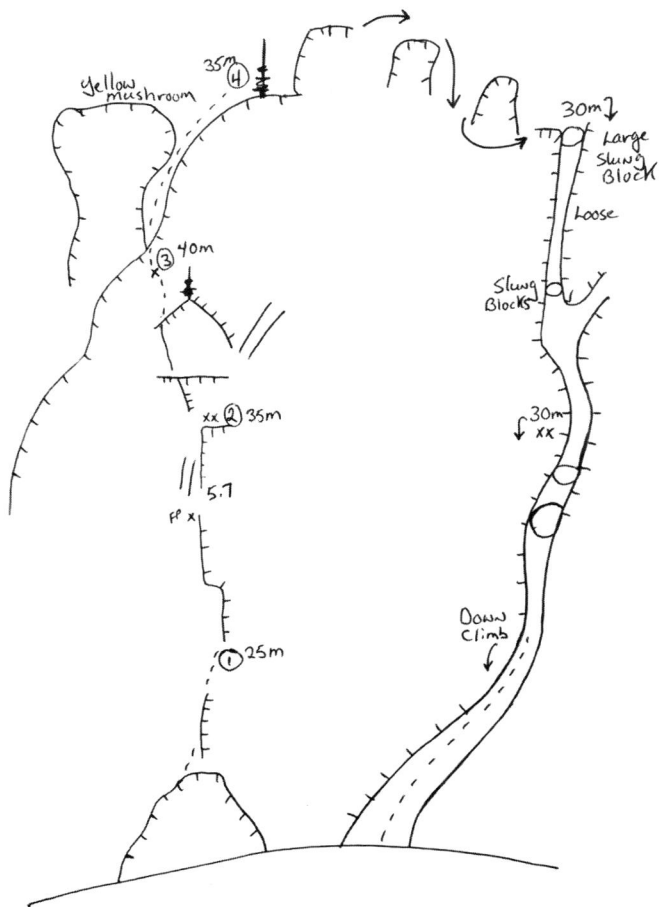

LITTLE EGYPT AMPHITHEATRE

Phoenix*   5.7, 135 m   gear rack to 3"

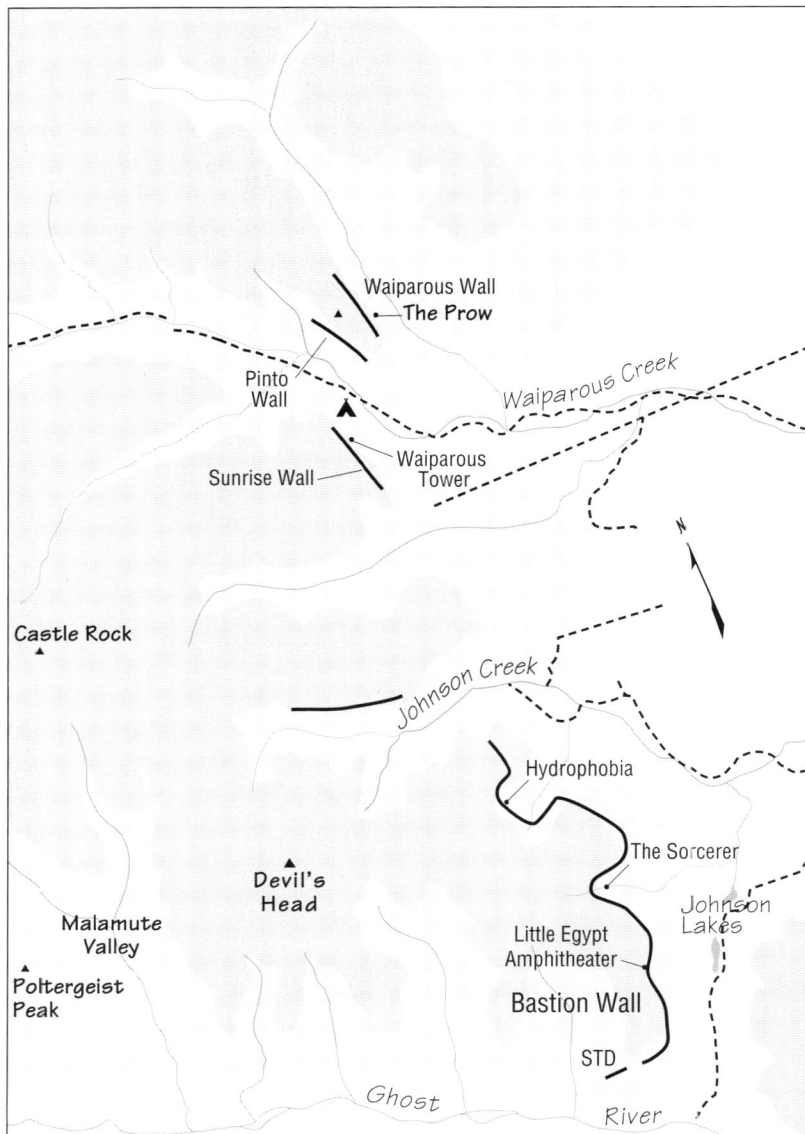

Waiparous Wall
The Prow

Pinto
Wall

Waiparous Creek

Sunrise Wall

Waiparous
Tower

N

Castle Rock

Johnson Creek

Hydrophobia

The Sorcerer

Devil's
Head

Johnson
Lakes

Malamute
Valley

Little Egypt
Amphitheater

Poltergeist
Peak

Bastion Wall

STD

Ghost

River

WAIPAROUS CREEK

The Waiparous Creek valley is the next major drainage north of the Ghost River. It has impressive cliff bands, similar to those in the Ghost, but they are less extensive and there are essentially only three major cliffs in the central climbing area. The rock is exceptional by local standards and there are a number of interesting features and impressive walls. However, the approach is difficult, being either a long walk or a true 4WD experience. Accessing Waiparous Creek makes the Ghost River approach seem easy.

All climbing routes with one exception have been established by Frank Campbell and a small group of friends who have mostly had the area to themselves. Only the obvious lines have been climbed and there are large sections of untouched rock. The routes done to date feature mainly crack climbing, often at a good standard and on excellent rock. Pitons are worth taking on most of the climbs.

Approach

Continue north on Forestry Trunk Road 940 past the Ghost River turn-off at the Bar Cee Ranch and into the forest reserve. 13.2 km north of the forest boundary, turn left (west) onto Waiparous Valley Road. Drive past Camp Mockingbird to a junction at 2.8 km. Turn left on to a rougher road (signed Margaret Lake trail), which is passable for another 4 km through Hidden Creek and past Camp Howard and Camp Chamisall. At the foot of a deeply-trenched hill, turn left into a parking area by the creek. At this point it is necessary to either start walking/biking or lock the hubs on the trusty 4WD. After the hill the road descends back down to Waiparous Creek and then twines around a driveable cutline/road for a further 6.8 km to the Margaret Lake junction. From here follow the most travelled track generally staying parallel to the creek, occasionally punctuated by yellow OHV and snowmobile signs to lead you through this tricky section. Cross over to the south bank of Waiparous Creek and continue on the "road" through several river crossings for about a further 4 km (excellent views of The Prow). A steep climb over a boulder-studded hill at a bend in the river leads to a final crossing and a good camping area between Pinto Wall and Sunrise Wall.

Sunrise Wall

A. Concord
B. Waiparous Tower & The Finger

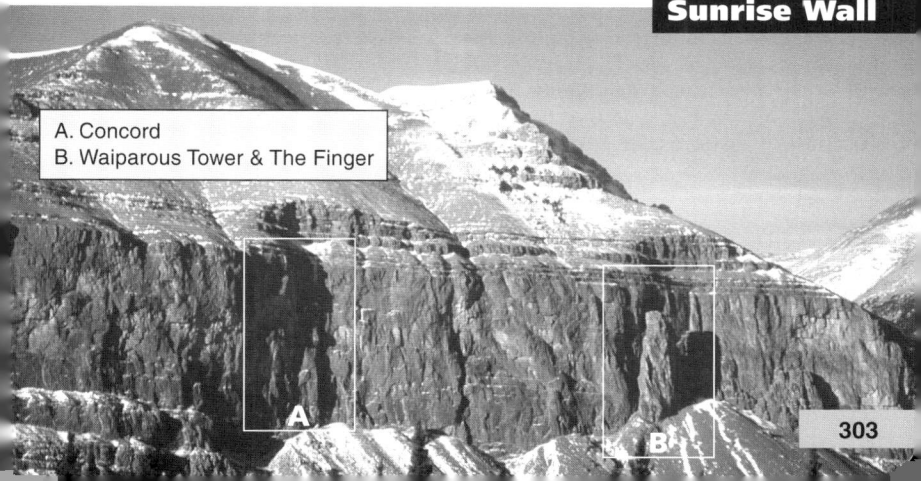

Sunrise Wall is a long, east-facing cliff that extends south from the upper Waiparous Valley. Waiparous Tower, a large, block-like tower is a prominent feature near the right-hand end.

Gutbuster 5.9, 95 m, gear to 4"
F. Campbell and J. A. Owen, Oct. 1987

Gutbuster climbs an obvious, right-facing corner system at the extreme south end of the wall. It begins at a large treed ledge, about one pitch up the face, which can be reached by scrambling up from the left.

1) 5.9, 40 m. Climb the lower corner to a two-bolt belay on the right.
2) 5.9, 45 m. Move up and left into the continuation corner and climb this to ledges on the left at the top.

Concord*** 5.11a/b, 190 m, standard rack to 4"
F. Campbell and R. Banard, Aug. 1996

This excellent climb goes up a corner system roughly in the centre of the wall and about 250 m south of the tower. In the lower section it climbs a prominent, clean-cut open book that faces right and begins about 10 m up the wall. Originally reported as going to the top of the wall it was discovered that the original grade of 5.10d was a sandbag so was the supposed top pitch, which doesn't totally exist. The second ascent party of Andy Genereux and Jeff Marshall found excellent climbing but mostly harder than the stated grades. They pushed past a bail-off biner on the last pitch but without bolts were not able to go much higher. After contacting Frank who couldn't remember what they had done, they got a hold of Ray Banard who was sure they hadn't reached the top. It was put down to the fact that the authors had pressured Frank for info on his secret stash of climbs for the last guide. The project never quite got around to being finished, more than likely Frank just forgot to go back. Here is the current info on this stellar route bring bolts and a drill to finish off this mega classic. Or at least to replace many of the fixed pins on the lower pitches and improve a couple of belays. Ray stated he would like to go back and complete this climb so maybe check with him.

1) 5.10a, 35 m. Climb up to the base of the open book and continue up an excellent finger crack passing several fixed pitons in the left wall to a ledge just left of a wide crack (two-bolt belay).
2) 5.10a, 45 m. Climb the upper portion of the open book to a fixed station at a small ledge on the left wall.
3) 5.10b/c, 20 m. Traverse right, back into the corner and climb an awkward crack to a large roof. Go out right around this and up to easier ground. Belay at a ledge on the left where the open book ends, piton and fixed wire belay.
4) 5.11 a/b, 45 m. Directly above the belay follow an incipient crack up through a bulge. Excellent but sustained climbing leads past two bolts to an overhang. Climb a notch in the overhang and go up through a second overhang bulging on sustained techni-

A. Concord

A

cal ground past a somewhat height dependant crux (bolts). Traverse right for 2 m and climb directly up to a two-bolt belay where the angle eases.

5) 5.10b, 25 m. Climb up to a rib on the left and go up this to a ledge (bolts). Move up to the top of a small pinnacle. From this point you will have to have bolting hardware to finish to the top. Lower off a single bolt or mank gear a few meters higher on the left from the second party.

Descent: Rappel the route using the fixed stations at the top of pitches 5, 4, 2 and 1. Two ropes will be required.

Waiparous Tower, South Side** 5.8, 130 m, gear to 4"
F. Campbell and J. A. Owen, Oct. 1987

This aesthetic, clean-cut formation is a prominent feature near the north end of the wall. Only the inside face on the south side has been climbed although other possibilities exist, most notably on the north edge. Photo on page 307.

The climb starts in the gully on the south side of the tower at a crack on the right wall.

1) 5.8, 50 m. Climb the crack to a ledge, move left and climb a chimney to easier ground. Move up to a ledge below a continuation corner system.

2) 5.8, 50 m. Climb the corner/crack moving slightly right toward a pinnacle on the edge. Continue up left following a corner to a ledge level with a traverse line leading right on to the front face of the tower.

3) 5.7, 5 m. Make a steep, exposed traverse right to a ledge and piton belay on the front face.

4) 5.7, 25 m. Climb the steep face above on good holds but minimal protection past a piton to a ledge system that leads right and up to the top.

Descent: Rappel from a large block on the summit (long sling required) into the notch between the tower and the main wall. A 50 m rappel reaches a single bolt station about 10 m above the notch. Rappel again into the notch and then scramble down the gully on the north side.

Sunrise Wall

A. Waiparous Tower
B. The Finger
○ Rappel Anchors

The Finger, Right Side*** 5.10b, 145 m, gear to 4"
F. Campbell, S. McDonald and S. Brucke, July 1988

"The Finger" is an obvious feature a short distance right of the tower. It begins at about two-thirds height, rises almost to the top of the cliff, and has impressive cracks on both its north and south sides. The quality of the rock hereabouts is exceptional and the last two pitches of the climb give some of the best, hard crack climbing in the guidebook area.

Start directly below The Finger at a right-facing corner system that curves over to the left.

1) 5.7, 50 m. Follow the corner system up and left to a corner crack that leads up to a belay at a block below an overhang.

2) 5.8, 25 m. Climb the overhang to gain an alcove above (5.8) and then make an exposed, horizontal traverse right to a short groove below the right-hand side of The Finger.

3) 5.10a, 20 m. Move up and then across right with difficulty to reach a break through the bulging wall above. Go up this and then over left to the base of the crack on the right side of The Finger.

4) 5.9, 25 m. Excellent crack climbing in the corner past several overhangs leads to a fixed rappel station at a small ledge on the right wall.

5) 5.10b, 25 m. Continue up the crack on superb rock to the top of the pinnacle (two-bolt belay).

Descent: Rappel to the station at the top of pitch 4 and then make two long rappels past a second station on the wall below the end of the long traverse—see photo page 307.

PINTO WALL

This colourful wall faces almost due south and parallels the creekbed. Only three climbs have been established to date, all near the upper, right-hand end. They follow prominent right-facing corner systems that begin just down and left of the highest point of a long scree slope. "Golden Cherub" is the classic of the crag and this follows a system of chimneys and corners directly to the top of the cliff.

Approach: From the campsite area, cross the river and climb easy, open slopes directly to the base of the routes.

Descent: Walk north and west to avoid cliff bands and then drop down into the drainage at the west end of the crag.

A. Golden Cherub Area

Fun Yet?** 5.7, 230 m, standard rack to 4" and pitons
M. Toft, F. Campbell and J. A. Owen, June 1988

"Fun Yet?" and "Compressor Fumes" are both reached by scrambling up and left across relatively easy ground from just below the high point of the scree slope. They begin at a long, horizontal ledge just over one third of the way up the cliff. "Fun Yet?" climbs an obvious, right-facing corner system that diagonals up left and it is the farthest west of the three climbs.

1) 5.6. From the ledge, move left and climb a corner. Go left again and then up into the base of the main corner (two-bolt belay).

2-3)   5.7. Climb the corner/crack for two pitches to a belay near the top.

4) Climb easily to the top.

Pinto Wall

Compressor Fumes* 5.9, 225 m, gear standard rack to 4" and p tons
F. Campbell, S. McDonald and S. Brucke, July 1988

This interesting route follows a corner system on the wall to the right of "Fun Yet?" It gives several pitches of good, sustained crack climbing.

Begin below and right of the upper corner system, at the long ledge noted above in the description for "Fun Yet?"

1) 5.7, 30 m. Climb a corner, move right and then go diagonally up left to the main corner system.
2) 5.8, 35 m. Follow the corner up to a ledge.
3) 5.9, 45 m. Continue up the corner system to where it eases near the top of the cliff.
4) 15 m. Exit up a short chimney.

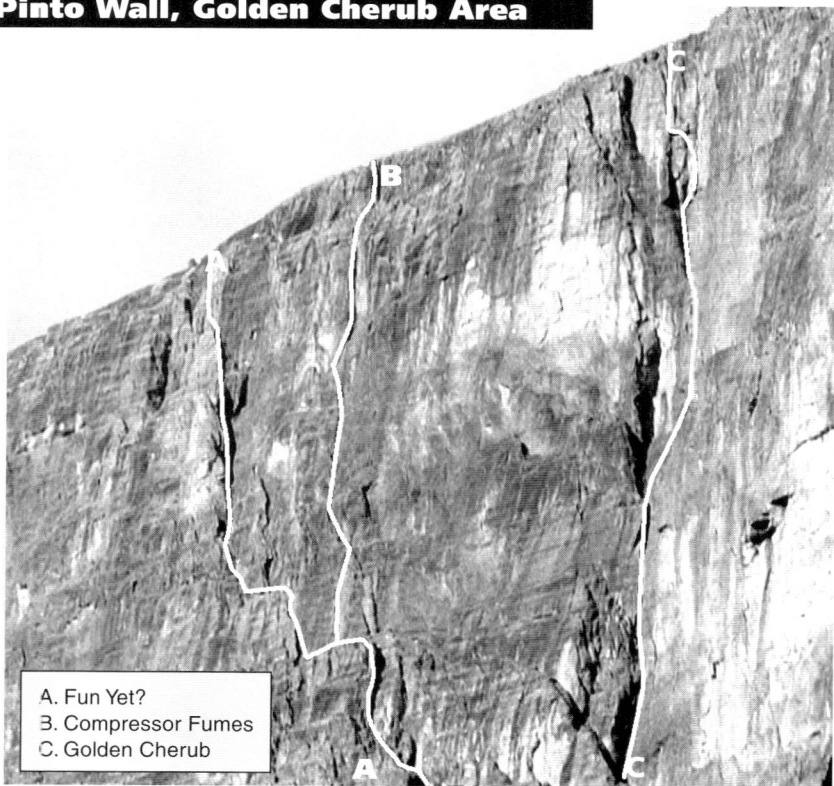

Pinto Wall, Golden Cherub Area

A. Fun Yet?
B. Compressor Fumes
C. Golden Cherub

Golden Cherub*** 5.10a/b, 190 m, gear standard rack to 4″ and pitons
F. Campbell and D. Dancer, Sept. 1987

Start to the right of the previous two routes below a right-facing groove that curves over left to the base of the lower chimney. Take a good selection of large gear. A bolt kit would be useful as Frank revisited the climb with Greg Fletcher recently and found the route stiff for the previous grade of 5.9+ and a couple of the belays were difficult to arrange. Greg felt the climb was a classic but would be even better with solid belays.

1) 5.7, 25 m. Climb the groove to a piton belay at the base of the chimney.

2) 5.8, 40 m. Climb the chimney past a fixed piton inside to a ledge (large gear required).

3) 5.10a/b, 45 m. Go diagonally up and right on easy ground to a ledge. Move right and climb a right-facing corner/crack to a belay below a wide chimney.

4) 5.10a/b, 45 m. Climb the chimney and move out right at the top to a grassy ledge and piton at the base of a right-facing corner. Climb the corner past a piton until an overhang blocks the way. An exposed traverse leads left to loose blocks in a major crack system. Climb the crack with difficulty to a small ledge.

5) 5.8, 35 m. Continue up the gully to the top.

A. The Ardent Heart

"The Prow" is the name given to a huge buttress of rock situated between Waiparous Creek and its north fork. It marks the southern end of a long line of east-facing cliffs that extends northward for some distance and is marked on the area map as "Waiparous Wall." The first section of cliff, which is readily visible on the approach, presented one of the most inviting pieces of unclimbed rock in the previous guidebook. This impressive wall had no climbs on it when the last Ghost guide was published. Only a picture to lure someone to something about it. Well a group did just that when another plan fell apart to climb "Concord" due it being a waterfall from the recent heavy rains. Climbing through several rainstorms they established the classic "Ardent Heart." The only new route in the area for several years. There appears to be a number of other possible lines on this 300-400 m face and the rock looks excellent.

THE PROW

The Ardent Heart ** 5.10+, 305 m,
  gear standard rack to 4" & pitons

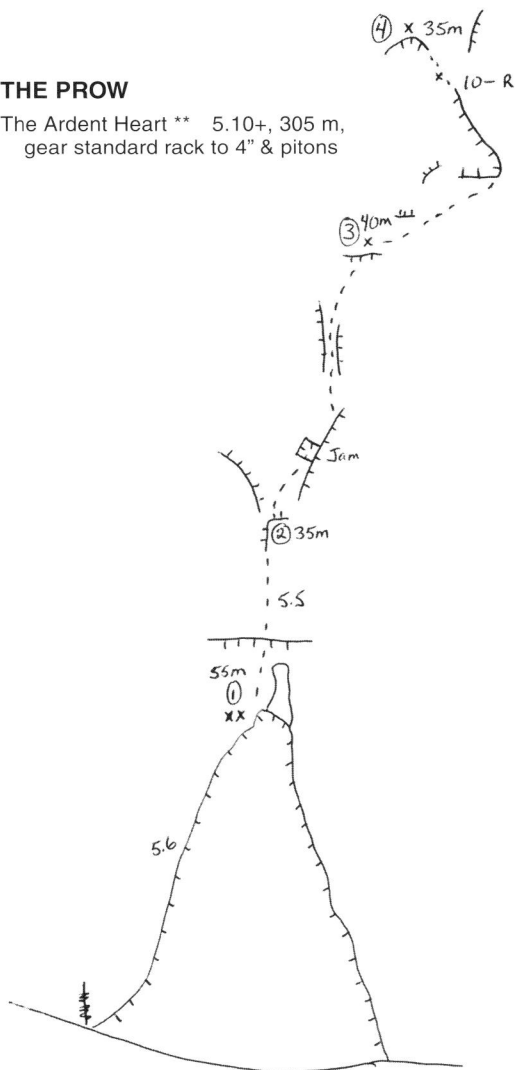

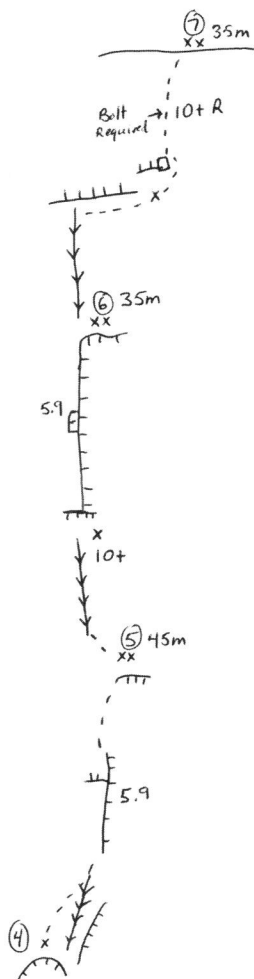

④ x 35m

10 – R

③ 40m
x

Jam

② 35m

5.5

55m
①
xx

5.6

⑦ 35m
xx

Bolt → 10+ R
Required

⑥ 35m
xx

5.9

x
10+

⑤ 45m
xx

5.9

④ x

The Ardent Heart

The Ardent Heart** 5.10+/R, 305 m, gear standard rack to 4" and pitons
Keith Haberl, Brian Spear & Ken Wylie, June 1998

This is a very good route with quality climbing and excellent exposure. The first ascent party likened the route to Kahl wall on Mt. Yamnuska. The first ascent was in true traditional style completed in a single day through three rainstorms. They were only able to scrape together a few bolts for this spur of the moment adventure. This climb has had one known repeat ascent to date, again by Keith along with Chris Robertson. Chris had the crux pitch. Unknown to them the piton protecting the crux had been removed on the first ascent making it very interesting. They recommended for the next party to contemplate doing this superb route to bring along a bolt kit to add bolts to some of the belays and on the crux of pitch 7 and for replacement of some of the fixed pitons. This service would up the star value and remove the "R" on this climb and be greatly appreciated by future climbers.

Approach: The route is located on the east face of the Prow. Park as for "Golden Cherub" and hike up through the trees to the left of a huge scree slope below that route. Traverse the cliffs east to overcome the shoulder of "Pinto Wall" and continue a descending traverse north passing a loose chimney system past a small tree to a gully that leads up behind a tower.

1) 5.6, 55 m. Climb the gully to belay on a ledge out right near the top fixed pitons.

2) 5.5, 30 m. Continue up and left to gain a very large scree covered ledge, from here there is a good view of the route above. Cross the ledge and climb up to a second smaller slopping ledge 15 m above to belay (pitons required).

3) 5.8, 45 m. Traverse right on thin slab moves (pins required) to gain a rising gully with a jammed block. Climb the gully stepping right at the top. Continue up a crack over a small roof into a wide slot. Climb this to the top and a single bolt belay on a small ledge.

4) 5.10-/R, 35 m. Traverse right on thin slab moves (pitons required) to step around a hidden corner to a groove. Climb up to a bolt, runout climbing leads up steep ground to a gully. Angle up and left to a belay with a single bolt.

5) 5.9, 45 m. Climb the slabby wall above, then angle right across the gully and up to an amazing left facing corner. Climb this superb feature overcoming two small roofs to a two-bolt belay.

6) 5.10+, 35 m. Move left and climb a friable groove to a bolt (crux) move past and angle left to a small ledge. Climb the corner above moving past a hollow block to belay at the top on two bolts to the right.

7) 5.10+/R, 35 m. Step left to regain the crack and climb this until blocked by overlaps. Hand traverse right on exposed moves past a bolt to make a hard move past a large shattered block. Thin face climbing continues (pin or bolt required) up to a two-bolt belay just below the summit of the crag.

Descent: walk north on the rounded summit then angle around southwest to descend as for "Golden Cherub".

THE ANTI-GHOST

As the name may imply, this venue is not really in the Ghost River. This east-facing cliff sits above the Ghost Valley is really an extension of the south ridge of Black Rock Mountain. The cliff is visible from only at a few locations along the access road, notably at a T-junction 4.6 km before the top of the Big Hill. It is totally non-visible from the Ghost itself. When this cliff was first explored, there were big hopes for a new venue without the rigorous approach endemic to the rest of the region. Those hopes were quickly lost with the long walk required to reach the crag and the scrappy nature of the rock itself. Only two small pockets have produced routes of any quality. Steep slopes directly below the climbs in the Bluebell Crack make it a bit of a thrutch to move around near the base. Don't drop your pack! These are worth considering if you discover the Ghost River too high to cross or when a cold wind is blowing in the lower valleys.

There are two sections of the cliff where climbs have been established and these are marked on the accompanying photograph. At the south end is the Motocross Crack area where two climbs have been done one on either side of a prominent gully. The other section that has been developed is the Bluebell Crack area situated in a prominent bay just to the right of the centre of the crag.

Parking Access & Approach
About 100 m before the top of the Big Hill, a dirt road heads off north and, after about 300 m, enters a large meadow and campsite area. From here, the cliff can be readily seen in profile to the north. The road continues but deteriorates rapidly and it is best to proceed on foot or mountain bike for about a kilometre to a small hill where a horse trail branches off to the right toward the cliff. Follow this to a steep hill that has been deeply gouged by motocross riders. Struggle up the hill and continue north along a treed bench below the cliff. A short uphill scramble will put you at the base of the cliff. The approach takes about an hour.

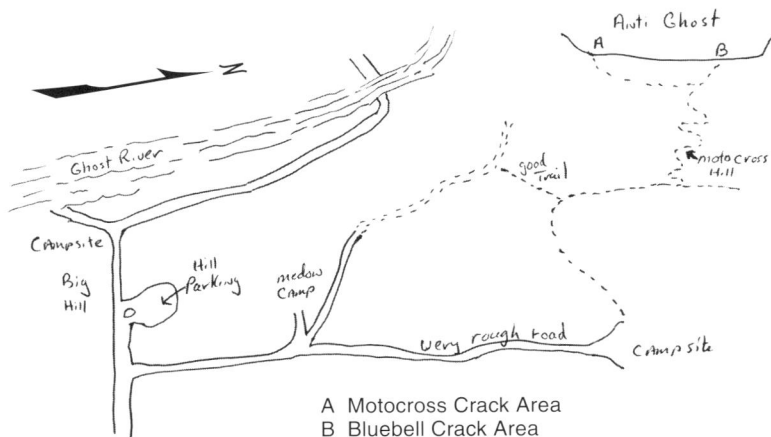

A Motocross Crack Area
B Bluebell Crack Area

A. Motocross Crack area
B. Bluebell Crack area

Chinook* 5.10d, 20 m, gear to 4"
F. Campbell, K. Doyle & Y. Leduc, May 1989

"Chinook" climbs the clean corner, capped by a roof, to the left of the prominent gully. Some gear is required for the lower corner. Climb the corner to the roof (5.9) and go out right to a bolt. Move over the overhang with difficulty (5.10d) past a piton and up into a short groove. Climb the groove and continue up and slightly left past more pitons (5.10a) to a good tree at the top.

Motocross Crack 5.9, 20 m, gear to 4"
F. Campbell & M. Brolsma, 1988

This route climbs the obvious groove to the right of the gully and requires a small selection of gear.

Descent: Descend both routes by walking off the back of the cliff to the south.

Bluebell Crack Area

All the routes here are descended by rappel. One 60 m rope is adequate.

British Bluebells Are Best 5.8+, 30 m, gear to 4"
O. Driskell & J. Hurst June 2002

Located 10 m down and left from the "Bluebell Corner". Scramble across some easy slabs, up a short corner then over an awkward bulge and round the roof to the right to belay off a tree on an obvious ledge. To descend, rappel from the tree a sling may be required.

Bluebell Crack** 5.10a, 17 m, gear to 2.5"
F. Campbell and M. Brolsma, 1987

Excellent, albeit short, crack. Either lower off the first single bolt or traverse left on a somewhat creaking flake to a small tree.

Bluebell Extension** 5.11c, 22 m, gear to 2.5"
A. Genereux and S. Mascioli, 1995

A desperate face climbing finish to Bluebell Crack. A recent visit by climbers found the extension bit to be rather stiff for the grade maybe it suits short fat people or maybe a hold broke off.

Bluebell Corner 5.9, 25 m, gear to 3.5"
F. Campbell and T. Mooney, 1987

It is unsure where the first ascensionist belayed but it is now recommended to traverse left to the bolt belay of "Bluebell Extension." If the crack were cleaned of dirt and vegetation, it would be rather nice. At present, however, the corner is quite dirty.

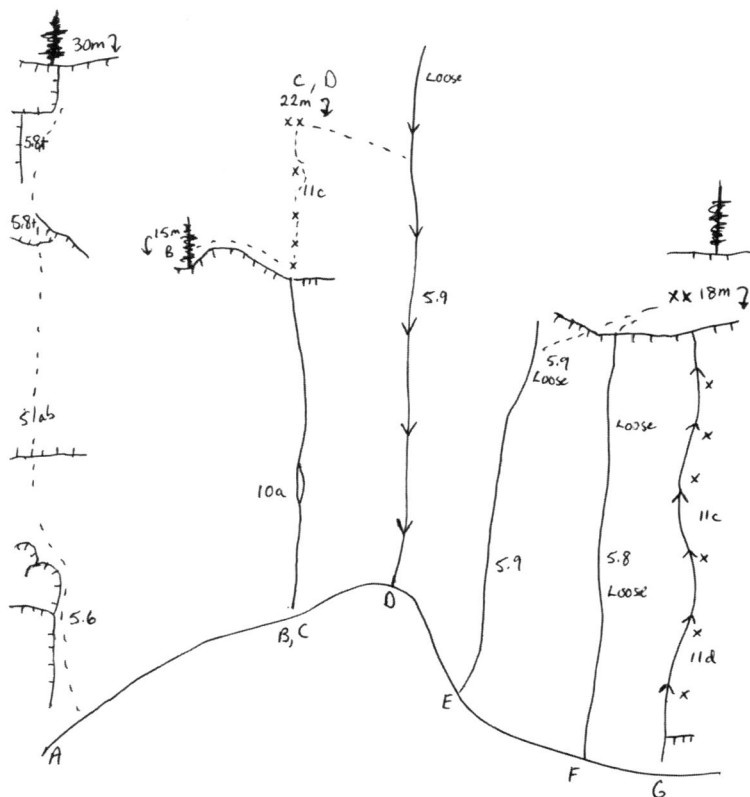

THE ANTI GHOST, BLUEBELL CRACK AREA

A	British Blue Bells Are Better *	5.8	gear to 4"
B	Bluebell Crack **	5.10a	gear to 2.5"
C	Bluebell Extension **	5.11c	gear to 2.5"
D	Bluebell Corner	5.9	gear to 3.5"
E	Handi Work	5.9	gear to 3"
F	The Handle	5.8	gear to 4"
G	City View *	5.11c/d	

Handiwork 5.9, 20 m, gear to 3"
S. Mascioli & A. Genereux, 1995

Immediately right of "Bluebell Corner" there is an obvious hand crack. It is rather loose and dangerous near the top but could become a good route if it was cleaned up. Use the "City View" anchor on top to the right.

The Handle 5.8, 20 m, gear to 4"
A. Genereux & S. Mascioli, 1995

A twin route to the right of the previous climb but a grade easier. Watch out for loose rock in the middle and near the top. Use the bolted anchor of "City View" over the top.

City View* 5.11c/d, 18 m, fixed gear
A. Genereux, 1995

A devious arête climb with hard face climbing on somewhat friable edges.

ALPINE ROCK

This is the beginning of what we hope is an ever-expanding chapter. Part of the wildness and scenery of the Ghost lies above the cliffs that grace the toes of the mountains. Over the years, numerous forays have been made into the upper reaches of the mountains and it is surprising how recently many of the peaks have received their first ascent. There is likely to be several (if not more) peaks or bumps on the ridges that remain totally unclimbed. As well, an almost endless supply of unexplored ridges and faces will undoubtedly burp up many more interesting routes of a general mountaineering bent. Here we have included the most technical of the completed climbs along with a variety of thigh-busting scrambles/climbs from the now out-of-print *Rocky Mountains of Canada South* by Glen Boles.

All of the climbs mentioned here lie north of the Minnewanka Valley (Palliser Range) and are on the Lake Minnewanka map sheet 82-O/6. To convert meter readings into feet (elevations on the map sheet are in feet), divide meters by 0.3048.

Orient Point, Saddle Peak and several unnamed points on the south side of the valley (northern end of the Fairholme Range) should present some interesting scrambles/climbs for those so inclined. See *Rocky Mountains of Canada South* and the Canmore map sheet 82-O/3 for more details.

Devil's Head

Photo: Glen Boles.

Phantom Crag Summits

A long ridge line extends westward from above the main climbing areas to the summit of Mount Costigan. Two rocky summits sit on top of this ridge at its eastern end and offer some interest to rock climbers "with a mountaineering problem." The eastern summit is marked as "Phantom Crag" (GR 265836, elevation 2,275 m) and its imposing east side is shown on the photograph of South Phantom Crag (page 114). To the authors' knowledge the peak has not been climbed from this side. West Phantom Crag Summit is a sister formation that lies about a kilometre to the west (GR 254837, elevation 2,365 m) and is not visible from many of the normal viewpoints. The two summits look very much alike and can be confused. From the Minnewanka Valley, the east summit sits directly above the Bonanza drainage whereas the west summit lies above the Aquarius/Recital Hall drainage. Both summits can be easily reached via their west sides and only the west summit has been climbed by its east ridge. This climb is reported to be a worthwhile outing.

East Ridge of West Phantom Crag Summit*, 5.6
F. Campbell, P. Roxburgh & D. White, 1984

The climb begins at the col between the east and west summits. This can be reached from Wully Canyon by hiking up the drainage that serves as part of the descent from North Phantom Crag (see approach) and descent details on page 159). Alternatively, East Gully (page 159) and then the South Phantom Crag descent gully (page 148) can be used to access the upper slopes. The ridge itself gives two pitches of 5.6 climbing on good rock and leads directly to the west summit. Descent can be made down the easy west side of the peak and then north down a relatively open drainage that leads back to the Ghost River just west of Sentinel Cliff (GR 245864). A much shorter descent can be made down the approach drainage although this requires a rappel. From the summit, scramble down to the north and locate a piton at the north end of a small cliff band. A 20 m rappel and easy scrambling allow the drainage to be reached, which is then followed down to Wully Canyon.

A. Thunder God Buttress, Mount Costigan
B. Costigan's Boil
C. East Phantom Crag Summit

Alpine Rock

Costigan's Boil (2,564 m, 8,410 ft.)

This aptly-named peak is on the ridge line that extends from the main summit of Mount Costigan east to Phantom Crag (GR 232834). It is a somewhat technical, blocky "boil" that sticks up above the surrounding scree slopes. The first (and perhaps only) ascent came in August 1960 by P. Duffy, J. K. Gray, Mr. and Mrs. Heinz Kahl. From *Rocky Mountains of Canada South*:

"From Devil's Gap pass Phantom Lake to the second canyon on the north side of the valley [Lacy Gibbet drainage]. Hike and climb up this canyon to its head bypassing two waterfalls [Lacy Gibbet?] to trees above canyon wall, one hour through the forest. Follow steep meadows to a ridge in about one hour. This ridge runs east to Phantom Crag. Follow the ridge west staying on the north side and use the rope again near the top. Descend by the same route. (*CAJ Volume 44, page 55*)"

Mount Costigan (2,980 m, 9,775 ft.)

Mount Costigan lies at the top of the long ridgeline that extends west from the Phantom Crag summits. The first recorded ascent came in June 1975 from the "Grizzly Group" of Don Forest, Gordon Scruggs and Glen Boles. Their description is from *Rocky Mountains of Canada South* page 432:

"From camp above canyon, below long south ridge, hiked up slopes west of south ridge to about 2,450 m, then traversed northwest over two ridges then climbed ledges and bands interspersed with scree to southwest ridge, ridge to summit. Found cairn and survey marker, 7 hours. Descend via southwest slopes and canyon, 2.5 hours. (*CAJ Volume 59, page 83*)."

Mount Costigan has a very impressive northeast buttress that can be seen from the top of the Big Hill or from the entrance to the Minnewanka Valley (see photo page 65). The buttress was first climbed by Frank Campbell and J. A. Owen and was named "Thunder God Buttress" to commemorate a rapid, unplanned, lightning-induced descent from the summit into the Minnewanka Valley. This resulted in a long hike back to their car which was in the North Ghost, giving a round trip of 25 km!

Thunder God Buttress is a prominent feature of the Minnewanka valley and the climb is included here despite its limited appeal to most Ghost River clientele. Perhaps a fun day out, which could be called the "Ghost River Integral," would be to climb the South Face of Phantom Tower, continue over the east and west Phantom Crag summits and Costigan's Boil, and then climb the Thunder God Buttress to the summit of Mount Costigan.

Thunder God Buttress 5.9, 250 m, gear to 4"
F. Campbell & J. A. Owen, Aug. 1986

The original approach was via the northeast drainage of Mount Costigan. To access from this direction, continue up the Ghost River past the "Alberta Jam" and "Sunset Boulevard" crags to a major valley on the south side (GR 206866). Head south up the valley and then angle left to gain the col between Costigan's Boil and the northeast buttress just to the west of a large block (GR 217834). A more logical approach, however, is from the Minnewanka Valley as the easiest descent from the summit is in that direction. Costigan's Boil is a small summit immediately east of the col that can be climbed (fourth class) by its east ridge. Access to this ridge from the Minnewanka Valley can be made easily via the major canyon beyond the Aquarius/Recital Hall drainage. The canyon is located just beyond the second Ghost Lake (GR 235811) and is home to a number of ice climbs including the long and popular "Lacy Gibbet."

From the col climb a step (5.7) on good rock to the base of the main buttress. Climb over an overhang (piton) to the right, loose and difficult (crux), easing off and then steepening to a groove. Belay 6 m below where the groove steepens. Climb up for 5 m and traverse right for 6 m to gain a crack system (#5 chock with no sling left in place). Climb the crack system (5.8) and belay where it eases. Continue up and left on a loose ridge (5.5), which becomes easier near the top. Descend to the south via an easy screed ridge that leads to the Minnewanka Valley.

MOUNT AYLMER, EAST RIDGE

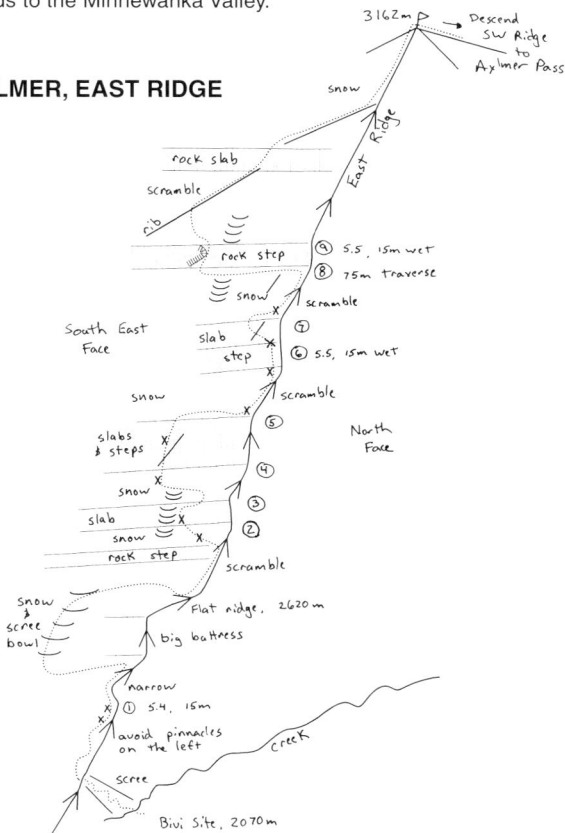

Mount Aylmer

Mount Aylmer (3,162 m, 10,375 ft.)

Mount Aylmer is the highest peak in the entire Banff region. It dominates the view to the west when you turn the corner into the North Ghost Valley near the Silver-Tongued Devil Crag. From this vantage, especially in winter or early summer, the east ridge is a particularly striking line. A popular hiking trail traverses the west side of the peak from Lake Minnewanka to Aylmer Pass and continues into Spectral Creek and the Ghost River valley. Aylmer Pass is best reached from the Banff end of Lake Minnewanka and is 13.5 km with 810 m of elevation gain from the Minnewanka parking lot. From the pass, a straightforward scree scramble leads to the summit, which was first climbed in 1889 by J. J. McArthur. (*CAJ Volume 10, page 32*)

East Ridge* alpine grade III, 5.5

M. Siska & P. O'Byrne, June 1994

The first ascent of this route came in mid-June when the lower-angled sections of the ridge were covered in snow. A later climb will undoubtedly find more scree ledges and dryer conditions (take water!), which may permit more direct variations on the ridge crest proper. Neither time seems more recommended over the other, it is simply a matter of preferences. If you go early to mid-season expect snowy, wet conditions and a certain amount of avalanche hazard—plan accordingly.

Approach

The first ascent team used a combination of biking and hiking to reach Aylmer Pass from Banff and continued into the upper reaches of Spectral Creek. They then traversed the north side of the peak on goat trails to a "lovely kettle lake" (GR 099888) and then headed down to a grassy bivi spot at 2,070 m (GR 106875). This approach took 9 hours. A slightly quicker approach may be from the Ghost River valley but it is untried. The base of the east ridge lies some 15 km west of the Silver-Tongued Devil Crag. The topo opposite and description were taken from the *Canadian Alpine Journal Volume 78, 199, page 82.*

From the bivi, ascend a brown scree slope to gain the ridge crest. A scramble and half a pitch of 5.4 leads to the base of a big buttress. Avoid the buttress by traversing left to a big snow and scree bowl, rejoining the ridge at a long, flat bench above the buttress at 2,620 m. Here the fun climbing begins. The ridge consists of a series of rock steps and snow slopes on the southeast face, intersecting with a huge cliff on the north face. The route climbs up short rock bands and stays on the ridge or within half a rope length of the southeast face for a total of eight pitches (5.5). A compact 10 m step is reached high on the ridge. Traverse left for 75 m to a weakness in the step that forms the final difficulties. Above the step, ascend a rib to regain the ridge for the final stretch to the summit. The first ascent took 14 hours from the bivi. Descend by following the regular route on the southwest slope down to Aylmer Pass.

Devil's Head

Alpine Rock

Devil's Head (2,997 m, 9,174 ft.)

This impressive block-shaped tower is a prominent feature on the Rockies skyline and guided early travellers to the route west through Devil's Gap. The first ascent came in 1925 when the legendary Edward Feuz Jr. guided two guests to the summit via the west ridge. The ridge is relatively easy by modern standards (some 5th class) but it is long and Feuz's time of 5.5 hours up from a camp at 1,670 m in the Ghost River (4.5 hours down) remains an impressive effort and is rarely improved upon even today. (*Alpine Journal, London, Volume 38, page 67*)

The imposing east face presents a much greater challenge and has been climbed only once to date. The face is broken by a large corner system that s easily seen, especially in cross-lighting, from a considerable distance away. The route "Devil's Bargain" follows the corner system and gives an excellent, exposed climb on generally good rock. The position in the upper part of the route is reported to be exceptional.

Approach

The normal approach to Devil's Head is from the southwest and begins where a major drainage called Malamute Valley joins the Ghost River from the north (GR 198865). Malamute Valley is about 6 km upstream from the "North Ghost" parking area below Sentinel Crag and a 4WD or mountain bike is required to follow the "road" through a series of river crossings and wash-outs. There have been some explorations reported in the Malamute Valley but concrete details were unavailable at press time. Hike up the drainage for a short distance and then cut up right onto a steep hillside that turns into a open rib higher up. The rib leads north toward the west ridge of Devil's Head and gives a long but easy approach. A shorter alternative is to begin at a smaller drainage on the north side of the river between the "Alberta Jam" and "Sunset Boulevard" crags (GR 228867) and about 2.5 km from the "North Ghost" parking. The drainage comes out of a small canyon that looks impassable higher up but can be climbed on its west side near the mouth. The east face of Devil's Head can be seen in profile above the head of the canyon on the left. Walk up the drainage for about one kilometre and ther angle up and back left to avoid cliff bands across a steep, wooded hillside. About 500 m higher an open rib is gained that can be followed easily to the base of the tower.

Descent

Scramble down the west ridge (some rappels—be sure to pay homage to Mr. Fuez as you rappel the sections he climbed up and down with little or no belay) and descend either of the two approach options described above.

Devil's Bargain* 5.9, 305 m, standard rack to 4" pitons

T. Jones & B. Gross, July 1984

The climb follows the corner system for much of the way and moves out right onto an exposed edge in the upper section. Pitons are recommended.

1- 2) 5.6, 100 m. Climb a series of short steps to a chimney where the corner system narrows.

3) 5.7, 40 m. Continue up the chimney to a good ledge at the base of a steep section.

4) 5.9, 45 m. This excellent pitch follows a crack system on the right wall that leads up to a 3 m diameter cave (The Eagle's Eyrie).

5) 5.8, 40 m. Move right and follow a diagonal line of short cracks and overlaps to the base of a steep corner/crack about 15 m right of the main corner system.

6) 5.8, 40 m. Climb the crack to the top of a very exposed pinnacle that overlooks the main east face. Continue up easier and looser terrain to a terrace belay.

7) 5.6, 40 m. Easy but exposed climbing leads to the summit platform.

Poltergeist Peak (2,970 m, 9,700 ft.)

Poltergeist Peak is the unofficial name of the complex peak that forms the west side of Malamute Valley. To the north it is joined to Peak 2975 West (see below) by a long ridge that involves several other summits that may not be climbed.

Several approach options exist including various eastern spurs that drop steeply from the southeast ridge into Malamute Valley. The first ascent team of M. Benn and T. W. Swaddle (June 1970) started in the Ghost River valley and followed a smaller drainage due south of the summit (GR 165868) into a cirque. From the cirque, they made the long climb up slopes to the east to gain the southeast ridge where "it terminates above a big, east-facing cliff band." The summit ridge was gained through an "ice-choked chimney (easier later in year)." Descent was pretty much via the same route, 9 hours return.

Castle Rock (2975 m, 9,700 ft.)

Northwest of Devil's Head there are many unnamed and rarely climbed mountains with numerous peaks exceeding 2,900 m (9,500 ft.). They form the headwaters of Waiparous Creek and in the past have been accessed via that drainage. See page 303 for access. Castle Rock is the unofficial name for a complicated peak that has several distinct summits of a similar elevation and ring the southwest corner of Waiparous Creek. A large drainage west of Devil's Head called Malamute Valley drains south into the Ghost River and may give access to a variety of these peaks and possibly some good new routes. The Ghost River Wilderness boundary lies just west of Malamute Valley so it may be possible to drive to near the entrance to the valley. See the approach description for Devil's Head on page 326.

The descriptions listed here are taken directly from *Rocky Mountains of Canada South* pages 432-33 in combination with the original reports from the Canadian Alpine Journal (CAJ). They appear to be the most interesting of the lot and we hope their inclusion here will rise them from the depths of "out-of-printism" and foster some exploration of this rugged, scenic and overlooked portion of the range.

Alpine Rock

Castle Rock East (Peak 2975)
Northeast Ridge and Traverse, 5.5
E. Grassman & J. Rokne, Aug. 1967

This climb came as part of an impressive tour-de-force that traversed several unclimbed peaks to the west and northwest. It was part of a large ACC camp in the area in August 1967. Castle Rock East lies 4 km northwest of Devil's Head. It is the southeastmost peak of a group ringing the head of Waiparous Creek.

From a camp at the junction of upper Waiparous Creek and a southern tributary at 1,800 m (approximate GR 209953) follow the south tributary then mount the northeast ridge of the peak. Follow the ridge to a rock band at 2,680 m that circumvents the north and east side of the mountain. Move left and climb rock to the left of a steep gully, then climb the upper part of the gully (three pitches up to 5.5) to the upper ridge, then to summit (GR 180919), 6 hours.

Descend to the west and scramble up Castle Rock West (GR 161923), some 2 km to the west, 2.5 hours. Continue to the northwest to Peak 2942 (GR 148932) almost directly at the head of Waiparous Creek. The party had to backtrack a considerable distance to circumvent a deep, wide notch on the ridge. A traverse was then made west of the ridge, then ascended easy slopes to the summit.

Cumbersome slopes made the descent to the northwest of Peak 2942 time consuming with a bivouac required in the cliffs below the col. Finish descent into Waiparous Creek. (CAJ Volume 51, page 211)

Peaks 2910 & Peak 2940

North of Peak 2942 there are three more summits that complete the ring at the headwaters of Waiparous Creek. Two peaks with the elevation of roughly 2,910 m (GR 141947 & 144953) dot the landscape while a larger Peak 2940 lies to the northeast (GR 155961). The middle of the three (Peak 2910) was climbed as part of the ACC camp in Waiparous Creek. The party of K. Kubinski, P. Lancaster and L. Guy ascended the southeast ridge. The key to the climb was a hidden chimney through a low cliff band, 10 hours return trip.

The obvious challenge found in these peaks would be a continuation of the Grassman/ Rokne traverse all the way around the main Waiparous drainage to create a grand horseshoe that would begin and end in roughly the same spot in Waiparous Creek (GR 220943). Check it out on map sheet 82-0/6.

INDEX

Index

Index

Index